FONDA, MY LIFE

is far more than a collaboration between an actor
and a writer. It is 200 hours of Henry Fonda
pouring out his most private thoughts on tape. It
is based on over 117 interviews with his family
and friends, revealing their innermost opinions of
the man.

You know Fonda the actor. Now, for the first
time, you'll meet Fonda the thwarted lover, the
disillusioned husband and the perfectionist father
of his controversial children, Jane and Peter. But
most of all, you'll meet Fonda, the man, a
multidimensional figure who has become a legend
in his own time.

"A STUNNER . . . VERY READABLE!"
—NEW YORK POST

"FIRST-RATE . . . CANDID, PLAINSPOKEN,
WHOLLY UNSPARING . . . CLEARLY
REVEALS FONDA THE MAN."
—LOS ANGELES TIMES

*(For more exuberant praise from the stars and the critics,
please turn page . . .)*

HENRY FONDA IS WHAT AMERICA IS
MEANT TO BE—complex, curious, forever
searching, improving, emerging, triumphant.
And it's all in the book!"

—*Lauren Bacall*

"SOLID, ENDEARING, HIGHLY
ENGAGING . . . HAS EVERYTHING FANS
WILL WANT TO KNOW ABOUT HANK'S
PRIVATE LIFE AND THEATER WORK."

—KIRKUS REVIEWS

"I AM ENTHRALLED WITH THE BOOK. I
feel that I'm coming to know for the first time a
man I've loved and admired for years. Fonda is
the greatest living actor today."

—*Lucille Ball*

"A CANDID, GRATIFYING 'TELL-ALL!' "

—SATURDAY REVIEW

"A MARVELOUS ACCOUNT OF HENRY
FONDA'S LIFE, WONDERFUL,
REMARKABLY HUMANE AND
ACCURATE ABOUT A MOST DIFFICULT
MAN TO CATCH ON PAPER."

—*Joshua Logan*

"UNSPARINGLY HONEST . . . IT HAS ALL
THE INGREDIENTS!"

—LIBRARY JOURNAL

Biography and Autobiography from SIGNET

(0451)

- [ ] **ALAN ALDA: AN UNAUTHORIZED BIOGRAPHY by Jason Bonderoff.** (114191—$2.75)*
- [ ] **FIRST YOU CRY by Betty Rollin.** (112598—$2.50)
- [ ] **SAVE ME THE WALTZ by Zelda Fitzgerald.** (056035—$1.25)
- [ ] **BOGIE by Joe Hyams.** (091892—$1.75)
- [ ] **KATE: THE LIFE OF KATHARINE HEPBURN by Charles Higham.** (112121—$2.95)
- [ ] **PENTIMENTO by Lillian Hellman.** (115430—$2.95)
- [ ] **ELEANOR: THE YEARS ALONE by Joseph P. Lash.** (112938—$3.95)
- [ ] **ELEANOR AND FRANKLIN by Joseph P. Lash.** (112318—$4.95)
- [ ] **SINATRA by Earl Wilson.** (074874—$2.25)
- [ ] **THE WOMAN HE LOVED by Ralph G. Martin.** (090748—$2.50)
- [ ] **THE ROCKEFELLERS by Keith Colher and David Horowitz.** (113705—$2.95)
- [ ] **IF YOU COULD SEE WHAT I HEAR by Tom Sullivan and Derek Gill.** (118111—$2.50)
- [ ] **GEORGE WASHINGTON: MAN AND MONUMENT by Marcus Cunliffe.** (620577—$2.50)
- [ ] **OFF THE COURT by Arthur Ashe with Neil Amdur.** (117662—$3.50)*
- [ ] **WITH MALICE TOWARD NONE by Stephen Oates.** (620771—$3.95)

*Price slightly higher in Canada

FONDA

MY LIFE

AS TOLD TO
HOWARD TEICHMANN

A SIGNET BOOK
NEW AMERICAN LIBRARY
TIMES MIRROR

Ⓞ

SIGNET TRADEMARK REG. U.S. PAT. OFF. AND FOREIGN COUNTRIES
REGISTERED TRADEMARK—MARCA REGISTRADA
HECHO EN CHICAGO, U.S.A.

SIGNET, SIGNET CLASSICS, MENTOR, PLUME, MERIDIAN AND NAL BOOKS
are published by The New American Library, Inc.,
1633 Broadway, New York, New York 10019

First Signet Printing, November, 1982

1 2 3 4 5 6 7 8 9

PRINTED IN THE UNITED STATES OF AMERICA

*This book
is
dedicated
to*

SHIRLEE

JANE   FONDA   PETER

AMY

PREFACE

For years I have resisted the idea of a book about my life — I simply wasn't interested. Editors have suggested I write it myself and I even labored over several pages before I gave up. I didn't think I was good enough—but mainly I realized that if I took the time to write a book there were hundreds of other things I wouldn't be able to do.

Then Howard Teichmann came into my life. I liked Howard at sight, and having read and enjoyed his other biographies, I agreed to the alliance—and alliance is what it has been. I have spent untold hours with him, spilling my guts out as I never thought I could to his tape machine.

I, of course, hope you'll enjoy the book—it is certainly there, warts and all.

HENRY FONDA
Bel Air

INTRODUCTION

It wasn't easy. Although I'd seen Henry Fonda dozens of times on the stage and in movie houses, we'd only met once and I was certain he wouldn't remember me when I telephoned him. He didn't.

"But I know some of your work," Fonda said. "You write plays and biographies. If you've got a play, I'll be glad to read it. If you want to do my biography, forget it."

I swallowed, and then jumped into the silence.

"Maybe if I fly out to California and discuss it with you . . ."

"Don't waste your money," Fonda told me, and I sensed our conversation was about over.

I hadn't been that intimidated in years. It must have been the Fonda voice! How could I sway Abe Lincoln, Tom Joad, Doug Roberts, Wyatt Earp, Clarence Darrow, an Admiral of the Fleet, a General of the Army, and a couple of Presidents of the United States?

"I'll be in New York next week," he said. "Call me at this number. We'll make a date to meet."

I had little sympathy for myself. Everybody had warned me that getting permission to do an authorized biography of Henry Fonda would be mighty improbable and damn near impossible. I got in touch with Walter Kerr, the dean of Broadway drama critics. I asked his opinion. His reply came in a *New York Times* envelope. Inside was a carbon copy of an unused review he had written in 1978. It began with:

Henry Fonda has been an actor, and a fine one on stage and screen for fifty years. Perhaps there's nothing so unusual about that. Other men, and many women, have done it. What was surprising, the last time he appeared on the New York stage, was to realize that he was no longer simply a fine actor. He had transformed himself—was still in the process of transforming himself—into a phenomenon, a legend, before our eyes.

Actors who look like Mr. Fonda, actors who perform as modestly, as soft-spokenly as Mr. Fonda normally does, do not tend to become legends. It takes extravagance to become legendary, it wants the death dealing grin of a James Cagney or the high-and-mightiness of a Bette Davis to bring it off.

Toward the end of his article Mr. Kerr made these observations:

Behind all the juveniles, inside all of those apparently placid leading men, there lurked a *permanent* stubbornness, a determination never to be persuaded beyond a point of principle. He may always have been a gentleman; he was never a pushover. The inner resolve, the tensile strength beneath the surface, had been there the whole time—and it was the strange mixture of spine and suppleness that has kept him interesting, even challenging, for the first fifty years . . .

On a rusty October day in 1979 I telephoned Mr. Fonda as arranged and went to his apartment on Fifty-seventh Street. He shook my hand and pointed me to a chair. He was taller than I had remembered and incredibly slim. His face had that Midwestern-prairie look to it and he was still very handsome. He wore cowboy boots, brown corduroy trousers, and a Texas-type shirt open at the neck. Depending on what was said, the color of his eyes changed from the soft blue of a summer sky to the icy look of the Atlantic in January.

"I've been married five times," he said abruptly, "and I'm goddamn ashamed of it."

During the pause that followed my ears popped as though I were in an express elevator going down.

Fonda leaned toward me and set his jaw.

"My life has been peppered with suicides and I don't like to think back on them. Dozens of writers and publishers have asked me to cooperate on a book about my life. I've always said no."

His long fingers grasped his knees and he eased himself into the thick pillows of the couch. I stood up to leave.

"Thank you very much for your time, Mr. Fonda."

He didn't invite me to stay.

"I've read two of your books," he said, "but I never got around to the one on George S. Kaufman. Do you have a spare copy? Shirlee and I could trade off reading it on the plane tomorrow."

Later that afternoon I dropped off two copies of the Kaufman biography with Fonda's doorman. Then I went home and turned on the television set. After a minute I turned it off. I could taste my disappointment but not my dinner.

The next day Henry Fonda telephoned.

"Let's do the book," he said. "I'm ready."

The exhilaration I felt could have powered the four jet engines that carried me to Los Angeles. Almost everyone in America and many people throughout the world know the public Henry Fonda. My job was to dig down and uncover the private man.

I arrived in California with a suitcase, a tape recorder, and dozens of probing questions that required intimate responses.

He met me in the courtyard of his Bel Air home, ushered me into the living room, and sat me down on a sofa. After he settled into his favorite easy chair, I turned on the tape recorder.

"Is this how you want to do it?" he asked.

I said yes if it was all right with him.

He began to talk. He talked about his father's job-printing plant in Omaha, Nebraska, how he flunked out of college, his first audition for the theater, his initiation into sex, the years of rooming with Jimmy Stewart, Josh Logan, Myron McCormick, and Johnny Swope.

He didn't disappoint me. John Steinbeck had been right when he described Fonda as "a piece of electricity." He spoke frankly, without hesitation. No questions offended him. Many answers caused him pain and brought tears to his eyes and to mine. He read me poems he'd written as a young boy, he sang songs, he told funny stories that had us both laughing right into hiccups. We established a routine that went from nine in the morning to eight in the evening seven days a week. The slipcovers on the sofa changed with the seasons.

All of his files, all of his letters were made available to me. During the course of these sessions, Henry Fonda accepted no telephone calls. The only interruption he tolerated was the occasional appearance of his attractive wife, Shirlee. Those blue eyes of his took on a tender hue whenever she stopped by the room. It was Shirlee as much as Henry who arranged for me to interview his family, his friends, his acquaintances, and his associates. But it was Henry who urged them to talk not only to the smooth texture of the Fonda marble, but to comment on the flawed side as well. All those kind people are listed alphabetically in the acknowledgments at the back of this book.

During one of my visits to California, Dan Sullivan, Walter Kerr's opposite number on the West Coast, wrote in the *Los Angeles Times:*

Audiences trust Fonda. They and their parents

have been doing business with him for years—at least as far back as *The Grapes of Wrath* and he has always given value. Fonda's name over a title somehow seems to speak well for a show.

The name over the title means the actor is a star, but never in the hundreds of hours of tape I have recorded with Henry Fonda is the word "star" mentioned.

In its own way that should be indicative of the man's character. He never thinks of himself as a star, only as an actor and a human being.

And that is how I hope I have written him.

HOWARD TEICHMANN
New York

CHAPTER
1

NATURE, which had pummeled New York City mercilessly with the blizzard of 1947, relented the following month. January had been white and impassable, then gray and miserable. The traditional January thaw arrived in February. The eight-foot-high banks of snow melted, the asphalt streets were potholed but clear once again, city traffic returned to its usual snarl, and by mid February Manhattan took on an early spring, freshly polished look.

Amid this atmosphere of relief and milder weather, a play was trucked into town. It would be a play that made theatrical history. All plays make theatrical history in one form or another, but this one would make a mark more permanent than most.

The man chosen to play the title role in that memorable production arose early. He showered, shaved, dressed quickly, breakfasted, and stepped out into the sunshine that tried to work its way down through the spaces between the tall buildings in front of the Lombardy Hotel.

Hailing a taxi, he got in, closed the door behind his long frame, and said, "Fifty-second Street between Broadway and Eighth."

The cabbie looked at his fare through the rear-view mirror.

"Which side of the street?"

"Downtown."

"Any address?"

"The Alvin."

The cabbie stared even harder, but his passenger deliberately averted the inquisitive gaze.

"You with that new show comin' in there?" In those days the men who drove New York taxis were riding encyclopedias. The passenger, however, was a shy man. Instead of answering, he turned his head and pretended to observe the well-dressed pedestrians on the fashionable East Side streets. It was only when they crossed Broadway that he relaxed enough to stretch his legs, put his arms up, and lock his long fingers behind his neck. Broadway was *his* territory. Already on the way down from the golden age of the American theater, the Times Square area still held more legitimate theaters in a dozen block area than any ten cities in the country combined. Looking to his left, the passenger saw the theaters that had been converted into movie houses and the movie houses that had slipped into shoddier pursuits. In the morning light, however, Times Square still retained its excitement and glamour for him. He remembered only the good times. The bad ones he kept locked in the depths of his mind. All that he could accept now was that he was back on Broadway.

"You got something to do with this show here?" the cabbie asked as he pulled up in front of the theater.

"Uh huh."

"I thought so. I noticed you when you got in the hack. You got that kind of face. Familiar, y'know?"

"I know," the passenger answered in a broad Midwestern accent.

"So what's with the show? You in it?"

The fare got out, paid the driver, and a big smile spread across his lean face.

"I sure am," he said. As the taxi pulled away, the actor gazed up at the marquee of the Alvin. The electric light bulbs on the sign read:

HENRY FONDA
in
MISTER ROBERTS

2

He grinned with satisfaction, entered the stage door and nodded to the white-haired doorman. Immediately, the odor of backstage reached his nostrils. The dust, the scent of hemp, of fresh paint and stale makeup was like perfume to the actor. He strode leisurely to his dressing room on the first floor, opened the door, and turned on the lights. The forty watters that ringed the mirror over his dressing table looked like Welcome Home signs. He looked into the mirror.

Nineteen forty-five, Lt. (s.g.) Henry Fonda, air combat intelligence officer in the United States Navy, flew stateside as soon as permission was granted following the victory over Japan. Waiting for him at his home on Tigertail Road in Brentwood, California, were his wife, Frances, and his two small children, Jane, age eight, and Peter, five.

Like millions of other Americans, Lt. Fonda became civilian Fonda as quickly as possible. His khaki trousers and his khaki shirts were placed in mothballs along with his officer's cap. Battered by rain, scorched for three years by the Pacific sun, the cap and other parts of the uniform were stored in the attic of the house on Tigertail Road never, it was hoped, to be used again.

Once out of his uniform, Fonda reverted to his life's work: acting. As an actor, he was a "type." Taller than Clark Gable, thinner than John Wayne, slower than Tyrone Power, Fonda, his long-time friend Jimmy Stewart, and Gary Cooper were the American versions of Robin Hood, of the gallant knights of Arthur's Round Table; these three played cowboys better than any other actors. They shared many traits. They were lanky, supposedly slow to anger, supposedly quick on the draw. Actually, Stewart was an ace bomber pilot, Cooper was a genuine bronco buster, but Fonda was quite different. He would have nothing to do with guns, he hated horses. Despite his slow speech and crinkling blue eyes, Fonda was more a closet intellectual than a cow puncher, but he hid this side of his nature almost as well as he concealed his shyness. There was nothing simple about him. He was as complex as the lighting charts backstage on Broadway and as complicated as the camera angles on a sound stage on the West Coast. Part dreamer, part painter, he was captivated by farming, politics, women, and above all by his work.

Both Cooper and Stewart were properties of the major motion picture studios. Fonda was a maverick. Always looking for better roles, more meaningful scripts, he battled the Hollywood Establishment with almost the same tenacity he fought the Japanese.

Awarded a Bronze Star by the Navy and a Presidential Citation for services to his country, Fonda gave the medal to his small son who took it out to play and promptly lost it. Motion picture contracts are not done away with in such an easy manner. Fonda made seven fast films after the war. The next script offered Fonda was a draft of *Rain Before Seven*. He did not feel it was right for him. He coaxed his friend, author John O'Hara, to adapt his novel *Appointment in Samarra* as a screenplay.

The studio was as indifferent to *Samarra* as Fonda was to *Rain Before Seven*. In an attempt to salvage *Samarra* Fonda rode the train to New York to visit his chum of many years Josh Logan, the stage director and play doctor.

Josh Logan, co-author and director of *Mister Roberts*, also lived at the Lombardy Hotel with his wife, Nedda. Logan stood six feet tall, an inch or two shorter than Fonda, but he had the solid body of a football player. Unlike Fonda's flat Nebraska speech, Logan's voice was soft and honeyed. He came from deepest Louisiana. His drawl had been sharpened by four years at Princeton and two decades on Broadway. Logan's wife, Nedda Harrigan, came from a prominent stage family. She was famous as a beauty and a leader in the upper echelons of theatrical society.

No one had a greater stake in the production of *Mister Roberts* than these two. Fonda had been Logan's close friend since both men had squeaked their way into the theater in the late twenties.

When Logan came across a novel of loosely knit short stories dealing with naval life in the Pacific during the war, he invited the young author, an ex-sailor named Tom Heggen, to collaborate on the dramatization. Mostly, they worked at the Logan country cottage in Connecticut. Both men agreed not to discuss casting until the play was finished.

"When we wrote the word *Curtain* at the end of the second act," Logan observed later, "we both began talking about Hank."

"I know it's crazy," Heggen said, "but when I was writing *Roberts* I kept picturing Henry Fonda."

"That's a terrible idea," Logan replied. "I ought to know because I've had the same terrible idea for a long time."

"I thought he was a pal of yours," Heggen said.

"Pal or no pal," Logan answered, "we can't compete with movie-star salaries or Hollywood contracts."

"But he's so right for Doug Roberts," the younger man persisted.

"Listen, we don't even know what Roberts looks like. I'll get Davey Wayne over to the hotel and see how *he* likes it."

"We drove down to the city," Logan recalled, "and when we walked into our place in the Lombardy, the phone was ringing. It was Fonda. In New York."

Logan threw back the covers on the morning of February 18, 1948, feeling good about everything, eager to hear the laughter a hit brings. No cause for worry, he told himself. The show had been a success in all three try-out towns they had visited. He listened patiently while his wife discussed the dress she intended to wear to the opening that evening. Then he left the hotel and strolled crosstown to the Alvin. He had every reason to expect great things from the night's work that lay ahead of him.

William Hammerstein, *Mister Roberts*'s stage manager, left his Upper West Side apartment earlier than usual that morning. In spite of the good out-of-town reviews, he felt uncomfortable on several counts. This was the first big show he'd ever stage managed. When he'd read the first draft of the script by Tom Heggen and Josh Logan he

5

hadn't liked it particularly and had been foolish enough to express his opinion to Logan. Moreover, he and his first wife were on the verge of a separation that would lead to a divorce. Finally, he remembered a matinee had been scheduled for two-thirty. Hammerstein, as Fonda, as Logan, as Tom Heggen, as almost everyone in the cast of *Mister Roberts*, had been in the service. Hammerstein had served in the Navy as a chief quartermaster. He slipped into his dungarees and walked to Seventy-second Street and Broadway, where he took the subway downtown to the theater. At the time he had no idea of the near disaster that awaited him at the matinee prior to the opening.

There was only one woman in the cast of *Mister Roberts*, Lt. Ann Girard, a nurse. Originally Peggy Maley got the part, but she didn't seem right. Her replacement was an unknown youngster named Eva Marie Saint. But Eva Marie Saint also brought a problem to the play. She was far too beautiful and when she walked off stage, the audience longed to go with her.

"I remember driving home with Josh and Leland in Leland's car and they were talking about it," Fonda says.

"The problem here," Logan pointed out, "is that Peggy was too tough and Eva Marie is too attractive."

Producer Lelend Hayward agreed.

"After that scene on the deck when she discovers the crew is looking at nurses on the island taking showers, she exits and the audience has to stay with those poor slobs on stage who haven't had sex in eighteen months."

"Have you told Eva Marie she's out?" Hayward asked.

"I've made an arrangement," Logan answered. "Jobs are hard to get and she needs the money so she can stay on as the understudy."

"How'd she take it?"

"Tears."

The three men in the car sighed.

"But, dammit," Logan continued, "it's three days before we leave for New Haven. There's got to be a young Margaret Sullavan, a young Dorothy McGuire. That's what we need."

Both men looked at Fonda. He'd been married for a

time to Sullavan and he'd discovered McGuire in his hometown.

"I remember another girl from Omaha," he said.

"Who?" the producer inquired.

"Her name is Tid," Fonda said.

"What?" Hayward asked.

"T-i-d."

"What the hell kind of name is that?" the producer asked.

"It's just her nickname," Fonda winced. "I knew her as a baby in Omaha, tossed her in the air and tickled her."

"Can she act?" Logan inquired.

"She understudied Dorothy McGuire in *Claudia*."

"Can you get her?"

"She's in town."

"Call her."

From his hotel Henry Fonda telephoned Jocelyn Brando.

"We've got a part," he told her, "and we don't know what to do with it. Do you want to take a whack at it?"

Two days before the company left to try out on the road, a new Lt. Girard went on stage.

The day of the opening in New York, she got up around six in the morning. She lived in a cold-water flat on Sixty-eighth Street and West End Avenue. She had a sore throat but was determined it would not interfere with her performance that night. She roused her three-and-a-half-year-old son, Gahan Hanmer, fed him, dressed him, and took him to his nursery school. Then she prepared to do gown to the theater. Jocelyn wondered if her brother would show up at the opening. She had sent him a ticket, but who could tell about Marlon Brando?

On orders from his employer, Leland Hayward's chauffeur slowed down the limousine as he swung into Fifty-second Street from Eighth Avenue. The car stopped in front of the Alvin Theater.

Born in the same state as his star, but three years earlier, the producer of *Mister Roberts* had gone to the best schools in the East, St. Paul's, Hotchkiss, Princeton. His first job was reporting for the old New York *Sun*. From there, Leland Hayward went into publicity for United Artists, and for ten years, beginning in 1934, he operated his own literary and theatrical agency. Among his clients were Fred Astaire, Judy Garland, Garbo, Hemingway, Dashiell Hammett, Lillian Hellman, Boris Karloff, Margaret Sullavan, and, of course, Henry Fonda.

Toward the end of World War II, Hayward sold his agency to Dr. Jules Stein's Music Corporation of America and went into producing Broadway plays. His first attempt, John Hersey's *A Bell for Adano*, met with great success. Next season he followed this with the Pulitzer Prize-winning *State of the Union* by Howard Lindsay and Russell Crouse.

Stepping out of his car, he checked the day's "wrap" with the treasurer of the Alvin, Irving Keyser. It gave him much satisfaction to hear that *Mr. Roberts* would open that night with an advance of three hundred thousand dollars, not an unsubstantial sum in 1948. After watching the double line of people buying tickets at the box-office windows, Hayward returned to his car and went back to the office to make last-minute plans for "dressing the house" for opening night.

Aside from the principals, the first member of the cast chosen had been Harvey Lembeck, a short, dark, barrel-chested boy from Brooklyn. When World War II erupted for America at Pearl Harbor, Lembeck looked for action and found it in the Submarine Service of the Navy. He spent three years in combat. With an honorable discharge and little else, he returned to New York to look for work. Acting is what he thought he might try, but few jobs were open to him.

"Leave your résumé," indifferent casting directors told him. He didn't have one.

The Hudson Theater was on Forty-fourth Street between Broadway and Sixth Avenue. A line extended from the front doors out onto the sidewalk. Lembeck saw a friend standing there. Without knowing why, Lembeck joined him. At the door a young man sat at a small table taking names, adresses, agents.

"Were you in the service?" he asked Lembeck.

Lembeck listed his service record. If he didn't have credits in the theater, he most certainly had them in the armed forces.

"Go right in," the young man said. The young man, he learned later, was the author of the novel, *Mister Roberts*, Tom Heggen.

Inside the darkened theater a tall, well-built man with a mustache and a soft voice waved him onto the stage.

"Take off your shirt," Josh Logan instructed Lembeck.

Lembeck did as he was told.

"We are looking for an Italian American kid from Brooklyn," Logan's voice came from the darkness of the house.

"That's me," Lembeck snapped.

"Okay," Logan answered, "take the script and go over it with our stage manager." Lembeck and Billy Hammerstein read the pages on which Sam Insigna's role had been typed.

"All right. That's enough," the voice from the darkened house said.

Lembeck waited for the usual words, "Thank you very much. We'll call you." Only this time the words were different.

"Please go upstairs," Josh Logan told him, "and see Herman Bernstein."

Lembeck had no idea who Herman Bernstein might be but he went upstairs. Inside the office there were three men. One was unfamiliar. The other two left Lembeck in awe. The week before, he and his wife had scraped together enough money to see the hit *State of the Union*. There, before him, sat the authors, Howard Lindsay and Russell Crouse.

"They were charming," Lembeck recollected. He explained how very much he had admired their work and they accepted his compliments graciously. Everyone was smiling only Lembeck didn't know why.

"You're the first one we're hiring," the third man, Leland Hayward's general manager, Herman Bernstein, said. "You'll be making a hundred and a quarter a week, a hundred and fifty on the road for expenses."

"Congratulations, young man," Lindsay said.

"Welcome aboard," Crouse told him.

"My God," Lembeck gasped, "if my wife could only see me now."

"Where is she?" Russell Crouse inquired.

"Brooklyn. She's pregnant."

"Call her up."

"No, it's okay."

"Well, I'll call her. What's the number?" Crouse asked. When he got it out of Lembeck, Crouse dialed the telephone.

"Hello, Mrs. Lembeck, this is Buck Crouse."

"Really?" Caroline Lembeck asked in disbelief.

"Your husband is here," Crouse said and he handed the phone to the shaking young actor.

"Honey," Lembeck said, "That's him. That's Russell Crouse, the fellow that wrote the play. And, honey, listen. I got a job. I'm in a Broadway play!"

On the morning of the opening, Mr. and Mrs. Harvey Lembeck left their apartment in Brooklyn's Sheepshead Bay and checked into the Taft Hotel on Broadway and Fiftieth Street. She was five months pregnant with their first child and he was prepared for anything.

In Greenwich Village David Wayne and his wife, Jane, slept late. Their twin daughters, Melinda and Susan, then three years old, had awakened them in the apartment they rented on West Twelfth Street. Wayne, knowing he had a matinee to play before the opening that night, dressed rapidly and left the house. The day was warm and sunny, and as he basked in the mild weather on his way to the Sixth Avenue subway, David Wayne, the pride of Traverse City, Michigan, the glorious Leprechaun in the previous season's hit musical *Finian's Rainbow*, reflected on how he, unlike everyone in the cast of *Mister Roberts*, had stepped from a hit in which he had captured the laurels of the critics into a new and untried comedy-drama. Before the war, Wayne had appeared in a series of not very successful revivals and a string of even less successful plays. With the start of hostilities, Wayne enlisted in the American Ambulance Service in Libya and Egypt; later with the United States Army. He wasn't discharged until 1946, but almost immediately upon his return he went into *Finian's* and became the sensation of the season.

One night in October he was sitting at Sardi's Little Bar nursing a beer after an evening's performance when Josh Logan stopped behind him and put his large hand on Wayne's small shoulder.

"I've been looking for you," the director said in a whispery voice that spelled Logan's brand of excitement. Wayne looked up from his drink.

"Yes?"

"Everybody said you might be here."

"Well, here I am. Sit down."

"Not now. Listen, Davey, I've got the greatest part in the world for you."

"I'm playing the greatest part in the world at the Forty-sixth Street Theater."

"No, you aren't," Logan contradicted him. "Tom Heggen and I are working on it right now, and there's no question that we've got to have you playing in the show. It's called *Mister Roberts*."

Wayne had never heard of it but that didn't dampen Logan's enthusiasm.

"Listen, Davey, Tom and I are getting ready to read a show to you. One of these nights I'll call you up and tell you we're coming to the theater, and afterward we'll read you this play."

"Okay, okay," Wayne answered. Dismissing the entire notion as folly on Logan's part, he finished his beer and went home to Jane and the kids.

Then came the Saturday when Logan called.

"Davey, Tom and I are coming to the theater tonight. We'll see your second act, pick you up and take you to my apartment."

"Wonderful, wonderful," Wayne answered. It's always pleasant for an actor to be courted by a director.

Following the performance, Logan and Heggen appeared in Wayne's dressing room. Behind them stood a tall, familiar figure. Wayne had seen him on the movie screen over and over.

11

"Davey," Logan began, "this is my good friend Henry Fonda."

"How do you do?" Wayne asked. "I've heard about you and Josh and Jimmy Stewart and all the guys from the University Players. How are you?"

"Fine," Fonda said, committing himself to nothing.

"Davey," Logan said filling in the sudden gap in the conversation, "do you mind if Hank comes along with us? We're very proud of this play and I'd like my old buddy to hear it."

"Sure. Why not?" The Leprechaun who could turn a white man into a black man eight performances a week could afford to be generous to a fellow actor.

At eleven-thirty they entered Logan's apartment.

Nedda Logan knew a cue when she heard one.

"Forgive me," she said to the four men. "If you don't mind, I'll leave you and head for bed."

Immediately, Logan laid out the scenes for *Mister Roberts*. Chairs represented gun turrets, end tables suggested hatches, lamps were to be companionways. The scene was an old tub of a freighter in the Pacific during World War II. Logan started reading the first scene. He finished at three in the morning.

Wayne was flabbergasted, absolutely overcome with the power and magnificence of the work. But he had already played a matinee and an evening performance and by now he felt drained. All he could get out were the words, "Marvelous, marvelous, marvelous."

Then he went by cab to Twelfth Street.

"Originally, I didn't have any interest in the play Josh had written," Fonda says regarding the script that had been read that night in Logan's hotel suite. "I went there just to talk to him about a movie. I'm a polite fellow, though. I thought I'd sit and listen and make a couple of complimentary remarks and then get the conversation around either to the property I had already signed to do or the O'Hara screenplay.

"God! What an overwhelming surprise and experience *Roberts* turned out to be. I listened and laughed and I cried and I felt everything an audience should feel. Wayne was wild about it, too, but he left because he was tired.

"After he went, I said, 'Josh, there's no way I'm not going to play that part. It's mine. I don't care if I get sued. Nothing's going to stop me.'

"I called California and told my agent, Lew Wasserman, 'Get me out of my contract with Fox.' Wasserman is a wizard. He did."

At four in the morning Wayne's telephone rang.

"Davey?" a concerned voice asked.

"Uh huh."

By now Wayne's wife, Jane, had turned on a light.

"What's the matter, Davey?"

"What do you mean, what's the matter?"

"You acted as if you didn't like the play very much."

Wayne sat up in bed.

"Josh," he began, realizing Logan's sensitivity, in fact, the hypersensitivity of almost all playwrights, "Josh, I think it's the most delightful comedy I've heard in my life."

"But you only said . . ."

"I think it's the most touching script I ever heard, too."

"Then why did you only say it was marvelous?"

Everybody in the theater knows about everybody else's ego.

"Josh," David Wayne spoke earnestly, hoping not to wake the twins, but still trying to convince Logan he had something, "Josh, it's the best modern play I've ever heard. There's just one little matter.

"On the way home I got to thinking in the cab."

"Yes? Well, what is it?"

"The guy sitting over there in the corner of your apartment, your friend Henry Fonda, should play Mister Roberts. I should play Ensign Pulver."

Logan beamed. Exactly the way he had planned it.

"You're right, Davey. Hank'll do Roberts, you'll do Pulver. Now, go back to sleep."

The man staring into the mirror in the star's dressing room in the Alvin Theater before the final preview did

13

not look forty-three years old. His eyes, the color of a high summer sky, showed a face youthful and still un-lined. His boyish smile, his thin body made it possible for Henry Fonda to play the role of Doug Roberts, a man in his late twenties, with ease and believability.

His dresser, T. R. Moss, had his neatly pressed cos-tume hanging nearby. The khaki uniform, lightweight trousers, lightweight shirt, came from a costume house. But the officer's cap, perhaps out of sentiment, perhaps because it had seen him safely through three years of war-fare in the Pacific, was Fonda's own. He and his wife, Frances, had gone to the attic of their home in Brent-wood, opened the box containing his naval uniform, and extracted the old cotton cap. When he packed for re-hearsals in New York, it went with him. He wore it throughout the run of *Mister Roberts*.

There was another entity in that dressing room not visi-ble to the eye but surely present. From the time he first appeared on the amateur stage in Omaha, Nebraska, in every play and every film he did, Henry Fonda wore the mask of the character that had been written for him. His shyness, his vulnerability, his insecurities vanished once he placed the actor's mask over his face. Behind it he be-came fearless. He was *not* Henry Fonda, he was another personality. With no trouble whatever he could become a sophisticate, an Okie, a United States senator, a Supreme Court justice—but *always* an American, *always* the hero. On this day he will become a lieutenant (j.g.) aboard a rusting freighter shuttling "from Apathy to Tedium with occasional side trips to Monotony and Ennui." That lieu-tenant will be more loved and better remembered than most parts written for an actor.

Fonda made him that way.

No jars or tubes of makeup rested on the table in front of the lighted mirror in that dressing room. The *Mister Roberts* company didn't use makeup, Joshua Logan had large sunlamps installed in the basement of the Alvin Theater and every member of the cast was under orders to take sun two or three times a week. If the war was in the Pacific, Logan wanted his actors to be tanned by ul-traviolet rays not by Max Factor Number Ten.

"One of the beautiful things about the theater for me," Fonda says, "is that it's therapy. I don't have to be me. I've got the mask on. And *Roberts* was one of the best masks I ever had. I knew that I had something they'd like. I was cool. And I was ready."

Billy Hammerstein had entered the theater moments before Fonda and experienced none of the leading man's coolness or readiness. By law an asbestos curtain had to be lowered after each evening's performance. A form of fire protection going back to the days when the footlights held candles and the flame from a single candle could ignite the hem of a lady's gown, the asbestos curtain was a large heavy object that hung on the pipe closest to the audience. Normally, such curtains are counterweighted with bars of lead equal to the weight of the curtain. A slight tug by a stagehand and the asbestos rides up or down. Except in the early afternoon of February 18, 1948.

No one remembers what went wrong, whether a line was fouled up in the gridiron of the house, whether a tackle had slipped, but Billy Hammerstein *does* remember that when he asked the curtain man to raise the asbestos it wouldn't budge. Hurried conferences with stagehands, stage managers, and the house manager resulted in the only alternative method of getting up the gray mass. A hand winch stood nearby and it required two men to turn the handle of the winch which would eventually raise the curtain.

Two men at a time, attempting to pull up tons of fireproofing, lasted about five minutes apiece on the winch. Then, dripping with sweat, their muscles aching, they would be replaced by another two men. Inch by inch the curtain went up. But it was now two-fifteen and the house was filling with an audience and the curtain was only a foot and a half off the stage floor. Unless the curtain could be raised, the audience could not see the actors.

That final preview before the opening of *Mister Roberts* consisted of a handful of theater friends of the producer, Leland Hayward. The remainder of the 1,341 seats were filled by enlisted men of the United States

Navy. Hammerstein looked out and saw a sea of white hats. Within fifteen minutes, half hour at the most, these sailors would grow impatient and from there, unruly.

To begin the play with a curtain cutting the actors off at the waist didn't seem wise. How could the audience see them? How could they hear them? Three feet off the stage floor, four feet off the stage floor. The time on Billy Hammerstein's wristwatch read quarter of three. When the asbestos had been raised to five feet, Hammerstein threw the first cue to Chief Johnson.

J. Russell "Rusty" Lane, the college drama professor who had left his wife, his children, and his tenure at the University of Wisconsin to marry a student, Sarah Anderson, played Chief Johnson. From an off-stage position he sung out, "Reveille . . . Hit the deck . . Greet the new day."

Harvey Lembeck had the next line.

"Okay, Chief, you done your duty—now get your fat can out of here."

Lane, ducking under the asbestos curtain, made his entrance. The play was under way.

The men in the house identified completely with the actors portraying sailors on the stage. Better than any audience before, they knew what it meant to be denied shore leave, what it felt like to serve under a martinet of an officer. When the play ended, thirteen hundred sailors shouted themselves hoarse.

To Fonda it had been very gratifying. He and Bob Keith, who played the role of Doc, changed and ran next door to a restaurant called Ruby Foo's where they enjoyed a sizable Chinese dinner.

Harvey Lembeck raced back to the Taft Hotel where he and his wife ordered room service. It was delicious. Only when Harvey Lembeck walked out of the hotel and looked at the lights and marquees of Times Square, he suddenly realized what the opening night of *Mister Roberts* might mean to him. Promptly, he lost his entire meal at the curb in front of the hotel. Feeling shaken, slightly feverish, and filled with anxiety, he made his way back to the Alvin.

For opening night Leland Hayward had handpicked the audience, Marlene Dietrich, Noël Coward, Oscar and Dorothy Hammerstein, Richard and Dorothy Rodgers, Howard Lindsay, Dorothy Stickney, Russell and Anna Crouse, Dorothy Parker, John Steinbeck, Dorothy McGuire, John Swope. Slowly, they inched along from the lobby of the Alvin into the theater's auditorium. Backstage, Billy Hammerstein spoke softly into the microphone of the public address system that carried his voice into every dressing room.

"Half hour, please."

The flowers, the telegrams, the gifts heralding an opening night filled Fonda's dressing room. Under orders from the actor himself, the stage managers allowed no one into his dressing room before the performance except Josh Logan His friend, his director, his author had a few words of hoarse encouragement.

"Fifteen minutes, please," Hammerstein's voice warned over the PA system.

Logan left. Was Fonda fretful?

"Hell, no!" he says. "They call me a frosty son-of-a-bitch, my peers in the New York theater, because I'm not nervous. They're throwing up in the corners and I can't wait to get on."

Looking out at the packed house and then glancing at his wristwatch, Billy Hammerstein flipped on the microphone for the third and last time.

"Places, please," he called gently to the actors.

As the cast assembled in the wings, Hammerstein spoke to the chief electrician.

"Take the house to half."

The lights in the chandelier dimmed. Gradually, the chatter of the audience diminished.

"Kill the house."

Even the lamps on the sides of the auditorium went out.

"Curtain!" Hammerstein called in much the same sense that crowds at race tracks call, "They're off!" as the horses leave the starting gate. The house curtain of the Alvin rose to reveal Jo Mielziner's marvelous set of the AK 601. Applause greeted it.

"Reveille . . . Hit the deck . . . Greet the new day," Rusty Lane's gruff voice sounded from off stage.

"Okay, Chief," Harvey Lembeck responded, "you done your duty—now get your fat can out of here."

Mister Roberts was under way.

Leland Hayward sat in a seat down front on the orchestra floor. Joshua Logan, smartly dressed in a dinner jacket, stood quietly at the rear of the house. While he listened carefully to each word spoken by his cast, he watched intently the reaction of the audience. On either side of Logan were his collaborator, Tom Heggen, and his wife, Nedda, the former in an ill-fitting tuxedo borrowed from Alan Campbell, Dorothy Parker's husband, the latter in an evening gown.

Nedda Harrigan Logan remembered, "Josh and I chose it when we were in Paris during the war. It was made by Lanvin and after *Mister Roberts* I called it my good luck dress."

The sailors at the matinee had been wildly encouraging; cast members worried that the evening performance could not match it. Within moments, the actors realized the opening night audience was even better.

There is a theory held by many theater people that a play becomes a hit or a failure within the first twenty minutes after the curtain goes up. In the case of *Mister Roberts* it didn't take that long. Fonda recognized the audience's initial reaction almost immediately. Everything, in the parlance of the stage, "worked" that night.

When the final curtain came down, the people in the Alvin leaped to their feet. Cheers overrode applause. The standing ovation the cast members received refused to die down. Noël Coward, author, Englishman, sophisticate, but also a former member of the Royal Navy, stood atop his seat shouting bravos. The actors stopped counting the curtain calls.

Finally, Henry Fonda appeared alone on the stage. His face wore that boyish smile, and he held up his hand, beseeching a moment of silence from the audience.

"That's all Tom and Josh wrote," he explained. "If you want us to do it again, we will."

The cheers grew even louder.

At that point Billy Hammerstein ordered the house-lights up full and the audience, still tingling from the play, reluctantly started up the aisles. By then, most drama critics were out of the house and on their way to the newspapers.

In 1948 eight daily periodicals flourished in New York. Half an hour after the curtain came down the future of *Mister Roberts* and Henry Fonda was being decided on the sheets of white copy paper on the rollers of eight typewriters in as many city rooms.

The Logans and Leland Hayward threw a cast party for the *Roberts* company in the ballroom of the Lombardy.

Fonda remembers little of it. Just bits and pieces. Logan is equally vague. Nedda Logan recalls being wrapped in a fog of happiness that parted only when Dorothy Parker came into the room. One of the wickedest wits of the old Algonquin Round Table had nothing to say. She marched in, stopped in front of Harvey Lembeck, got down on her knees, and salaamed before him. The Waynes, Davey and Jane, also were aglow.

When the company press agent appeared ninety minutes later, his arms filled with the morning newspapers, the hum in the ballroom died down. All the crewcut heads of the cast bent over the drama pages while they read the reviews. Then a roar went up. *Mister Roberts* didn't get ordinary notices. It received ecstatic raves.

Referring to Fonda's curtain speech, John Chapman, the *Daily News* critic, wrote, "I hung around awhile, hoping they *would* do it again."

Brooks Atkinson of the *Times* noted, "Now that Mr. Fonda is back after eleven years, it would be nice to have him back for good."

Handshakes, hugs, and kisses were exchanged. Fonda touched his wife's elbow and they rode up in the hotel elevator.

"Did you see that audience?" he asked Frances. "Did you hear that applause? Did you read those notices?"

He opened the door, danced his way into the suite, and twirled his wife around the sitting room.

"You know what? I've rehearsed forty-three years for this night, and it sure as hell was worth it!"

The management had sent up a bottle of chilled champagne. Frances reached for the glasses and Fonda eased the cork up with his thumb. Pop! The wine foamed out over the lip of the Piper Heidsick '36.

"It's a long way from Nebraska," he said, and started to pour.

CHAPTER
2

It is 1,296 miles from the stage of the Omaha Community Playhouse to the boards of the Alvin Theater in New York, but Henry Fonda made it. It took more than talent, it took years of patience and labor and luck, but he got there, his name billed over the title of the play, a handsome salary, the star's dressing room.

Henry Jaynes Fonda and the nickelodeon both made their appearance in the same year, 1905. The nickelodeon first saw light of day on the streets of Pittsburgh, Pennsylvania. Henry Fonda was born in Grand Island, Nebraska.

His father, William Brace Fonda, proprietor of a job printing plant, moved his wife, his son, and his presses to Omaha within six months of Henry's birth. Once there they remained permanently fixed, permanent for Fondas.

Early records show the family ensconced in northern Italy in the sixteenth century where they fought on the side of the Reformation, fled to Holland, intermarried with Dutch burghers' daughters, picked up the first names of the Low Countries, but retained the Italianate Fonda. Before Pieter Stuyvesant surrendered Nieuw Amsterdam to the English the Fondas, instead of settling in Manhattan, canoed up the Hudson River to the Indian village of Caughawaga. Within a few generations, the Mohawks and the Iroquois were butchered or fled and the town became known to mapmakers as Fonda, New York,

It was from there that a seventeen-year-old boy volun-

21

teered for service in the Union Army during the Civil War. Young and quick, he learned telegraphy and was instrumental in carrying a message, family lore has it, that helped save the army of General Meade.

Family lore misses the fact that General Meade commanded the army of the Potomac only once, but that conflict was the greatest battle ever fought on the North American continent. From July 1 through July 3, 1863, Meade opposed Lee at Gettysburg. Army records list Fonda, Ten Eyck H., Henry's grandfather, and Douw's grandfather, as being promoted by Ulysses S. Grant to the rank of lieutenant after Gettysburg.

Today, Fonda, New York, is principally known as the town in which Henry Fonda "was almost born."

Following the birth of her son, Herberta Fonda bore her husband two daughters, Harriet and Jayne.

"No one could have nicer sisters," Fonda says. "No sibling problems there."

"As a matter of fact," Fonda says, "my whole damn family was nice. I don't think I've imagined it. It's true. Maybe it has to do with being brought up as a Christian Scientist. Half of my relatives were Readers or Practitioners in the church.

"If you got sick, you sent for Granny or Aunt Bess or Aunt Ethelyn, and they'd come and read Mary Baker Eddy to you and you'd get well. We steered clear of doctors."

One night, five-year-old Henry recalls being awakened by his mother. "Shhh," Mrs. Fonda cautioned, "Don't let the girls hear us. They're too young to be interested, and father works too hard to lose his sleep." She clasped his hand in hers and drew the barefoot child to the landing halfway down the stairs.

"A window faced west," Fonda says, "and we looked out and saw this long, brilliant streak moving across the sky, ten, fifteen degrees above the horizon."

His mother put her arm around him, squeezed his shoulders and said, "Remember this . . . Halley's Comet. It comes around only every seventy-six years. Seventy-six years is a long time. I didn't want you to miss such a sight. Now you'll always remember it."

Mrs. Fonda was right. Henry never forgot. The year was 1910.

Another of his early memories has to do with the wooden sidewalks in Omaha. Cement hadn't reached many Nebraska streets and the sidewalks were covered with slats.

"After dinner in the summer when we kids had been put to bed," Fonda recalls, "Dad and Mother would walk three or four blocks to a drugstore to get ice cream sodas. Then they'd walk home. The girls were asleep, but I'd generally wait up until I heard their footsteps clomping on those wooden boards, faintly at first, then nearer and nearer and louder and louder as they got toward the house. When they started up the steps, I'd nod off."

He stretched in his chair and reached back into his memory.

"Our first car was a Hupmobile," Fonda says, "and on Sundays, Dad would go out to the driveway and take apart the motor. He'd get under the car, and those oil cans they had in the old days would drip all over him, but he didn't care. He'd clean the motor and put it back together again.

"Then we'd go on picnics, three cars loaded with people. It was a real adventure because there were bumpy, dirt roads, and we'd often get flat tires. We'd pile out, find the jack, and the women and girls drank lemonade while the men and boys changed the tires.

"We were a big family, five of us, and generally uncles, cousins, aunts, nieces, nephews joined the group.

"When we arrived at the picnic grounds, my favorite cousin, Douw, and I played ball, or cowboys and Indians, or cops and robbers, and when I'd be hiding behind one of those big elms pretending to be someone else, I'd start to loosen up and get that good feeling that would come over me years later on the stage."

The years slipped by and the Fonda girls grew tall and strong. The boy was healthy, wiry, but throughout the better part of his childhood, short. Fonda was a bashful boy, only too aware of his lack of height, eager to please, devoted to his mother and sisters, and in constant awe

23

and admiration of his father. Too often his self-consciousness forced him to walk across the street to avoid saying hello to a girl. He fared better among boys. He swam well, sprinted the dashes at track meets, even ran a respectable five-minute mile.

The searing dry heat of the Midwestern summers, the tree-cracking cold of the winters he accepted as a normal way of life. In June and July he went to camp. Before and after those months, he worked as a printer's devil in his father's shop. Between Thanksgiving and early spring Henry and his young friends skated, tobogganed, and molded snowmen. When they were a bit older, they built snow castles or forts. Always they engaged in snowball fights during the months with short days.

At age ten he won a short-story contest sponsored by the local newspaper.

"I thought when I got to college I'd major in journalism and eventually take over the school paper. Never happened." .

Instead of a city room Henry Fonda made his first appearance on the screen. It had not been a previously prepared event. No talent agent, no Hollywood scout, no West Coast producer was involved. Still, Henry Fonda made his film debut.

"There were these totem poles at scout camp," Fonda says. "Every year a new totem pole was added. When I got there, five or six of 'em stood around. A local newsreel operator came up with the idea of photographing the Indians marching away from the totems and heading down a little path to the Missouri River. We were all brown from the summer sun, and I suppose we wore little loincloths in front, but the cameraman had us turn away from him.

"Being the smallest, I was last in line. Well, sir, I went down to the Strand Theater one Saturday afternoon to see the totem ceremony, and there I was, covered a bit where I should be covered, but from the rear, naked as a jaybird as I went down the trail.

"The first movie I was ever in was X-rated. I was so ashamed to see a closeup of my bare little twelve-year-old bottom that I just slid down on my seat and hid my face

24

in the darkness of that movie house. Soon as the newsreel was over, I scooted out. I thought I never wanted to have anything to do with movies again!"

Young Henry had skills other than those recorded on film. Quite early he began to draw. By his teens, his sketches took on more advanced techniques. Midway through his adulthood, the artistic talent exhibited as a child would bloom and Henry Fonda the painter would emerge.

When he reached thirteen or fourteen an incident happened that remained with Henry forever. Usually, W. B. Fonda came home from his plant, dinner would be served, the girls would giggle at the table, father, mother, and Henry would exchange small talk, and when the meal was over, the family would adjourn to the living room where W. B. Fonda played his guitar or read until the children's bedtime rolled around.

On this particular night Henry's father arrived home with most disturbing news. Talk of it occupied the entire dinner hour. Fonda's printing shop looked out on the courthouse square. Across the way stood the alabaster county seat. Sometime earlier, by midmorning, a young black man had been accused of rape. He'd been hunted down, arrested, and lodged in the temporary jail in the courthouse. By late afternoon a large crowd of men gathered. They were unruly and angry. When the family finished eating, William Fonda stood up.

"Henry," he said, "I want you to come with me."

The boy and his father climbed into the car and drove to the plant. They got out and mounted the stairs to the second floor. Once inside, Henry looked about. He had always been there during the day. Lights were on, machinery clanged, men did their work. Now, however, his father refused to turn on the electricity. Presses stood silent, printers were gone, his father's old wooden rolltop desk was closed, the same smells of ink and benzine drifted up into his nostrils, but the darkness, the eerie shadows from the glow of the torches held by the men in the crowd below, plus the added roar of the citizens out of control frightened the boy.

His father called him over to the window. Beneath

them, choking the courthouse square, cursing, waving guns and clubs, the mob screamed for the alleged rapist's blood. No charges had been filed, no grand jury action had been taken, but as the minutes passed, the shouts grew wilder and more insistent.

Now the mayor, the sheriff, and a few aides pushed their way through the crowd. They rode horseback and attempted to quiet the mob. Henry watched in terror, fearing that the men astride the animals would be pulled from their saddles and trampled.

At last the door to the courthouse opened and a small group of heavily armed men pulled the black man out. It took very little time to get the job done.

"A great huzzah went up when they saw the poor fellow," Fonda says. "They took him, strung him up to the end of a lamppost, hung him, and while his feet were still dancing in the air, they riddled his body with bullets. It was the most horrendous sight I'd ever seen. Then they cut down the body, tied it to an auto, and dragged it through the streets of Omaha.

"Aside from the lynching, there was something else. It was my father. He never said a word to me. He didn't preach, he didn't make a point, he just made sure I saw it!

"We locked the plant, went downstairs, and drove home in silence. My hands were wet and there were tears in my eyes. All I could think of was that young black man dangling at the end of the lamppost, the shots, and the revulsion I felt. I could not sleep that night and a lot of other nights after that."

Henry's brush with violence wasn't limited to observation. Dundee is a suburb of Omaha. The Fondas moved there and found an Irish family with a battling reputation. The Vaughans, they were named, and they had six sons, each tougher than the next. Henry knew the Vaughans and lived in fear of them.

One Halloween night Fonda and the group of youngsters with whom he associated were raising their mild sort of cain, waxing windows, soaping streetcar tracks, when who should confront them but the six mean Vaughan brothers? To everyone's surprise the biggest Vaughan boy stepped forward.

"Would you like to be joinin' us?" he asked.

None of the boys Fonda was with knew what to expect.

"The bunch of us could be havin' a fine time together," he smiled the warmest of Irish smiles.

Evidently he meant it and the two groups merged.

"How very exciting," Henry thought. "I'm with the Vaughans." On the one hand he couldn't believe it, on the other hand to be with the toughest kids in Dundee seemed exhilarating. What the Vaughans did was always a little more daring than any of the other boys.

"It was nine-thirty, ten o'clock, at least," Henry said. "I couldn't stay out too late. My father and mother would wonder where I was. Anyway, we were walking along and someone behind me started stepping on my heels. I looked back after a while and it was one of the Vaughans.

"I couldn't say, 'Stop it,' because he was deliberately provoking me and everyone knew it. My guys weren't saying anything and all the Vaughans were snickering because I wasn't taking up the challenge. Now, look, I was small for my age still, and not an aggressive boy, surely not a fighter, but I was being put on the spot. So I turned and faced him. All the other fellows, my group and the Vaughans, formed a circle around us. Everybody was happy because everybody liked to see a fight.

"We squared off. Now, I'd never fought before. I didn't know what to do really. I didn't take by mackinaw off, I didn't take my mittens off, I didn't take my stocking cap off. But there I was, fighting one of the vicious Vaughan brothers.

"Well, he swung first and missed, and then I swung and missed, and he swung again, and I swung and hit him! I hit him right on the button and he went down!

"Everybody yelled like hell. He sat on the sidewalk rubbing his chin, and looked up at me."

"Fonda," he said, "if there's blood here, I'm going to kill you."

"Then he got up," Fonda remembered, "and we fought some more. A few more wild swings and I caught him again. And he went down for the second time. And the biggest Vaughan stepped up to me and, to my complete astonishment, told me I'd won fair and square. My guys cheered and even the Vaughans applauded me."

Fonda's sister Harriet has never forgotten that night.

"They carried him home on their shoulders," she said, "all the boys he went around with in Dundee. They were so proud of him. And I'll have to confess, we were proud of Henry, too. It was the first and last time he fought, but he came home a winner."

Fonda's first date with a member of the opposite sex was more comical than notable. Since Henry was too young to drive, his father wheeled out the four-door touring car and whizzed his son over to the girl's home.

"It wasn't black tie," Fonda says, "but it was dress-up. She wore her best dress. At least she was dressier than I'd ever seen her before. I rang the doorbell, she came out, and we walked down the steps and across the front lawn and down some more steps to where the car was parked on the street there beside the sidewalk. The car had a front seat and a back seat and I opened the back door and she got in.

"I closed the back door and reached for the handle of the door to the seat next to my father, but I couldn't open it. I tried, but it wouldn't budge. Then I saw my father holding the door shut. He didn't say anything, he just wouldn't let me sit beside him on the front seat.

"Finally, I realized what the hell was wrong and I got into the back seat. The girl had settled herself in the middle of the seat so I sat as far in the corner as I could get. It was typical of me. I didn't know how to handle a date. I was not a lady's man."

To his everlasting amazement, in his senior year in high school, Henry Fonda began to grow. He did more than grow during that year. He sprouted. In less than twelve months he shot up from being a runt to six-foot-one and a half.

The added height, however, did nothing to change his personality. He remained timid and skittish, unobtrusive and restrained. Blushes came quicker than scowls, brashness appeared rarely, sheepishness and modesty flanked each side of him.

"That was the year I fell in love," Fonda says, "with Helen Moore, puppy love, of course, but what a feeling! You think it's gonna break you wide open. It's the kind of thing that just wants to burst out of your skin. Yes, I was shy, but when I danced with Helen at the prom, she was like a feather in my arms. Wow!"

W. B. Fonda and his family lived comfortably, but he could not sow cash like kernels of corn on the Nebraska plains during the spring. His boy, Henry, had to find work after school. Henry held a variety of odd jobs; the most important was with the Northwestern Bell Telephone Company.

After graduation from Central High School, Henry chose the University of Minnesota—not that he held anything against the University of Nebraska, but the home office of the telephone company was in Minnesota, and he figured chances of getting a full-time job there were good. He figured wrong. After enrolling at Minnesota he went around to the Northwestern Bell Telephone Company and learned to his dismay that the best they could give him was part-time employment as a troubleshooter. He accepted, but it paid little. The problem of working his way through college still lay before him.

"I tried out for the freshman track squad and the coach put me onto a job at the Unity Settlement House at the north end of Minneapolis," Fonda says. "The house was a three-story brick building with an enormous playground in back. Inside, it had a huge gym, a track, basketball courts, and underneath lockers and a pool.

"I was interviewed by the head resident, a woman, and she hired me." Apple-cheeked with wavy black hair, young Fonda must have been irresistible to women, but he didn't know that.

"They ran my tail off, those kids at the Settlement House. I'd finish up my classes at the University and then take a streetcar. Cost a nickel for a forty-five-minute ride, but when it was thirty degrees below zero and you had to wait on a corner to transfer to another car and you had to blow on your gloves to keep your fingers from freezing and stamp your feet to keep the feeling in your toes that damn forty-five-minute ride with a ton of books on your back or in your arms seemed one helluva lot longer. First, I'd coach softball or touch football or whatever the sport was outside in the playground if the weather was pleasant. If it wasn't, we'd go inside for basketball or track or maybe swimming. Then dinner. For two years I worked in that Settlement House and never got to the last course. For two years I never had time for dessert.

"After dinner there'd be three games of basketball, and while the kids were showering, I'd stand around and shoot baskets until they were finished. By eleven-thirty, I'd get upstairs to my room and the homework for the next day. It wasn't much of a room, just two cots, a dresser, a little unpainted desk, and a chair. Every night I'd fall asleep over my books, dead tired. My roommate, Glen Doty, would shake me awake and I'd crawl onto my cot.

"At the end of my sophomore year I was so exhausted that when they passed out the blue books for the final exams, I just sat in class and drew pictures instead of answering the questions. That did it! I flunked out of Minnesota."

"For me, college wasn't a breeze. I had eight o'clock classes, I worked from three to eleven at the Settlement House. On the weekends, if Northwestern Bell needed me, I'd troubleshoot for them, and I had a steady girl. God! I never even kissed her *once*. Scout's honor."

Fonda reached the rank of Eagle Scout in his youth, and to this day, to emphasize a point, he frequently raises his right hand and makes the three-finger salute of the Boy Scouts of America.

This is not to infer that Fonda remained a Boy Scout forever. The transition from boy-child to man-child came during the summer after he returned from Minneapolis. A group of high school chums, after a bout with the needle beer of Prohibition, lured the virgin Henry to a disreputable part of town and a two-dollar whorehouse.

"It was a horrible experience," he says. "I knew what you were supposed to do, but I'd never done it. I was

30

just curious and it wasn't at all what I thought it should be. It was just 'Wham, bam.' I was repulsed. It turned me off for quite a while."

With sex ever so temporarily out of his life-style, there was nothing for Fonda to do in Omaha but wait for opportunity. She knocked almost immediately in the person of Dorothy "Do" (pronounced "Doe") Brando.

Marlon Brando was still a bottle baby when his mother coaxed twenty-year-old Henry Fonda into trying out for the Community Playhouse.

"It came about this way," Fonda says. "I was lying around the house when my mother came in and asked, 'Do me a favor, Henry. Do Brando's on the line. Just listen to her.' "

Mrs. Fonda's friend, Mrs. Brando, a talented woman, was one of the founders of the Omaha Community Playhouse. The 1925 season was about to start and the company needed a juvenile. The "company" meant a theatrical company and the "juvenile" meant a young actor.

"I went to the Aquilla Court Apartments," Fonda says. "It was a new building in the center of town with stores on the first floor and apartments on the second. I knocked and a short red-headed man asked me in. His name was Gregory Foley. He was the director. I looked up. It was the first time I'd ever seen a skylight. He walked over to a table, took a book, and handed it to me.

" 'Read Ricky,' " he said.

"I don't know what you mean. What is this?" the puzzled Fonda asked.

"We're doing Philip Barry's *You and I*. What you're holding is the published version. The juvenile is Ricky. You read that and I'll read the rest of the parts."

The man who in time would become one of the most distinguished actors in America hesitated. Then, looking down at the book, he read aloud. "Ricky. But why not? Other people have. Life shouldn't be all gravy, anyway. After ten years of . . ."

"No!" Greg Foley interrupted. "You don't say, 'Ricky.' "

"But you told me . . ."

" 'Ricky' is the name of the character," the director explained. "You just read the dialogue after the word 'Ricky.' "

Fonda blushed and stammered, ashamed of his own ignorance. Picking up the book, he started afresh. He hardly knew what he was reading. He stopped only when the director said, "Okay, you've got it."

"I was too self-conscious to say I didn't want to do it or I didn't know *how* to do it," Fonda says. "I was so painfully introverted that I tucked the book under by arm, mumbled a few words, went home and memorized the part."

As in most amateur theaters all of the men except Fonda had other jobs. The cast rehearsed nights and weekends. The beginner felt a distinct sense of inferiority. He squirmed at his own lack of experience. Still, he was fascinated with the life backstage.

"On opening night," Fonda says, "I could hear the stage manager giving orders. The hum of the audience went down as the lights in the theater dimmed. It got quieter and quieter and then the curtain went up. I get all emotional because that's when it started for me. When the curtain went up, it was black out there, and then the lights from the railing hit me and the play began.

"I couldn't have been very good. No way at all. It was my first time out. But this strange new atmosphere, I was hooked. Good.

"I don't think we played more than a week, but I stuck around the Playhouse for the rest of the season. I became totally involved. I built the scenery, I painted it, I swept the stage, I pulled up the curtain, I ushered, I borrowed a station wagon and picked up a couch that was used on a set. I did everything, anything."

From September 1925 to May 1926 Henry Fonda relished the mysteries and wonders of small-town amateur show business.

Then, gently and without any vast amount of pressure, William Brace Fonda sat his boy down.

"Henry, it's been a fine year. You've had a lot of fun, but now, let's face it son," the elder Fonda said, "you're not going back to school and you've got to figure what you're going to do with your life."

Henry hadn't given a thought to his future. His father, however, had. Dutifully, the young man looked through the want-ads in the local newspaper. He answered one.

"I was hired by the Retail Credit Company of Omaha as a clerk," Fonda says. "They paid me thirty dollars a week. That was a lot of money in 1926."

Henry worked regular hours at the Retail Credit Company. Eight in the morning till six at night with half a day off on Saturdays. Life outside the Playhouse seemed solid but uneventful. He filed the cards then cross-filed them and told himself this was like detective work which, of course, it wasn't.

One afternoon the telephone rang at the Retail Credit Company. Gregory Foley was calling.

"Hank," the director said, "we're going to open the new season at the Playhouse with *Merton of the Movies.*"

"Uh-uh," Henry replied softly. He wasn't supposed to get personal phone calls at the office.

"I want you to play Merton."

"Who?"

"The lead."

The employee who wasn't supposed to take personal phone calls shouted into the receiver.

"The lead? God!"

That night Fonda broke the news to his family.

William Fonda, who until now had never had a confrontation with his son, suddenly turned into a first-rate antagonist.

"Absolutely not!" he told Henry. "You're not going to sacrifice your job for some make-believe world."

"I can do both," the son argued.

"You cannot," his father retorted. "In no way can you do justice to both of those things. You've got a good job and a real chance for a future in business. And to waste time trying to do both, the job and the play, and I know how much time it takes, you can't do it!"

It was one of those quarrels that began with, "Yes, I can," "No, you can't," and ended with, "I'm twenty-one years old and I'll move out."

33

"Go ahead."

"I'll move to the YMCA."

"Do that."

"I'll stay there and won't bother you."

"All right with me."

"I'll be independent."

"Fine!"

Henry's mother, always the diplomat, made a sort of truce between her husband and her son. The latter didn't move out, and the former didn't talk to his offspring for six weeks. Henry avoided his father, arising early, going to work, grabbing a malted and a soggy sandwich at a drugstore counter, and rehearsing until late in the evening. By the time Henry returned home each night, his parents were asleep. Sometimes, father and son passed each other in the bedroom hall. They didn't even nod.

"We were both stubborn," Fonda admits.

Rehersals for *Merton* flashed by. At the initial performance, Fonda experienced a sensation entirely new to him.

"The short hair on the back of my neck felt like live wires and my skin tingled. That was the first time I realized what acting meant. It also dawned on me that for a self-doubting man, this was the answer. Writers give you words and you can become another person."

All the Fondas went to see Henry. When he returned home aglow from what he thought had been a successful performance, he found the family in the living room. His father, to whom he hadn't spoken since the start of rehearsals, sat in his chair, deliberately ignoring the discussion of Henry's performance by holding up a newspaper in front of his face.

Superlatives poured down upon the actor's head from the three women in the family. At length Harriet started to say something that sounded as though it might have been the slightest bit critical of her brother.

"Henry," his sister suggested, "instead of . . ."

Putting down his newspaper, William Fonda spoke across the living room.

"Shut up," he ordered. "He was perfect!"

"That's the best notice I ever got," Fonda says. His voice catches. He stops and swallows. "I'm going to cry before I finish this. I always do. Fondas are like that. We're teared around the edges."

Mrs. Hunter Scott, Sr., was the dowager of Omaha society. Her dearly departed husband made a fortune in real estate and left her with stacks of cash and a wayward son. The faint scent of lavender trailed after Mrs. Scott as she rode about Omaha in her electric car. Painted black, surrounded by four large glass windows, the interior of the car was upholstered in gray velvet. Twin bud vases were placed on either side of the doors. A fresh rose bloomed in each one each day. The electric car moved silently through the streets. In place of a wheel, the double-chinned matron guided it with a long steering handle. Mrs. Scott, in addition to lavender, reeked of money, and in the twenties, that was the sweetest smell of all.

Hunter Scott, Jr., "the most spoiled kid in Omaha," suffered through almost two years of Princeton. Toward the end of his sophomore year, he was ready to give up the Ivy League. Princeton allowed no cars on its campus; Hunter Scott garaged his in nearby Kingston. His mother, prepared to give in to her son's every whim, flinched at the thought of his driving back to Nebraska alone.

An old acquaintance of the family, Mrs. Scott stopped her electric car outside the house in Dundee, opened the door next to the curb, stepped out, and swept into the Fonda home. Following the usual amenities, she turned her lorgnette in Henry's direction.

"Hunter is not going to stay at Princeton," Mrs. Scott sighed heavily, "and he wants to drive home the long way."

"What way is that, Mrs. Scott?" Fonda asked.

"Princeton to Florida, around New Orleans, and then up to Omaha."

"New Orleans. I hear that's pretty wild."

"So is Hunter. Now, Henry, that's why I want you to go with him."

Henry looked at his father. No reaction there.

"Thank you, Mrs. Scott," he answered, "but I can't afford to take the time off. I have a . . ."

Mrs. Scott held up a pudgy finger.

"Henry, if you go East to drive with Hunter, I will pay your way to New York, and you can spend a week there at my expense seeing all of the Broadway shows."

"Well, I . . ."

"You *do* like the theater, don't you?"

"Yes, ma'am."

"Think it over, Henry dear, and let me know by this time tomorrow." And with that, she made her exit.

Henry turned his attention to his parents.

"New York," he said. "I've never been east of Council Bluffs, Iowa."

"You haven't been much farther west, either," his father noted.

"Then you wouldn't mind my going?"

William Fonda swung around toward his wife. She said, "Do it."

Henry went to work Monday morning. Almost immediately he knocked on the frosted glass door that led to the small office occupied by his boss. He had intended to ask for two weeks off with pay, his annual vacation, and two weeks off without pay. After he entered, to his own astonishment, he heard himself saying words he hadn't planned on speaking.

"Sir," he said, and his voice seemed to go up an octave. "Sir, I've come to give my notice."

His employer almost went into shock.

"I'm quitting. I've decided the business world isn't for me."

"But, Fonda, we're about to promote you."

"Thank you very much, but I'm going to try something else."

"We're about to send you to the home office in Atlanta."

"That's very nice, sir."

"Someday you might even wind up like me, a branch manager of the Retail Credit Company anywhere in this country."

"Thank you. Sounds very tempting, but I've made up my mind."

New York had everything Henry Fonda expected. In 1927 a record 268 productions opened on Broadway. The country boy plunged into the theatrical waters and saw nine shows in six days. He still remembers most of them. Helen Hayes in *Coquette*. Otis Skinner in *The Front Page*. Ethel Barrymore in *The Constant Wife*. Florenz Ziegfeld's *Rio Rita*. And Glenn Hunter in *Tommy*. He was particularly interested in Glenn Hunter because that actor had played the original Merton in *Merton of the Movies*.

With the lights of the Great White Way flashing before his eyes and the tunes of *Rio Rita* humming in his head, Henry Fonda walked back and forth in front of the Ziegfeld Theater under the Sixth Avenue "El." The crowd thinned out, and for a while, Henry thought perhaps his friend had forgotten about him.

"Hunter Scott was a typical F. Scott Fitzgerald character," Fonda says. "He never really bothered to get engaged. In those days they called it 'pinned,' and Hunter Scott pinned girls all over the country. Anyway, he told me he'd pick me up after the matinee of *Rio Rita*. And sure enough, I caught sight of his long Packard convertible. He pulled up to the curb, I got into the car, and he introduced me to his passengers.

"There were three females. A Mrs. Davis and her two daughters. Hunter was 'pinned' to the one called Bobbi. It seemed he'd invited them to come down with their mother for a weekend at Princeton.

"The drive down there was rough going, a foggy night and you couldn't see ten feet in front of the car. I figured any minute we'd hit something. None of us talked. I sat in the back with Mrs. Davis and this girl who looked about seventeen.

"We arrived at Princeton, and Hunter put them up at the Nassau Inn, and then we went back to his dorm on campus.

"Right before we fell asleep, Hunter said, 'I've got a great idea. On this long drive we're taking, let's have a match. Every time you kiss a girl, you get a score. Every time I kiss a girl, I get a score.' Not score in the sense that we use the expression today," Fonda stresses. "That's a sample of how juvenile Hunter was.

"But what the hell! His mother told me to do whatever

he wanted, and if he wanted to play this crazy game, I'd go along.

"The next morning, we took the girls and Mrs. Davis on a tour of the college, then to lunch, and eventually to dinner. Afterward, we drove Mrs. Davis back to the Inn, and Hunter asked permission to show her daughters the Princeton Stadium by moonlight.

"Mrs. Davis was a stern New England lady but she knew Hunter well enough, she thought, and she trusted him, so she allowed us to drive them to the stadium.

"Well, after we parked, Hunter got out with Bobbi and left. I was sitting there with a girl I didn't even know.

"God! I'd dated a girl at the University of Minnesota for two years and I'd never kissed her. I was afraid. But there I was in the back seat of a car with almost a complete stranger, and Hunter was off getting his first score of the contest.

"I knew I'd never win, but I didn't want to disgrace myself by not having one point. I sat there thinking, 'I've got to kiss her. I've got to!'

"She looked up at me with those enormous saucerlike eyes and what the hell.

"Well, I sort of leaned over and gave her a peck on the lips, not a real kiss, but what a relief to me. One point! I felt like Casanova.

"In the morning, we put the girls and their mother on a train for Boston. Before Hunter and I left on our trip, I received a letter that my date had written on the train and mailed on a stopover at Penn Station in New York.

"It said, 'I've told mother about our lovely experience together in the moonlight. She will announce the engagement when we get home.' It was signed, 'Bette Davis.'

" 'Holy Shit,' I thought, 'One kiss and I'm engaged.' That's how naive I was, and that's what a devil Bette Davis could be at seventeen.

"For years, whenever I saw Bette Davis, I'd give her a wide berth.

"Yes, it's the one you think it is. In no time at all she became very attractive with a dynamite personality."

By the end of April the ex-filing clerk and the playboy returned home. Fonda relaxed a bit listening to the hand-cranked victrola, read play after play, and did chores around the house. Often, after trimming the hedges and watering the lawn, he'd treat his sisters to penny candy. His preference was licorice.

Then Greg Foley came back into the picture.

"I want you to be my assistant next season," the director of the Playhouse told him. "More importantly," he added, "we'll pay you five hundred dollars."

"Man! Even my folks thought that sounded great," Fonda says.

The five hundred dollars kept him in carfare, clothes, and cigarettes. He lived at home and ate most of his meals at his parents' table. He reached his twenty-second birthday and the bright future his father sought for him still seemed a long way off.

Although he fulfilled his duties as Greg Foley's assistant, a disturbing thought began to gnaw at him. Was this as far as he was meant to go? A small frog in the small pond of amateur theatricals?

Then, suddenly, a professional opening appeared. Not what Fonda had fantasized as he lay in his bedroom in his parents' home in Dundee, but a real chance with a legitimate theatrical venture.

George Billings had been a carpenter in Hollywood. He'd been working on the set of a Lincoln movie one day when the leading man stormed out of the studio. The lights and the cameras stood by, the cast waited, the director fumed when someone noticed George Billings. He had a long, lean, melancholy face, a head of black hair and a beard to match. They put him into a Prince Albert coat, gave him a stovepipe hat, threw a shawl across his shoulders, and there he was. Abraham Lincoln!

Critically and financially the Lincoln film was a hit, but George Billings never made another picture. There were two reasons: first, only one or two films about Lincoln can be made in each decade, and second, George Billings had a great fondness for alcohol.

To look after the latter Billings trouped across the country playing at fairs, carnivals, movie houses, always acting the role of the Great Emancipator. He traveled alone and recited either the Gettysburg Address or the

Second Inaugural Address or both. In Omaha a newspaper reporter came up with an idea.

"This fellow stopped me on the street," Fonda says. "He was with the Omaha *World Herald* and he told me that an actor named Billings was staying at the Fontenell Hotel. I went there and here was a man who was the spitting image of Abe Lincoln.

"He told me how he'd been playing all over the country as a single and how he'd gotten an awful lot of mail from Lincoln fans and Lincoln scholars. Then he told me there was a bigger and better act than his single, but it would need another actor to play John Hay, Lincoln's secretary. He stared pretty hard at me and said that Hay was a tall, skinny young man. I nodded. He said he thought of the set as being a tent near the White House. Lincoln and his secretary would be going through the daily mail.

"Anyway, it was his idea and he gave me the material and I took it home and put together a little fifteen- or twenty-minute sketch. I went back to him with it the next day. He read it and liked it and told me he'd sign me to play John Hay.

"What about money?" I asked him.

"Pay you a hundred dollars a week." Billings told Fonda.

"A hundred dollars. Brother! I didn't make that again for ten years. I remember I rented the Civil War uniform at the local costumers and I went out on tour with this Billings customer throughout Nebraska, Iowa, and Kansas.

"We'd do three a day, and for the first eight or ten weeks, we were a howling hit. We'd do the mail. I'd be in uniform and I'd hand him a letter and he'd dictate an answer. And then he'd pull the Second Inaugural out of his coat pocket and read it aloud to me. Or the Gettysburg, whichever he felt like. And then I'd hand him Mrs. Bixby's letter begging Mr. Lincoln to spare her son's life. He'd been found asleep on sentry duty and they were going to stand him up in front of a firing squad. And then the house orchestra'd play 'Hearts and Flowers.' I tell you, you can't get much more cornier than that, but he was effective. When he was right, he had 'em, tears streaming down his cheeks and beard. I was absolutely fascinated. Where did he get those tears from? Every performance. It was like he turned on a faucet. The audiences we played to loved it. They cried right along with him.

"He was picking up about a thousand a week when the trouble came. He'd show up at the theater drunk. Now, I don't mean an occasional nip. He came in so stewed he wouldn't even bother with the stage door. He'd come in through the lobby and down the side aisle and up onto the stage.

" 'Can't you control this son-of-a-bitch?' the house managers would yell at me.

" 'Are you kidding?' I'd yell back. 'I'm twenty-two and he's sixty and dead drunk. You think he's going to listen to me?'

"There were times when he never showed up. I couldn't play *both* parts. I could just read the letters. And I'd do it. But I couldn't cry. And I couldn't read the Gettysburg Address or the other one, so right after 'Hearts and Flowers' one evening I left and went home."

Fonda wasn't destined to remain in Omaha for very long. What he wanted was the theater he'd seen when he'd been back East. Specifically, he'd heard about summer-stock companies that were then springing up on Cape Cod. The problem appeared to be how to get there. The solution followed almost at once.

In his junior year in high school Henry had worked after-school hours as an office boy in the stock brokerage firm of Burns, Brinker & Company. Both Mr. Burns and Mr. Brinker had been best friends of his father's. Burns had died recently and Mrs. Burns, who had a summer place just beyond New Bedford, was anxious to find someone to drive her out of Nebraska and onto Cape Cod.

"I had a hundred dollars left from my tour with George Billings," he says. "With that and my parents' blessings I said good-bye. I had no idea when I'd be back so I took a long look at them before I stepped on the clutch of Mrs. Burns's car.

"Gentleness was a quality my parents shared. They

both stood tall. They had attractive features, and like so many people who are married for a long time, they resembled each other. Sometimes, when I round a corner and see my reflection in a store window, I think, 'My God, there's my father.' On the other hand, people say I look very much like my sister Harriet, and I know she takes after my mother. Father was dark-skinned, mother fair; blue eyes, high cheekbones, thick eyebrows, dimples, but gentleness, that's what I remember about them most."

Fonda depressed the clutch, pulled the stick shift on the floor into first gear, and he and Mrs. Burns were off, she to her summer place, he, he didn't know where or what, but for the moment, at least, Omaha disappeared in a cloud of dust from the road heading east.

Millicent Burns, a remarkable birdlike woman, knew if she mothered Henry and smothered Henry she'd do him no good. She allowed him to drive out of Nebraska, all the way across Iowa, Illinois, Indiana, Ohio, Pennsylvania, New York, Massachusetts, right over the Cape Cod canal. Although her place was close by, she insisted Henry drive the full length of the Cape to Provincetown. Then she made him open the door and get out. Sliding across the seat, she slipped behind the wheel of the car, waved good-bye, and Henry Fonda was on his own.

"I've never been able to sell myself," Fonda says. "Without the playwright's words, I'm not much of a talker, let alone a convincing talker. But I picked up my suitcase and walked out onto the wharf where the Provincetown Playhouse was."

It took him a while to get up the nerve, but eventually Henry, because he knew of no other way at the time, approached the box office.

"Something for tonight's show?" a man behind the small grill asked.

"I'm looking for a job," Henry answered. The man in the box office "humphed" loudly.

"As what?" he snorted.

"As an actor!"

"We don't cast here."

"Well, where *do* you cast?"

"New York."

"Oh." His voice failed to conceal his disappointment.

"Besides," the box office man added, "we're all cast for the summer."

"Thank you," Henry said.

"Anything else?" the man in the box office smirked with self-satisfaction.

"Is there another summer theater near here?"

"Sure," the man said. "At Dennis."

"Where's that?"

"Halfway down the Cape."

"When's the next train?"

"Couple of hours."

"Thanks."

With nothing to do, Henry Fonda walked along the beach. He watched the gentle surf come onto the sand. This soft, giving ground felt nothing like the Nebraska prairie. He breathed deeply. The tang of salt water filled the air. The screech of the gulls sounded not at all like the sweet chirps of the birds at home. The stunted trees didn't compare with the giants that stood proudly, their roots deep in the Midwestern soil. He should have felt homesick. He didn't. He had several good reasons to feel rejected. Curiously, he felt as though he belonged.

By asking questions, Henry found his way across the dunes close to the home of Eugene O'Neill. The house rested on Pecked Hill Bar. Henry gazed long and hard at it. He had read everything the great American playwright had written to date. He had even acted in *Beyond the Horizon* at the Omaha Community Playhouse.

Standing there, he faced the house of genius, wondering if the great man was home, and if he was, was he writing a play, and if the play had a part for an actor who . . . A train whistle interrupted his reverie. Henry ran to the station and rode back to Dennis.

He arrived late in the day.

"I made my way walking from the station across meadows," Fonda says, "to the Cranberry Highway and found the Cape Playhouse. I went up the long driveway to the box office. It was empty. There was a door open to the auditorium. I went in through the open door and they were rehearsing down on the stage. I sat in the back row, sort of waiting until I could find a person to talk to.

"I was so innocent I didn't know what a homosexual was, but after a while, a young man came over to me."

"Can I do anything for you?" he asked and raised an eyebrow.

"I knew something was different about him but I couldn't figure it out," Fonda says, "so I told him I was looking for work as an actor."

"Oh," the young man said sweetly. "We cast in New York."

"Okay."

"Besides, we're all cast for the summer."

"Okay," Fonda said as he got up and started out of the Playhouse.

"I'm sorry," the young man called after him. "I really am."

The late afternoon sun hung over the ocean warming the Cape and the people on it. In half an hour it would set. Henry walked to a large white frame house that had a sign on its scruffy lawn reading Rooms. For a dollar and a half he got a single for the night on the second floor in the rear. At an adjoining diner, Henry ordered a meal.

"I'll bet mine was the only hamburger served that night," he says.

Upstairs in his bed Henry heard animated voices from the rooms below. Everyone knew everyone else. Only Henry knew nobody. He stared up at the ceiling.

"What will it be like in the morning?" he asked himself. Then, being young, he fell asleep.

CHAPTER
3

A FRESH wind off the Atlantic rattled the shade and allowed the midmorning light into his room. Fonda stayed in the too-short bed listening to sounds of running water, doors opening and slamming shut, and knives and forks clattering against dishes. He smelled bacon frying and coffee brewing. That got him off the lumpy mattress. The bathroom was down the hall. He showered, dressed, and with his hair still wet, he took the stairs down two at a time. He was hungry. The dollar and a half for the room included breakfast.

"My God," Henry says, "what a sight, all of the actors from the Cape Playhouse were sitting at the long table in the dining room. I recognized some of them from their pictures in papers and magazines."

The assemblage included Peggy Wood, who had played on Broadway and in the West End of London in *Naughty Marietta, Maytime, Candida*, and *The Merchant of Venice;* Laura Hope Crews, the star of *Raffles, Mr. Pim Passes By,* and *The Silver Cord*; Romney Brent who delighted audiences in *He Who Gets Slapped, The Devil's Disciple, Androcles and the Lion*; and Minor Watson, who appeared in *Ready Money, Undercover*, and *Why Men Leave Home*. These were professionals. The closest Fonda ever had been to Broadway actors was the balcony. The rest of the company was made up of ingenues and juveniles, but even they had more training than Henry.

Peggy Wood motioned him to fill his plate. After the meal, as they lounged in white wicker chairs on the lawn, they smoked, talked, and read *Variety*, the show business newspaper. The young man who had raised an eyebrow during rehearsal the previous afternoon, sauntered up to Fonda.

"Still looking for work?" he asked.

"Sure am," Fonda answered.

"Well, we've discussed it and we can't give you any money to start, but how would you like to be the third assistant stage manager?"

Now in summer stock, particularly in those days, a third assistant stage manager carried about as much weight as the second driver of an automobile or the fifth pilot on an airplane, but Fonda accepted immediately.

"In the beginning, I was in charge of props," he says. "I had to make sure the right number of cigarettes were where they should be, matches, ashtrays. Things like that. It sure as hell wasn't acting, but it didn't take long for my time to come.

"When they started casting *The Barker*, the director called me over.

" 'I've got a kind of problem,' " he said. " 'The actor I hired to play the boy took another job. Think you can handle the juvenile?' "

"Now I'd never heard of *The Barker*," Fonda admits, "but I said, 'Sure.' "

"I think you're the right type," the director went on.

"I'm ready," Fonda told him.

"That doesn't mean I'm going to give you the part," the director cautioned. "I'm going to let you read for it Tuesday morning."

"Minor Watson played the lead," Fonda recalls, "and three guys in addition to me were auditioning. The scene called for some dialogue between Minor Watson and the character I was reading for. The other three already had their shot. Then I walked onto the boards. The script had Minor getting angry and swinging at me. Which he did.

You understand, he didn't touch me but I fell flat on my face. I was that eager a beaver.

"Minor peered at me and then out at the director. P.S. I got the part.

"We opened *The Barker* and I guess I must've been all right because John Weaver, Peggy Wood's husband, came back and congratulated me. Romney Brent gave me a letter of introduction to Daniel Frohman, the Broadway producer, and you'll see how important that comes to be in my life."

During the fourth week of his stay in Dennis, the mysteries of the opposite sex finally became apparent to Henry Fonda. He had been drinking a considerable amount of beer with the cast following a performance when one of the ingenues approached and asked if he would care to take a ride in her car. Fonda appreciated the suggestion and off they went bumping across the beach in her sedan.

Some twenty minutes later Fonda, because of the number of steins of beer he had consumed, asked the girl to stop the car.

"I felt very self-conscious," Fonda says. "She stayed in the car and I got out, and I was, well, ashamed of the noise it would make if I stood up, so I lay down on the beach and dug a little hole in the sand and relieved myself.

"When I buttoned my fly and went back to the car, I opened the door to the front seat and she was gone. I couldn't believe it. Left the car and the keys and went. Then I turned and looked in the back. There she was, lying on the rear seat stark naked!

"It took a girl to practically pick me up and put me there because I was too backward. But there she was and I just stood there, looking, and finally she said softly, 'Get your ass in here!' "

It turned out to be a long, arduous, and pleasure-filled night.

"Next afternoon," Fonda says, "she came by after I was finished work and told me that Laura Hope Crews wanted her to pick up some records. We got into the car and drove to Miss Crews's cottage. Only Miss Crews had gone back to New York for a week. I found that out later.

"Well, there I am, looking through the record collection, and I turn around and there is this ingenue lying on top of a couch, bare-assed again.

"It was a good thing for me that Bernie Hanighen came by that night and took me to see a play in Falmouth. Many more days like that and I would have grown old before my time."

Bernard Hanighen, an Omaha friend who had stayed in the East to make up unfinished scholastic work at Harvard, dropped by unannounced and said, "Come on. There're some Cambridge pals of mine putting on a show not far from here. Let's drive over and see it."

Fonda didn't appear in the Dennis cast that week. He and Hanighen drove off. He wasn't impressed when they arrived in Falmouth. The theater was a little old movie house, not at all like the well-appointed one at Dennis. The boys couldn't get seats together. They flipped a coin for the tickets. Bernie settled for a row in the rear. Fonda found himself down front. He was surrounded by well-dressed, middle-aged "summer people" who fanned themselves with their programs and wiped their foreheads with linen handkerchiefs. They were not an ideal audience for George Kelly's comedy *The Torchbearers*.

The curtain went up and the audience remained uncomfortable and apathetic until a Princeton sophomore named Joshua Logan made his entrance. As Huxley Hossefrosse, a fatuous old man, something about Logan's performance caught the interest of at least one member of the audience. From a seat near the stage came a laugh, a scream, a sort of unearthly sound.

"I can't really do justice to that sound," Logan reported, "but it saved my acting career. It started as a sort of wave of hysteria. It was a laugh that became a sob that went way up in the air, and then there was a strangulation of some sort.

"The audience picked it up and went wild," Logan continued. "The evening turned into a triumph. Afterward, Bernie Hanighen brought a man backstage."

"May I present my friend, Henry Fonda," Hanighen said.

"We glanced about," Logan remembered, "and saw this boy standing there. He was lean and lanky and had an extraordinary chest. His chest was caved in and his pelvis stuck out, and his lower thighs went back and his knees stuck out. He was in a black pullover sweater and the typical white golf pants of the day, which were supposedly plus fours, but his were minus two. He was very skinny. Black stockings and black shoes. Nobody had ever seen anybody dress that way before. We couldn't figure it out. He was either terribly chic or didn't know what the hell he was doing.

"But this beautiful man's face looked down at me and said, 'Were you Huxley Hossefrosse?' And I said yes, and he let out that yell again, that laugh that brought me such great success. And, of course, I loved Henry Fonda from that moment on, and nothing has ever shaken that love."

They gathered around him, the two directors, Bretaigne Windust and Charlie Leatherbee, and the entire cast, and they asked if he would care to join the University Players Guild.

"A pittance a week," Windust told him.

"What's a pittance?" Fonda asked.

"Five dollars plus room and board."

That was five dollars more that he was getting at Dennis. Besides, he felt an empathy toward these people. They were his age and not at all like the "pros" at Dennis. Fonda signed on immediately Of course, he returned to the Cape Playhouse to thank everyone, collect his few belongings, and say good-bye.

The boy with the raised eyebrow and the girl with the naked body were both depressed at his departure. The one hadn't started, the other hadn't finished.

At the time there were less than half a dozen summer-stock companies in the country: Elitch's Gardens in Denver, the Lakewood Playhouse in Skowhegan, Maine, Henry C. Potter's and George Haight's theater in Easthampton, Long Island, the Cape Playhouse at Dennis.

The University Players were a group composed of Ivy Leaguers and Seven Sisters, mostly Harvard, Yale, and

Princeton males and Radcliffe, Vassar, Barnard, and Smith females. Of their two directors, Charles Leatherbee was a Harvard boy whose grandfather owned the Crane Plumbing Company, and whose mother divorced his father and became Madame Jan Masaryk, wife of the Czechoslovakian Minister to the Court of St. James. Although he had some artistic talent, Leatherbee served as the primary producer of the project, raising the money, eventually building a theater for the University Players.

From Princeton came Paris-born, English-educated Bretaigne Windust. "Windy" served as president of the Intime Theatre at Princeton and held concepts of glory for the group. The idea Leatherbee and Windust had was that college-educated men and women suffered an initial disadvantage in the theater because four years of their lives went into academic pursuits. To make up for this loss of experience, the University Players came into existence.

The Elizabeth motion picture theater was dark on Monday and Tuesday nights. For 50 percent of the gross, an outrageous sum, the owner leased the nine-hundred-seat house for two nights a week to Windust and Leatherbee. Female members of the cast lived in a cottage five miles away. Males stayed aboard the *Brae Burn*, a 110-foot World War I submarine chaser that had been converted by Leatherbee's grandfather into a yacht for his honeymoon, and since those happy days, had lain idle at a pier in Falmouth harbor.

Fonda's first appearance with the University Players was a monumental piece of miscasting. The vehicle was *The Jest*, and Henry played an Italian nobleman, dreadfully. Fonda has played hundreds of roles since then, and if there is one matter directors and producers have learned it is that Fonda can act rich or poor, powerful or weak, a pauper or a President, but always he does best as an American.

Following his disastrous performance, Fonda busied himself in an area familiar to him—paints, scenery. He did so well that Windust approached him one afternoon.

"Listen, Hank," Windy began.

"Yup?"

"Why don't you consider becoming a scenic designer?"

Fonda looked at the slim man with the blond hair and the bandanna wrapped around his forehead.

"I mean, you're so awfully good at it, Hank."

"Maybe I'll do both, design *and* act."

And he did for a while, but when he learned that the next play was to be *Is Zat So?* Fonda filched a copy of the script, read up on the part of the dumb boxer, won the right to play it, and scored a knockout. Grinning and confident, this boy from Nebraska won the applause of the audience and the acceptance and kudos of the critics.

"That's where I became a leading man," Fonda says. "From then on, I played the leads with the University Players. And I mean the leads that I *should* have played."

The season ended after the first week in September. The amateur actors had had enough theater for a while and were ready to return to college, double rooms, occasionally a suite, fat allowances from the folks at home, football games, raccoon coats, hip flasks, and other niceties of the university life during the Prohibition era. They bid one another fond farewells and went back to the cloistered life. Everyone, that is, except Fonda. To quote his contemporary, Norris Houghton, "Hank Fonda went down to New York and spent the autumn discovering how hard it is to get onto Broadway."

For Fonda New York meant a ten-dollar-a-week room with a family on the Upper West Side. With letter in hand, he entered the Lyceum Theater and rode the elevator to the top floor where Daniel Frohman had his offices. Timidly, he drew close to the secretary and handed her his letter of introduction. She glanced at it and allowed it to float onto her desk.

"But that's a personal letter for Mr. Frohman," Fonda said.

"I know," the bored woman answered.

"It's from Romney Brent, personally."

"Romney Brent. I know. He was in here trying to find work yesterday."

A subdued and bewildered Fonda rang for the elevator. Show business in New York was not nearly as easy as show business on Cape Cod.

At Christmastime, a University Player named Kent Smith returned to New York. Fonda was the first one he contacted.

"Henry," Kent Smith told him, "I'm through with Cambridge."

"Why?" Fonda asked.

"The University fired me because I didn't attend enough classes."

"Gee. What're you going to do now?"

"Get a job acting. Isn't that what you're doing?"

"Kent, what I'm doing is making the rounds. That isn't acting. That's wearing out shoe leather."

Fonda, who had been in New York since the first week in September, knew where everything was even if he couldn't get it. He knew the producers' offices, the agents' offices; he knew how to cut through the rain by ducking into the subway at Fortieth Street and emerging at Forty-fourth Street; he knew how to kill a day with a Coke and a package of Camels in Walgreen's basement, a drugstore where all the other unemployed actors hung out. "Henry Fonda," Josh Logan said, "was the best known unknown actor in New York."

"Sorry, Henry," the agents would call out. "Nothing for you this morning."

"Sorry, Henry," the producers' secretaries would sing out. "We're through casting for this one."

Henry was as big a hit as you could be in New York without notices from the drama critics.

The Actor's Union is called Equity. Its headquarters is at 1500 Broadway. In late December 1928 on the first floor of the Equity building hung a large bulletin board. On it were tacked the names of all new plays that were being cast, the producers, their offices, and the number of actors wanted in the cast. To this bulletin board Henry steered Kent Smith late one afternoon.

As the two men studied the board, two little old ladies approached them.

"Are you seeking work?" one of them asked.

Fonda and Smith turned.

"If you are," the second little old lady said, "we have it."

52

"Where?" Smith asked.

"Washington, D.C."

"As what?" Fonda asked suspiciously. He'd been around longer. Waiting on tables, emptying garbage, bell-hopping, yes. Acting? No.

"We operate the National Junior Theater," the first dear soul said. "You are actors, aren't you?"

"Naturally we are," Fonda replied quickly, "with great training and experience."

"That's just what we're looking for," the second one said.

"Would you be willing to come to Washington?"

"Well, I dunno," Fonda said, trying to conceal his eagerness. Kent Smith kicked him, but Fonda remained firm. "For how much?"

"Five dollars a week, plus room and board."

"We seem to be typed," Fonda told Smith.

"We'll take it," Smith snapped.

They left on the midnight train for the nation's capital.

The National Junior Theater was in a wing of the old Wardman Park Hotel. Two teachers from the National Cathedral School, Mrs. Tinnin and Miss Brown, operated an ambitious children's theater.

Mildred Natwick, later one of America's finest character actresses, was, at the age of seventeen, an original member of the National Junior Theater.

"It was my first job," Miss Natwick recollected. "We had performances on Saturday mornings, Saturday afternoons, and Sunday afternoons. I played one of the pirates in *Treasure Island* and I was ready to do the male lead in *Twelfth Night* when Henry Fonda came to Washington and took away my part."

The role given to Fonda was that of Sir Andrew Aguecheek.

"I'm not sure that I'd read much Shakespeare," Fonda says. "I don't think I could have spelled it properly. As for iambic pentameter, hell! I didn't have the foggiest notion of what it was. They just handed me Sir Andrew Aguecheek, told me to put on a putty nose, a funny hat, and fake eyebrows. I didn't know what I was doing, but

53

went out and read the damn lines. Evidently they couldn't tell good from bad so they kept me on."

Kent Smith, who sounded the way one would expect God to sound, and resembled one of the men in the Arrow collar advertisements, roomed with Fonda that season.

In April Henry received a telegram from Bernie Hanighen. Hanighen and Harold Adamson had written the libretto, the words, and the music for a show at Harvard called *Close Up*. Bernie, president of one of the theatrical clubs at Cambridge, wired:

> WE ARE STUCK STOP NEED A COMIC
> STOP CANNOT FIND UNDERGRAD
> STOP WILL YOU COME UP AS A
> RINGER

Since the children's theater was about over, Fonda packed and left for Boston. *Close Up* called for Fonda to walk across the stage, encounter a young woman, try to pick her up, and get slapped by her for his impertinence.

The actress was Charlie Leatherbee's girl friend. She was short and pert with honey-colored hair, a good figure, a throaty voice, and a way of laughing when she threw back her head that seemed irresistible. She called herself Margaret Sullavan.

"We rehearsed that bit for a week or ten days," Fonda says, "and every time she slapped me, she rocked me. Every time she hit me, I saw a flash. It seemed to say, 'You better, by God, notice me.' And I did. I fell in love with her, too."

Fonda and Sullavan were taking a breather one evening when she came up alongside of him. She hardly reached his shoulder.

"Are you Harvard or Yale?" she asked in that cracked, husky voice.

"Are you Radcliffe or Vassar?" he countered, trying his best not to sound too Midwestern.

"I sell stationery at the Coop in Cambridge and go to a secretarial school in Boston."

"I flunked out of the University of Minnesota."

"Hello."

"Hello."

From then on, Charlie Leatherbee had to find another girl. The romance between Fonda and Sullavan would have gone nowhere had it not been for Leatherbee. He invited the Virginia-born girl to join the University Players at the theater he was building for them on Old Silver Beach.

Immediately, the question arose, could the University Players accept someone who had not attended college? Miss Sullavan solved the problem promptly.

"I went to Sullins College," she informed a dubious Bretaigne Windust.

"Sullins?"

"For a whole year."

"Sullins?"

"It's one of the finest colleges in Virginia," she said firmly.

Windust, like everyone else, was captivated by Margaret Sullavan.

For the University Players the 1929 season began hectically. The opening of the new theater was a producer's nightmare. Nothing was ready except the actors. And they hadn't slept in days. The audience waited patiently, some knitted, some did crossword puzzles. About nine-thirty Windust rushed out to make an agonized apology. No one left.

"When the play started," Fonda says, "it was disaster from beginning to end. Sullavan and I were supposed to be the leads, but a vicious sea robin who tried to claw me to death and a crazy tortoise who wandered on and off stage at will stole the damn show.

"The people out in front were good-natured about the whole thing. They just applauded and said, 'The kids'll get it right eventually.' And we did."

In addition to events on stage the new house required more muscle than rehearsal. Fonda painted the murals in the large adjoining area they called the tearoom. Actually, it was a nightclub. Bernie Hanighen brought down a jazz band from Harvard. After the evening's performance, coffee, tea, and soft drinks were served with sandwiches.

55

The female members of the cast waited on tables, the men cooked, washed dishes, functioned as busboys, and provided entertainment.

Fonda and Logan created a series of sketches. The audience's favorite act featured Logan portraying Professor Huxley Hossefrosse and Fonda as his simple-minded stooge, Wilbur. A fifty-pound cake of ice was put at the back of the platform in a dishpan and covered with a towel. Professor Hossefrosse would come out immaculately attired in a tuxedo but barefoot. He was an oddball who supposedly had dashed in from Boston to lecture on "Health and Body Building." He moved about, gesturing, pointing, reprimanding.

One of the lines Fonda still recalls is, "Let me tell you about Camp Junaleska. It's a camp for boys between the ages of fourteen."

Suddenly, Logan gave the impression that he was about to sum up his theories. "Now, you've learned this at your mother's knee, and it's the honest-to-Jesus truth," Logan's lecture went. "Early to bed, early to rise . . . makes a man . . ." and then he'd roll his eyes toward the ceiling as though he'd forgotten the rest.

"Makes a man healthy, and . . . and . . ." And then Fonda entered. He'd slouch beside Logan, wearing a small silly hat and a deadpan expression.

"Josh would keep trying to get rid of me," Fonda says, "because I interrupted his lecture, but I wouldn't budge. In desperation, he'd turn around, pick up the ice, and give it to me. There I was, holding this block of ice, shifting it from hand to hand, it was getting colder and colder and it was dripping all over the floor. I showed no reaction. Josh kept talking, but you couldn't hear him anymore, because the audience was howling."

They did their act on the dance floor in front of the orchestra, now known as "Hanighen's Kings." Work in the tearoom went on from the end of the show until two A.M. Not too much time for romance, but Fonda and Sullavan somehow found it.

"Josh and I had just finished our act when the band took a break," Fonda says. "There were five musicians and they were on the porch smoking. I went out and joined them and found they were passing around a kind of cigarette they called a reefer.

"I didn't know what a reefer was, I didn't know anything about pot or marijuana then, and they told me to take it, just inhale and hold it. Well, I did a couple of times. I got so high. I'll never forget it. I remember walking across the dance floor when it was empty and thinking it took half the night to get there. Floating on a cloud and never happier, I went up to Sullavan. She didn't smoke, and I don't think she drank either. But I was so emboldened by my high I asked her to go swimming in the moonlight.

"Because we had lockers right there and dressing rooms in the theater, we got into our suits, crossed the beach, and went into the surf swimming, just the two of us.

"When we came out, we kissed a little and hugged some, and then fell asleep in the sand dunes. The sunlight woke us up."

Days later, when members of the company saw Fonda and Sullavan lying on a rock near the shore, their heads close together, they assumed the couple was memorizing their lines. Then their fellow actors noticed that the two exchanged winks and laughed at private jokes.

As a kid Fonda had learned to walk on his hands. He tried to teach Sullavan how to do it. When they fell, it was into each others arms. Between kisses, talk of marriage entered into their conversations, but for two actors making ten dollars a week between them, the subject was rapturously attractive but practically impossible.

By the end of summer, over the vociferous protests of her family, Sullavan followed Fonda to New York.

Although he didn't know him personally, Fonda had heard of a dynamic press agent. To impress Sullavan with his worldliness and knowledge of the New York theater, Fonda overcame his timidity long enough to reach the agent's office and make appointments for Sullavan and himself.

In the fall of 1929, Leland Hayward showed no interest in Henry Fonda or Margaret Sullavan. After two weeks of trudging the streets of the theatrical district, Sullavan heeded the entreaties of her parents and went home to Norfolk to make her debut into the genteel society of the South.

A much more exciting event occurred to Fonda. The co-directors of the University Players landed jobs as assistant stage managers with the Theater Guild. Bretaigne Windust was sent out with a road company of *Strange Interlude*. Charlie Leatherbee, always considered to be the more fortunate one, ended up in New York with the production of *The Game of Life and Death*, starring Claude Rains. Fonda strung along with Charlie, figuring with a name as important as Claude Rains, he would be certain to get at least a year's run out of the play.

Henry signed up for fifteen dollars a week as a walk-on. The stock market crashed that month, panic ran through the streets of the country, but the great shock to Fonda came when the closing notice was posted on the call board backstage at the Guild Theater. No matter how big a draw Claude Rains was *The Game of Life and Death* lasted only six weeks, the length of the Guild's subscription list.

Nothing remained for Fonda but to return to Washington and the National Junior Theater where he received a joyous welcome and a twenty-five-dollar a week raise. Clearly, the Crash hadn't reached the Wardman Park Hotel yet.

After adapting, directing, designing the scenery and costumes for *The Wizard of Oz*, Henry played the Cowardly Lion. Following that, he'd had it with children's theater.

"I wanted Margaret Sullavan, I wanted a play to act in, I wanted Broadway," Fonda says, "but Sullavan was as out of my reach at the time as Broadway. That left a play, and a chance for me to do one turned up."

Tired and homesick, he returned to Nebraska when the Omaha Community Playhouse offered a round-trip railroad ticket and allowed him to choose a vehicle for himself.

Henry lived with his family during his stay in Omaha. He noticed the contrast between the Depression in New York and in his home state. The spring didn't seem as green as he remembered it. Riding in on the train, he looked out the window and the land lay fallow, the farmhouses shabbier. The streets in town were emptier, quieter. A great many store fronts were boarded up. For Rent signs were everywhere. Fewer and fewer trucks from the farms showed up on Saturdays. A large share of his father's business consisted of printing foreclosure notices. As the banks had repossessed most of the land and equipment, farm machinery, tractors, rakes, and harrows rusted in the open, often untilled fields.

Henry's family was happy to see him, although his mother expressed an immediate concern about his weight.

"Mother," he explained patiently, "ever since high school I've eaten every bit of food you set in front of me. I've stuffed myself with malted milks and ginger ale with heavy cream. I've stuffed myself till I'm green, and the needle on the scale always stops at the same number, one-forty-six."

His father had doubts of a different nature.

"Henry," William Fonda began, "are you still sure you want to continue with this acting business? Not that I consider it a business, mind you."

"I don't suppose I'll ever make a fortune," Henry said, but a new confidence in his voice replaced his earlier uncertainty. "Dad, things aren't bad enough to give up. I keep thinking, it's just around the corner, then it's going to happen."

W. B. Fonda was kind enough not to point out that Mr. Hoover's prosperity was eluding the country from rounding the same corner. His father couldn't put up much of an argument against his son's acting career. During the forlorn days of the early thirties, doctors twiddled their thumbs, lawyers sold neckties, if they could land the jobs—engineers with college degrees offered to dig ditches, and were turned down. From the day he left Omaha, Henry had never written home asking for money. In some way, his father didn't know how, he had sustained himself. And if the senior Fonda's wife complained about her son's weight, well, working at the Retail Credit Company hadn't fattened up Henry.

And here he was, back as the lead in the Community Playhouse.

"They decided to bill me as their guest celebrity," Fonda says. "Guest celebrity. God! This was the place where I'd started, where I learned the difference between stage left and stage right. Okay, if that's what they wanted, I'd sure be pleased to oblige.

"Henry Fonda in *A Kiss for Cinderella*, the posters read. I liked Barrie's play. I'd done it before. The only problem was who could play Cinderella?"

"They had auditions in the Playhouse one Sunday afternoon and I read with dozens of girls. I didn't have to hold a script in my hand because I knew the part. As I read with woman after woman I noticed a girl sitting on a high stool in the wings. I asked the director who she was."

"Oh, that's the kid who played Snow White for me last season," he told me.

"Well, she looks awful pretty."

"You think she's old enough?"

"She sure seems right to me."

"If that's what you want," the director told Fonda.

The girl had been sitting with her feet on a rung of the stool, listening as each Cinderella read. When they called her over, *she* didn't need a script either; she'd memorized what the others had been reading.

"She came center stage," Fonda says, "and we did the scene together, neither of us using scripts. And that was it. There was no more contest. Her name was Dorothy McGuire and she was wonderful."

He and his thirteen-year-old discovery truimphed. She wanted to go on to New York, but Fonda persuaded her parents to keep her in school until she was older, a decision Miss McGuire never regretted.

Then, making use of his railroad ticket, Fonda hurried back to Manhattan and from there to Old Silver Beach on Cape Cod. Summer was starting and so were the University Players. Despite the Depression, Charlie Leatherbee's grandfather still had cash to reopen the theater.

New to the company were a Phi Beta Kappa from Princeton, Myron McCormick, Millie Natwick, and Aleta

Freel. Ross Alexander, a sly twenty-four-year-old, wandered in one day and charmed the entire company, particularly Aleta Freel. He'd done some professional acting on Broadway, but they wouldn't allow him to join the group because he'd never attended college. He didn't seem to mind. He participated in the skits at the tearoom and slept in the men's house when he wasn't sleeping with Aleta Freel, whom he later married.

That summer Logan was late in coming back to Falmouth. He had been delayed at college because of academic problems. Specifically, he owed a major paper to the university.

Windust telephoned Logan.

"What's keeping you Josh?" the director demanded.

"I have a paper to do, a big one," Logan explained.

"Get up here! I've cast you as the corpse in *The Wooden Kimono*."

"Windy," Logan reasoned, "if I don't finish this . . ."

"For Christ's sake," the impatient director shouted, "I've got a Vassar girl here writing essays for everybody. Come on!"

Logan didn't arrive in time to play the corpse and Fonda drew the assignment. He proved not to be the best of all dead men. At the big Saturday night performance, as he lay lifeless on the stage floor, Fonda was seized with a case of hiccups. When the cast saw Fonda's body involuntarily bumping up and down, they went to pieces. At best *The Wooden Kimono* was a mediocre mystery. Fonda's hiccups turned it into a comedy. The Saturday night's performance, everyone agreed, was the best of the week.

Having played *A Kiss for Cinderella* in Washington and Omaha, Fonda took on the triple chore of directing, painting the scenery, and acting the male lead in the production of Sir James M. Barrie's work for the University Players in the early summer of 1930. Originally, Susan Gill, a Radcliffe girl, had been assigned to act the part of Cinderella, but Fonda, more in love with Sullavan than ever, persuaded Miss Gill to withdraw. He and Sullavan managed to get through three days and nights of rehearsal and opened as a couple thoroughly entranced with each other. The words of the play called for their romance to blossom and the audiences caught the spirit. Fonda as the policeman-prince and Sullavan as the invalid-Cinderella couldn't have been better.

"Sullavan took direction well on stage, but offstage she was a true Southern rebel. Peggy was Scarlet O'Hara before Margaret Mitchell even dreamed of her," Fonda says. "In fact, at times she made me feel a little like the Leslie Howard character. All that girl needed was a hoop skirt. She had everything else Scarlet had, particularly her temperament."

In August of 1930, the innocents in the University Players asked themselves why the audiences grew smaller. The real truth of the Depression arrived slowly for them. January 1931, however, as the nation dug itself deeper into social and ecomonic chaos, Fonda realized how bad things were and how much worse they could become. He moved from one cheap rooming house to another. To erase the sordidness of his living conditions, when Charlie Leatherbee was in town and living at his grandfather's apartment on Park Avenue, Fonda indulged himself by staying with Charlie, thus saving himself a week or two of sorely needed rent money.

A major break came when Leatherbee and Logan went to Russia to study under the director of the Moscow Art Theater, Konstantin Stanislavsky. Before Charlie left, he and Windust had rented a terrace apartment in the newly constructed Tudor City complex overlooking the East River at Forty-second Street. Since Windy traveled about the country with the touring company of the O'Neill play, Leatherbee offered the apartment to Fonda and Goury Ivanov-Rinov, one of the designers of the University Players.

This was luxury on a high floor. In a closet Fonda found cans of paint. The copper was meant for the walls, the black for the ceiling. But as Leatherbee had entrusted the design of the apartment to Fonda, the process was reversed.

"I decorated the place," Fonda says, "and it was wild. I painted the walls a glossy black and the ceiling copper. Not sheet copper, but paint that looked like it. Quite modernistic and not at all like me. The effect was quite startling."

Fonda neglects to mention that he spent all that time painting because there was little else for an actor to do in the winter of 1931. The theatrical season crept along on feet paralyzed by a lack of backing. The exceptions were *Private Lives* with Gertrude Lawrence and Noël Coward, Lunt and Fontanne in *Reunion In Vienna*, and Katharine Cornell in *The Barretts of Wimpole Street*. If productions were few, so were the chances of a job. Moreover, talking motion pictures became firmly established as a powerful entertainment medium. Hollywood began the process of catching much of the best of Broadway with its nets of gold.

Millions of Americans starved during those cold, hopeless months, and Fonda went hungry right along with them. All he and his expatriate Russian roommate could afford was rice.

"Goury didn't have a job and I didn't have one," Fonda says, "and if we had a dime between us, we'd buy rice. Just a small box of rice or a tiny bag of it. We would boil rice and it would swell up and there was a great deal of bulk to it. There was no salt to put on it. We couldn't afford sugar or milk. We just ate rice to fill us up. Nothing was wrong with it. The Chinese and the Japanese have been doing it for centuries. It was filling, all right, but after a few weeks, it became boring as hell."

Occasionally, Erik Barnouw, one of the founders of the University Players, would telephone Fonda and ask if he might stop by and bring some dinner. The answer was always yes, and always the generous Mr. Barnouw would bring steak and potatoes not only to feed the hungry pair in Tudor City, but enough extra food to relieve the rice diet for a week.

"Of course, every day I'd walk from Tudor City to Times Square to make the rounds. This wasn't walking for exercise, I didn't have a nickel for the subway. You can't imagine how sad Times Square looked in those days. Half or more than half of the theaters closed. Veterans selling apples on every other corner. Broadway Rose trying to peddle her flowers in Shubert Alley. The old-timers said she was the only one allowed in the Alley because she'd danced in an early Shubert chorus line.

"Late one afternoon I was walking home from the theater district and I passed Grand Central Station. The placards out in front announced an art show in a gallery on the sixth floor. I knew about it. I'd always hang around the art shows when I wasn't hunting for a job. So I took the elevator to the sixth floor and went into the Grand Central Art Gallery.

"It was about five-thirty in the afternoon and I found myself outside a large room that had about a hundred people in it. Some of them were looking at the paintings, but most of them were standing and talking to each other or nibbling. At first, I couldn't see it. And then, suddenly, I did. In the center of the room was this table loaded with drinks and hors d'oeuvres. It looked like the kind of set that Cecil B. DeMille would do in a banquet scene. That table must have been twenty feet long, and at one end was a cornucopia with stacks of sandwiches pouring out; cakes, fruits, cookies. Everyone in the room looked so well fed and so well dressed.

"Now, the party was by invitation, only I didn't have one. Still, no one was at the door collecting them. I thought to myself, 'Well, Henry you just step in. Nothing'll happen.' But then, quick as that, I said right back to myself, 'You do that, Henry, and they'll arrest you.' But they didn't. I walked in and went all around looking at the paintings and all the while edging closer to that table with all the food on it. I thought of Goury waiting at home for me with the boiled rice, and I wondered what would happen if I slid a couple of those sandwiches into my pocket, one for Goury, one for me. But I didn't. I thought that would be too obvious. Then I wondered if I could get up enough courage to, you know, nonchalantly pick up a sandwich with one hand and a drink with the other.

"I went around that entire room twice. Nobody would have paid the slightest bit of attention if I'd devoured a platter of sandwiches. But I never touched a thing. I didn't have the nerve."

Winter melted into spring and spring opened up into

summer. The University Players returned to Cape Cod with another busy schedule. Since many of the regulars were graduated from college in June 1931 they had rightful apprehensions about their futures. When a theater in Baltimore put out a nibble of interest for a repertory company, Windust, Leatherbee, and Logan grabbed it. They felt they were set.

Between Labor Day, when they closed the theater on old Silver Beach, and a week or two before they opened in Baltimore, the members of the troupe rehearsed the plays they intended to present, swam, sailed, and had the best postseason anyone could recall. For Fonda, a most important member of the company had left.

Margaret Sullavan had gone on the road as an understudy in *Strictly Dishonorable*. That he missed her was evident to all. Their spirited quarrels and fond reunions had been a major source of conversation for three years.

An understudy is an unrehearsed, ill-prepared actor who almost never gets to go on. Sullavan was fortunate enough to disprove the rule. She actually did appear in Philadelphia, and Lee Shubert, senior partner of the two brothers who controlled the theater, saw her. And liked her. And signed her to play the lead in a Broadway comedy.

"Christ, I was happy for Sullavan," Fonda says, "but I sure had my doubts as to what would happen to us if she made it."

He didn't have to wait long. Margaret Sullavan opened on Broadway featured in a play called *A Modern Virgin* and walked off with the notices. Fonda was understandably fearful of his future relationship with Sullavan. Mr. Lee, as the older Shubert liked to be called, put the play into his best house for comedy, the Booth Theater. But despite the good reviews for the leading lady, *A Modern Virgin* ran for a mere forty-five performances and closed. Miss Sullavan rejoined the University Players shortly after they opened at the Maryland Theater in Baltimore.

"When I saw Peggy come backstage," Fonda says, "I was sure glad to see her. The expression they used in those days was, 'She looked like a million,' and she sure did. When she smiled at me, I thought, I ain't ever gonna let this girl get away from me again!"

At first the group at the Maryland fared even worse than Sullavan at the Booth. Their idea of repertory was to present one play on Monday evening, a different one on Tuesday evening, and still another at the Wednesday matinee. They succeeded in confusing audiences so thoroughly that almost no one bought tickets, and when they did, they saw the wrong play. The only two happy people were Fonda and Sullavan.

Neither one was much for public billing and cooing, but during the early winter their romance grew to the point where Fonda proposed, Sullavan accepted, and they took out a marriage license. "I flipped," Fonda says. When a sharp Baltimore newspaper reporter interviewed Miss Sullavan on the subject of her forthcoming marriage, she denied it.

"Good heavens, no!" she exclaimed. "Who on earth would want to marry Henry Fonda?"

At twelve o'clock noon on Christmas Day 1931, with Kent Smith as the best man and Bretaigne Windust playing the little upright piano, in the dining room a sunny Margaret Sullavan and an elated Henry Fonda were joined in holy matrimony at the Kernan Hotel in Baltimore, Maryland.

The beginning of the thirties ended the fashion of the flapper. The bound breasts of the women, the long waists, the skinny John Held, Jr., sticklike girl gave way to a woman whose skirts were six inches longer and whose clothes allowed the natural curves of her body to be seen once again. Though she was not a New York high fashion model, Sullavan quickly adopted the new styles. A little hat, a tiny veil, her best dress, a soft silk crepe with a V neckline, a string of pearls, and a saber slash of bright red across her mouth served as her wedding costume. A lapel corsage of two gardenias provided a touch of white. The fragrance it emitted also helped to cover the odors of cooking emanating from the nearby kitchen. No need for face powder. Her natural complexion, glowing at the start of her first venture into matrimony, did what no cosmetic house could do. She was radiant.

Fonda, his blue-black beard shaved as closely as possible, wore his dark suit and an expression of wonder.

Sullavan's bobbed hair bounced as she nodded in assent to "I do." Fonda could barely be heard. Present was the entire company of the University Players. They were as much family as the bride or bridegroom wished.

A bridal luncheon followed the ceremony.

"We ate like we were in the army," Josh Logan said.

There was good reason for this haste. The wedding cake had to be cut and eaten in the wings of the theater. A matinee was scheduled for that afternoon, and if the show had to go on, and it did, well, Fonda tells it this way:

"I went on stage and played the lover. Sullavan sat in the last row of the house and watched. We thought we'd kept it all a secret. Well, shit! It was on the news before the audience came in for the matinee. They went crazy because they knew about it and found it a lot of fun. After a while Johnny Swope took Sullavan out to see a movie, Greta Garbo in *Mata Hari*, but all of a sudden, he grabbed her arm and whispered, 'I forgot! I'm in the last act.' And he flew out. There she was, the bride on her wedding day, sitting in Loew's Whatever."

Joshua Logan, now the leading director of the University Players, saw it this way:

"That day there was a matinee of *The Ghost Train* by Arnold Ridley. Fonda played the bridegroom in it. The news of the wedding had spread via the lady ushers, so that when Fonda accidentally scattered rice by pulling a handkerchief from his pocket [part of the plot], the audience applauded . . ."

For their honeymoon Fonda bought a secondhand two-toned blue Stutz Bearcat roadster. Amid many joyous farewells, the couple started out. Fonda had paid seventy-five dollars for the car. Shiny nickel bumpers, nickel freestanding headlights, grill, balloon tires—what a buy! He drove it from the garage to the theater where he picked up his wife. They got no more than two or three blocks when the Stutz coughed, sputtered, and came to a final halt. Taking their bags out of the trunk, Mr. and Mrs. Fonda returned to the hotel where Myron McCormick moved out of the room he and Fonda shared and Mrs. Fonda moved in.

"He got the choicest article we had," Logan said, "and that was Margaret Sullavan."

The prize and the man who won her stayed out the season in Baltimore, and then, early in March, moved to a small garden apartment behind a big house in New York's Greenwich Village. Although as lovers Fonda and Sullavan had fought and made up, as husband and wife their arguments reached heights Fonda had never anticipated.

Living with Sullavan was like living with lightning. Her tantrums struck at any hour and on any subject. Scenes are what actors play best, and Sullavan created them over everything, the weather, the food they ate, the clothes she wore, the plays they tried out for, anything. Fonda reacted to this in atypical fashion. He began to match her, argument for argument.

"I never knew I had a temper until I got married," he says.

"She was too fiery to handle," was Kent Smith's opinion.

"Time after time that slender girl's words stung me like a wasp," Fonda says. "It got to the point where we didn't live on love. We were at each other constantly, screaming, arguing, fighting. It's all a blur now. I don't know whether I stamped out in a rage or whether Sullavan threw me out."

Whichever way it was, less than four months after their marriage Fonda found himself in a single room in a fifth-rate hotel below Forty-second Street. Cockroaches were his only companions, plaster hung from the walls, dirty sheets covered his bed, a dim bulb swung from a dusty chain suspended from the stained and cracked ceiling. This was not the worst he had to endure.

"In an agent's office," Fonda says, "I overheard an actor say Margaret Sullavan was having an affair with the producer Jed Harris.

"I left that place fast. I had to get into the cold air before I passed out. That was rough. That was hard. Even after I'd heard it, and I realized everyone else knew, I was drawn back to that Greenwich Village area.

"I'd wait until night and then I'd go by the main house down from the sidewalk and into the garden. I'd lean against the fence and I'd stare up at our apartment with the lighted windows on the second floor. I knew Jed Harris was inside with her and I'd wait for him to leave. But instead the lights would go out.

"More nights than I care to remember I'd stand there and cry, and then wipe away my tears so that I wouldn't look like a wino on the subway riding uptown.

"I'd go back to that flea-bitten hotel room and I'd sit in the dark. I couldn't believe my wife and that son-of-a-bitch were in bed together. But I knew they were. And that just destroyed me, completely destroyed me. Never in my life have I felt so betrayed, so rejected, so alone."

CHAPTER
4

ON a gray day in May 1932 a cruel wind howled its way in through the window frame of his hotel room and a constant rain beat a tattoo on the glass panes. Henry Fonda, needing to escape the wretchedness he felt within himself, left the room and walked east on Fortieth Street. By the time he reached Madison Avenue his shoes squished with rainwater that flooded the gutters of the New York streets. Turning, he started uptown. He had no idea where his soaking shoes would take him.

"My thinking was scrambled when Sullavan and I separated," he says. "Something happened to me that had never happened before. I didn't seem to be able to handle it. I couldn't cope. It was heartbreak time and I thought it was the end of the world.

"I stopped when I found myself facing a Christian Science Reading Room. My God! It had been eight years. There had never been any renunciation of religion on my part, but like so many people, it was a gradual fading away.

"It didn't take me long to decide what to do. I was desperate. I opened the door and went in. A man was sitting behind a desk."

"May I help you?" the man asked.

Fonda didn't even glance about to see if anyone else was present. He simply spilled out all of his agony and the story of the conflict that had gone on between Sullavan and himself and how it had climaxed in their separation.

"I don't know what it was," Fonda says. "I must have had faith that day. I don't even know who the man was, but he helped me to leave my pain in that little reading room. When I went out, I was Henry Fonda again. An unemployed actor but a man."

When he returned to his hotel to change into his other pair of shoes, he found a message waiting for him. Henry C. Potter, producer of the Easthampton Playhouse, had telephoned.

Fast as a firehorse and just as determined, Fonda raced to the Potter office.

"Hello, Hank," the producer began. "Going back to the University Players again?"

"Nope," Fonda answered truthfully. "I've had four years of Falmouth. The only people who've seen me are visitors to Cape Cod."

"Good. I have a part here that's right for you."

"Well, I'm never going to isolate myself again."

"Our policy is different than Windy's and Charlie's"

"How?" Fonda asked.

"We do new plays. If they work, you go right to Broadway with 'em."

"Fine."

"Here," Potter said, handing Fonda a script. "We'll use you."

The rain had cleared and Fonda returned to the hotel which suddenly didn't seem so terrible. That night he wrote his mother.

"At last," a portion of his letter said, "I've been discovered!"

The play called for Fonda to take a fall or two. Ted Sherdeman, a friend from Omaha, was in town. He knew nothing of Fonda's rehearsal tactics. All he knew was that he and Fonda were riding atop one of those old open-air double-decker buses.

"We were going down Fifth Avenue one Sunday morning and we must have been around Twelfth Street, near Washington Square, when BAM! Henry fell right off the top of the bus. Scared? I almost fainted. Then I looked at the conductor. He almost died.

"We stared at the street, two floors below, and there stood Henry, pleased with himself."

"Holy Christ," Sherdeman shouted. "What the hell do you think you're doing?"

"I'm practicing falls for a play I'm going to be in," Fonda yelled back.

Sherdeman got off at the next stop. Although Prohibition was still the law, he managed to get himself a drink.

"I sure as hell needed it," he claimed.

A few days later, Fonda strolled into the Potter office.

"Hank," the producer began uneasily, "I don't know how to make this easy, but the author has decided to cast someone else."

"You're telling me I don't have a job," Fonda said hollowly.

"The author always has the last word, Hank. You know that as well as I do."

His latest opportunity disappeared as easily as a magician's rabbit. A dejected Henry Fonda headed toward the Sardi Building. On his way, he took stock of his situation.

"It was the second week in June," he says. "Most summer theaters were starting rehearsals for their opening plays. Everything was set. I remembered only too damn well those lines I got from people in Provincetown and Dennis four years earlier. 'We cast in New York and we're set for the season.'"

For a brief moment he thought there might be a chance of his returning to Falmouth, but he recalled the conversation he had held with Josh Logan.

Logan had used a young Princeton undergraduate in one of the Triangle shows he had written and directed. When Fonda had announced his retirement from the University Players, Logan tried to get a commitment from the gangly youth.

"You're going to follow Fonda," Logan advised him.

"Oh, no. Hold on a minute," the Princeton sophomore backed off, shaking his head and holding up his outstretched arm. "I couldn't."

"Why not?" Logan demanded.

"I promised my father I'd help run the hardware store in Indiana, Pennsylvania, this summer. Besides," he added, "I'm not good enough to replace Fonda."

But Logan had prevailed and Jimmy Stewart joined the University Players. Fonda had accepted this, and by now he knew his acting career had hit bottom.

Taking the shortcut through Shubert Alley, Fonda arrived in front of the Sardi Building. Above the famous restaurant are a warren of little offices. On a lower floor one of the kindest talent agents in New York, Sara Enright, made her headquarters.

"I went into Sara's place and told her the shape I was in," Fonda says. "She began poring over her lists, she always had lists of everything that went on in show business. Finally, she stopped turning the pages and pointed an index finger at a name."

"You poor boy," she commiserated with him. "I have something here, but it's not much."

"What is it?"

"I can send you to a theater in Surrey. That's in Maine, dear. You won't be acting, but you'll get twenty dollars a week and keep. It's just driving a sation wagon and stooging around backstage. You'd only be a hired hand, Henry, but it's a job."

Henry took a deep breath. "I'll take it," he said. "I have to exist somehow."

Surrey is just above Bar Harbor. The theater was set back in the woods and what Fonda did at the beginning was exactly what the agent had told him. He chauffeured and picked up Joseph Cotten's trunk at the railway station.

"It was a real comedown," Fonda says. "There I was doing the same sort of odd jobs I'd done years ago in Omaha. Still, I was glad to have the work."

Fonda did these menial tasks without complaint until the middle of July when the set designer, in a fit of temperamental creativity, packed up his T-square and his pencils and left.

"I can do that job," Fonda volunteered. "I've done it before."

Out of necessity, the producer said, "You're it."

73

Rather than spend the rest of the season driving about, moving trunks, and picking up furniture, Fonda busied himself with the paint pots and canvas that turned into scenery. The summer passed quickly, as most summers do. Fonda made his good-by and returned to New York.

Autumn of 1932, while President Hoover and the governor of New York were battling for the White House, four young men decided to move into the same apartment. In alphabetical order they were Henry Fonda, Joshua Logan, Myron McCormick, who was rapidly becoming one of New York's most successful radio actors and who would one day play Luther Billis, the Seabee in *South Pacific* whose rotating belly dance stopped the show at every performance. Finally, there was James Stewart who had no intention of ever becoming as actor. He had studied and received his degree at Princeton as an architect, and if buildings weren't going up very often, there was always the hardware store at home where he could help out. His father was an unusual sort of businessman. He took odd items in trade in place of cash. As a result, he once got a ten-foot-long python from a carnival that went broke while in town. This he displayed in the window of the store. Another time, he accepted an accordion that his son, Jim, learned to play. Not that Jimmy Stewart became one of the greatest accordion virtuosos of the world, but his mother played the organ in church on Sundays, and she taught him a few chords. That was enough to get him into a Triangle show that Logan wrote and directed. As for acting, he laughingly thought of it as a way to pass the time before graduate school. The only reason he hung around with the two Princeton boys and the fellow from Nebraska was they were such good company.

The four of them moved into a two-room apartment on West Sixty-fourth Street. The notorious New York gangster Legs Diamond made his base of operations in a hotel two doors up the street. The name on the hotel's neon sign changed every week or two—probably to bewilder the police.

Aside from Fonda, Logan, McCormick, and Stewart the other tenants of the apartment building were prostitutes. A kind of nonaggression pact served to keep peaceful relations between both sides. What problems did occur generally came from the hotel two doors up the street.

"We were on the third floor of this seven-story building," Fonda says. "We'd be sitting there, after the theater, drinking a beer or two and the door would open. We'd turn around and three characters that looked like they'd just walked in from a Warner Brothers gangster movie would appear: Chesterfield coats with black velvet collars up and white Borsalino hats pulled down, dark glasses, and hands in their pockets; they'd walk over to the bedroom, glance around, shrug, never open their mouths, and leave.

"It happened so often, always with different guys, but they all were after the same thing. When they couldn't find the girls, they'd go down the hall or the floor above."

One morning, next door to the apartment, a small-time hoodlum was shot to death on the stoop, but after the police and the reporters and the photographers left, the gangsters returned, and as the prostitutes had never left, business continued as usual.

Business for the girls may have been good. For the boys it was only promising. Arthur Beckhard, a Broadway producer who took over the University Players, brought many of the men and women from Cape Cod to New York. Stewart and McCormick played in his cast, Windust served as the stage manager, Logan was his assistant. The play, which featured Beckhard's wife, Esther Dale, was called *Carrie Nation*. Mixed reviews and a scarcity of hard cash at the box office closed the production after three and a half weeks.

Stewart prepared to give up acting; shovels and nails appeared to be steadier. McCormick went beck to those quiet carpeted radio studios at NBC and CBS. Logan looked about desperately, but found nothing worthy of his talents in the theater. And then Beckhard opened a hit, *Goodbye Again*, and everyone had walk-ons or a job of some sort. Everyone except Fonda. Henry played winter stock in East Orange, New Jersey. As the leading man he was entitled to ten percent of the gross, a sum acceptable on Broadway. But in East Orange, the weekly gross brought Fonda seven dollars a week, sometimes as much as eight. To make up for this palpable inequity the producer, who owned a sizable orchard, quite frequently gave Fonda a jug or two of applejack to even up matters. That applejack kept the boys on West Sixty-fourth Street warm for the better part of the winter, although it must be noted that Fonda, who served as cook, lurched from the kitchen time and again to join in the four-part harmony as they sang "Sam the Old Accordion Man."

The hard cider helped numb his hurt after he received his finalized divorce papers from Margaret Sullavan's attorney. That last wrench, despite the hot and cold periods of their marriage, despite the bickering and the battles called for liquor stronger than applejack.

"For serious drinking," Fonda says, "we'd buy raw alcohol and mix it with gelatin. There was always a question if the stuff was wood alcohol or grain. We'd test it by pouring just a little bit on the metal running board of a car. Then we'd light it. It the flame was blue, we'd drink it. If it was red, we'd throw it away."

Another opportunity came to Fonda when he appeared as a supernumerary in *I Loved You Wednesday*. The drama, with Humphrey Bogart, opened on Broadway. Fonda played a bar patron who had no lines but sat opposite a teen-age Arlene Francis. During the traditionally "dead weeks" in December, the production folded.

They celebrated Christmas early that year. Fonda prepared a dinner from a menu sent east by his mother. They finished what remained of the applejack and went to bed without much cheer. There were no presents.

The new year held no more prospects than the old, but in February 1933 Fonda got another chance. Arthur Beckhard was directing the great Tallulah Bankhead in *Forsaking All Others*. Her leading man, Fred Keating, needed an understudy, and Fonda waited backstage with the other hopefuls. Of course, it wasn't Mr. Keating who saw the candidates but Miss Bankhead.

Taken into Tallulah's dressing room, Fonda politely removed his hat while the southern belle stared at him through her mirror. Then she whirled around.

"How the fucking old are you?" Miss Bankhead drawled.

"Twenty-eight," Fonda answered truthfully.

"You're a fucking liar!" she lowered her voice and lifted her eyes to meet his.

But there was something about Henry Fonda that Tallulah Bankhead liked, and he got the part. Unfortunately, even Bankhead's sorcery couldn't beat the critics' reviews and that play closed, too.

In the spring, when Franklin Delano Roosevelt told Americans the only fear they had to fear was fear itself, Henry Fonda earned his only dollar outside the theater.

"We pooled our resources at the apartment," Fonda says, "and I contributed the least. I didn't have any money and I knew I had to make a buck. I was willing to do anything, address envelopes, anything. I heard there were ads for that kind of thing. Help wanted. Cheap. So I scanned the classified ads of the *Times*, and there it was: 'Florist's Assistant, Goldfarb's, My Florist, southwest corner 72nd & Third.'

"Easter was coming and florists were doing more business than they normally did during the year and they needed extra men. I thought it would be to work as a salesman or to handle the flow of traffic.

"So I answered the ad and I got to the shop and I was directed to the second floor. A line of men waited outside Mr. Goldfarb's office. There had to be thirty or forty, and it took half an hour for me to get near the front. I had a lot of time to think. What do I have to offer that these other guys don't have? How am I going to sell myself to Mr. Goldfarb? How am I going to convince him that I'm the fellow to hire because I hear from the other men in the line that he's taking only one or two.

"Anyway, it's my turn next and I go into the office. It wasn't much. Not very big, a desk with a vase of flowers on it, and a chair on the other side of the desk. Goldfarb was a chubby little man and sort of cheery. Fifty, sixty years old."

"Well, young man," he said to me, "what do you have to recommend you?"

"I looked him right in the eye, pulled back my shoulders, and tried to use as much sincerity as possible. 'Mr. Goldfarb, I've been in the theater. I've been trying to be an actor, and it hasn't panned out. And . . . ah I've got to change my life. And ah . . . Mr. Goldfarb, I've decided I want to be a florist.' "

"You're a sensible person," Goldfarb nodded.

"I tell you," Fonda says, "I put on the goddamnedest performance you've ever seen. I was selling him the idea that I had given up this dream of mine and all I wanted now was to go into the flower business.

"He shook my hand. 'The job is yours,' he told me. I never saw Goldfarb again, but I did learn something important. Never lie during a job interview. There were nights I could hardly move. I had to lug large pots of lilies, tulips, hydrangeas, and other plants they sell at Easter from the cellar to the counter on the first floor. This meant going up and down the stairs carrying those fucking lilies all day until my legs were about to give way.

"I did this for two or three weeks, and then my knees went completely. Those pots were heavy, and I simply could not make it anymore. I went to the floor manager."

" 'Yes, Fonda, what is it? What're you doing up here? Why aren't you carrying the merchandise?' "

"So I explained, and he was sympathetic, and from then on, my job was to carry the plants from the center of the store out to the cars at the curb where I'd get tips, ten cents from the Chevys, a quarter from the Cadillacs. That part was all right. Of course, when Easter went, so did the job."

The news that his ex-wife signed for a part in a Hollywood motion picture did nothing to encourage Fonda. He did not begrudge Sullavan her contract. It seemed to him simply part of the cycle both were on, she on top, he, for the moment, below.

Fonda and his roommates organized a once-a-week steak and beer party. A friendly Irishman who owned a speakeasy on Forty-first Street allowed them to use the lower floor for their supper—"all you can eat and drink for a dollar."

Steep stairs led down to a place furnished with long

wooden trestle tables and benches to match. In the corner there was even an upright piano.

"Some of the keys didn't work," Fonda says, "but that was all right, neither did we, very often. Johnny Morris, an ex-University Player, taught us how to make hobo steaks; huge thick slabs of beef with sides of salt on top of them. Johnny would slide the steak into an iron grill and then he'd take them out and lift off the salt like a hunk of plaster."

After this, Fonda sliced the steaks, covered them with butter, and placed the rare meat on chunks of bread; that and mugs of beer gave the young theater people about town something to anticipate every Thursday night.

"I was a jazz freak," Fonda admits, "and still am. I was terribly impressed when Benny Goodman would come over from NBC where he was a house musician, and he'd bring a couple of the other guys from the orchestra, and they'd eat and then jam for an hour or two. Great!"

Those were friendly suppers, but by late May or June, the big downstairs room started to retain heat and become uncomfortable. The customers disappeared, and the boys from Sixty-fourth Street took off to resume their summer-stock careers.

Fonda's fame as a scenic designer landed him at one of the finest new summer theaters in the country. Day Tuttle, an actor, director, and writer, headed the Westchester Playhouse at Mt. Kisco, New York. For the summer of 1933 Tuttle engaged Fonda to do the sets. As nothing loomed on the horizon, Fonda accepted.

He sketched and drew, painted and built the scenery for twelve productions. He also found the furniture and set decorations, and to make it appear the way he wanted, he did the lighting, too.

The Westchester Playhouse was on the Lawrence Farm Country Club's acreage, a millionaire's estate. Tuttle and his partner, Richard Skinner, managed the theater, and Monty Woolley, later to make his name in *The Man Who Came to Dinner*, directed there for a season.

It was at Mt. Kisco that Fonda heard the story of Mrs. Cornelius Vanderbilt and the governor of Rhode Island.

Tuttle and Woolley were present at the grand lady's marble and bronze "cottage" in Newport. Tuttle described it.

The Depression was just beginning to pull itself out of its depths when Mrs. Vanderbilt invited the governor, Tuttle, and Woolley to lunch with her. To the surprise of everyone, she inquired about economic conditions in Rhode Island.

"How are things in the industrial world of your dear state developing, Your Excellency?"

"Ah, very well. Very well, indeed," the governor answered, astounded that Mrs. Vanderbilt should condescend to interest herself in anything as mundane as a reviving economy. But as long as she had done so, he would allow her an overall view of fiscal conditions.

"Indices of employment are rising," he informed his hostess. Mrs. Vanderbilt picked at her cold fish.

"Bank clearances are definitely on the upswing," the governor proclaimed. Still no reaction from Mrs. Vanderbilt.

"Car loadings are increasing and in towns and cities throughout the state, the mills are doing ever so much better." The great lady stopped eating at once, and smiled with the pleasure of one who can at last follow the thread of conversation.

"The Mills are doing better," she mused. "How gratifying."

And then she gave a pleased sigh.

"Dear Ogden," she said and returned to her fish.

This tale, told under the grove of maples where the cast rehearsed and relaxed after lunch, always brought great merriment. Although Fonda laughed at it and other stories, he did not laugh the way he had when Josh Logan performed Professor Huxley Hossefrosse that first night at Falmouth. The days at Mt. Kisco were sunny and the nights were cool black velvet, but Henry Fonda had retreated within himself.

Day Tuttle said, "I think he had been terribly hurt by Sullavan's success. For a while, he built a quiet place around himself and walked into it and didn't let anyone come very near."

A scenic designer works alone. He imagines, creates, draws, and paints alone. Fonda's contacts with the actors were, therefore, at a minimum.

One reason for his withdrawal from the social life of the acting company was that his former wife, Margaret Sullavan, played leading roles at Mt. Kisco. They rarely spoke, and it took until midsummer before Sullavan told Day Tuttle, "That ex-husband of mine is really a very good actor."

The dapper Tuttle, eager to please his leading lady, cast Fonda in the next production, *Journey's End*. He played a stretcher-bearer.

The proximity of his former love and the personal and artistic differences between them—she, the leading lady, he, a name that appeared toward the end of the program, left him quieter and more desolate than before. He found some solace with a girl who ushered at the Playhouse.

"Two or three times a week Hank would borrow our station wagon," Day Tuttle said. "In the back of the wagon were three enormous lengths of heavy blue moire that made a cushy mattress. After the girl was finished with her ushering duties, Fonda would pick her up and they'd drive out somewhere deep in the woods and park. It was nothing serious, just a light summertime fling."

Labor Day weekend Sullavan returned to films in Hollywood. Fonda went to New York where he and Jimmy Stewart rented a pair of rooms in the old Madison Square Hotel down in the twenties. Both sitting room and bedroom were furnished in early East Lynne, faded ruby and permanent gray.

There are those people living in New York who believe autumn is the best of the four seasons. The heat of the summer is gone, the foliage in Central Park turns from green to yellow to a brilliant red, schools start up, plays open, opportunities for actors to find jobs begin afresh.

Fonda and Jimmy Stewart were optimistic, particularly when they both landed roles in a play scheduled to open at Henry Miller's Theater early in December. It was called *All Good Americans* and it went through its casting period in October, rehearsed through November, and previewed the first week in December. Luckily, the play ran through Christmas and New Year's. Then the inevitable closing notice was posted. The management, generous beyond expectation, held a party following the last performance.

"I played the accordion a little bit those days," Jim Stewart said. "And the party lasted pretty late. It was three o'clock in the morning I suppose, and we were on our way across Times Square to get a subway to go home.

"And Fonda stopped in the middle of Times Square—there was nobody, it was completely deserted, and he said, 'I wonder if you started playing your accordion now if you'd get an audience.'

"Well, that's Fonda's idea. So I said, 'There's only one way to find out and that's to start playing.'

"So I took out the accordion and began. And in two or three minutes a couple of people came up. And I played another number and some more people came up. Pretty soon we were surrounded and they started giving requests.

"Then the next thing I saw Fonda passing the hat. Well, as far as the first part goes, we agree. I say we got thirty-six cents. Fonda says we got twelve to fifteen cents. So we disagree on the box-office receipts for that night.

"But it ended up very quickly. I felt somebody hit me on my backside with a club and it was a policeman and he was furious. I wouldn't exactly call it disturbing the peace, except that's what *he* called it. He said, 'It's taken me three or four hours to get all these people asleep in those doorways, and you come along and start that noise.'

"I've always felt he could have used a kinder word.

"'Now,' the policeman said, 'it'll take me another four hours to get them to sleep again.' Anyway, that was it. But all this originated with Fonda."

Fonda and Stewart were fortunate that the cop did nothing worse than refer to Stewarts' music as noise. Stewart packed up his accordion, and he and Fonda dove into the Seventh Avenue subway and took the first southbound train to Madison Square and home.

Unemployed again, Fonda and Stewart returned to the steak and beer parties in February.

"I'm afraid Jim and I overdid it a bit at one of those parties," Fonda says. "The slogan might have been 'Eat as much as you want and drink as much as you can,' but that particular night, we did a helluva lot more drinking than eating. We drank beer by the pitcher instead of the mug. We finally decided to go home, and we went outside. There had been a snowstorm during the evening, and it already had been shoveled into high banks along the curbs and against the buildings.

"We caught a subway train, and we were sitting there, and I said to Stewart, 'I can't straighten up. My bladder's so tight from beer.' And he said, 'That's how I feel.'

"When we left the subway, we had about four blocks to reach the Madison Square Hotel. Stewart said, 'Hank, I don't think I can make it to the hotel. There's no place open, and there're no people on the street. Let's do it here.'

"I said, 'It's a good idea. Let's have a contest. We'll see who can piss the longest continual line in the snowdrift. If a car passes, it'll look like we're walking along, admiring the snow.'

" 'It's a deal,' Stewart replied.

"Then I had a better plan. 'Say, let's write our names in the snow.' We must have been pretty pie-eyed because he agreed.

"Now I walked two blocks going real slow, and Stewart walked about three blocks. He complained later that my name was shorter than his, but I had broken the rules anyhow, I only printed my initials. He wrote his whole name in those drifts. Come to think of it, Stewart must have had a helluva lot more to drink that night than I did!"

In March Fonda's fortunes took a swing upward. Leonard Sillman, the boy impresario from Detroit, had pulled together a revue called *Low and Behold*. Featuring Tyrone Power and Eve Arden, it hit in Pasadena and bombed in Los Angeles.

Lee Shubert stopped by long enough to sign Eve Arden for the next edition of *The Ziegfeld Follies* and promised Sillman backing and a theater if he brought the show to New York. As Angelenos were staying away by the thousands, Sillman shrewdly closed his operation and brought it east. Tyrone Power stubbornly remained in Hollywood.

Sillman considered this a proper move. Manhattan was not only the theater's capital, but more pure talent could be found in the canyons of Gotham than in the arroyos of Los Angeles. Furthermore, had not Lee Shubert promised money and a house? Actually, financial backing wasn't what Mr. Shubert had in mind. What he neglected to mention was that his offer really would consist of moral backing. However, he did lend the fledgling producer a series of empty theaters in which to audition. What he neglected to mention was that the heat would not be turned on. Very often, what Mr. Shubert didn't say was more important than what he did say.

Glenn Anders, a Broadway actor of long experience, had toured in O'Neill's *Strange Interlude*. Bretaigne Windust, the stage manager of the production, had introduced him to Fonda when the company returned to New York. Learning of Sillman's venture, Anders invited Fonda to accompany him to the Algonquin Hotel where Sillman was living. Once inside the door, Anders called Sillman on the house phone.

"Leonard," he said, "I know an actor who needs a job."

"Where is he?" Sillman asked.

"In the lobby."

"Send him up."

Sillman occupied a one-bedroom apartment that doubled as his office. When he heard a knock on his door, he called, "Come in."

A young man in a turtleneck sweater stood on his threshold.

"Yes?" Sillman asked. The young man waited for a time and then murmured his name.

"Do you sing?" Sillman inquired.

"Nope."

"Do you dance?" The applicant was tall and slim and adopted the odd stance of a dancer.

"Nope."

"Well, what *do* you do?" the producer asked impatiently.

"I do imitations of babies from one week to one year,"

Henry Fonda said. At parties, at steak and beer suppers, almost at the drop of anyone's hat, Henry Fonda would oblige with his baby imitations.

"Well, can you do one of them now?" Leonard Sillman asked.

Without a word Fonda went into his act. He pantomimed a man driving a car and simultaneously changing a baby's diaper. Within minutes, Sillman was lying across an armchair collapsing with laughter.

"What did you say your name was?"

"Henry Fonda."

"Well, Henry Fonda, I'm going to put you into my show."

"But I don't sing and I don't dance. What're you going to do with me?"

"You'll sing and you'll dance by the time I'm finished," Sillman promised.

Leonard Sillman gathered about him a group of highly talented young people: Charles Walters, who later became one of MGM's great musical directors; Nancy Hamilton, who would write the sketches and lyrics for many of Broadway's most successful revues; Imogene Coca, who went on to fame in theater, films, and television.

Sillman had a first-rate revue and a first-rate problem. He didn't have the money for the production. To keep the cast, he improvised backers' auditions, casting calls, everything a good producer can invent during a bad spell. Each time Sillman telephoned a wealthy friend and offered him "the chance to get in on a great show," he heard the same question, "Who's in it?" And then, "Oh? Sorry."

Money on Broadway has always gone to sure things. If Sillman had announced Fred Astaire and his sister, Adele, Marilyn Miller, or even Clifton Webb, he would have had checks sliding under his door with each morning's mail.

After months of frustration, the imaginative producer came up with an idea good enough to use for years.

"What do you mean who's in it?" he would answer back, "Why, Henry Fonda and Imogene Coca and Nancy Hamilton, new faces. That's what we're calling it. *New Faces*." That did it. After 196 auditions, the exhausted cast heard the exciting news: Sillman raised the necessary fifteen thousand dollars. Rehearsals began.

Because Lee Shubert still failed to provide heat, the company shivered. Tiny Imogene Coca stood around in a man's camel's hair coat that Sillman said was "eighteen sizes too big for her." Far over, stage right, one of the dancers, Marvin Lawlor, wrapped up in a hat, coat, muffler, and gloves, was moving about a bit, just to keep warm. Coca, thinking the steps he was doing were interesting, silently slipped beside him, and started to follow. Fonda joined them, and then Chuck Walters. The four began using the same little steps, and then Fonda began putting in little bits of pantomime for them.

Out of the corner of his eye, Sillman noticed the group. He stopped rehearsal and called out.

"What're you doing?"

Immediately, all movement, stage right, ceased.

"Nothing," Coca's timid voice replied.

"What was that?" Sillman demanded.

"Just having a little fun," Fonda explained lamely.

"Fine," the producer answered. "We'll put it in the show. Three times in the first act, three times in the second. It's just what we need when the scenery changes. Very amusing. Just play deadpan, look right at the audience, and do those silly little things you were doing."

Coca began to weep.

"What's the matter, Imogene?" Sillman asked.

"I don't want to be funny."

"But you are."

"I don't want to be. I'm a classical dancer. I was hired as a dancer."

Coca cried for days, but fortunately the producer remained firm.

"Opening night was a success," Sillman recalled. "Those days, the men wore high silk hats, and the women, orchids. In the first row sat Katharine Hepburn, Mary Pickford, Tallulah Bankhead, Robert Benchley, Louis Bromfield, Libby Holman, Aleck Woollcott. And Tallulah was so excited she smoked throughout the show."

The critics complimented the entire production but

singled out Fonda and Coca for particular praise. He had made it. At last. Not as the great dramatic actor he had hoped to be, but there was his name in all the New York papers. He clipped the reviews and mailed them back to his folks in Omaha. From 1928 to 1934. Suddenly, it didn't seem like such a long time after all!

With few exceptions the company of a show becomes akin to family. The company of a hit becomes a closely knit family.

"I was at a party one evening a few weeks after we opened," Fonda says. "Everyone was sitting on the floor. There was hardly room for me to stretch my legs. So I crawled under the grand piano and propped myself up on my elbow. Coca was at the party, too, passing around highballs and canapes. When she came to me she got down and offered me a glass of something. Well, hell, I didn't want a drink. I just reached up and took her by the wrist and pulled her under the piano next to me.

" 'Listen,' I said to her. 'This doesn't have to mean anything to you. It just means something to me, and I think maybe you might want to hear it. I've been crazy about you ever since we started rehearsing. Just thought you might like to know.'

"Well, she smiled her crooked little smile at me and said, 'See you later.' And I saw her later."

It is often difficult to reconstruct a romance of forty-six or forty-seven years ago. Fonda says he was enchanted with her. "She was an adorable little clown, with so much talent!" Coca denied the affair meant anything. "Oh, I don't know," Fonda says. "We both felt guilty as hell. We were always afraid her mother would find out."

A different Henry Fonda returned to Mt. Kisco in June 1934. Now Fonda was more relaxed and more emotionally secure. He *had* been discovered. His name could be found in the newspaper columns of Danton Walker, Walter Winchell, and Leonard Lyons. Perhaps not as often as his ex-wife, Margaret Sullavan, but some New Yorkers were starting to recognize him on the streets and ask for his autograph.

Henry hadn't been able to resist returning to the Westchester Playhouse, especially when he learned that

Sullavan was coming in from Hollywood. Other old friends would be there, too: Mildred Natwick, Aleta Freel, Ross Alexander. The magnet that drew him was Sullavan. Once again he would be her leading man. Let the student apprentices worry over the scenery, the props, and the lighting.

The company lived together in a beautiful sprawling inn called The Kittle House. The inn had a large dining room, two tables with linen placemats, crystal goblets, silverware, and good china. Tuttle had inherited a fortune from his father and preferred luxurious surroundings.

The summer did not start exactly as Fonda had anticipated. The Fourth of July began with a bang but not from the usual source. In 1933 Tuttle and Fonda had knocked together a trough of boards from the scenery dock. They used it for sky-rockets. Day Tuttle said, "Our view was magnificent. You sat on the terrace and there were Fontainebleau-like brick stairs that went down to a lower terrace, and you could look over the brook and the 18th and 1st holes of the Lawrence Farm Golf Club. Way over, about three hundred yards, were the cupolas of the Playhouse coming up out of the maples.

"The year before we had put the trough down on the lower terrace and sent the rockets up. They were spectacular."

Now, on July Fourth, as they sat in the dining room, ten people to a table, Tuttle said to Fonda, "Let's do the fireworks again this year." Fonda agreed. During dinner the leading man carried his beaten-up felt hat from actor to actor, taking up a collection. They needed only about twelve dollars. The men dug into the pockets of their white duck trousers. The women snapped open their change purses. Dimes, quarters, a dollar bill now and again. Then Fonda reached Sullavan. He held the hat before her. She shook her head no. He thought she was being facetious. He moved his hat closer to her shoulder. Sullavan shook her head more vigorously.

"You mean you're not going to put in anything?" Fonda asked in a stage whisper. Sullavan refused to answer. Instead she munched another bite of her salad.

Tuttle observed that though Fonda continued around

the table, "You could see he was smoldering." At last he turned to Ross Alexander and said, "Christ! And with the money some people are making."

Sullavan didn't wait ten seconds. She pushed back her chair, picked up a goblet of ice water and poured it over Fonda's head. He didn't flinch. Slowly, he reached over and picked up a napkin from the table. Everyone laughed except Fonda and Sullavan.

That night they played sweethearts in the Mt. Kisco production of *Coquette*.

"The love scenes were perfect," Tuttle said. "Off stage they didn't speak."

Fonda had a week or two off at Mt. Kisco when Leonard Sillman telephoned.

"Hank," his caller spoke warmly, "I hear you're killing them in Westchester. Are you ever coming back into New York?"

"Gotta see Dwight Deere Wiman," Fonda told him. "Tomorrow."

"Here's my problem. Jimmy Shelton is sick. Could you do his soliloquy?"

"You get it up here. I'll learn it in the car on the way down."

"But it's a whole thing," the producer said. "How can you memorize it in the car?"

"Just send it, Leonard. I'll know it."

That night he took Shelton's place and flawlessly did the number, "She's Resting in the Gutter and She Loves It."

Sillman says he was twenty times better than the man who wrote and performed it, and Sillman must have been right. Sitting in the audience was Leland Hayward. Hayward had graduated from press agentry and was now a top-seeded artist's representative.

"You were terrific, kid," he told Fonda after the performance. "See me in the morning. I want to sign you."

At ten A.M. Fonda arrived at Hayward's office and before the agent could get out a word, Fonda explained his second reason for coming into Manhattan.

Dwight Deere Wiman, whose primary fortune came from the manufacture of Deere tractors, and whose secondary fortune came from producing *The Little Shows*, *The Vinegar Tree*, *The Road to Rome*, and many other successful plays, had seen Fonda at the opening of *New Faces*. He had instructed his lawyer to draw a contract. Wiman would pay Fonda one hundred dollars a week for an entire year, plus tuition for dancing school, in return for which Fonda agreed to allow Wiman to make him into a leading man for musical comedies. One of Fonda's fantasies had been to glide through the air and tap his shoes rhythmically on the floor like another Omaha boy, Fred Astaire. He couldn't wait to get started.

Hayward leaped out of his chair.

"Never!" the best agent in New York and Hollywood shouted. "I am *never* going to let you put your name on a contract like that!"

"But Mr. Hayward," Fonda argued, "a hundred a week for fifty-two weeks, that's financial security."

"That's financial crap! I'll find you seven hundred and fifty dollars a week. Now get the hell back to the country, stay away from Dwight Wiman, and let me handle you."

Fonda drove to Mt. Kisco wondering how Leland Hayward intended to obtain that kind of money for him legally. He'd heard Hayward could sell chewing gum to a man with lockjaw. Now he'd wait and see.

A week later Hayward contacted Fonda again. This time from California. By telegram. The wire was three pages long, and it explained in detail why Fonda should come out to the West Coast to be in the movies. Fonda sent back a one-word answer, "No."

"It wasn't my ambition to be in the movies," Fonda says. "No way would I go out to Hollywood, but Leland never accepted no from anyone. He called me in Mt. Kisco. 'Listen, you son-of-a-bitch,' Hayward said. 'I'll pay your fare out here, come and just spend the day. You'll meet some people and then go back to your fucking theater.' He sent me a plane ticket and met me at the Burbank airport."

LAX was years in the future. The field in Burbank had a few hangars, a windsock, and some pumps for high octane aviation fuel. As they rode into town they passed acres and acres of citrus groves, and the air which was dry and burning smelled of oranges, grapefruit, eucalyptus, and pepper trees. What wasn't irrigated in Southern California was desert. For the most part, the highest structures were oil rigs. There were no highways, no freeways, smog didn't exist. Nor did air conditioning nor private swimming pools nor high-rises. Sunset Boulevard consisted of two unpaved lanes alongside of which ran a bridle path. The famous hotels were the Ambassador in downtown Los Angeles, the Garden of Allah in far off, mostly unpopulated Beverly Hills, and the Beverly Hills Hotel itself. Perched on its own hill, it could be seen in its pink splendor for miles around. The Brown Derby Restaurant, begun by Wilson Mizner and financed by Jack L. Warner, stood across from the Ambassador. It had been named for the headgear worn by Mizner's two favorite men, Bat Masterson and Governor Alfred E. Smith. The new Beverly Wilshire Hotel looked down on a Rodeo Drive choked with tumbleweed rather than elegant shops.

It was to this hostelry that Hayward drove Fonda. When they arrived in the suite Hayward had reserved, the agent grabbed the phone to make calls, Fonda went into the bathroom, took off his wrinkled seersucker suit, showered and shaved. After he dressed, he came out into the living room to talk with his representative.

"There was a man there with Leland and he introduced me to Walter Wanger. Now," Fonda says, "the name meant nothing to me, and frankly, Wanger didn't know who the hell *I* was. It made no difference to Leland. He said to the man, who I found out later was an important Hollywood producer, 'Listen, you better sign this kid because he's going places.' Anyway, Wanger and Leland talked, I listened, and all at once I found myself shaking hands with this man on a deal to make two pictures for him next year. He knew I wasn't eager, but he made it clear that I could do theater work *and* movies. He wouldn't stop me. God! This was really like having two cakes and eating them both.

"Mr. Wanger held out his hand to me again. 'It's settled then, isn't it? We'll start you at a thousand a week.' I couldn't believe what I heard. I turned to Leland.

He nodded. 'You've got yourself a deal, Walter.' I don't even remember saying good-bye to the man. I was in a complete daze. Leland and I took the elevator to the lobby and walked down Wilshire Boulevard."

Neither of them spoke. Hayward smiled. Fonda frowned.

"Is that handshake binding?" Henry asked the agent. "What did I get myself into?"

Hayward stopped walking, shaded his eyes and said, "You're a silly son-of-a-bitch, but yes, it's binding, yes, it's a deal. Next year this time you'll be working in California."

Fonda boarded a plane for New York with prospects as limitless as the skies in which he flew. Two weeks later, however, everything in California seemed as small as new potatoes grown in Maine.

Tuttle cast him as the tutor opposite Geoffrey Kerr in *The Swan*. Kerr's wife, June Walker, had a new play by Marc Connelly that needed a leading man. After two performances Miss Walker came back to visit her husband who shared a dressing room with Fonda.

"We said hello," Fonda says, "and then June Walker sat with Geoff while he removed his makeup. 'He's marvelous!' She sounded excited and I had a feeling she was referring to me. 'He's ideal for the part. I'll phone Marc when I get home.'"

The next night Marc Connelly and his producer, Max Gordon, appeared at the Westchester Playhouse. Following the final curtain Connelly invited Fonda to read for the title role at his suite in the Gotham Hotel in New York. It was as simple as that.

Marc Connelly, an ex-newspaperman who had collaborated with George S. Kaufman, the drama editor of *The New York Times*, on a number of plays, was well on his way toward becoming bald, heavy around the waist, and puckish. His apartment on Fifth Avenue and Fifty-fifth Street gave testimony to his profession as a playwright; chairs, tables, couches, and the floor were strewn with discarded pages of manuscript.

Connelly, a habitual late riser, greeted Fonda in his pajamas and directed him to the den.

"You know Marc," Fonda says. "He wrote more stage directions in between dialogue than the usual playwright. He's like Sir James M. Barrie, beautiful writing, description of the characters, description of the set. It wasn't just stage direction. It was literature. And he wanted me to appreciate it. So he waved me to a couch, script in his hand, and he started reading it to me.

"He got through maybe a page and a half of the set, and then he went into the description of Molly, the girl. Pretty soon he was reading her dialogue. Only he couldn't play Molly sitting on that couch, so he stood up.

"Then still in his pajamas, still playing Molly, he held his hand on his pajama bottoms, only now he made me believe it was a skirt, and from there he began playing all the other characters. He was absolutely spellbinding.

"He read the whole damn play to me and then he plopped down on the couch. 'How was I?' he asked. And I told him the truth. 'Great.'

"You've got the part," Connelly said as his face lit up.

"I have?" Fonda asked doubting his luck.

"You like the play?"

"Absolutely!"

"What was your last salary on Broadway?"

"Well, I've never made more than thirty-five dollars a week, but this is a leading part, isn't it?"

"It most assuredly is, the male lead," Connelly answered emphatically. "Now you go over to Max Gordon's office. I'll call and tell him you're coming. And you walk in there and ask for two hundred dollars and don't you settle for a penny less."

If he'd been a boy in Omaha Fonda would have skipped on his way over to Max Gordon's office, but as he was a man and about to play the lead in a first-class Broadway production he walked as fast as he could without arousing the attention of the police who might have thought him a thief fleeing the scene of a crime.

When he entered the Gordon office the contract was already on the producer's desk. Two hundred dollars a week. For a fleeting moment he thought of Leland Hayward and how he would not allow one of his clients to sign for so paltry a sum, but he repressed the thought of what Hayward would do to spoil his chances for a lead in a Marc Connelly production. He signed all four copies of the contract for *The Farmer Takes a Wife*.

In later years Margaret Hamilton played the Wicked Witch of the West in Judy Garland's *The Wizard of Oz*. *The Farmer Takes a Wife* was her third Broadway play.

"I remember Henry as a very sweet person," Miss Hamilton said, "very quiet. He was endowed with enormous patience, great courtesy, and incredible concentration. All of us in the cast admired him greatly."

The happiness Fonda experienced during the first two weeks of rehearsal was blurred by the shock of his mother's sudden death. Herberta Fonda had fallen, broken her leg, and developed a blood clot that traveled to her heart and ended her life.

"It was a cruel blow," Fonda says, "and I felt so badly that she didn't live to see me move ahead." His father and sisters insisted he continue to work and he obeyed their wishes.

The Farmer Takes a Wife, by Marc Connelly and Frank B. Elser, adapted from Walter D. Edmond's novel *Rome Haul*, dealt with life along the Erie Canal. The play bowed at the scene of Fonda's earlier efforts, Washington, D.C.

"We opened on Monday night," Fonda says, "and Tuesday morning we woke up to top-notch reviews. The cast call was eleven o'clock and I got there a few minutes ahead of time, and just as I strolled into the stage door, there was Max Gordon's general manager, Ben Boyar. Ben was a toothpick of a man, sharp, bright-eyed, encouraging, but always on the side of management."

"Just a minute, young fella," Boyar said.

Fonda stopped. What could be wrong now?

"I've got some good news for you."

"What is it?" Fonda asked.

"Max Gordon might be willing to give you a run-of-the-play contract. In fact, he *is* willing. Here. Sign it."

Until then, Fonda had the usual Equity contract. Two weeks' notice and he could be fired. But with the reviews the critics had showered upon him, Max Gordon wanted him tied to the length of the production.

The wise Fonda, the shrewd actor, considered his position. He exercised every ounce of show business acumen he had acquired over the years.

"A run-of-the-play contract," he pondered. Then he knew exactly how to play his cards.

"I've got 'em by the short hairs," he told himself. "I can get more money!" He began to stall, not a great deal, just stutter enough so that Boyar knew he wasn't dealing with an amateur.

"Well, what've you got in mind?" the general manager asked wearily, knowing that Fonda had read the same reviews as Max Gordon.

"What am I making now?" Fonda asked.

"Two hundred a week."

Who needed Leland Hayward?

"How about making that two twenty-five?" Fonda asked boldly.

"You got it, kid," Boyar said, and shoved the papers at him. "Ink it here."

In retrospect, Fonda says, "Shit! I could have asked for a thousand a week and gotten it. But I was smart. I knew!" Then he sighs and says, "Story of my life."

New York turned out to be better than Washington. Applause for June Walker. Acclamation for Henry Fonda.

"He had that gee-gosh, foot-dragging quality about him that Gary Cooper and a few other have always had. But likable, very American, and very good," Marc Connelly observed.

A couple of weeks into the New York run, Margaret Hamilton arrived at the theater for a matinee. "I must have been early," Miss Hamilton said, "the stage door was locked. It was about an hour and a half before curtain. I went up to the man in the box office and asked him if he'd buzz open the lobby door for me. He did and I went in. It took a moment for my eyes to adjust. It was quite dark. But the stage had the usual work light on, one bulb hanging in the middle of the set. There was sort of an eerie look to it. And then I realized someone was there in the back. I didn't say anything, because I didn't know whether there was a rehearsal going on or not. But pretty soon from the stir of the shadows emerged Henry. He stood on one side and he carried a pile of folded papers. And then I noticed he'd folded them into little airplanes and he started to shoot them across the stage. I've watched small boys do this hour after hour to see how far they could make the paper airplanes go."

Margaret Hamilton didn't move; she studied Henry Fonda. "He was graceful and beautiful. He stood there for a long time throwing those folded pieces of paper into the wings and I thought, I'll bet that was something he liked to do when he was a youngster, he seemed so at peace with himself. He never knew I saw him."

Fonda's photograph decorated the front of the Forty-sixth Street Theater. There were invitations for Mr. Henry Fonda from people he didn't know, the telephone rang constantly, everyone wanted him for everything.

Early in December of 1934, an exuberant Henry Fonda wrote his sister:

> Dear Harriet—
> Let me practice my typing on you—I rented an Underwood last week and feel ambitious as hell. Last night was one of the biggest thrills of MY life. We broadcast in the big studio theatre in Radio City with an audience of 1500—but all I could see was Dad and the rest of you sitting around the radio at 454. We rehearsed our little scene yesterday morning, and in the afternoon we had a dress rehearsal—that is the whole program was put together and rehearsed with mikes. I don't know how funny she seems over the air, but Beatrice Lillie had us all in hysterics at the rehearsal. And Cole Porter is a real right guy. He hasn't a voice, but he certainly writes songs. Bill Hart was so nervous that he was shaking all over. The script shook in his hands so I don't (sic) see how he could read the words. I don't (sic) know whether I'll be shattering any dream pictures—but Mr. Vallee is NOT the prince his crooning makes him seem. We had to be all made up and

dressed for the broadcast because we didn't get back to the theatre until 8:40 . . . I got three wires by 9:15.

I'm going to be in a Benefit Sunday night for unemployed newspapermen. June and I will do a short scene from the show.

Gosh, I hope you can come in January. It would be swell. I'll swing a special Beer Party for you.

We haven't found anything in the way of apartments that we like. Coca looks like Lily Pons. Sullavan: Cream and sugar on a dish of hot ashes.

Love,
Henry.

After the negotiations he had conducted personally in Washington, all business matters were referred to Leland Hayward. Social affairs were held to a minimum. Fonda and Stewart still lived at the Madison Square Hotel, but as Fonda had a job, and as Stewart had one also, they began serious work on a new project: the assembling of model airplanes.

Each man would rush home from the theater, unroll the plans, read the complicated directions, "Strut 'A' fits snugly onto Wing 'B 1', three eighths of an inch from the forward flap. . . ." Balsa wood would be carved by hand, glue would be applied, both men took their labors to heart.

The play at the Forty-sixth Street Theater, a heavy show in terms of cast and stagehands, made money for its backers and producer, ran a respectable one hundred four performances, and closed.

"By then," Fonda says, "Stewart and I were so into model airplane building that we wouldn't allow any of the hotel maids into our rooms. It was ankle deep in balsa shavings and we were afraid if they came in to clean, they'd wreck our plane which, as I remember, was a replica of a United States Army Air Corps Martin bomber.

"We finished the framework and covered it with silk, and the instructions called for us to paint it. The paint came with the kit, but *Farmer* folded and Hollywood wanted me, so I left the decorating job to Stewart."

March 1935 may have come in like a lion for some but for Fonda it came in like a little orange kitten. The night before he was scheduled to leave for California, Jim Stewart and José Ferrer, another Princetonian, treated him to a night on the town. They wound up in Ralph's, an actors' popular hangout.

"Say, you wanna see what we got in the basement?" the bartender asked. "Our saloon cat had kittens a couple of days ago."

The three customers went down to inspect the scene. There, on a gunnysack, lay a contented tabby and her litter.

"I want one," Fonda said.

"You're leaving town tomorrow," Ferrer protested.

"I still want one."

"I dunno. They're not weaned," the bartender warned.

"Trust me," Fonda said. He picked up a tiny purring object about four inches long and tucked it into his woolen scarf. Despite the cold, Fonda and his kitten reached the Madison Square Hotel safely.

"I called him George," Fonda says, "because my dad always called cats George. The next evening, along with my luggage and three hats piled on my head, Joe Ferrer and Jim Stewart taxied me and my new friend to the train. I wanted to fly, but the studio wouldn't hear of it.

"Stewart and Ferrer steered me through the mass of commuters in Grand Central Station to the gate where the Twentieth Century waited to roll. Passenger planes to California were few and unreliable in those days, but the Twentieth Century, well, that was the crack train to Chicago.

"I showed my ticket to the man at the gate, said goodbye to Stewart and Ferrer, and walked down the red plush carpet that ran the length of the train. Clouds of steam hissed out from under the cars, people were shaking hands and kissing, a porter looked at my reservations and waved me into his pullman.

"I had a bedroom on the train, and the first thing I did was to send for a pint of warm milk. Naturally, they brought me a glass and a napkin, and by the time the conductor and the brakeman yelled, 'Board!' I had the bottle open, the edge of the napkin twisted and dipped into the milk, and as the train pulled out, I fed George.

"He sucked on the end of that napkin until he'd had enough. Then I rang for the porter again. When he came I explained about the cat. He was a nice man and he made up my berth and I put George to sleep in one of my hats and I went into the dining car."

The dining car steward met him with a mixture of hospitality and efficiency and seated him opposite a fellow passenger. The man who shared the table with Henry kept his nose buried in an early afternoon edition of the New York *Sun*. Not being the most loquacious of men, Fonda shifted his attention from the silverware to the newspaper and finally to the constantly changing scene outside. The view of the river from the window of the dining car was reminiscent of the Hudson River Valley School of painters; swamps and marshlands below him on the east bank, then the silvery ribbon that was the river, topped by the Palisades towering above the west bank.

At Harmon, while Fonda enjoyed his appetizer, the train crew switched engines from electric to steam. Thereafter the roadbed became slightly rougher. Henry was happy the water glasses and the wineglasses were only half filled. The speeding train caused the car to sway slightly, and passengers walking down the aisle frequently brushed up against his shoulder.

"After paying my check," Fonda says, "I went back to my room and rang for the porter again. He brought a cup of warm cream this time. I gave the kitten his ten o'clock feeding. Then I laid out my pajamas, brushed my teeth, and without disturbing George too much, slipped into bed, switched off the ceiling lamp, and raised the window shade."

Fonda watched the lights on the bridges along the Erie Canal flickering by like fireflies on the Nebraska prairie in the summer.

He thought of Marc Connelly and June Walker and

the play that was responsible for his going to California. Hollywood had purchased *The Farmer Takes a Wife*, and in keeping with its custom, ignored the players who had brought the vehicle to life on Broadway. The West Coast moguls had substituted Janet Gaynor for June Walker. Miss Gaynor had scored very high at the box offices in *Seventh Heaven*, *Sunny Side Up*, and *Daddy Longlegs*.

For the Fonda role they had wanted Gary Cooper or Joel McCrea. Since both men were busy, the Broadway leading man would re-create his original role on the screen.

As the Twentieth Century roared forward, publicity wheels already were grinding in Hollywood, but the only wheels Henry Fonda heard that night were those of the train as they clicked along the rails. He could not forget the curtain line of the first comedy in which he played the lead back in Omaha. It had been written by the same Marc Connelly who collaborated on *Farmer*, only the production in Omaha had been by George S. Kaufman and Marc Connelly. It was called *Merton of the Movies*. Fonda had played Merton.

And at the end of the first act Merton, a clerk with acting ambitions, blows out the lamplights in the general store, pulls his cot out from under the counter, and in the moonlight, kneels beside it. Fonda could still remember those lines.

"Oh, God," Merton prayed, "make me a good movie actor! Make me one of the best. For Jesus' sake, amen!"

As the earth's crust in California is given to tremors and occasional quakes, so the people and events in the Golden Bear State presented Henry Fonda with a series of surprises and a shock or two. He had gone out west under contract to Walter Wanger to play *Farmer*. Upon his arrival, Mr. Wanger explained that he had loaned out Henry to the Fox Studios for five thousand dollars a week. Through that legerdemain by which actors act and producers grow wealthy, the five thousand was payable to Mr. Wanger. Before Henry could open his mouth or even ask to consult with Leland Hayward, Mr. Wanger offered to split the difference with Fonda. All the time *Farmer* was filming, Henry would receive three thousand dollars a week.

For a man subsisting on rice three years before, a weekly salary of thiry-five dollars two years before, and two hundred twenty-five dollars cleverly wrung out of Max Gordon's general manager last year, Henry suddenly felt like a lucky King Midas. A good meal at a fine restaurant cost three dollars and fifty cents, admission to a neighborhood movie house went for twenty-five cents, and the Ford roadster with the rumble seat that Henry bought new cost nine hundred dollars.

Eulalia Chapin, a guest of David O. Selznick, who later became the best friend of Fonda's second wife, Frances, received a call.

"Walter Wanger phoned me one night," Mrs. Chapin remembered. "We were going to Carole Lombard's party at the Fun House at the beach. I was down with the Selznicks for the weekend. Wanger called and said, 'Eulalia, I have a young man here from New York who knows no one. Would you mind taking him under your wing at the party and introducing him around?' Of course I didn't mind. I was delighted. I did as he asked me, introduced Hank to everyone, and he made such a big hit, I didn't see him for the rest of the evening."

"Carole Lombard," Fonda says, "took over an entire amusement park on a steel pier that jutted out into the Pacific. Boy! Was I impressed. She'd invited a thousand people or more. Everybody in the industry was there. And every time you passed a popcorn stand, it was a bar. And if you went into the House of Mirrors, you'd see a terribly fat Clark Gable, or a pencil-skinny eight-foot-tall Myrna Loy. And you could go on every ride as often as you wanted—free."

In the beginning of his Hollywood days, Fonda stayed with Ross Alexander and his wife. Ross and Aleta Freel had carried their lovemaking from Cape Cod to Baltimore to Mt. Kisco. Finally, one autumn day, they were married in her parents' home in New Jersey with Henry Fonda as the best man. The best wedding gift was a Warner Brothers contract for Ross. The couple migrated to Los Angeles, where they installed themselves in a house high in the sparsely populated hills through which wound Woodrow Wilson Drive. Ducks, dogs, and goats surrounded their place. Fonda considered it a miniature farm. George, the cat, thought of it as a dangerous jungle.

Aleta, who had little to occupy her time during the hours when Ross went to the studio, offered to help Henry find an apartment of his own in Beverly Hills. Fonda suspected that the Alexanders' married life had flipped from passionate to pallid. Ross supposedly spent days, even nights, at Warner's. Aleta seemed too eager to help her husband's career at the expense of her own. Their teasing had an edge to it that never existed before. Henry hoped it was all his imagination; life in California had an unreal quality.

In between his apartment hunting Fonda met with the director of *Farmer*, Victor Fleming. Tall and handsome, a former leading man himself, Fleming, who would eventually direct *Gone With the Wind*, gave Fonda a shooting script of the film they were about to do.

"Puzzled the hell out of me," Fonda says. "Now I know who the two leads are, Dan and Molly. But suddenly, they've written in a third character. 'Dan and Molly go into the hotel. Dolly with them.' Show you how dumb I was, and I'm serious, I never for the longest time figured out what the fuck Dolly was doing in there. She was always there, but never opened her goddamn mouth!"

Fonda learned quickly that dolly meant a camera direction and not a character.

"Cameras and camera angles enthralled him," his costar, Janet Gaynor, noted. "He studied them and everything else on the set. He was a serious young man and interested in almost everything that happened on the lot. Big red-headed Charlie Bickford was cast as the heavy. He and I would gossip and play practical jokes, but Henry would have none of it."

The Fox lot was on the site of the old Tom Mix ranch and the present location of Century City. A brook had meandered through it originally but had been induced by a series of culverts to run underground. For *Farmer* the brook, allowed to rise to the surface again, was channeled into the Eric Canal. The reality of the set captivated Henry. On stage in New York all scenery had been painted canvas. In California the blacksmith's shop was constructed of genuine lumber and the forge contained real fire. Live horses pulled the canal boats. The sky was not a blue cyclorama but the blue of the heavens, the sound of the birds came not from a record or a whistle blown by a stagehand but from the actual winged creatures. The cows on the set reminded Fonda of the cow that his father had kept in the yard next door to his home in Omaha. Hollywood at first blush seemed friendly if somewhat mechanical, high priced yet familiar.

In one respect Henry Fonda was no different from anyone else. Even before they began shooting the picture he was guilty of nepotism.

"You say you need a cat for the canal boat?" he asked Victor Fleming. The director agreed. "I've got just the fellow you want. Brought him out from New York myself." That's how George, the kitten from Ralph's saloon, got into show business.

The picture proved no real problem for Fonda except for the first day when Fleming called, "Cut!" The shooting stopped, and taking his leading man aside, the director said, "Hank, you're mugging a bit."

"I'm what!" the startled Fonda shot back. To any actor the accusation of mugging is thoroughly objectionable. It smacks of scene stealing, of upstaging, of hamming it up, of unprofessionalism.

"Mugging," Fleming repeated.

"That's a dirty word," Fonda stated flatly.

"I know it is," the director explained, "and it really isn't your fault. You're playing the farmer the way you did in the theater. You're playing to the back row of the orchestra and the rear row of the balcony. That's stage technique."

Fonda nodded.

"That's the biggest message I ever got in Hollywood," he says. "I just pulled it right back to reality because that lens and that microphone are doing all the projection you need. No sense in using too much voice, and you don't need any more expression on your face than you'd use in everyday life."

In almost a hundred films the technique Fonda employs has not varied. Some say he underplays, some say he's not even acting. Quiet, calm, even in anger or desperation, whether in comedy or drama Fonda uses as little facial mobility as possible. Whatever he does he makes you see inside the character he plays.

"That was the big lesson for me," Fonda says, "and I will always bless Victor Fleming for being kind enough to tell me, rather than let me go and have somebody else say it in a review."

During the filming of *Farmer,* Fonda moved from the Alexander's into his own apartment. There was no comparison with the place on Sixty-fourth Street where he and Stewart and Logan and McCormick had lived; everything was new: the rugs, the furniture, the dishes, orange and beige color inside; outside, a patio where trees allowed the sun to peek through.

When he heard that his ex-wife, Margaret Sullavan, married the film director William Wyler, Fonda was pleased at his lack of interest. Of course, by now, he and a singer named Shirley Ross were involved in the mildest sort of infatuation.

"Oh, I might have kissed her a lot," Fonda says, "but I'm really a lousy kisser. Ask any of the girls I married. They'll tell you."

"Don't let him try to fool you," James Stewart said. "He must have done something right. Fonda did very well in the women's department. Of course, he never wrote me about his social life. All he wanted to know was how far I'd gotten with the airplane. In the meantime I'd sort of gone through the movie tests and suddenly I got a call from MGM to go to the Coast for a final test. So I wrote Fonda I was coming and he wrote back, 'Be sure to bring the airplaine, and get something to bring it in so you won't break it on the train.'

"Well, I went home first to Indiana, Pennsylvania, and I held it in my hands the whole way. And then I got a helper at the hardware store to build a case for it. The only trouble was the case looked like a machine gun carrier. I painted it black. It looked exactly like a machine gun. It was quite a trick, sleeping with it in the upper berth of a Pullman. The conductors kept saying, 'What do you have in that thing?' Everyone was trying to figure it out.

" 'It's a model airplane with the wings folded back,' I told them, and they'd say, 'That's too good an answer for us, so we'll let it go.'

"Fonda met me when I got off the Super Chief in Pasadena.

" 'Where's the airplane?' was all he wanted to know."

Once he'd been assured the Martin Bomber was in the machine gun case Fonda returned to Fox and Stewart was dropped off at MGM where he remained for thirty-five years, taking time out only for World War II.

Together Fonda and Stewart decided to renew the living arrangements they had had at the Madison Square Hotel. Now, however, they could afford to rent a Mexican-style farmhouse in Brentwood. Their next-door neighbor was Greta Garbo.

"The day we moved in," Fonda says, "we found a cat in the little kind of greenhouse out in the back. Now, George, my cat from New York, had gotten a better offer from Fox and stayed on there, and here was a cat that had just had a litter. And Stewart and I both love cats.

"So this was a good omen, a ready-made family of pets. Well, it didn't take us long to discover that they weren't pets at all. They were wild. They hadn't been pets for Christ knows how long. And we couldn't get close to them. We'd put out food for them, but the cats never would come close to a human being.

"Well, sir, you wouldn't believe how fast it took those little kittens to grow up and procreate. And although you could never count them, a good ball park estimate after a year or so was thirty to thirty-five cats.

"By this time John Swope was out in California and living with us. Now I ask you. Can you picture three grown men sitting around at home trying to tackle the problem of thirty to thirty-five cats?

"We'd be relaxing after work, drinking beer and trying to think of the various ways of getting rid of 'em.

"Stewart would say, 'Well, we don't want to put out poison. That'd be mean, and they'd crawl under the house and die, and then it *would* stink.'

"And Swope'd say, 'If we don't get rid of them soon, the couple we have looking after the place will clear out.'

"And then Stewart, carried away with the situation, suggested we catch one and paint it purple, the theory being it would scare all the other cats and they'd leave.

"Stewart said we should call the ASPCA. Well, I did and the man there said they'd come and get 'em if we boxed 'em, but how in the hell are you going to box thirty-five cats if you can't catch 'em?"

The howling, the caterwaulling, and the nightly prowlings of the mating felines proved too much for their neighbor. To the consternation of all three men Miss Garbo actually had a large fence erected dividing her property from theirs. This put the problem of the cats into a subordinate position. Top priority went to the fence. After dinner, as more and more beer was consumed, the means of retaliation grew more and more fanciful.

"We finally decided to tunnel under the goddamn fence," Fonda says. "Stewart says we actually did start digging until we hit a water main and flooded the whole damn place, but I don't remember that. It might have happened. Of course, what Stewart doesn't remember he invents."

Stewart's memory is every bit as good as his friend's, and he can match Fonda story for story.

"There are some things Hank and I don't have in common, but love of work isn't one of them," Stewart said. "I think if the studios hadn't paid me, I would have paid them. Hank pretends he's not crazy about moviemaking, but when we lived together, I never heard one complaint out of him. We liked to play and we liked to work, and they were both fun for us.

"It was a six-day week then, and every Saturday night we'd go over to the Trocadero or the Coconut Grove. They were wonderful sorts of nightclubs. We didn't get very good tables because the maître d's didn't know who we were."

Ringside tables were held for the owners of the studios, their favorite producers or relatives, and the biggest money-making actors, Harold Lloyd, William Powell, Norma Shearer, Dolores del Rio, and those others who inhaled the rarefied air of moviedom. Directors, slipping stars, and featured players were placed around the middle of the room. Writers, contract players, and starlets were given either the cold shoulder or seats near the exits.

"They stayed open all night," Stewart reported, "and the most famous people just got up and performed. Mary and Jack Benny, George Burns and Gracie Allen, Red Skelton, and I remember one night Judy Garland's mother brought her. Judy wore pigtails and bobby sox and she sang for an hour. Absolutely terrific! I don't know why people have the impression that California is a cold, unfriendly place. There was a real sort of camaraderie, and Hank and I had great times."

Great times. Lucille Ball and Ginger Rogers used to date Fonda and Stewart.

"We worked long and hard, Ginger and I, in front of our mirrors. We used eye shadow, plenty of mascara, pancake, deep red lipstick, rouge, everything we'd been taught in the studio cosmetic department. Then we went out to Brentwood, that's where the boys lived," Miss Ball recollected. "My date was Fonda. Ginger's date was Stewart. Henry cooked the dinner, and after we ate, Ginger and the boys turned on the radio in the living room and Ginger tried to teach them the carioca. I was left doing the dishes.

"When I finished, we went out dancing at the Coconut Grove. Freddie Martin's orchestra. There we were, Ginger and I in our long organdy dresses, looking just as summery and smooth as we could. The date stretched into daybreak. We'd had a hilarious, wonderful evening that came to an end at Barney's Beanery which still exists where Santa Monica twists and goes east into North Hollywood. Well, it was dark when we went in and light when we came out. Hank and Jim took one look at us and said, 'What happened?' We said, 'What do you mean what happened?'

"And Jimmy Stewart said, 'Well, your nighttime make-up is on awful heavy for this time of the morning.'

"And Henry Fonda said, 'Yuk!' "

And that's the way it ended for Miss Ball.

Fonda, in retrospect, has his own thoughts,

"Shit!" he says, "if I hadn't said, 'Yuk!' if I'd behaved myself, they might have named that studio Henrylu not Desilu."

Farmer came in on schedule, and Fonda went into his second film immediately. *Way Down East* had Rochelle Hudson, Spring Byington, Slim Summerville, Andy Devine, and Henry's good-luck charm, Margaret Hamilton, in its cast. *The New York Times* called it "the personal triumph of Henry Fonda."

Before the year ended, Fox put him in another picture, *I Dream Too Much*, with Lucille Ball, Lily Pons, Eric

Blore, and Osgood Perkins. Of this effort *The New York Times* thought, "Henry Fonda, the most likable of the new crop of romantic juveniles."

After three pictures Fonda fell easily into the rhythm of filmmaking. It is, he believes, largely a director's medium interspersed with technicians ranging from cameramen to film editors. Actors are two-dimensional figures to be used in the exposing of raw stock to its best advantage.

"When you do a film," Fonda says, "you come in the first day and, let's say, you've been told to learn scenes fifteen and seventeen, and you learn them, and that's usually not more than three pages, but that's considered a day's work. Three pages, three minutes on film. That's what they figure. That's not a lot and certainly not a big deal to learn.

"Now, when you get there and you're ready, the director and the cameraman and the other actors rehearse to the extent that the cameraman knows the positions you're going to be in. What I'm leading up to is that usually before lunch you've played that scene for a few takes or however many the director wants, and that film has gone to the laboratory, and that is your performance, you never get to do it again. Directors are satisfied usually if nothing goes wrong, if all the words are said and you look intelligent enough and nobody drops a hammer.

"In the theater, you feel you've created something, and you get to do it better the next night."

For the first time in his life Fonda did not feel the cold of winter. A few weeks of wind from the desert, palm trees shedding, and the seasons scarcely seem to change. In December 1935, however, the cold ice of tragedy struck close to him. The marriage of Aleta Freel and Ross Alexander came apart. The nights supposedly spent at Warner Brothers turned out to be nights spent by Ross in the arms of other women. When word of this confirmed Aleta's suspicions, she took her husband's rifle, turned it on herself, and committed suicide.

"Somehow," Fonda says, "my life has been peppered with suicides." Aleta Freel Alexander's was only the first.

"We took Ross out of the house up there and brought him to Brentwood. He gave up women for port, and drank bottle after bottle. He was rocked, obviously, and he had a real guilt feeling, because I'm sure he knew. I don't think she left a note, but he must have known why she did it. A few weeks later he told us he was well enough to go back up to that house on Woodrow Wilson Drive. A year and a month later, using the same gun, Ross put it into his mouth and blew his head off."

Between those two tragic events came much more work for Fonda and further development of the problem of the ungovernable cats who lived and bred beneath the Mexican-style farmhouse in Brentwood. The trouble may be summed up in a single word: fleas. Fleas on the cats. Fleas in the rugs. Fleas in the furniture.

Greta Garbo immediately put her house up for sale. Not to be outdone, Fonda, Stewart, Swope, and the latest arrival from New York, Joshua Logan, went to a rental agent seeking to sublet their house.

"One of the first people to look at the place was Jeanette MacDonald," Fonda says. "And I can remember walking around outside with her and you could literally see black clouds of fleas jumping up onto her stockings."

Miss MacDonald did not rent the house. Instead, she chose one four doors away. According to Fonda Garbo moved and then the boys located another house. They never did sublet it, apparently the cats and the fleas were the only interested parties at the time. Where Garbo went, of course, remained a mystery. The boys, however, resettled in another rental in Brentwood.

To celebrate Joshua Logan gave a house party. Actually, it was Fonda's original Hollywood sponsor, Walter Wanger, who provided the food, the drinks, and the girls. Wanger was about to shoot a film with eight of the loveliest "models" in the world, and the notion of all that pulchritude going to waste seemed sinful to him. Knowing that the four men had a house of their own, he urged Logan to find three other eligible men. Wanger would make the eighth. Logan, then an assistant director well on his way to becoming one of the greatest theatrical directors of his time, had little difficulty in corralling Dick Foran and Alan Marshall. When he tentatively approached Humphrey Bogart with the notion of spending an evening with such luscious ladies, Bogart accepted with a wicked smile.

Of the eight "lovelies" a few of them chewed gum, most of them were sheathed in clinging satin backless evening gowns and wore dangling rhinestone earrings; all of them were ready for anything. The men took their cue from Bogart, who had brought the Broadway critics to their feet with his performance as Duke Mantee in Robert E. Sherwood's *The Petrified Forest*, and was now in Hollywood carving out a matchless career for himself. Bogey, however, behaved in a fashion that astounded everyone at the gathering. He kept to himself, said little, and barely glanced at the girls. Logan told the story of the party with great delight and detail.

"When the party was over and we had driven the eight magnolia petals home, we came back into the living room and found that everyone had gone but Bogey, who was sitting there in an inkily thoughtful mood.

"Thought I to myself, Oh, my God, he'll never speak to me again. He was expecting a good wrestle in the hay with one of these girls and he got nothing. He'll be so frustrated I'll hear about it at the studio for months to come.

"Jimmy and Hank and I went over to him to offer him a drink to lift his spirits. 'What's the matter, Bogey. Did you have a bad time?'

"He looked up at us with the most profound emotion and said, 'Anybody that would stick a cock in one of those girls would throw a rock through a Rembrandt.' "

All four occupants of the house hooted and freshened his drink. Wanger made the picture with the eight lovelies and it turned out to be one of his lesser efforts. Fonda's next project did not include a film of importance either. *Trail of the Lonesome Pine* was the third remake of a film originally shot in 1916.

In the spring of 1936, however, Wanger produced a comedy notable for the reunion of Fonda and Sullavan. *The Moon's Our Home* brought the former man and wife together for the first time since she had angrily poured ice water over his head at Mt. Kisco. Separated from her second husband, William Wyler, Miss Sullavan became extremely friendly with her former spouse.

The first day on location in Lake Tahoe she edged up to him and said, "Hello, Hank."

"Hello, Peggy," he answered.

"They call me Maggie out here."

"Maggie? I'll still call you Peggy. Okay?"

"Okay."

As is the case with Fonda the woman always has to do the leading. Margaret Sullavan's daughter, actress-author Brooke Hayward, many years later said of her mother, "She was rather a flirt, a southern belle, and men were enormously engaged by her. She was not a flirt in a serious way. It was something that had been bred into her in the South. I always found it charming and completely innocent."

Innocent or not, her charm flowed as easily as maple syrup onto hot pancakes, and the words she spoke melted Henry like butter. Her wit, her allure proved irresistible to many men. She held off most of them with a laugh or a shake of her lovely head. Not Fonda. They had loved before, and now, thrown together in the ski lodges of snowy Lake Tahoe night after night, they found the emotions they had once held for one another continued to exist. James Stewart's explanation is simple and effective.

"The whole setup in Hollywood was such that you'd get about half stuck on your leading lady," Stewart said, "or some gal in the picture, and they'd generally turn out to be your dates."

With Fonda and Sullavan nothing was "half stuck." When they returned to Los Angeles it had grown serious enough for the two of them to go house-hunting together. Fonda considered a second marriage to Sullavan. Sullavan did not fight the idea. The premarital honeymoon ended typically and abruptly with Sullavan's quick temper exploding and destroying the romance.

"There was a party at the West Side Tennis Club," Fonda says. "It was a place we went to often. It had sort of countryclub dances. Johnny Swope and Jim Stewart were there, and I took Sullavan. At one point during the evening I cut in on another girl. And that triggered it. Sullavan blew. She wouldn't even let me take her home.

"The next time I saw her was on the set, and she said, 'This is a mistake, Hank. This thing between us—it's not going to work.'

"She was smart enough to realize we couldn't make it happen again. But breaking up with her the second time," he says, "was not the tragedy it had been originally."

Moon turned out to be neither a smash nor a failure. Moviegoers in the thirties craved zany, escapist comedies, and Fonda and Sullavan had played that sort of fare for years. The press paid less attention to the picture and more to the unusual circumstance—that a former husband and wife were playing a couple who meet and marry.

With Sullavan out of his life Fonda busied himself with other pursuits. The Martin bomber turned out to be a fragile craft that had cracked up during a flight around the backyard. A friend gave Fonda a sixteen-millimeter motion picture camera. That provided him with a new hobby. Swope, too, was fascinated with the camera. He eventually became a fine photographer, but at this time he took over the filming of a home movie. Fonda and Stewart were the cast. Logan wisely refrained from direction. Stewart played the villain in a melodrama the three men improvised.

"I got shot," Stewart said, "but Hank wasn't satisfied. 'What'll we use for blood?' Fonda asked. So I searched the kitchen shelves and found a large can of beets. I opened it and poured beet juice all over me. Johnny Swope and Hank liked the effect, but when we finished shooting the scene, I realized some of the stuff had gotten into my sinuses."

The following afternoon Stewart went to see a highly recommended nose and throat specialist. The physician made a thorough examination. Then he announced, "Yes, it's cloudy, very cloudy up there. I'm not quite certain yet what's causing the condition."

"Beet juice," Stewart told him.

The man in white removed his eyeglasses and wiped them slowly, but, as Stewart observed, "He didn't even venture to ask how beet juice happened to be in my sinus cavity."

"We'll try to clean it up," he told his nurse wearily.

When Fonda hears this story he scratches his neck and says, ."Doctors do like actors, but don't trust 'em a lot. Ever notice that? By the way, why didn't Stewart use catsup like all sensible people? We must've been out of it."

Early that summer Fonda sailed for England aboard the *Ile de France* with his friend Charles Boyer. With Boyer was a young Frenchwoman, a friend of his family. She could speak no English and Fonda knew absolutely no French. While he admired the aplomb with which Boyer ordered a champagne called Pommery et Greno, 1926, from the sommelier in the first-class dining salon, Fonda caught the eye of the French girl. She was most definitely looking at him. They dined together for two nights, once at Boyer's table, once at the captain's table, never exchanging a word, but later on that second evening, she tapped discreetly on the door to his cabin, and for the remainder of the voyage, speech was unnecessary.

The beauty of the English countryside burst upon Fonda when he debarked at Southampton and took the train to London. He had signed to do a film called *Wings of the Morning* with an unknown actress named Annabella, principally because he had wanted to see England and Ireland where the picture would be shot.

Annabella, much admired in France as an actress, was a name unknown throughout the rest of the world, and needed, therefore, a strong, well-recognized American leading man. The producer, working out of Denham Studios in England, insisted upon such support as the picture would be the first film in England shot in Technicolor. Harold Schuster, who had edited Fonda's two previous films, was chosen to direct *Wings of the Morning*. By mutual agreement he had gone ahead and rented a thatched-roof English cottage in Buckinghamshire for himself and Fonda. It had a rose garden and was surrounded by a white picket fence. Once they settled in the two Americans engaged an elderly man servant to see to their needs. They also got hold of a car that would take them to the primary set ten minutes away, or, if they wished, up to London.

For Fonda, London had been historic, exciting, visually just as he had imagined. Annabella turned out to be something else. She had a french haircut, a French accent, and a very French approach to life. She was thoroughly bewitching on and off camera. And it was off camera that Fonda's problem began. His leading lady wanted more than his acting. When he learned she was married he fled the set the moment the shooting ended each day. Although it was difficult to dodge so fetching a woman, Fonda thought he had managed rather well until he walked toward the commissary for lunch one noon. The rest of the cast were still before the cameras when a strange man approached him.

"M'sieur Fonda?" the man asked.

"That's right," Henry answered.

"I am the husband of Annabella."

Fonda stopped.

"I must ask you, m'sieur, no, I must demand that you stop making love with my wife."

Now a man cannot be an actor for a dozen years without recognizing a dramatic situation when he is confronted by one. And he cannot be a leading man for all that time without having some notion of how to handle that situation.

"I am not making love to your wife," Fonda began.

"But she has written me," the husband stated.

Fonda fell into step with him and the two men walked across the fields. The man was a fellow actor from Paris. He was very much in love with his wife and to lose her would be both unthinkable and unbearable.

"Listen to me," Fonda said, deeply moved by the man's words. "I'm going to tell you the truth because I know exactly what you're going through. Not too long ago I was married to a beautiful woman. She was an actress, too, and I know how it feels when a man finds someone else making love to his wife." The Frenchman looked into Fonda's earnest face.

"I give you my word," Fonda continued, "nothing has gone on between Annabella and me and nothing will go on. She will make this picture with me and then go home to be your wife. Will you believe this? Can you trust me?"

Tears came to the Frenchman's eyes. He shook Fonda's hand vigorously, thanked him profusely, and left. Fonda and Annabella made the film and that was it. Unfortunately for the Frenchman, and through no fault of Fonda's, she divorced her husband three years later, fell in love with another actor, and married him. He was a friend of Fonda's named Tyrone Power.

Fate helped the Frenchman as much as Henry's promise. A group of American tourists came to England and asked to see the shooting of a British film. On the set in Denham Studios Henry Fonda met Frances Seymour Brokaw.

What the Lowells were to Boston, the Seymours, on a slightly smaller scale, were to New York. Before the American Revolution, there had been Seymours as governors general of the colony of New York. Following the establishment of the new government, Seymours had been active in the social and political life of New York. In fact, Horatio Seymour, a former governor of the state, had been defeated for the Presidency by the incumbent, Ulysses S. Grant.

Frances Seymour, tall, blonde, brown-eyes, and aristocratic, had married multimillionaire George T. Brokaw following the divorce between Mr. Brokaw and Clare Booth.

To her most intimate friend, Frances spoke frankly about her attitudes and achievements with the opposite sex.

"I've always gotten every man I've ever wanted," she told Eulalia Chapin. "Do you know what I did with George Brokaw? First of all, I'd made up my mind as a teenager that I would become the fastest typist and best secretary anyone could hire. Then I'd descend on Wall Street and marry a millionaire."

When Frances arrived at her twenty-second birthday, Brokaw had just been divorced by Clare Booth. Mrs. Chapin thought Brokaw may have been introduced to Frances by her wealthy uncle, Henry Rogers, one time head of Standard Oil.

"George and I went together for about six months," Frances told her friend, "and when he didn't pop the question, I became impatient. I took a taxi to Tiffany's and bought a gold ring. Then I went home and found a long piece of satin ribbon. I slipped the ring onto the ribbon and tied a pretty bow at the top. That day George and I had a luncheon date. Just before dessert, I took the ring and ribbon out of my handbag and dangled it before his eyes. Then I said, 'George, I think it's time now.' His mouth fell open. 'Why, Frances, do you want to marry me?' "

Frances Seymour nodded. Within a short time they were husband and wife.

George Brokaw died in 1936, leaving a young widow and a small daughter whose nickname was Pan, a contraction of Panchita, Spanish for Frances. For her trip abroad Mrs. Brokaw left her daughter in the care of her mother, Sophie Seymour. Accompanying Mrs. Brokaw was her brother's fiancée, Fay Devereaux Keith—also a Buick touring car that had been stored in the hold of the ship on which she had crossed the Atlantic.

Of course, Henry knew nothing of the Brokaw money, or the Seymour background, or the Buick touring car. All he saw was an extraordinarily attractive young woman.

Sitting on the set, Mrs. Brokaw appraised Henry Fonda. Handsome? Yes. Talented? Definitely. But reticent, very reticent. Once again it had to be the woman taking the lead.

"Do you ever come up to London?" she asked.

"I can," Fonda replied tentatively.

"Let's have dinner," she suggested.

Harold Schuster didn't get to use that car he and Fonda had rented. Henry started making regular trips to London in it.

Frances Brokaw proved to be an enchanting woman.

"She had a winning personality and I find that important," Fonda says. "I think a sense of humor is next. And I suppose somebody who's attracted to me. I'm very impressed or influenced by somebody's being attracted to me. I'm easily seduced.

"If I have a feeling she likes me, likes me for myself,

not because I'm a movie actor or I can take her to a good place for dinner, but a feeling that she enjoys me, enjoys being with me . . . well, she has to send me some sort of rays."

Frances Seymour Brokaw met all the requirements Fonda sought in a woman and obviously sent out the right sort of rays. They went to the theaters in London where she introduced him to pink gins during the intermissions. He took her to pubs where they drank warm English beer. They visited the best restaurants and dined on Scottish salmon and beef Wellington. They went punting on the Thames. They ate at the Savoy Grille, drank at the American Bar, visited the British Museum, the Tower of London, the Houses of Parliament. They watched the changing of the guard at Buckingham Palace, saw the Marble Arch, Nelson's Column in Trafalgar Square. They did it all.

Of course the touring car, the companion, the suite overlooking the Embankment, slowly it began to come to Henry that he wasn't seeing just an American widow, but rather a wealthy widow. Henry was still the Fonda who had worked his way through two years of college, who had been paid pittances for performances for which he was now receiving sizable chunks of money. But the wealth and social position of Frances didn't do it. It was the terribly intelligent, sensually exciting woman, not the riches that drew him.

Wings of the Morning was still being shot when she made a startling announcement to him.

"I'm leaving London," she said calmly one evening.

"Why?"

"I'm going to Berlin."

"Berlin? What's in Berlin?"

"The Olympics. Why don't you come, too?" she asked, blowing a smoke ring into the air.

"The picture isn't finished."

"When it is," she suggested, "why don't you join me?"

"I hadn't thought about it," he said. He noticed her head was tilted but she was leaning toward him ever so slightly. He made up his mind at once.

"Sure," he said. "Why not?"

Frances left two days later, and then he realized how much he missed her. He couldn't wait for the "wrap" of the film. When it came, he went directly to Croyden Airport, boarded an old Ford Trimotor plane (or was it a Fokker?), and left England.

He landed at a postage stamp of an airport called Templehof in Berlin.

"Jesus, I hated it right away," Fonda says. "All those guys in brown uniforms and black uniforms and all of 'em wearing these crazy red and black arm bands. Getting through customs was hell. I didn't have anything to declare but there was some damn rule about how much money you could bring in or take out. Finally, they registered the number of reichsmarks I was allowed to spend each day on my passport and let me in."

Berlin was a city on its best behavior. The atrocities of the past three years came to a temporary end for the summer Olympics; clean, orderly, outwardly jovial and friendly, there existed, in spite of everything, an undercurrent of tension. The swastika-festooned Brandenburg Gate symbolized the Nazi power.

The lobby of Frances's hotel, the Adlon, was filled not only with visitors to the games, but with swaggering Brown Shirts and black uniformed SS men. Fonda felt uncomfortable. The only time he'd seen so many uniforms was at the Decoration Day Parade in Omaha.

"My first night in town Frances got us reservations at the best restaurant on Unter den Linden. That was their main drag," Fonda says. "Well, up to that point, I thought Charles Boyer was the most worldly gentleman I'd ever met, and when he ordered that champagne on the *Ile de France*, it had a sort of style and what you might call savoir faire to it. So when the wine steward in this restaurant came up and asked if I'd like to look at the wine list, I just waved it away and said grandly, 'Pommery et Greno, 1926.'

"That impressed Frances, I guess. It impressed the wine steward, too, because he told me what a fine selection I'd made. When the bottle came, I was mighty pleased with myself because it turned out to be the same stuff as Charles Boyer had ordered. But when the check came, I damn near fell over. On the *France* Pommery et Greno sold for seven and a half or ten dollars a bottle. In Germany, where it had to be imported, and where all the prices had been jacked up for the Olympics, it cost four times as much. Hell! I'd spent five days rations of reichsmarks on one dinner."

They went out to the recently constructed Olympic Stadium that held one hundred thousand spectators. The athletes and the games seemed of secondary importance. Center stage was held by the Führer's box, draped with the ever-present swastika. Whenever he arrived or left, whenever he stood or spoke, thousands upon thousands of arms shot into the air and voices screamed out, "Heil Hitler!"

"Son-of-a-bitch!" Fonda swore. "I can't stand this. Let's get the hell out of here." Frances found Berlin oppressive, too. They left with the high-pitched fanatical voice of Adolf Hitler ringing in their ears.

By now the companion who had been accompanying Frances discreetly disappeared, and Frances and Henry drove to Munich. Schnitzels and wursts and dark beer drunk in large blue-veined earthenware steins were good. The company was not. In every beer hall the crowd linked arms and sang a song Fonda could not understand. They called it *"Horst Wessel."* Fonda had no stomach for it. Getting into the car, he and Frances drove east.

"Once out of Munich," Fonda says, "the roads were choked with soldiers. They were marching and carrying rifles and bayonets. Motorcycles were zipping in and out. I asked what was happening and all they'd ever say was, 'Military maneuvers.' The fields were filled with them. And not just troops. Tanks creaking and artillery rolling around. Every little town you'd go through was filled with soldiers. You didn't see it in England. You didn't see it in France. But in Germany there was a lot of military action going on.

"In retrospect I think, shit! I wasn't the only one who saw that. Why didn't somebody else notice and get smart and say, 'Hey, fellas, something's going on!'"

Fonda and Frances drove through the Black Forest and out of Germany through the still peaceful hills and valleys of Austria and on to the plain of Hungary. Located on both sides of the muddy brown river that poets and lyric writers persist in calling the Blue Danube is the city of Budapest.

To Frances Brokaw and Henry Fonda Budapest was the most romantic city in Europe. Although Hungarian is a tongue almost incomprehensible except to language students or those born within the national boundaries, the couple who fled Germany found it as entrancing as the violins that gypsies played in almost every eating place in the city. Goulash, chicken paprikash, strudels, strong Tokay wine, and the music. Hungarian music was fiery yet soothing, carefree and caressing.

If August is the month Parisians leave their city to the tourists, Budapest in the thirties accepted them most hospitably. Henry Fonda and Frances Brokaw couldn't have enjoyed each other more. Each was a new experience to the other.

With precious few exceptions most of the women Fonda had known as an adult had been in the theater or in pictures. Although she was born in Canada and spent much of her life in New York, she had never seen him act on the stage or in films.

Frances was drawn to Henry because he was handsome, virile, soft-spoken, gentle, different than any of the other men she had known, and possessed, she thought, a secret streak of vulnerability.

Henry knew little of Manhattan debutantes, of the people included in the New York social register, of high finance and inherited wealth. Blue bloods, Blue Books were unknown to the actor from Omaha. Frances captured his interest because she showed interest in him. She was witty, she was beautiful. They visited the Opera House on the southern bank of the city, the citadel on the higher northern bank; they listened to the violins, drank at the cafe houses, and made love. The setting was romantic, the time was right. He proposed in Budapest. She accepted in Paris. They married in New York.

CHAPTER
6

AMERICA crawled out of the Depression. The Chrysler Building and the Empire State Building raced one another skyward. The old townhouses on the Upper East Side had been reclaimed from the banks and their original occupants continued to live in the style to which they had grown up and become accustomed. The apartment buildings lining both sides of Park Avenue and the east side of Fifth Avenue had their doormen back, attired in green or blue uniforms with white piping, starched shirt fronts, white cotton gloves, and silver whistles to hail taxis tenants could afford once again. The stock market had begun its recovery.

When Henry Fonda stepped off the gangplank of the ship that brought him back to New York, he plunged into an alien world. The people to whom Frances introduced him talked about stocks and bonds, debentures, and what to do about "That Man in the White House" running for a second term. The names and addresses of the family and friends of Frances Seymour Brokaw were people and places found in the society pages of the eight New York dailies. Fonda had always read the theatrical pages.

"God!" he says. "John Mason Brown, George Jean Nathan, Brooks Atkinson—those were the mighty to me. The high were the Barrymores, the Lunts, O'Neill, Max Anderson, Bob Sherwood, Sidney Howard, Philip Barry, Kaufman and Hart, Lindsay and Crouse." Instead he was introduced to the people in Frances's circle, the Van Wycks, the Ten Eycks, the Stoutenburghs, the Belmonts, the Stuyvesants, the whipped cream of New York's social establishment; quite a contrast for a fellow who had lived in two cramped rooms in the Madison Square Hotel and had run steak and beer parties, "all you can eat and drink for a dollar."

Ten days after Fonda returned to Manhattan, the newspapers carried the story that, "Mr. and Mrs. Eugene Ford Seymour of 315 East Sixty-eighth Street and Fairhaven, Mass., have announced from Mt. Kineo, Maine, where they are passing the summer, the engagement of their daughter Frances Seymour Brokaw of 646 Park Avenue to Mr. Henry Jaynes Fonda of California."

The parties he attended now were held either in those townhouses he had never entered, at the Plaza or the Waldorf, or in those elite private clubs he never knew existed. The ebullient Frances glowed. Her high forehead, her quick, gracious smile, her light brown hair, the aristocratic manner in which she carried herself bespoke her happiness.

At the dinners given by her relatives, seated between two women whose names he couldn't remember, couldn't even recognize from the place cards on the table, Henry grew silent. More than likely after the meal concluded he would retreat to the library in the home where the dinner was held. He could be found there, to the consternation of his bride-to-be, thumbing through a magazine.

Henry apologized to Frances and she forgave him. When the formal evenings were over and the happy couple thanked their hosts and hostesses, they would walk for a while in the fresh air. Then, hailing a cab, Henry would order the driver to take them down to the jazz joints in Greenwich Village.

If they stayed late enough they heard the musicians jamming at Jimmy Kelly's on Sullivan Street or Eddie Condon's on Sheridan Square. Or they would taxi up to Harlem to the Savoy Ballroom on Lenox Avenue to hear Ella Fitzgerald sing the blues and Louis Armstrong blow the trumpet as only Satchmo could do it. That kind of music made Henry happy, and Frances saw it as a reward for his sitting through the dinner parties that pleased her and bored him.

Henry spent a few afternoons with a new person. He had been wary of meeting Frances's little daughter, recalling the sticky-fingered audiences in Washington who liked to unwrap candy bars during his big scenes. The slender, four-year-old child seemed as serious-minded as an adult. She even spoke of becoming a ballet dancer.

"My first recollection of Henry Fonda," Pan said, "was when he came to meet me. He kneeled down so as to be at my level. I must have like him because I asked him right away to read to me. He did."

At three o'clock on a warm Wednesday afternoon on September 16, 1936, Frances and Henry were joined in holy matrimony at Christ Church on Park Avenue and Sixtieth Street by the Rev. Dr. Ralph Stockman. It was as high stylish and ultra-fashionable as a New York wedding can be.

"I don't know if I was ready for that kind of fancy-dress wedding," Fonda says. "They got me into a black coat with swallowtails, a pair of striped pants, an ascot around my neck, and a high silk hat on my head. Shit! I thought any minute a director would yell, 'Roll 'em! Action!'"

Joshua Logan apparently was quite at home in his clothes. He performed his functions as best man most efficiently. Logan hovered near Fonda's elbow, lit his cigarettes, straightened his ascot, and prior to the ceremony, whispered words of encouragement to the bridegroom. Leland Hayward, elegant as always in his Saville Row clothes, served as Henry's usher. H. Roger Seymour, a brother of the bride, was also an usher.

Frances was attended by her sister, Miss Marjory Capell Seymour, and escorted by her brother, Ford de Villers Seymour. Her young daughter, Pan, walked in front of her strewing petals as properly as a flower girl should. The bride wore a gown of pale blue taffeta and tulle with a wide-brimmed hat of a matching shade and carried a bouquet of delphinium and pink roses.

"She was as good-looking as a model from *Vogue* or

any actress I'd met," Fonda says, "and bright as the beam from a follow-spot."

The pews on the left side of the church were filled with relatives of the bride: the Pells, the Howlands, the Fishes, and the Biddles of Philadelphia.

Outside, in the fading sunlight, three hundred fans had gathered, and they were obviously in a holiday mood. They called "Good luck" to the couple, clapped, and threw rice.

"My God!" Fonda says, "I had to restrain an urge to pick up the rice grain by grain and cook it!"

Following the ceremony, a reception was held at the Hotel Pierre Roof Garden. One hundred and fifty persons attended, including Henry's two sisters who trained in from Nebraska for the nuptials. Everything about the affair was lavish. The orchestra played "The Way You Look Tonight," the hit tune by Jerome Kern and Dorothy Fields. Henry danced the first dance with Frances. When the orchestra segued into Cole Porter's "I've Got You Under My Skin," Henry danced with his wife's mother. Then came his two sisters, and on and on and on. When the newly married couple left, Irving Berlin's "Cheek to Cheek" was playing.

The new Mr. and Mrs. Fonda spent their wedding night in her apartment at the Sulgrave Hotel. The next day they flew to Hollywood where he began a new picture.

Their first lodging was a two-room suite in the Beverly Hills Hotel. The management sent large vases filled with flowers and baskets of fresh fruit to make them welcome. Henry spent the entire first day with his wife. It was like being in Budapest again. Only now it was airy and sunny and the tall palm trees guarded the driveway up to the porte cochere and down to Sunset Boulevard. Henry took her through the hotel, to the shops, to the Olympic-size swimming pool, to the cabanas. At night they drank in the dimly lit Polo Lounge.

After that he left her at six-thirty every morning. Picture making is an early business.

Frances's daytime loneliness ended after a week. Pink notes from the bell captain's desk would be slipped under her door. Their wedding gifts began to arrive. She spent hours opening them, closing them, fighting a losing battle to find a space to store them. The rest of her day went to writing thank-you notes.

A person without an automobile is a person isolated in Southern California. After six days of thank-you notes and shifting the wedding presents about so Henry could find a place to sit down after a day's shooting at the studio, Frances went out and bought a car.

"A Buick," Fonda says. "Frances always had Buicks."

It didn't take her long to discover an attractive furnished house in the Pacific Palisades on Monaco Drive. As soon as she negotiated the lease, they moved into it and sent for Frances's daughter, Pan. The small child took to the semi-rural life of California as promptly as Fonda took to her. When she started school, she signed the name, "Pan Fonda" to her finger paintings and drawings. Henry liked her so much he was ready to adopt her as his own, but Frances's lawyers argued against it. They pointed out that her adoption might prohibit her inheritance of Brokaw money. Years later, when Clare Booth Luce's daughter was tragically killed in an automobile accident, Pan received a portion of her half-sister's estate.

By the greatest of coincidences, Fonda's agent, Leland Hayward, married his ex-wife, Margaret Sullavan, and by an even greater coincidence, the Haywards rented a house a block away from the Fondas.

As it is with most couples, particularly those who marry following a short courtship, Henry and Frances began to learn about each other. He found out his wife's father hit the bottle a bit too frequently. So had her first husband. In addition Mr. Brokaw, while in his cups, took pleasure in whacking his women from wall to wall. According to Frances, her predecessor, Clare Booth, suffered four miscarriages at his hands. Mr. Brokaw spent the last year of his life at a sanitarium in Connecticut. Even there he managed to stash away countless decanters filled with liquor. He was discovered facedown, floating in the swimming pool one morning. The newspapers printed, "Heart." The newsmen muttered, "Scotch."

Henry also discovered that while Frances's family abounded in notable ancestry, she grew up the poor relative. Instead of attending college she had chosen Katharine Gibbs Secretarial School, and after a year, rushed to Wall Street to make her way in the world of finance. Henry didn't give that a thought, because while they were in Europe she had told him she once worked at the Morgan Bank. What did cause him to raise his eyebrows was when she confided that the only real money she had came from the estate of her late husband. And then she explained that the amount was over a million dollars. The rest, alas, had evaporated in the Crash.

"I was floored," Fonda says, "but Frances wasn't satisfied. She wanted more." Because money in Hollywood came in like water flowing from an open tap and went out just as easily, many movie actors retained business managers. Frances suggested that she handle his financial affairs personally. Well, why not? No commissions, no percentages, no risk of knavery. Here was someone with Wall Street experience who was capable of managing her own money. Why not his?

As for the further education of Frances Fonda, she was aware her husband, particularly when he worked, immersed himself so deeply in his current role that when he came home from the studio, he would take a light supper, say little, and then hide himself off to study his lines for the next day's shooting.

His wife didn't feel much like a bride. In two or three weeks Frances grasped the order of her husband's priorities. "A" for acting stood at the top of the list. She had to face reality. Movies and theater meant little to her.

"Frances is interested in only two things," Leland Hayward observed, "sex and money."

"Hell," Fonda replied when he heard the comment, "I'm certainly interested in both of 'em."

Henry's West Coast friends took an instant liking to his East Coast wife. She was knowledgeable on almost every subject except picture making. Talk of rushes, of key lights and grips and close-ups, of billing and distribution bored her. While she was a most affable woman, she failed to fit in with most of the movie wives.

In a land where women wore slacks and sandals during the day Frances wore suits and oxfords. Where women dressed in chiffon at night Frances wore black velvet. When the wives of movie executives sparkled with diamonds Frances wore pearls. When the envious conversations were as green as imitation jade, her soft Eastern accent rang as true as a sterling bell. The "darlings" and "dears" and "honeys" that show people threw at each other like confetti were not in her vocabulary.

While it took Frances about twenty seconds to tell an original Duncan Phyfe from a copy, it took her ten seconds to recognize a phony compliment. She was far more comfortable with men than with women. She preferred business talk to gossip. In a day before Hollywood columnists wrote about "class," Frances had it.

Invitations streamed into the house on Monaco Drive. The Fondas hit the party circuit regularly.

"There were always one or two women at every gathering who tried to interest him in something more than the hors d'oeuvres," a friend of his said, "but Hank was always like a block of marble in those drawing rooms, present, polished, but immovable. He was as warm and faithful to Frances as a golden retriever."

Frances could be found on the patios chatting easily with the men about American going off the gold standard, labor conditions, foreign and domestic policy. Truly, they were a most unusual pair. While his career as an actor shot up, their popularity as a couple grew apace.

One spring evening Frances lighted the candles at the dinner table, blew out the match and told her husband she was pregnant.

Fatherhood! Henry was jubilant. He telephoned his sisters in Omaha. He called his friends in California, in New York. He began making lists of names, one if the child was a boy, the other if it was a girl. Frances had to quiet him down. It would be many months before she gave birth. He controlled his exuberance and returned to work on second-rate pictures with first-rate actors.

A regular paycheck could not keep Fonda from yearning for the legitimate theater. He recalled the excitement he felt as the curtain went up before a live audience.

When Day Tuttle sent him a telegram, he ignored Hayward's opinion and Frances's advice and flew to Mt. Kisco to play the title role in *The Virginian*. Based upon the celebrated novel by Owen Wister, *The Virginian* is the play with the ultimate cowboy role.

"This town ain't big enough for both of us."

"When you call me that, mister, smile."

"You got till sundown to get out. Then I'm a-coming' fer ya."

These are only a few of the classic lines of dialogue given the leading man. Tough, fearless, he *is* the original American folk hero. There isn't a villain he won't outdraw or a horse he can't gentle. Fonda knew the part and was ready to play it with both guns blazing.

"There was a stable attached to The Kittle Inn," Fonda says, "and I suppose it was the press agent's idea that the whole cast get dressed up in cowboy costumes and go out riding. Now I've never liked horses. They never do what the director tells 'em to do. But there I am, on top of this big fella, leading Henry Morgan and the entire cast down this back road in Westchester County. We're on our way back to the stable and the horses know it and they're in one helluva hurry to get there.

"Suddenly, a couple of cars are coming at us. My damn horse jumps over a station wagon and slams into a sedan that's following it. I go flying through the air, land on my hand, break my wrist, and think the poor animal is dead or about to be destroyed. But no. He's got a slight scratch on his chest and the front of the car he hit is totaled. And the owner sues me for a couple of thousand dollars and collects. And I play *The Virginian* with a cast on my wrist and my arm in a sling. God! You wonder why I feel the way I do about horses."

At the Westchester Playhouse Fonda received a script he wanted to do. It was an opportunity to return to Broadway. Even Hayward agreed.

Blow Ye Winds opened at the Forty-sixth Street Theater and proved to be as bad as its title. Fonda hurried back to California after thirty-six performances.

He was happy to be home, happy to be with Frances, happy to start a film with Bette Davis.

Bette Davis, the girl he had "scored" with in the back seat of Hunter Scott's car as it overlooked the Princeton football stadium, had shot so high to stardom that she could dictate the choice of her leading man. She and Fonda had already made one picture together, *That Certain Woman.* Now, in 1937, for one of her most memorable films, *Jezebel,* she again picked Henry Fonda. This time he insisted on a clause in his contract. His wife planned to return to New York because she had great faith in the obstetrician who had delivered Pan. If, during the course of shooting, Fonda's wife should go into labor with his child, he had the right to go to her side. Sure enough, Frances checked into Doctors Hospital in Manhattan and Fonda flew to New York, leaving Bette Davis to play several love scenes to the camera without the presence of her leading man.

On December 21, 1937, Jane Seymour Fonda was born by cesarean section.

"That was a great day," Fonda says. "I took dozens of snapshots with my Leica. Every night the floor nurses had to kick me out."

From the time she was old enough to understand until she was old enough to complain effectively her parents called her "Lady Jane," a name she disliked "because," she said, "it sounded sissy."

In its time Doctors Hospital might very well have been called Patients Hospital. To those socially prominent individuals who were admitted the place was more like a hotel. Many patients brought their own sheets, pillows, blankets, even drapes. Whiskey and meals could be ordered up from the downstairs dining room for patients and their visitors. Some of New York's finest chefs maintained the quality of the cuisine in the restaurant on the first floor. Many passersby strolling along East End Avenue dropped in for lunch without knowing any patients in the building.

Even the panoramic view from the rooms provided a form of nature's cure. The East River with its tankers and tugboats cutting through the winter mists was tranquilizing and peaceful. And in the distance the spidery silhouettes of black and silver bridges loomed up majestically.

Peaceful or not two weeks in any hospital is enough. After that time Mr. and Mrs. Henry Fonda and their daughter, Lady Jane, returned to California.

Both Henry and Frances reacted positively to parenthood. Henry bragged endlessly to anyone who would listen.

"As for me," Pan admitted, "I was quite jealous of the new baby."

Frances, slender again, filled with energy and enthusiasm, said good-bye each morning to the household staff, settled into her light blue convertible Buick, and headed out in search of a new home—one they could own. She drove slowly from Sunset to Wilshire trying to find a place that appealed to her eastern tastes.

In 1938 in Los Angeles and its environs real estate firms had planted signs deep in the soil of the front lawns. In many sections For Sale signs stood block after block like sentries.

In Brentwood, south of Sunset Boulevard on Chadbourne, she spotted a Cape Cod cottage that pleased her. The next Sunday Fonda followed his wife into a residence that he says, "looked little on the outside, but Lord, it was plenty big inside. It needed extensive remodeling, but we bought it. A two-story house with rooms for three children and a nurse, a dining room, living room, den, and kitchen. We even put in our own pool."

When Fonda came home at night he could smell the raw lumber, the fresh paint, and the varnish.

Eventually, the carpenters, electricians, floor scrapers, and painters left, and the Fondas had their new home to themselves. To no one's surprise the Haywards again moved a block away. The Fondas spent Sunday afternoons luxuriating beside the pool with their friends. They swam, listened to his collection of jazz records, and, when allowed by the nurse, photographed the baby.

"Lady Jane was even prettier than her mother, and precocious. I would have liked to play with her and pamper her," Fonda says, "but the nurse was strict." Strict and as stiff as her white uniform. She commanded the children's wing with a general's power.

"We had a cook and a chauffeur and a nurse, and, you

know, for this boy from Omaha, it was like showing off when I was a kid. I felt like calling out, 'Look, Ma, no hands!' I had everything, but I needed permission to see my own baby. Jane was quarantined. I often had to put on a mask when I went in to see my kid, not because I had a cold, it's just the way the nurse and Frances wanted it. It makes me sad when I think about it. She grew up without ever being hugged or fondled. I choke up when I remember what I missed and what she missed."

In 1938 Fonda moved over to RKO for a single picture. There he met one of his favorite women. *The Mad Miss Manton* was just another little comedy with a murder mystery running through it, but the girl who played opposite him was Barbara Stanwyck.

"Everyone who is close to me knows I've been in love with Barbara Stanwyck since I met her," Fonda says. "She's a delicious woman. We've never had an affair. She's never encouraged me, but dammit, my wife will verify it, my daughters and son will confirm it, and now you all can testify to the truth. Stanwyck can act the hell out of any part, and she can turn a chore into a challenge. She's fun, and I'm glad I had a chance to make three movies with her. *The Lady Eve* was the best."

"Yes, *The Lady Eve* was a good picture," Miss Stanwyck agreed, "but about the rest of Fonda's talk, he was single when I was single and where was he?"

It was around this period that Fonda came into contact with two other persons who became as dear to him as Miss Stanwyck, but they were men and they influenced his life much more directly and much more strongly than the talented actress.

The first man to capture Fonda's imagination was John "Pappy" Ford, the son of immigrant Irish parents. Ford's older brother, Patrick, ran away to California where he became a serial star at Universal Studios. His eighteen-year-old brother followed him and got jobs as a stunt man, an assistant cameraman, and eventually a director.

Tall, craggy, with thin legs, a pale complexion, bad eyes, and worse language, Ford found John Wayne, put him into *Stagecoach* as Ringo, and made two careers, one for Wayne, another for Ford. His pattern was to turn out three pictures a year. One for the Internal Revenue Service, a second for his boat, the *Araner*, and finally, a third for himself to live on until the next year.

In 1939 Lamar Trotti, a screenwriter, and Kenneth McGowan, a producer, approached Fonda with a picture they were putting together. They called it *Young Mr. Lincoln*. Did Fonda know anything about Lincoln?

"Know about him? I'm a Lincoln nut. I've read three quarters of the books that have been written about Lincoln," Fonda answered.

"Well, can we come over to your house tonight and read the script to you?" McGowan asked.

"Why not?" was the answer he received.

That evening McGowan, Fonda, and Frances listened as Lamar Trotti read his script aloud. When he finished the writer waited for approval of his work.

Mrs. Fonda thought it engrossing. Turning to her husband she said, "Hank, you'd make a marvelous Lincoln."

"Nope. Not a chance," he replied. "Sorry boys, thank you very much, but I'm not your man."

"At least," McGowan argued, "come down to Fox and test for it. See for yourself."

Two weeks later Fonda strode into the studio. The makeup crew went to work. Fonda had Lincoln's long face but not his nose. Within forty-five minutes, an hour at the most, he had not only Lincoln's nose, but the wart on his face, too. Fonda had enough black hair on his head for the hairdressers to part it, tease it up, and suddenly his hair was Lincoln's. Then they turned him over to wardrobe. There he received the standard stovepipe hat, the unpressed black trousers, the white shirt, the string necktie, and the knee-length frock coat.

"Ready on the set!" the test director called.

A young studio actress played opposite him, but Fonda had most of the lines. They did it twice.

"Cut!" cried the director. "Print it!"

That afternoon Fonda, McGowan, and Trotti sat in a projection room and watched the blank screen. A group of numbers appeared, 5-4-3-2-1. Then the slate, "Henry Fonda, Lincoln Test, Take One, Scene One."

Abraham Lincoln filled the screen in black and white.

Fonda's jaw went slack. It *was* Lincoln, really Abraham Lincoln! And then Lincoln turned to speak to the girl, and to Fonda's astonishment and distress, it was *his* voice coming out of Lincoln's mouth. For him, the illusion ended abruptly.

"Fellas," he said as he stood up, casting his own shadow onto the screen. "I can't do it. When my voice comes out of that figure, I can't stand it." And with that he left the projection room, got into his car, and drove home. He was an independent actor now and no one was going to make him do what he didn't want to do.

Some months later the phone rang. It was John Ford's secretary-script girl. Mr. Ford had just returned to town and wanted to see Mr. Fonda immediately.

"I'd never met him," Fonda says. "I'd stood in the background and watched him direct Duke Wayne. But now I'm going in to see Ford. I was in a sports jacket with a sweater under it, and there was Ford sitting behind the desk, with a slouch hat on the back of his head. His clothes looked like they came from the Salvation Army, too large for him, too ragged for anybody. He had either a pipe in his mouth or a handkerchief all of the time. This was typical for Pappy. He'd chew a hankerchief or chew a pipe. He'd have a cigar after a meal, but otherwise it was a pipe, and he'd fill it and refill it and smoke all day long.

"Anyway this is the man who's sitting at the other side of this desk when I come in and I'm standing there. I'm sure he's putting on an act for me, or he's being as dramatic as he can be, because he looks down, and then he looks up at me.

"'What the fuck is all this shit about you not wanting to play this picture?' Ford growled. 'You think Lincoln's a great fucking Emancipator, huh? He's a young jack-legged lawyer from Springfield, for Christ sake.'

"Anyway that's the way the guy talks. I mean he was full of the words you don't use in polite society. He talked that way naturally, but for God to sit there and talk to me like that was awesome. What happened was he was trying to shame me into playing Young Lincoln, and that was the point he made. He *wasn't* the Great Emancipator. He *was* a young jack-legged lawyer from Springfield. We don't know at the end of the movie what's going to happen to this guy. That's not it. It's a good movie about a young lawyer in 1830. Anyway Ford shamed me into it, I agreed, and I did the film."

The impression Fonda, Ford, and the movie made on *The New York Times* was, "Mr. Fonda supplies the warmth and kindliness, the pleasant modesty, the courage, resolution, tenderness, shrewdness and wit that kindles the film, makes it a moving unity, at once gentle and quizzically comic."

A second man who influenced his life was the writer John Steinbeck. Someone, Fonda is unable to recall who, sent him a collection of short stories by the California-born author. It was called *The Long Valley.* Fonda was entranced by what he read. When he completed the book he drove to a Brentwood bookstore.

"May I be of service to you, Mr. Fonda?" the middle-aged salesperson asked, flattered that a famous actor had set foot in her shop.

"Yes, indeed," Fonda answered. "Let me have a copy of every book in the store by a man named John Steinbeck." He left with three volumes and read one after the other. Then he began combing the bookshops of Beverly Hills and Westwood for more work by the man who wrote simply but realistically about the lives of rural Americans. Fonda could appreciate and identify with this more than the literature of Greece, Rome, England, France, or even contemporary American authors.

It was a joyous moment when Leland Hayward telephoned him.

"Ever hear of *The Grapes of Wrath*?" the agent asked.

"Sure have," Fonda answered readily. "It's about the farmers who were driven out of Oklahoma by the dust storms and made their way to California and . . ."

"I didn't ask for a book report," Hayward said, stopping the enthusiastic actor. "I just want you to know Zanuck bought it for Fox. Nunnally Johnson is going to do the screenplay and John Ford is going to direct. They want you for Tom Joad."

"Great!" Fonda's word practically scorched the telephone.

135

"Not so fast," Hayward cautioned. "Zanuck wants to talk to you."

Darryl Francis Zanuck had begun his hollywood career as a screenwriter. His earliest scripts were for the dog Rin Tin Tin. More an executive than a screenwriter, Zanuck founded Twentieth Century Productions in 1933, merged it with Fox Films in 1935, and became vice president in charge of production.

A short man, he rode horses well and played polo whenever possible. His fixation with the game caused him to carry a polo mallet in his office and swing it at will. Tough, shrewd, harsh, Zanuck made himself a major individual power in motion pictures.

When Fonda entered his office Zanuck nodded toward a chair.

"I hear from Leland you like *Grapes of Wrath*," Zanuck said.

"You betcha," Fonda replied.

"Like it well enough to sign a seven-year contract with me?"

"Hell, no!" Fonda jumped to his feet. He wasn't going to allow this arrogant man to tie him up like a calf ready for branding.

"I'm a free-lance actor and I intend to stay one," Fonda declared.

"Well, I'm not going to give you Tom Joad and let you go off and do some picture with MGM and Joan Crawford," Zanuck snapped.

Fonda bit his lip and sat down in the chair again.

Zanuck swung his polo mallet once or twice and then softened his tone.

"I've got big plans for you, Fonda," the producer said, "and I want to be able to control you and keep you and I've got to have a contract with you to do it."

The bait was irresistible. Hayward got Fonda as good a deal as he could, but Zanuck held the high cards. Henry Fonda had no choice. He signed the seven-year contract reluctantly. But he signed. And he played Tom Joad in *The Grapes of Wrath.*

After forty-five years of filmmaking *The Grapes of Wrath* stands as Fonda's masterpiece. The elements were all there: John Steinbeck's shattering novel of the social injustice of the "Okies" during the Great Depression, the talent and craftsmanship with which Nunnally Johnson adapted the novel for the screen, Gregg Toland's revolutionary camera work, Alfred Newman's moving use of "The Red River Valley," as the musical theme, and, ultimately, John Ford's direction.

"Ford was a giant as a director," Fonda says. "He rarely made more than one take. He wanted the freshness of the first time. The emotion would be there if it wasn't rehearsed to death, and that's what Ford felt would happen if he did it too much. 'You'll leave the performance in the locker room,' he'd warn.

"The second unit went out and shot all the footage between Oklahoma and California. The river outside Needles, California, where we take our bath was the farthest away we went. The rest of the picture was shot in real 'Okie' camps in the vicinity of Los Angeles; let's say Pomona, for instance."

The picture, in a matter of weeks, with a budget that would barely pay for a single week of filming today, ended with a farewell scene between mother and son.

"Ford didn't even watch the rehearsal," Fonda says. "That last scene in *The Grapes of Wrath* was standard Ford.

"Both Jane Darwell, who played the mother, and I knew the scene was coming up this particular day; it was on the schedule. We knew that this was the key scene in the picture for both of us. It was an emotional scene and we were looking forward to doing it. We each knew our lines and we thought they were incredibly fine, we were eager to get on with it.

"We both had sense enough not to tell Ford how we felt, though, because we'd worked for him before and you didn't make suggestions to Pappy Ford. He'd say, 'You want to direct this film, huh?' And you were on the shit list right away. He didn't like to have anybody ever recommend anything.

"Are you aware that Ford was an admitted alcoholic who got falling-down piss-eyed drunk when he wasn't filming a movie? When he worked, he was cold sober, and I mean cold.

"Well," Fonda continues, "the scene I'm talking about started in the tent where Tom Joad goes in and wakes up Ma. He's going away, and he wakes her up. Without waking the other people in the tent, Pa and the kids.

"I had to light a match, and then the cameraman, Gregg Toland, rigged a light in the palm of my hand with wires going up my arm. The light, which was supposed to be the glow from the match, had to light Ma's face just right. It took a half an hour to set up that piece of business.

"Then I tapped her and she opened her eyes and she went outside with me. We walked around the tent and up to the bench that was at the foot of the dance floor. Ford wouldn't let us get into the dialogue. By the time he was ready Jane Darwell and I were like racehorses that wanted to go. 'Hey, boy have we got a scene. We want to show you.'

"Then with Ford's intuitive instinct, he knew when we were built up. We'd never done it out loud, but Ford called for action, the cameras rolled, and he had it in a single take. After we finished the scene, Pappy didn't say a word. He just stood up and walked away. He got what he wanted. We all did. On the screen it was brilliant."

That final scene of the film, played with extraordinary skill, cannot be shown on the page, but the words ring true over the years.

TOM: I thought it out clear, Ma, I can't, I don't know enough. Maybe it's like Casey says—if a fella ain't got a soul of his own—just a little piece of a big soul that belongs to everybody, then . . .

MA: Then what, doll?

TOM: Then it don't matter. I'll be all around in the dark—I'll be everywhere. Wherever you can look—wherever there's a fight, so hungry people can eat, I'll be there. Wherever there's a cop beating up a guy—I'll be there. I'll be there in the way guys yell when they're mad.

I'll be there in the way kids laugh when they're hungry, and they know supper's ready, and when people are eatin' the stuff they raised, and livin' in the houses they built—I'll be there, too.

The open, honest acting of Henry Fonda rose above the entire production, and still shines from the celluloid to make it one of America's classic films.

While *The Grapes of Wrath* was being filmed in California the true wrath of Europe exploded early in September 1939. The war blew in like a rainstorm sweeping across the lake. It could be seen in the distance, and then the curtain of water drew even closer. Henry and Frances had expected it. They had heard the hobnail shoes of the infantry pounding the paving bricks of Germany. They had watched as the jackboots of the officers goose-stepped in Berlin.

Now that the Stukka dive bombers and the Wehrmacht tanks had destroyed Poland in seventeen days, now that Britain and France were at war with the Nazis, the Fondas tried to make the days of peace at home as pleasant for their children as possible.

Margaret Sullavan Hayward had given birth to a daughter, Brooke, around the same time as Jane had been born. Jane's nurse knew Brooke's nurse. Jane played in the Haywards' sandpile one day and Brooke played in the Fondas' sandpile the next day. While the two girls became best friends, their mothers maintained neutral positions. The Fondas were invited to the Haywards for dinner only once. Frances refused to reciprocate. Although the distance between the two houses was only around the corner, the gulf between Fonda's first wife and his second wife was unbridgeable.

Children notice signs that their elders often ignore. When Fonda stopped by to collect his daughter at the Haywards', he and Sullavan instantly became a team once again.

"They had a look of naughtiness when they came together," Brooke Hayward said about her mother and Henry Fonda. "They could stand on their heads and walk on their hands. They seemed so inseparable that for years Jane and I would wonder what might be going on between them. Of course, in reality, nothing went on, but we took their horsing around and showing off for more than it actually was. Jane and I got around to where we'd make up stories about how we could get my mother and her father back together again.

"My mother thought Henry was the best actor she knew and told us so very often. She was enormously loyal to him. She had to be because she knew if she ever said anything against him, I'd go straight to Jane and tell her. She had to be careful. Mother and Hank were two fabulously attractive people. We had fun watching them."

At the stroke of noon, on February 23, 1940, Peter Henry Fonda arrived at the LeRoy Institute in New York. His parents were ecstatic, but Frances's recuperation period from her third cesarian was slow. The attending physicians suspected a kidney problem. After fourteen weeks, Fonda and a nurse flew baby Peter home to California. Frances remained behind with her mother and her medical advisers.

"Can you visualize me changing Peter's diapers on an airplane?" Fonda asks. "Well, I did!"

Henry had filmed home movies of his wife feeding his son in the hospital. He took them home to show Jane and Pan.

"I remember that movie," Jane said, her eyes narrowing. "I looked at it and I burst into tears and ran from the room. I was not happy, I can tell you."

The return of Frances allayed Lady Jane's fears of being nudged from the nest. There was room for three children, Pan, Jane, and the newly born Peter.

To bring his family closer together, Henry arranged a series of picnics. He remembered them from his own youth and took his wife, their daughters and their son, Peter, and the nurse up into the hills. With hampers of food and drinks they would picnic away a Sunday afternoon.

"There were just dirt roads there," Fonda says. "We'd drive to the end of 'em and take our baskets and walk up those paths onto quiet lovely oak hills. We'd spread out blankets and paper tablecloths and napkins, put out assorted sandwiches and pickles and potato chips and fruit—milk for the kids, iced beer for the grownups. While the nurse cared for Peter, Jane, and Pan and I'd play ball or climb or just sit and watch the water. Frances and I fell in love with some property and kept thinking how much we'd like to build a house there.

"It overlooked the ocean from that vista. You could see the Pacific, that's how high it was. It was a lot of property but it wasn't for sale. It was owned by the Bell family and they made their billions in real estate that's now called Bel Air. But they weren't ready to partition this property until they were sure what land values were going to be. In order to sell the property they had to guarantee utilities and sewers and gas lines and electricity.

"Finally, the knoll we liked, Tigertail it was called, became available. It cost three thousand dollars an acre and we bought nine acres. That was expensive and I had to figure: 'I think I can afford it, and I think it would be lovely and great for the kids.'

"Well, I laid out twenty-seven thousand dollars and hired an architect, but Frances and I knew exactly what kind of house we wanted. A Pennsylvania Dutch farmhouse. We had scrapbooks full of clippings of houses and furniture—Early American we were dreaming about. So the architect didn't have a helluva lot to do."

To pay for all this Henry gave Frances permission to sell some or all of his stocks. She sold all, paid for Tigertail, converted a portion of the rest into a chain of neighborhood motion picture theaters that she turned over at a loss. From the remaining funds she bought some beachfront property. Another poor investment.

Her own stock and bond portfolio increased in value steadily, but it disturbed Frances that her business acumen failed when it came to her husband's holdings.

Buying and selling, selling and buying. Fonda noticed a subtle change in Frances. This lovely woman he married became obsessed with dollar signs and decimal points.

When he arrived home from the studio at night Fonda found her sitting in bed, surrounded by stacks of ledgers and account records. She'd be checking and rechecking the figures in them. These special books were kept in the bedroom all the time now. Frances barely glanced up when Fonda entered.

Her conversations with her acquaintances were vague instead of animated. Frances no longer kept up with the financial or political news.

The medicine chests were filling up with pills of every assortment and shape. In 1940 physicians prescribed cod liver oil capsules and "tonics" for people suffering from "nerves."

While Fonda worked, Frances went to doctors. During dinner she ate little. She complained she felt ill. Fonda tried to be understanding—he did notice that she tired easily these days and had lost weight. Henry suggested she consult another physician. He failed to realize the symptoms were more mental than physical. Whenever a doctor told Frances she was a healthy woman, she changed doctors.

Eventually, one medical man humored her by going along with her hypochondria. He told her he suspected she had developed undulant fever, and recommended that she enter a hospital for a few weeks. She agreed and went to Scripps Clinic on the outskirts of La Jolla.

Late at night Fonda would sit at his wife's desk in their bedroom and write letters to her; news of the children, news of their "dream house," funny stories he'd heard.

While she remained at Scripps, Henry ran the construction of the house, the children, the servants, and he made movies Darryl F. Zanuck decided he should make.

"Remember all that talk about those plans he had for me? And not allowing me to go to MGM and make a picture with Joan Crawford?" Fonda says. "Well, the first film after *The Grapes of Wrath* Darryl F. Fuck-It-All Zanuck had me make was *Lillian Russell* with Alice Faye!

"Now I've got only good things to say about Alice Faye. But shit! I was only one of ten men in that picture! I swear it. Count 'em. Don Ameche, Nigel Bruce, Eddie Foy, Jr., Weber and Fields, Edward Arnold, Warren William, Leo Carrillo, and Ernest Truex.

"Zanuck not only had me making dogs at Twentieth

Century-Fox, he loaned me out to Paramount, Columbia, Warner Brothers, and RKO.

"I'll admit a few of the pictures were pretty good: *The Lady Eve, The Male Animal, Jesse James,* and *The Ox-Bow Incident,* but as for the rest, I wouldn't even want to mention 'em!"

After three weeks of rest and tests, Frances returned home.

"It was as though she'd been away on a vacation," Fonda says. "She looked refreshed and ready to get back to the preparations for the house."

In 1941 they moved to 600 Tigertail Road. Their place was designed and built to look like a hundred-year-old rambling Pennsylvania Dutch farmhouse. It was surrounded by vines and flowers. Beyond them were flagstone walks that allowed grass to crop up between the stones. Inside, it was a combination of antiquity and efficiency. While everything appeared to be Early American, one of the first deep freezers stored the Fondas' food. Upstairs, Frances converted a closet into an office and keys to every lock in the place hung from a ring as a testimony to her good housekeeping.

Outside there was a pool that had the appearance of an old-fashioned swimming hole, and a smaller building they called the playhouse. Pan, Jane, and Peter and their companions used it during the day, but at night Frances and Henry took over.

"The playhouse had an enormous mantel at one end of the main room with a fireplace so huge you could walk into it," Fonda says. "There was a barbecue inside of that. We copied it from pictures of old fireplaces. The kids' toys were all around, rocking horses, dollhouses, sets of blocks, everything boys and girls collect during their childhood. Then there was a round table in the center of the room where we sometimes laid a green felt cover, and we'd have poker games."

Fonda cultivated most of the nine acres. He planted grass and cut it and put it into haystacks. "The kids liked to bounce on the hay." He had chickens in a coop and four or five elevated rabbit hutches. He collected his own eggs from his chickens, and he grew his own vegetables.

"This was the beginning of the war crunch," Fonda says. "The President told us to have Victory Gardens and I had one of the first.

"Around this time, a little magazine was published called *Organic Gardening and Farming*. I was one of the earliest subscribers. That's when I decided to be an organic farmer, and I still am."

Henry bought Frances's daughter a horse. Then he had a stable built to house it. After that he bought two burros for Jane and Peter. "Peter never liked horses any more than I did," Fonda says, "but Jane became a real horse-woman."

When the treacherous Sunday of December 7, 1941, arrived, Hollywood along with the rest of the nation went to war. The disgrace of moving Americans of Japanese ancestry to relocation camps in the desert was matched by the censored but truthful stories of Japanese submarines surfacing and shelling the California, Oregon, and Washington coastal towns and cities. Los Angeles browned out streetlamps, black air-raid curtains went up on all windows that showed light at night. Air-raid wardens patrolled the streets, the Stage Door Canteen for servicemen opened, and the production of almost all movies went over to what the Germans called propaganda films and what Americans dubbed public service pictures. They all dealt with how we were on the verge of beating the Axis Powers, or *were* beating them even when we were not.

A Hollywood joke circulated around town. "In case of an air raid," the story went, "go directly to RKO. They haven't had a hit in years."

Hollywood's leading men began entering the armed services. James Stewart went into the Air Corps. Tyrone Power into the Marines, Clark Gable into the Army; Robert Taylor, Gig Young, Robert Montgomery—all went into uniform. The dressing rooms at the studios emptied out as the ranks of the armed forces swelled.

"I registered for the draft right off," Fonda says. "I had another idea, too. Frances and I talked it over."

"The Navy?" Frances asked, hardly believing his words.

"That's it," Fonda told his wife after the children had been put to bed one evening.

"But you're exempt."

"I know."

"You have three dependents. Why, Hank?"

"I still look like a baby."

"You mean you're self-conscious about being out of uniform?"

"I mean," Fonda said, "that the wives and mothers of a lot of soldiers and sailors'll see me on the screen and say, 'Why isn't he out there?' "

"What about the picture you're shooting?"

"It'll end soon enough. Frances, I don't want to do any more movies. I don't want to sell war bonds or be photographed with soldiers and sailors. I want to *be* a sailor."

"Duty?"

"You said it. I didn't."

"Patriotism?"

"Frances, this is my country and I want to be where it's happening. I don't want to be in a fake war in a studio or on location. I'm not crazy about the idea of getting hurt, but I want to be on a real ocean not the back lot. I want to be with real sailors not extras."

"In other words," Frances sighed, "you want the genuine article."

"That's just about it."

Husband and wife thrashed it over endlessly in the snug playhouse up in the hills. Their conversations always ended the same way.

"If you must, you must," Frances said, "and if you do, you'll go with my blessing."

The picture being shot at the time was a film Fonda had chosen and fought to have made, *The Ox-Bow Incident*. The day after he completed it, he drove to Naval Headquarters in downtown Los Angeles, volunteered for active service, and signed his enlistment papers. No photographers had been tipped off, there was none of the usual hoopla attending the induction of a screen personality. A group of young men stood before an office who administered the oath.

"I, Henry Fonda," he repeated, "do solemnly swear that I will support and defend the constitution of the United States against all enemies, foreign and domestic;

that I will bear true faith and allegiance to the same; and that I will obey the orders of the President of the United States and the orders of the officers appointed over me, according to the regulations and the uniform code of military justice. So help me God."

Because he enlisted as opposed to being drafted, he was given a twenty-four-hour pass and told to return the following morning. After dinner that night he packed a small hand case with a toothbrush, toothpaste, razor, shaving soap, comb, and hairbrush. When he slipped in the snapshots of Frances, the children, and his two sisters, his wife left the room for a few minutes. When she returned she was composed again.

As ordered, he returned to the induction center and was sent to boot camp in San Diego.

"When I got there," Fonda says, "the Shore Patrol picked me up and shipped me right back to where I'd come from.

"Why? Because Darryl F. Fuck-It-All Zanuck had pull in Washington and demanded, 'I want Henry Fonda for a picture I'm planning. It's for the war effort and I need him.' And he had enough weight to swing it.

"So there I was back in Imperial Valley, California, in the hottest part of the desert, making a film called *The Immortal Sergeant*.

"It was a silly picture. You want to hear the plot? I won World War II single-handed!

"They let me go back to Tigertail for one last night. It was harder to leave this time than before. After dinner I went upstairs and kissed Jane and Pan good-bye. To hell with the nurse and her wishes. These were my kids and I was going off to war and I honest to God didn't know what would happen, so I kissed Peter; he was too little to know, but he kissed me back. Jane had some idea of what was going on and I gave her an extra hug and left before either child could see my crying.

"In the morning I dressed slowly. While Frances and the children slept, I walked through the house, and then outside around the grounds. A last look, I suppose you'd call it."

By ten A.M., Henry Fonda, thirty-seven-year-old actor, sat in a bus filled with nervous but noisy college-age boys and headed south toward San Diego, the United States Navy—and a real war.

CHAPTER
7

In the vast machinery of the Navy, Apprentice Seaman Henry Fonda went from being a celebrity to a serial number. He began at boot camp in San Diego.

"Orange juice and oatmeal, bacon and eggs, steak, a baked potato, and milk. That was breakfast," Fonda says.

For a man who in private life ate a piece of toast and sipped a cup of coffee, his diet switched overnight.

"In the Navy," Fonda says, "it was up at four in the morning, run a mile the first week, two miles the second week, three miles the third week. Back to the parade ground, calisthenics, and then the chow line."

Had he been presented with a breakfast the size the Navy served two months earlier, Fonda would have left the table. In boot camp all that running, all that climbing, and all that jumping made it easy to wolf down the calories.

"For the first time in my life I gained weight," Fonda says. "In the old days Jim Stewart and I were both rakes, we were so skinny. We'd actually gone to the 'Strong Man' at MGM who'd given us special exercises to build muscles onto our skinny arms. We tried everything and nothing worked for us."

In boot camp it made no difference that Henry Fonda had been a movie actor. Now he was just another trainee—a man three years away from forty. On one side of the fence around the base were salutes, on the other side slogans.

"Loose Lips Sink Ships," wall posters warned.

"Praise the Lord and pass the ammunition," radios blared.

"Hurry up and wait," servicemen muttered.

At the end of eight weeks he got his white cap: Ordinary Seaman Third Class. It had been years since he'd had such lowly billing. Even more astonishing, he had absolutely no lines, nothing to say at all. Others gave *him* orders; petty officers, chiefs, lieutenants, commanders. Still, Henry Fonda was more than satisfied with that white cap he'd earned. He was a full-fledged sailor in the United States Navy, ready to serve under wartime conditions.

"At first I wanted to be a gunner's mate," Fonda says. "We were in a shooting war and gunners did the shooting, so I thought I'd like to be where the action was, but in boot camp, you not only ran and drilled, you also had to fill out questionnaires and take tests."

Over the public address system one evening he heard his name.

"Fonda, Henry J.," the metallic voice boomed. "Report to Company Headquarters."

He ran on the double, vaulted the three or four stairs to the Headquarters building, and threw open the door. There he faced a grizzled, old Chief Petty Officer who had red service stripes going up his right sleeve from his cuff to his elbow.

"Fonda?" the chief rasped.

"Yes, sir."

"I see here you put in for gunner's mate."

"That's right, Chief."

"You know what the fuckin' gunners' mates do in this man's fuckin' Navy?"

"Well, I thought . . ."

"Trouble with guys like you, Fonda, is you think too much at the wrong time. Listen, for Chris' sake, to an old China hand and you'll learn somethin'. Now these here tests you took . . ."

And the Chief held up a batch of papers.

"You remember 'em?"

"Yes, sir."

"Well, they say you're too smart to be some fuckin' gunner's mate. You're officer material."

"I don't want to be an officer," Fonda spoke up. "I'll be stuck on some damn shore station doing public relations work for the rest of the war."

"And you wanna go sailin' on the pretty ocean?"

"I'd like to, Chief."

"Okay, wise-ass," the Chief said as he stamped Fonda's orders. "Sixteen weeks in Quartermasters' School. Outside!"

"Now, a quartermaster is an assistant to the navigator," Fonda says. "In grade school I'd been really lousy in arithmetic. I had to learn trigonometry, square root, and how to use navigational equipment. That meant cramming math every free hour I had. I bought two or three books and studied like I'd never studied in college.

"I also had to learn Navy communications, wigwag, which is not semaphore, but Morse code with flags, blinker signals, and flag hoists, and you'd better, by God, have it right! Sixteen weeks in San Diego and I came out a quartermaster third grade. That's as low as you can get, and I was as qualified as a signalman third. The Navy shipped me to Seattle, where I was to become a member of the crew of a new destroyer, the U.S.S. *Satterlee*."

The *Satterlee* stood in the ways of the Todd Shipyard.

On a day early in May 1943 the captain of the *Satterlee* arrived and the sea trials of his ship began.

"I don't remember his name," Fonda says, "but he looked about eight feet tall. Years later, when Herman Wouk wrote *The Caine Mutiny*, I understood it right off. My first commander was a Captain Queeg."

The ship was commissioned and steamed to San Diego. It had a full complement of men save one. A signalman third grade was missing. Could Quartermaster Third Fonda also stand the signalman's watch? The phrase at the time was "There's a war on!" Fonda assumed both responsibilities.

Standing double watches, as a quartermaster third and a signalman third, meant Fonda had twice the work of any man on board. He was grateful for the time he spent below deck asleep in a hammock or gulping down the ever-present coffee that the Navy keeps hot through all watches. The weight he put on in boot camp began to disappear. When they made port at San Diego the crew was given a week's liberty. Thumbing his way up the coast highway, Henry Fonda returned to his family.

He couldn't remember a better week. Mike, the Great Dane, barked and leaped high at the sight of his master. Three-year-old Peter rode triumphantly on his father's shoulders. Jane grabbed his hand and tugged him up the driveway. Pan raced down to meet him, and Frances waved from the doorway, her cheeks actually blushed.

Fonda changed into his civilian clothes, dug in the garden, played with his children, made love to his wife. He checked the hundreds of bushes and dozens of trees he'd planted before they moved to Tigertail. Some evenings at sundown the family sat outdoors and Henry felt enveloped by the aromas of sumac, wild strawberries, and pine. After he returned to the Navy, a letter from home could bring back those sweet-smelling odors and remove him from the world of war for a moment or two.

Back in San Diego Fonda was told to report to the ship's executive officer. He knocked on the exec's door, entered, and saluted.

"Quartermaster Third Fonda reporting as ordered, sir."

"Fonda," the exec said, "I've got a piece of paper here instructing me to send you to Ninety Church Street."

"Sir?"

"That's Naval Headquarters in New York. It seems they want to make an officer out of you."

"I don't know anything about that, sir."

"But," the exec glanced up, "it's going to put us in a spot if we have to send you back now because we're going to be shoving off tomorrow and we'll be leaving without a quartermaster third and a signalman third."

"Well, sir," Fonda explained, "if the department wants me to be an officer, I'd like a chance to get as much Navy under my belt as possible."

"Good," the executive officer nodded. "That'll be all."

"Yes, sir." Fonda snapped off a salute, did an about-face and left the cabin.

The next day the *Satterlee* and three other destroyers got under way as escort vessels for the British aircarft carrier *Victoria*.

"I enjoyed the navigator's duties, but the signalman's part was a nightmare," Fonda says. "I had to stand out on a little platform off the bridge. It was just a small slab of gray metal with holes punched into the bottom of it so that it drained easily if we took on water. It had a low chain to protect you from falling overboard. Next to you was the blinker light, and below you was your striker, an ordinary seaman who bent on the flag signals you ordered or wrote down the code coming in from the blinker light on the flagship—in this case, it was the *Victoria*.

"Now, about ten feet in front of me was the surface lookout. He was an apprentice seaman who was given a pair of binoculars and told to look for a ship, a torpedo, a submarine. On this four-hour watch going south to the Panama Canal we ran into some heavy weather, and the *Satterlee* was bucking and tossing like a horse with a burr under its saddle. And the lookout was some towheaded kid from the Kansas wheat fields who'd never seen salt water before. In about twenty minutes, he started to get seasick, and gale-force winds blew it back at me.

"I had enough trouble squinting through the long glass trying to read the signals and ordering what flags to be bent on without him. I didn't know how he could eat, but sure as hell I knew he did. He was all right when we went through the Panama Canal, but as soon as we got into the Atlantic, he started up again."

Nobody was more relieved than Henry Fonda when the *Satterlee* tied up safely in Norfolk, Virginia.

"I was one of the men who got shore leave," Fonda says. "The signalman first and I had become very good friends, and we both went out and got reeling drunk together. I hadn't been that liquored up since the Madison Square Hotel. It was daylight when we came back aboard. I had my seabag packed and I don't think I saw anybody except the officer of the deck who winked as I left the ship.

"I had the orders the exec had given me to report to Ninety Church Street in New York, and about eight o'clock in the morning I zigzagged into the naval training station in Norfolk. It was a big place with yeomen, WAVES, and officers. One of them recognized me. He also recognized I was blind drunk, so he put me into a room and sent in black coffee until I was at least sober enough to take orders. Eventually, they got me onto the northbound train. I can't tell you how long the ride was because I was so hung over, but by the time we got to New York, I was able to check myself into a YMCA and sleep the night through.

"Next day I pulled myself together and reported, as ordered. Everything after that happened fast. First, I had to be discharged as an enlisted man, and a second later I was sworn into the Navy again as a Lieutenant Junior Grade. Then they handed me my new orders which were to report to the Navy Department in Washington. Before I left, though, I got some officer's uniforms, blues and whites. In the early winter of 1943 I reported to Washington.

"Dammit! They informed be I'd been assigned to make training films," Fonda says. "There I was with a gold stripe and a half on my sleeve bellowing and bitching to a three-striper, a full commander. But luck was with me. The commander, stuck behind a desk himself, understood how I felt. And when I told him about air combat intelligence, he had orders cut that sent me to Officer Candidate School at Quonset, Rhode Island."

Quonset was boot camp all over again, but instead of farm boys and kids fresh out of high school, Fonda found himself with mayors of towns such as Henning, Mississippi, or district attorneys from large cities in Ohio or young judges from Philadelphia—grown, mature, highly intelligent men. As he had over a year earlier, Fonda turned up at the head of his class. He became drillmaster of his company, and as he had drilled his ROTC boys in high school, and the apprentices in boot camp, Fonda barked his fellow trainees into the best drill team on the base.

When his training period as an officer was over, Fonda had his choice of duty. He selected air combat intelligence.

One day an ACI officer, who had served a tour of duty in the Pacific, returned to lecture the new men.

"Don't fill up your seabags with blues and whites," he told Fonda's class. "You won't need them and they'll just get in the way. Take tropical khakis and take lots of them because they're going to be in the wash most of the time.

"More importantly, take all the liquor you can carry," the officer said, lowering his voice. "Now, it's a well-known fact that liquor is not allowed in the United States Navy, not on any shore installation, not aboard any ship. But you will find that it is barter. Don't take it because you want a drink, but you might find yourself in a position where your admiral wants a jeep or a shore boat or whatever it is, and the only way you can get that jeep or that shore boat or whatever is with a jug of something."

That was experience talking and Fonda listened carefully. Work in the ACI rooms intensified. The silhouettes of aircraft and ships flashed on and off the screens in shorter bursts.

"I'm going to brag a little," Fonda says. "When we graduated, I was at the top. It was the sort of work that required almost instantaneous reaction in addition to a helluva good memory. That's one thing I've always had: the ability to memorize. If I read the theatrical page of the Los Angeles *Times* twice and concentrate, I've got it down cold!"

Upon completion of the course, Lt. Fonda was granted a week's leave. Before Fonda caught the crowded train to California, he stopped at the Post Exchange and loaded up with items that were hard for civilians to come by: Hershey bars for the kids and cartons of cigarettes and nylon stockings for Frances. And following the advice of the veteran ACI officer who had returned from the Pacific, he bought fourteen bottles of the best bourbon and wrapped them carefully in shirts and other goods that insured them against being broken. All of this he lowered carefully into a parachute bag with two canvas grips on the ends. Clear across the country, Fonda allowed no one to carry that bag except himself.

The children were rapturous about the Hersheys and the sight of their father. Of course his appearance in an officer's uniform puzzled them a bit. The blue of the seaman's uniform hadn't been much different from the denims he'd worn around the house, but the brass buttons on his coat now and the insignia on his collar and cap didn't fit in with their image of Daddy.

He watched them do laps for him in the swimming pool and he encouraged them to do more. He'd even get into his own trunks and swim beside them. The week drifted away as easily as the water sloshed over the sides of the pool. Without the children realizing it, Daddy had his last dinner at home . . . for quite awhile.

By now each child had a private room.

Henry knocked at Pan's door. She was a big girl, ready for adolescence. He entered, went to her bed, and kissed her good-bye.

Next he barged into Peter's room and caught him out of bed. His father carried him back and tucked him in. A long good-bye kiss for Peter and many promises by Daddy to write. Peter was not yet four and not quite certain yet why Daddy was going and where.

Jane sat up in bed waiting for him.

"Sing me a song, Daddy," she asked.

"Well," Fonda says, "her mother or the nurse had been singing songs before they kissed her good night, and I wondered what she liked. I couldn't think of a song for a child, and then I finally remembered one Harriet and I used to sing.

"When I finished," Fonda says, "Jane sat there smiling. And then I asked her to sing me a song. Well, she looked at her doll for a minute and then she nodded. She was attending the Brentwood Town and Country Day School at the time and their song went to the tune of 'Anchors Aweigh,' and out of this sweet little mouth came this strong earnest voice.

'Heads up and shoulders back,
That's the way to stand.
Fill up your lungs
And let them hear you shout to beat the band.
No matter where you are,
Make people say:

That child's a credit to
The Brentwood Town and Country School. Hooray!'

"I'm supposed to be this unemotional, immovable character," Fonda says, "but after I kissed Jane and left her
room, I stood outside her door, pulled out a handkerchief,
and wiped my eyes. Isn't that a crazy thing to react to? I
listened to her singing that song and suddenly, I didn't
want to leave my family."

Frances accompanied him to San Francisco where they
spent a week at the Mark Hopkins Hotel awaiting further
instructions. When his orders arrived, they took a taxi to
the naval base. Fonda kissed his wife good-bye.

"Take care of the kids, Frances, and take care of yourself," Fonda told her.

Frances squeezed his hand.

"I'm not going to war, Hank," she said. "You are.
Good luck."

"Thanks." He started toward the restricted area, and
when he turned around to look back, Frances was gone.

In Seattle a Dutch freighter took Fonda and a group of
ACI officers to Pearl Harbor.

All the while, from Rhode Island to Los Angeles to
San Francisco to Seattle to Honolulu, Lt. Fonda carried
his parachute bag with its precious cargo of bourbon for
barter.

In Kaneohe, Hawaii, he received a two-week intensified
course in antisubmarine warfare, how to search and
destroy enemy undersea craft by sea and air. A crash
form of instruction, it came close to but not really near
combat. Upon completion of the course, he was assigned
to the staff of Vice Admiral John H. Hoover, who served
directly under Fleet Admiral Chester W. Nimitz, the U.S.
Naval Commander in the Pacific.

Along with his orders he was given a dispatch case and
made an officer-courier. In February 1944 Naval Air
Transport flew him directly to the recently taken atoll of
Kwajalein, key to the Gilbert Island Group. There Lt.
(j.g.) Henry Fonda got his first glimpse of the fighting
Navy.

"It was an awesome sight," Fonda says. "The lagoon

was enormous and it was filled with battleships and carriers and cruisers and destroyers. That lagoon stretched so far out I couldn't see all of the ships.

"My first duty was to report to the carrier that flew Admiral Nimitz' flag. The dispatches were for him. A shore boat stood ready to take me out to the *Essex* where Nimitz made his headquarters. There was a Quonset hut nearby, sort of a ticket office, only it was Navy.

"I've got to go out there and deliver this stuff," Fonda told the Chief Petty Officer in charge of the Quonset. "Is it all right if I stow this parachute bag back underneath your counter?"

"Of course, sir," the Chief answered. "May I give you a hand, sir?"

"No, no, no, no," Fonda told him quickly. "I'll do it myself."

"Yes, sir. Anything the lieutenant says, sir."

After Fonda had secured his gear he drove down to the docks and presented his orders to the officer in charge. He received immediate attention and was assigned to a launch about fifteen or eighteen feet long. An ensign stood behind the wheel, and when Fonda sat down, the junior officer called, "Cast off fore and aft!" And with that they were under way to the *Essex*.

"Even in the lagoon," Fonda says, "the water was so choppy that within minutes my hat and face were taking spray from every third wave. By the time we came alongside the *Essex* I needed a towel. A couple of sailors grabbed the lines of the launch and I hopped onto a little platform. I looked at the companionway on the carrier. It was a shaky set of steps with a heavy rope running upward. It was like climbing five flights of stairs on the outside of a building, straight up.

"Well, I got through the ship and into the executive officer's quarters. He took the packet for the Admiral, I saluted and started back.

"When I returned to the Quonset hut, I found that some son-of-a-bitch had loaded my parachute bag onto a departing plane. Then someone else figured it didn't belong there and hurled it onto the steel-webbed runway. After that, it was chucked back under the counter.

"I had carried that bag in my lap for eight thousand miles, on trains, troopships, trucks, jeeps, and airplanes. Like a baby. I had five changes of khaki and fourteen bottles of Old Taylor. And when I reached under to get my gear, the bag was dripping and I could smell whiskey all over the Quonset hut. I felt free to beat the beejeesus out of all hands but I figured it was wrong for enlisted men to see an officer crying.

"Now I want you to get this picture. There goes Henry Fonda, boy scout, eager beaver reporting for his first sea duty as a naval officer, slightly damp from the voyage to the *Essex*, my parachute bag dripping the best bourbon money can buy.

"But that was not enough. The coxswain of the boat that was taking me out to Admiral Hoover and the *Curtis* thought I was still a movie actor and forgot all his lessons. He took so much water over the side that we had to stop and bail out four times to keep from swamping. Drenched to the skin, I finally climbed the ladder of the *Curtis*, saluted the flag, saluted the officer of the deck, and asked for permission to come aboard. He looked at me as though I had come out from shore using the sidestroke.

"The hour that it took me to check in with all departments seemed, at the time, like the sorriest hour of my life. Standing there dripping salt water and Old Taylor and trying to brave the looks of disbelief by acting as though that was the way I always reported aboard, I allowed myself to be shunted from place to place.

"Once in my room I took off the seaweed and unpacked my bag. There was one shirt and one pair of pants on top that looked all right except for some big blue stains from a leather shaving kit that had dissolved. The rest of my clothes were soaked. Four or five bottles of whiskey had exploded. They were just like sand, not glass.

"I gave up trying to wring out my clothes and put them all in my laundry bag and staggered out onto the deck for some fresh air."

That night Fonda says he slept with his head out of the porthole. The next day the odor from the laundry bag reached the bridge. The third day the Executive Officer of the *Curtis* homed in on the odor.

"Mister Fonda?" he asked.

"Yes, sir?"

"Where's that stink coming from?"

"What stink, sir?"

"Mister Fonda!" the exec glowered.

"From my laundry bag, sir."

"Are those the only clothes you have?"

"Yes, sir, except for the ones I'm wearing."

"Mister, we can't have the ship smelling of Kentucky bourbon. It's not only against Navy regulations, it'll make the damn crew thirsty as hell. Understand?"

"I do, sir."

"Then strip to the buff and I'll send a hand for your laundry. We'll have it done right away."

"Thank you, sir."

"You understand, laundry on this ship goes out once a week."

"Yes, sir."

"But these are emergency conditions. That'll be all, mister."

Aboard the *Curtis* Fonda developed a greater reputation because of "l'affaire bourbon" than because of his previous film and stage appearances. As soon as he was properly attired he reported to Admiral Hoover. COM-FORPAC, or Commander Forward Area Pacific, gave no sign of acknowledging the junior officer who stood rigidly before him.

"He was abrupt, aloof, superior—just like a top officer should be," Fonda says. "He sat there behind the desk—in a way, he reminded me of Pappy Ford. It seems my life is full of going someplace and facing the Admiral!"

Following this brief meeting with his ranking officer Fonda was assigned to the ACI group aboard the *Curtis*. He was also reassigned to new quarters. In the five-by-eight cabin was a set of double-decked bunks, a small desk, a chair, and a pair of lockers. No question existed as to who would occupy the lower bunk and who would have the upper, inches away from the gray ceiling. His roommate was Lt. Commander John Dinkelspiel, formerly a prominent San Francisco lawyer, who presently served as Flag Secretary to Admiral Hoover.

"I was on the ship when Hank Fonda came aboard," Dinkelspiel remembered. "He was a modest man at all times—a calm customer and a very competent naval officer. He stood his watches along with the other officers and did his chores to a point where one would not know he was a quote unquote famous personage."

Throughout the time Fonda served in the Pacific Theater of Operations the white hats, the enlisted men, whispered about who had come aboard. Everyone knew who Fonda was. Everyone except senior officers. Not one of them ever recognized him as anything but a Lieutenant (j.g.). And that was fine with Fonda. He went to war to serve as an ACI officer and that's just what he did.

Admiral Hoover had what in theater parlance would have been called a running gag with Admiral Nimitz. Whenever it became necessary to deliver written messages from COMFOR to COMPAC, Mister Fonda almost always would be assigned to carry them from the *Curtis* to whatever ship flew Nimitz' flag. Nimitz never let on to Fonda's civilian identity. He would receive the dispatches Fonda handed him, nod, and return the salute.

Hoover finally broke down and started talking to Fonda, but not about movies.

"The doorways on ships are called hatches," Fonda says. "They're watertight and fireproof sections that can be sealed. There's about a foot of steel you have to step over when you're going through one, and about another foot of steel you have to duck under if you're the slightest bit tall.

"I'm six-foot-one-and-a-half inches, and on my way in to see the Admiral one morning I forgot to duck while going through one of the hatches and I gave my forehead a helluva smack. I mean I went into Admiral Hoover's cabin with blood streaming down my face."

"Mister Fonda?" the Admiral asked in astonishment. "Is that blood I see?"

"Yes, sir."

"Your own?"

"Yes, sir. I just bumped my forehead on a hatch, sir."

"I don't know if this vessel was built to take that kind of punishment, mister. After this please be more careful with my ship. Report to sick bay and have 'em stop that blood. Dismiss!"

Fonda did as ordered. After the doctor had staunched the flow from his forehead, several of his fellow officers urged him to put in for a Purple Heart.

"The doctor had lots more to do than worry about me," Fonda says. "There were men going ashore on those islands taking small-arms fire, mortar rounds, grenade fragments, and artillery shrapnel.

"A couple of weeks later our ship moved on to the next island, Eniwetok. We steamed in and made anchor—the Navy calls it swinging on the hook. It was terrible to see how battered everything was, but the Seabees went right to work. They leveled the ground and built an airstrip and Quonset huts before you could say, 'Where's the warm beer?'

"The route we were carving out became the Broadway of the Pacific. It began in San Francisco, went due west to Hawaii, then onto Kwajalein, Eniwetok, Guam, Saipan, Tinian, Iwo Jima, and Tokyo."

There were side streets to Broadway and they were called Guadalcanal and New Guinea and the Gilberts and Wake.

Every time General Quarters sounded aboard the *Curtis*, most hands rushed to battle stations.

"When we were under bombardment everyone had to go on deck. I was assigned to battle stations only three or four times in the whole war. But I still had to get up there. I'd put on my helmet and life preserver according to naval regulations and move fast!" Fonda says.

At first the incoming bombs and outgoing gunfire was a truly frightening experience for Fonda.

"Our guns would be firing and bombs would be dropping all around, and I'd crawl onto the flag bag. That's where the flags were stored, and it had a canvas cover over it," Fonda says. "Well, yes, in the beginning I was scared as hell, but I was so exhausted that after a while the goddamn noise lulled me to sleep."

When short periods of liberty came Fonda would go

ashore at whatever island the *Curtis* dropped anchor at and enter the nearest officers' club. With luck there would be a bar. With greater luck there would be a piano. When "Anchors Aweigh" was banged out, Fonda taught his fellow officers the version his daughter sang.

"Months afterward, when I'd walk into an officers' club on Saipan or Tinian or Guam," Fonda says, "I'd hear men singing about 'The Brentwood Town and County School. Hooray!' They didn't know what the school was or where it was at, but it reminded them of kids, and they hadn't seen kids in months, maybe years. Many of them had children of their own, and those who didn't thought it was a funny version of the Navy song. It became popular all over the Pacific."

Shortly before the battle of Leyte Gulf where the Japanese lost twenty-six combat ships and the Americans only six, Fonda found time to write his son, Peter.

His words were solicitous and caring. In letters Fonda could reach out and touch the hearts of the people he loved—and even reveal much that he kept hidden and couldn't express in person.

Tuesday, 10 October

My Dearest Son—

I had a letter from Mummy today, and she said that you had been thinking of me—and wondering what I was doing. And now I am sitting here and wondering how I can tell you what I am doing. I am thinking about *you* so much and so often that it never occurs to me to think about you thinking about me. When I think about you I always put myself right near you, at home—I think about working in the garden and having you work beside me—and every now and then you will say to me, "Daddy, I'm a good boy." And when I go down the hill to the stable you call out to Mackie. "Mackie, I'm going with Daddy!" So you see I think of myself as being at home when I think of you—and I forget that it must be hard for you to realize how far away I am—and what I'm doing. I am living now on a big ship, and we are anchored in the harbor of an island way across the

Pacific Ocean—this island was held by the Japs until a short time ago. I don't mean to give the impression that I took it away from them by myself—there were quite a few Marines that helped me.

I have a little room about as big as your bathroom that I share with another officer and I sleep in the top bunk of a doubledecked bunk like in a Pullman train—but of course you've never been in a train, that's silly. Most of the walls of the room are covered with pictures of you and Lady and Pan sitting on the blue seat out by the pool—and if I look a little to the right, there you are when you were just a baby, sitting on Mummy's lap with your finger in your mouth and Little Lady is standing behind Mummy playing with her hair—and Pan is sitting on the grass beside you patting Mike—and just a little more to the right and I can see you leaning over the bars in your play yard, laughing and looking right at me, and I can almost hear you say, "Hi, Dad!" And if I listen real carefully I can hear somebody say, "Look what I'm doing, Daddy" and I look over to the left and there is Lady leaning on her bicycle—and further over I can see you and Lady sitting on a haystack—and if I turn around I could see all of you playing together—but I won't turn around now or I won't ever finish this letter.

I know there is no good in my trying to explain to you why I am away from home—war doesn't make any sense even when you are grown up—but I think that someday you will understand why I had to be in it.

It's not natural for a father to be away from his family as long as I have had to be—ordinarily a boy grows up and has his father right with him all the time—but we are unlucky, because a war had to come along, and a lot of fathers had to go away—and a lot of young sons have had to puzzle it out and wonder where Dad went and what he is doing.

I'm not always sure of what I'm doing—but I know *why* I'm doing it—to get the whole thing over with as soon as possible so that I can come home again and live with my family and watch my children grow up.

Good night, Son—give Mummy and Lady a big hug and kiss for me and be a good boy—Dad.

Two weeks later, he wrote his six-year-old daughter an appreciative, warm, funny thank-you letter.

Tuesday, 24 October

My Darling Lady—

I was so surprised the other day to get a big brown envelope in the mail—and I couldn't imagine what it was—it was much bigger than the envelopes that Mummy's letters come in and it felt very heavy and mysterious—I was very busy when it arrived, and I had to leave it on my desk unopened—but all the time I kept wondering what it was and who had sent it to me—and finally my curiosity just got too much for me and I asked everybody to stop fighting the war long enough for me to go to my room and open the envelope.

Nobody felt like stopping fighting just then because they were fighting a pretty good war and the Japs were running away and they didn't want the Japs to get a chance to catch their breath—but a friend of mine said to me, "Why don't you run down to your room as though you were going to get a gun or something and the Japs won't know you are just going to open an envelope."

So that's what I did.

And when I opened it—first I found a little red, white, and blue hat box, and inside that I found a licorice kiss and an orange kiss and some green mint candy and a candy Easter egg.

Well—whoever in the world is sending these to me, I thought—and then I unfolded some papers that were in the envelope and there were drawings on all of them and one of them was a picture of a woman standing beside a fireplace and crying because her husband was away to the wars.

But why am I telling you all this, because you certainly know all about it because *you* drew them and *you* sent them to me. I ate all the candy except a small piece of mint that I left for a cockroach friend of mine who lives in my desk—and I took the pictures with me to show to some of my other friends—and when I got back the Japs were still running and everybody got a chance to look at the drawings—and they admired them very much—especially the one of the woman crying by the fireplace—and nobody would believe that I had a daughter who could draw like that—and when I told them that you could swim, too, and play the piano and went to Brentwood Town and Country School—they said, "You mean 'Brentwood Town and Country School, Hooray!'" And I said, yes—and we all sang two choruses and the Japs couldn't understand why were singing and so they ran faster.

> All My Love and Kisses—
> Dad

Stateside, as men on the ships called home, life was almost as different as it was for the fathers, husbands, sons, and sweethearts overseas. Civilians worked harder than they ever had before. They were more congenial and more comfortable sharing a common enemy. Their neighbors and acquaintances turned into family. They wept for each other when tragedy struck. When times were good, they went to every movie, scrambled for theater tickets, and at parties, some lost their inhibitions. Frances lost hers.

"Just between us . . ." and "Don't say I said so, but . . ." Fonda's friends confided to each other. Apparently,

Frances knitted for soldiers and sailors, wrapped bandages for the Red Cross, and to soothe her loneliness—had love affairs. Henry Fonda heard not a word of this for many years. The V-letters Frances sent him were cheery and optimistic. She told him about the movies she had screened for the children's birthdays. She was considerate enough not to write that when Jane saw him in *Drums Along the Mohawk*, the child grew terrified as the Indians chased her father, and hid her face in her hands.

Peter had a more agitated reaction to one of his father's films.

"I was four years old," Peter said, "and I went to see a movie with Lady and Pan and Mother. I looked up at that screen and there's Henry, my dad. I know it's him. I recognize him. I sat clenching my fists, watching this guy who looks like my father, sounds just like him. If he'd only give me a sign so I'd be sure.

"Now he's in a place with a lion. Big cage, big lion. Then the lion is out of the cage and he comes to a little door, and I realize my father is going to be eaten by a lion! I scrambled out of my seat, I raced up to the screen and started pounding like a mad banshee. I yelled, 'Watch out, watch out, Daddy!'

"My mother took me out of the projection room and told me, 'That's not your father, dear. That's a character named Chad Hanna.' I was hysterical. I wanted to explain that my dad ran away with the circus but I knew that I was four years old and they wouldn't take my word. 'Okay, you're right. My father is at war far away. That guy I just saw is Chad Hanna, Chad Hanna.'"

In addition to letters from his wife and children Leland Hayward sent him a cable informing him that John Swope and Dorothy McGuire had married.

"I couldn't believe it. They didn't even know each other when I went into the Navy," Fonda says. "My two dearest friends! I was delighted."

He saw Swope before he saw McGuire again. Swope had joined the Navy, and he and Fonda met in the Pacific. Tyrone Power, another of his friends, came through. Power was a Marine who ferried planes onto the island airfields. Inevitably, Bob Hope crossed his path.

166

Hope was on one of his many tours entertaining servicemen. Fonda requisitioned a jeep (perhaps some of that
bourbon was still around) and the two men drove from
one base to another.

"How do you like it out here?" the famous quipster
asked.

"Fine," Fonda replied.

The remainder of the ride went by in complete silence.

Letters from home proved pleasant interruptions to the
alternating hazards and tedium of war. During the quiet
times Fonda kept track of everything concerning his
family. He wrote notes for birthdays, anniversaries, and
on one occasion, when he'd heard his sister Jayne and his
brother-in-law John had become parents, this:

> Dearest Aunt Jayne and Uncle John:
>
> I sat at this same typewriter about five days ago
> and put a date to it and fingered out the same saluta-
> tion as above, and then as I sat choosing the immor-
> tal words that I was about to knock off to you, the
> war caught up with me in a censorable shape, and it
> all died aborning. It had come to me that you were
> about to foal, and I felt strongly that the occasion
> called for a few words chosen at random from Uncle
> Henry.
>
> Today, enclosed with a letter from my bride, comes
> Harriet's telegram about somebody arriving with a
> seven-pound bundle. I figure she's probably chair-
> man of an old clothes or wastepaper drive, and I'm
> very proud and show the telegram to all hands, but
> my yeoman, who went to teacher's college, said he
> thought she meant that somebody had a baby! Well,
> I immediately put two and two together.
>
> It's a fine and noble thing you are doing, and it's
> fun, too. I can barely remember.
>
> Can you remember Grandpa Fonda swinging his In-
> dian clubs and telling about the Civil War? I can. I

have been thinking about it just now while I sit stupidly in front of this machine. Thinking about your children and Harriet's children and when we were children and trying to recapture our childhood impressions. Grandpa's war was all drummer boys and carrying messages to the general on horseback. What am I going to tell my children . . . ?

What with this letter and fighting the war, it is now long past midnight and I'm beat. I think I might get home for thirty days in a couple of months. I wish I could tell you that I think it will all be over soon so that I won't have to come back out, but I don't.

Bless you both and think kindly of me.

Your loving brother,
Henry

Fonda did *not* get back in a couple of months, but the war lasted a shorter time than he had expected. The closer the Americans came to the home islands of Japan, the more intense the fighting grew. The *Curtis* no longer "swung on the hook." She followed directly behind the advancing troops during the "island hopping" strategy.

As the Americans recaptured Guam and conquered Saipan and Iwo Jima, the Japanese response took a dramatic form of retaliation: the kamikazes. These picked pilots had sworn to die with their planes as they attacked American ships. The first one Fonda saw was brought down by the gunfire from the *Curtis*. It plunged into the sea twenty-five yards from the ship.

As an intelligence officer Fonda felt it was his duty to salvage what information he could from the Japanese plane. The day after it hit the water Fonda and another officer rigged up a shallow-water diving gear and swam down to the fallen plane.

"It was down about thirty feet," Fonda says. "The two Japanese in it, the pilot and the bombardier, were upside down in their harnesses, hanging in their seats. It was an eerie sight. We got the maps and the flight plans and whatever else seemed of value and returned to the *Curtis*."

Kamikazes weren't the only offense the Japanese put up. Submarines came out of Tokyo Bay with increasing regularity. The closer the Americans approached, the shorter the run for the subs. The Americans, having broken the Japanese code, knew when a sub left its base and what its destination would be.

The Anti-Submarine School at Kaneohe, where Fonda studied, did the job well. Off Saipan Fonda received information on the movement of an undersea craft. On a thick sheet of Plexiglas he plotted a search pattern. Knowing the date of the submarine's departure and its estimated speed, he determined its location. Surface ships and airplanes were deployed. The search planes, PBYs and PB2Ys, converged on the area Fonda had reported.

He had done this dozens of times before for a parade of Admirals and other high-ranking officers.

"Where's the quarry, mister?" he would be asked.

"Where's the enemy, Fonda?"

He would point, they would nod and leave, and he'd hear nothing more about it. This time the surface ships went in, depth charges exploded in a variety of patterns.

The planes spotted the debris first. Floating on the sea were the remains of the Japanese submarine. Then the sub chasers and the destroyer escort vessels confirmed it. For his participation in the action Fonda was recommended for a Presidential Citation, and a Bronze Star.

"I must say," Lt. Commander Dinkelspiel recollected, "receiving a Bronze Star from Admiral Hoover was almost like the Congressional Medal of Honor from anybody else." Hoover had been an Annapolis graduate, and under his command everything went by the book. To get the medal Henry Fonda had to earn it.

The *Curtis* put in at Guam and Fonda and Dinkelspiel were given liberty.

While Fonda and Dinkelspiel were ashore, their ship headed out to sea. There a kamikaze pilot slammed his plane into the side of the *Curtis*, demolishing the photo lab and the cabin in which Fonda and his roommate bunked.

She came limping back into Guam battered and unseaworthy.

"I went down to look at her that evening," Fonda says. "Jeesus! If we'd stayed aboard we'd have been kilt!"

Admiral Hoover transferred his flag to a shore station and his command went with him. It was on Guam that Fonda heard of V-E Day.

"The German surrender meant just one thing to us," Fonda says. "More men and more ships would be coming out to us for what we believed would be a hard fight to take Japan."

A few days later Fonda and his immediate superior, a commander in charge of Air Operations under Admiral Hoover, flew up to Tinian. On that island they met the crew of a B-29. It was named *The Enola Gay.*

"I knew why we were there and I had a vague notion of what was going to happen the next day," Fonda says. "We had access, a very few of us in intelligence, to that kind of information. And we were the only ones. And when we returned to Guam, we didn't tell our shipmates."

They didn't have to. On August 6, 1945, *The Enola Gay* dropped the first atomic bomb over Hiroshima.

On August 15 Fonda pulled night duty at the communications desk.

"It was like the night shift at the Telephone Company in Omaha," Fonda says. "Eleven to seven. There wasn't much to do. Every fifteen minutes or every half hour a guy from Communications would come over with the dispatches. There never was anything urgent. If there was you'd wake up your commander. If it was *really* urgent you'd have him wake up the Admiral. That was pretty much night duty.

"That night I'm sitting there quietly when the guard comes in with a bunch of dispatches. And I'm going through them.

"And this one goes into this basket. And this one goes into Commander Koepke's basket. And this one is for Fonda, Lt. (s.g.) Henry, serial number so-and-so. 'Report

Number Two Priority, Washington, D.C. Duty Naval Radio Hour. Effective immediately.'

"Well, I am pissed off. I mean I am really pissed! Only the President of the United States has a Number One priority, and here I am—a man doing a job he's been trained to do. And now I'm sitting there steaming because I'm on a Number Two Priority. And that means, *go*. Now! To the goddamn Naval Radio Hour. I'd spent the whole war trying to avoid jobs like that, and while I'm sitting there I hear the loudest shout I ever heard going up from the Communications Quonset. And I can't imagine what the hell is happening until a guy comes in with the dispatches and the biggest grin you ever saw.

" 'Japan's given up,' he tells me.

" 'Are you saying the war's over, sailor?'

" 'It sure as hell is, sir. Hirohito just went on the Jap radio and told 'em they were finished.'

" 'This isn't just a lot of Navy shit, is it?'

" 'No sir. It's the real thing!' "

The sailor left and Fonda leaned back in his chair, lit a cigarette, and thought of what he and millions of others like him had been through.

"I wasn't pissed off anymore," Fonda says. "I was happier than I had been in years."

For the men who fought in the Pacific the battles stopped and another struggle began: how to get home? For some poor devils it was a matter of months.

Fonda, Lt. Henry, held a Number Two Priority. There was no question of who went first. He simply followed orders.

"I was out the day after the dispatch came in," Fonda says. "Like the night before leaving the *Satterlee* in Norfolk I got blind. There was a party and everyone was telling me what a lucky son-of-a-bitch I was, and I knew it and I agreed.

"And before I got on the plane there was a ceremony. They pinned these medals on me, and then we took off. I was drunk all the way to Christmas Island. And then, at the next stop, Johnson Island, I got off and drank all the water I could swallow because I had this hangover that was really terrible.

"Eventually, we reached Honolulu. I spent the night there, and because of my priority, they put me on a commercial plane for San Francisco. Suddenly, on that flight, I wasn't 'Mister Fonda' anymore. I was 'Hello, Henry.' "

"How are you, Henry?" an Admiral asked.

"I'm just fine, sir."

"Where're you headed?"

"I'm on my way to Washington, sir."

"Aren't you from Los Angeles?"

"Yes, sir. I am, sir."

"Well, Henry," the Admiral said, "I've got a little eight-seater waiting for me. How'd you like to fly down to Los Angeles and see the wife before you report to Washington?"

"Yes, sir. Thank you, sir." And then Fonda paused. "Does the Admiral mean I can have a lift with him?"

"That's the idea. If you'd like it, Henry."

"Yes, siree, sir. Thank you very much."

"I knew the war was over," Fonda says. "That Admiral did everything except ask for my autograph.

"We landed in Los Angeles just as President Truman made the official announcement of the Japanese surrender, and every siren and automobile horn in Greater Los Angeles went off. I thought to myself, 'Oh fellows, you didn't need to do that. Aw, you're overdoing it.'

"Anyway, it couldn't have been a more marvelous time to set down on United States soil. I took a taxi home.

"Frances didn't have any idea I was back until I kissed her. Jane was home and I gave her a hug and a kiss, too. It was about four o'clock in the afternoon and I took the station wagon and drove to the Brentwood Town and Country School to get Peter. I was able to park at the foot of the driveway where the kids always traipsed out of school.

"And sure enough, down came Peter. He recognized the station wagon, but not the officer who was standing beside it. He stopped. After looking at me for a moment, his eyes got as big as balloons. He remembered the man from the movie."

"Chad?" he asked cautiously.

"I picked him up and held him tight."

"No, son," I whispered. "Dad."

"And he threw his arms around my neck. Imagine! 'Chad.' That just cut me to pieces."

CHAPTER
8

COVERING everything and everyone like the fog that rolled in each morning from the Pacific was the quiet of peace. No more ship's bells for Fonda, no more klaxons calling all hands to General Quarters, no more living in cramped cabins and wardrooms with dozens of men. Now he gloried in the *real* rewards of victory.

Added to the simple joy of being home were the sights and sounds of civilian life—children's giggles, a lazy screen door squeaking shut, the swish of the automatic sprinkler spraying water over the thirsty August grass, a lawn mower in the distance, the dialing of a telephone, the voice of a friend.

Jane and Peter were allowed to stay up late and eat with their parents. Pan was at camp. Under the wartime food rationing that still remained in effect, meat was hard to come by. The cook and Frances had pooled their red ration stamps and managed to wheedle the butcher into locating and delivering a leg of lamb for the returning serviceman's first dinner.

After three years Henry Fonda sat at the head of his table. The faces of his family were as bright as the lighted tapers, and Jane had picked fresh flowers from the garden for the centerpiece. Peter was too excited to eat. Jane couldn't stop chattering. Frances was quiet and far more attractive than he remembered. But then none of them looked like the people in the photographs; Fonda had forgotten that time at Tigertail was not a still picture packed in his wallet or pasted on the gray steel bulkhead above his bunk aboard the *Curtis*.

Two days at home and Daddy left for Washington, D.C., and the Naval Radio Hour.

"That experience wasn't something I pigeonholed in my memory," Fonda says. "It lasted only four weeks. What I waited for was my honorable discharge from the Navy. I couldn't stand it till I shed those khakis. When I was mustered out, I bought me a white shirt and a charcoal-gray suit, and still sporting my crewcut from the service, I went up to New York looking for Jim Stewart.

"Now, Stewart had come back from the war a certified hero. I mean he was a chicken colonel in the Army Air Corps. He'd led the 703rd Squadron of the 445th Group in hundreds of bombing raids over Germany and he wore campaign ribbons with battle stars and oak-leaf clusters from above his left pocket damn near up to his shoulder.

"Did you know that Stewart's hometown in Pennsylvania gave him a hero's parade? The mayor invited *Life* magazine to cover the occasion. Well, the guy from *Life*, a famous photographer, Peter Stackpole, wanted more than just pictures of a parade, so he said to Jim, 'You're a small-town fella. I'll take pictures of you fishing.' Now, let me tell you, *I'm* a fisherman. Stewart ain't never been near a fish, maybe to eat one, but that's all. But you know, he wanted to be accommodating to *Life* magazine, and he felt too sheepish to say he couldn't fish.

"Stewart had a pal of his run over to the hardware store and pick up some tackle. Well, they wound up in a rented boat on a small lake near town." At this point Fonda tries to smother a laugh. "Stewart's in the middle of this boat, his friend is at one end, and the photographer is at the other end ready to take pictures. But Jim doesn't know how the hell to fish. He's staring at the hooks and the line and he finally thinks, 'Well, what can I lose? I'll try it.'

"Stackpole starts snapping the pictures and Stewart whips up the rod, there's a backlash, and the next thing he knows, he's caught Peter Stackpole, famous *Life* photographer, and hooked him right under the eyebrow. And

I don't have to tell you, Stewart's reactions aren't too fast. He just sat and looked.

"Jim told me that story during lunch at '21' and I practically slid under the table.

"We took in a couple of shows while we were in New York and then flew back to the Coast. Stewart had a slight problem.

"He'd rented his house while he was away, and according to the lease, he couldn't get rid of the tenants till the lease terminated. Well, hell! You can't leave a full colonel, who's a genuine hero, who's also been your roommate in New York and California, who double-dated with you and made the sacrifice of getting beet juice up his nose, you just can't leave that kind of guy out on the street. In Brentwood the police take a dim view of that. Especially if they see him wandering around after dark.

"So Frances and I invited him to stay in the playhouse until he got back his own place."

"Well, now, hold on, hold on," Stewart said. "There was a couch there that made up into a very comfortable bed, a kitchen, and a bathroom, and a shower. The Fondas thought they'd invited me for a weekend, and darned if I didn't stay for a month."

"It was *three* months," Fonda says emphatically. But how would he remember? After the war it was party time in California. Everyone gave parties.

"Marion Davies gave an annual to-do for the movie people. It was generally held at Miss Davies's beach house in Santa Monica. This one year the engraved invitation read, 'Costume Party. Theme: American Revolution.'

"Well, God! Just my kind of thing," Fonda says. "I suggested that Jim Stewart and Johnny Swope and I go as the Spirit of '76, but with a switch, the Marx Brothers dressed up as the Spirit of '76. They thought it sounded good.

"I collected the props, all kinds of stuff from the studio wardrobe department. Blue and white gold-buttoned Revolutionary uniforms, a Chico-kind of hat for Stewart, and a bandage for his head with the blood spot on it; a Harpo wig for Johnny, a Groucho cigar and a big mustache for me.

176

Beneath the X in the center of the second row stands Scout Fonda. He makes the mistake of closing his eyes before the camera. In later years he made sure this never happened.

HARRIET WARREN

The Fonda family in an arbor behind their Omaha home. William, Harriet, Henry (who knew how to take center stage), Jayne, and Herberta.

BETTMANN-SPRINGER ARCHIVE

His first paying job as an actor. Fonda toured the midwest with George Billinsa as Abe Lincoln. Fonda played Lincoln's military secretary.   BETTMANN-SPRINGER ARCHIVE

Sedate during the Roaring Twenties. Henry, Harriet, and Jayne Fonda.   OMAHA COMMUNITY PLAYHOUSE ARCHIVES

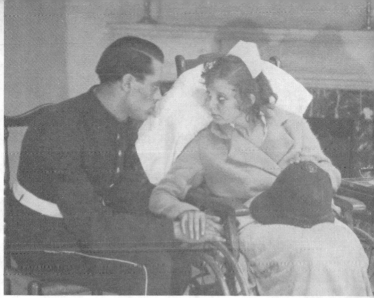

Henry Fonda and Margaret Sullavan in *A Kiss for Cinderella*. On stage he was earnest, she was ill. Off stage, they were falling in love.   PATRICIA SCOLL

Following his success in the Broadway production, Fonda played opposite Janet Gaynor in the film of *The Farmer Takes a Wife*. 1935.   BETTMANN-SPRINGER ARCHIVE

A really high society wedding. Frances and Henry Fonda as they left the church. New York. 1936.

John Steinbeck's character Tom Joad in *The Grapes of Wrath,* as interpreted by Henry Fonda, is probably the actor's single greatest dramatic role on the screen. 1940.

The seventeen-year-old he kissed near the Princeton stadium turned into Jezebel in the picture of the same name.
Bette Davis beams upon a supine Henry Fonda.

"I've been in love with her for years. Shirlee has gotten
used to it." Barbara Stanwyck tempts Henry Fonda in *The
Lady Eve*.

Peter Fonda's christening picture. Left to right: Harriet, Pan, Henry, Jane, Frances, Peter, Jayne, Grandma Sophie Seymour. PETER FONDA

See Jane jump over Daddy. Outside the house at Tigertail. California. 1940. BETTMANN-SPRINGER ARCHIVE

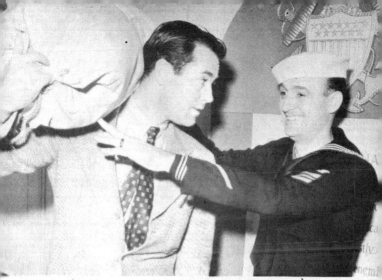

He's in the Navy now. Boot camp. San Diego, California. 1942.
BETTMANN-SPRINGER ARCHIVE

As quickly as they could, Lt. (s.g.) Henry Fonda, U.S. Navy, and Col. James Stewart, U.S.A.A.F., got out of their uniforms and into the Stork Club, 1945
BETTMANN-SPRINGER ARCHIVE

Back at Tigertail. Frances, Peter, Pan, Jane, and Henry—still sporting the flat-top from the Navy.
BETTMANN-SPRINGER ARCHIVE

At a costume party given by Marion Davies, three friends came as the Marx Brothers in the Spirit of '76. John Swope is Harpo, Fonda is Groucho, and James Stewart is Chico.
JOHN SWOPE

At Pearl Harbor, en route to the filming of *Mr. Roberts*. Jane, Peter, Henry, and Susan Fonda.　　SUSAN ADES

Mister Fonda as Mister Roberts, aboard the AK601 somewhere in the Pacific.　　BETTMANN-SPRINGER ARCHIVE

In the only film he produced, *12 Angry Men*. New York. 1957.   BETTMANN-SPRINGER ARCHIVE

Henry, Amy (the "White Sheep" of the family), and Afdera on the Riviera. 1956.   AFDERA FRANCHETTI FONDA

Never a lover of horse flesh, Fonda as *The Deputy*, the
first of two television series, approaching his mount with
something less than trust. BETTMANN-SPRINGER ARCHIVE

His agent, his producer, his friend, Leland Hayward earned
the right to joke as Fonda bathes.
BETTMANN-SPRINGER ARCHIVE

Wedding portrait. Mr. and Mrs. Henry Fonda. 1965.

If he didn't have the stage and the screen, Fonda would settle for the brush, the paints, the canvas, and the easel.
BETTMANN-SPRINGER ARCHIVE

"Ripening," an oil by Henry Fonda, in the collection of Norton Simon and his wife, Jennifer Jones.
BETTMANN-SPRINGER ARCHIVE

Henry Fonda and James Stewart are the mangy, scruffy cowpokes in *The Cheyenne Social Club*. Stewart inherits a house of ill-repute, Fonda tags along to keep him in trouble.

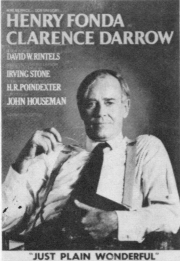

The window card tells the story. 1975.

"Frances gave me Jane and Peter. Susan gave me Amy, and I wouldn't give them up for the world, but my wish is that I'd been married to this one girl, Shirlee, all of my life." Outside their home in Bel Air.   JOHN SWOPE

Coloring Easter Eggs. Left to right: Troy Hayden, Jane, Tom Hayden, Shirlee, Henry, and Vanessa Vadim.
    SUZANNE TENNER

Half of the cast *On Golden Pond*. Katharine Hepburn, Henry Fonda, and Jane Fonda. Laconia, New Hampshire, during the golden summer of 1980. JANE FONDA

Jane, Henry, and Shirlee at home with Henry's Oscar. As many people predicted, he won the 1981 Academy Award for Best Actor for his performance in *On Golden Pond*. 1982. WIDE WORLD PHOTOS

"At Swope's we put on the outfits and the elaborate makeup. We were a sight. Swope announced, 'I've gotta get a picture of this.' He set his Rolleiflex up on a table, put the timer on, jumped back into position with us, and we took the proper poses."

Dorothy McGuire Swope and Frances Fonda tagged behind while the '76ers made their entrance. Swope and Fonda ruffled their drums to a marching rhythm, Stewart blew the fife, and limped in character.

The threesome received a great deal of attention and the second prize.

"God knows who won first prize," Fonda says, "probably Mr. Hearst. Seems he had some influence with the judge—Miss Davies."

Everyone entertained that season. Phyllis and Fred Astaire, Lillian and Fred McMurray, Ruth and Walter Pidgeon.

"Night after night," Fonda says, "Frances, Jim, and I'd come home from these parties and Frances would go to bed and Jim and I would sit in the playhouse and listen to our collection of records."

After the parties Frances did not go directly to bed. She undressed, slipped into her nightclothes, and sat before her mirror.

"My mother was very beautiful," Peter Fonda remarked. "But she was preoccupied with her beauty to the point that she would wear those funny little things on her face to keep lines from forming—little triangular pieces of adhesive tape. I guess she was very concerned about aging."

At forty her husband looked like a rosy cheeked youth who only recently had arrived at his majority. Frances, three years away from forty, considered her age, for a woman, to be on "the back nine" of life. In addition to the adhesive triangles Frances applied rich creams under her eyes, on her throat, and alongside her mouth. A final few pats to her chin with the back of her hand and she'd turn off the dressing-table lamps.

Afterward she would lie in bed in the darkness listening to the music drift up from the phonograph in the playhouse.

"Jim and I would spend hours," Fonda says, "Scouring the music shops for oldies. Johnny Mercer, Hoagie Carmichael, and Nat King Cole used to come over and listen with us. Nat even taught Peter to play boogie-woogie on the piano. This was quite an accomplishment. All of my children took piano lessons, but Peter is a 'lefty,' and in a right-handed world, Peter feels 'lefties' are the real minority.

"There was no work. Only parties and pleasure."

From September 1945 to June 1946 Fonda and Stewart socialized, played their records, and made up for lost days of leisure.

"This was our kite-building period," Stewart recalled. "We were like kids. The kites kept getting bigger and bigger. One night I got home later than usual. It was seven o'clock and it was pitch black out and Frances came up to me and said, 'You'd better go back there. Hank's in trouble with the kite.'

"Well, I looked out. We'd used swordfish tackle for the kite and the tackle was going straight up in the air, and it was almost off the reel, and Hank was holding this enormous kite. The wind was strong and it was pulling him off the ground. Boy! I grabbed him and the two of us got it down inch by inch.

"I take full credit for saving Fonda. Y'see, that kite was ten feet by ten feet, and if I hadn't arrived in the nick of time, well, Fonda would've made Nebraska by morning."

The kite that had almost carried off Fonda was constructed for adults. The children flew smaller versions. Young Peter, in addition to his soaring paper toy, was the proud owner of a dog, a cat, and a chipmunk. Of course he also possessed a burro named Pedro, but the only riding Peter really enjoyed was on an antique wooden horse that his parents had once bought in Greenwich Village and shipped west.

"Peter was a sad youngster," Fonda says, "very thin, sensitive, and sick more than most children."

Peter didn't like school, even nursery classes, and he made up excuse after excuse as to why he shouldn't attend.

"One of my neater tricks," Peter confided, "was to put the thermometer next to a hot light bulb to convince them I had a fever."

"Today they'd call him a problem child," Fonda says. "My absence from him *did* have a bad effect. Sons need fathers. When I got back home I couldn't seem to make up for the time the war had taken away from us."

"Dad didn't mention that my mother probably was responsible for my behavior and my fears," Peter remarked. "I'd be running across the grass to the swimming pool and I'd hear her voice calling from the second-floor office, 'Don't run, Peter. You'll get overheated.'

"I'd be ready to dive into the water and she'd call down, 'Peter, stay out of the sun. You'll be burned, and then you'll have a chill.' I'd stand there looking up at her helplessly, and then she'd add, 'As a matter of fact, dear, you'd better take a nap now. You're wearing yourself out. I'll have a tray brought to your room, milk and cookies.'

" 'But I'm not tired,' I'd insist. 'Peter,' Mother would pause for a second, the tone of her voice would change, 'I've heard that for proper growth, rest and sleep will help weak children sprout right up.'

"And then the phone would ring and I'd duck away so that mother would lose sight of me."

Frances Fonda almost convinced her son that he was one of the sickliest boys ever born.

Jane, on the other hand, was a barefoot, independent tomboy, as firmly planted in her world as the large old oak tree that overlooked the pool.

"My mother already had a daughter, and wanted a son, but had me instead," Jane insisted with bitterness. "She could have only one more child. I didn't know this then, but we were three cesareans, and at the time, that was it. I had been told by my grandmother, Sophie Seymour, that mother wanted a son so badly that if she'd had a third daughter, they were going to have a baby boy at her bedside, a boy she could adopt. When she came out of the anesthetic, there would be two children. She didn't have to worry, she had a son, and that was Peter. And she preferred him, I believe.

"My father was not a demonstrative person, and never

said, 'I love you' and didn't hold you on his knees. In those days his major emotion was rage."

Rage when Peter flushed the goldfish down the toilet, rage when they sailed to Catalina and Peter locked every door on the boat and flipped the key overboard, and righteous rage when Peter took the Bronze Star his father had been awarded in the war, carried it out to the field, and tossed it into the air. It was never found.

"Dad only spanked me once," Peter said, "but that was enough for all time. It shows the character of the man. I lied to him. I lied to him about something silly. He saw me stuffing pieces of licorice in my mouth, and he said, 'Where'd you get that?' Well, I'd taken it from a big brandy snifter where he kept pennies on the bottom and licorice on the top. Now there was plenty of candy in the house, but—Dr. Freud—I took my father's candy and when he asked me I lied.

" 'I found it.' This was said with the bravado of a seven-year-old.

"He just looked at me and I shot up the stairs to my bathroom where I bolted the door and spit out the half-chewed candy.

"It didn't take long. He knocked, and when I didn't answer he gave that door a shove with his shoulder, I guess. My father had enormous strength, and the lock just gave way. He paddled the shit out of me with a hair brush. I never lied to him again."

"His rages were terrifying," Jane recalled, "not the kind of Mediterranean rages where it's just part of the culture, where you scream and you yell and then it's forgotten. I think his were from tension, frustration, and repression. They were as much against himself as anybody else."

A knowledgeable child, Jane felt her father's anger at Peter was balanced by her mother's lack of interest in her.

"It was tense for both of us," Jane asserted.

As Peter came more and more under the influence of Frances her emotional illnesses brought on his anxieties. There was no question their mother liked to be a patient and to have her children as patients. Peter, naturally, received the focus of her attention. Jane, instead of resorting to self-pity, grew self-reliant.

Jane became an accomplished horsewoman. She rode on a western saddle at five, and displayed such ability that her instructor at the Riviera Riding Club switched her to the smaller English saddle where she learned to post as she trotted her horse and sit back as she cantered it. Soon she was wearing the black cap, the velvet jacket, the breeches and boots of a polished rider. In 1946 her parents beamed as she jumped the hurdles, her two long braids flying behind her.

"I'd go down to the Riviera Club and watch Jane jump," Fonda says, "with my heart in my throat!"

Before long her bedroom was festooned with the blue ribbons Jane had collected at horse shows. An occasional white or even red one was dispersed among the blue, but Fonda's daughter's room took on more and more the character of a rider. She even had a separate closet for her dirty jeans and the battered cowboy hats she liked to wear around the house.

"Jane's four-poster bed," Fonda says, "with its patchwork quilt, didn't seem to match the girl who occupied the room. For a while there, I was afraid my daughter would grow up and marry a horse."

Boots, spurs, riding crops, gloves; a persistent trace of stables pervaded the room. Although Jane couldn't be considered messy, her surroundings did not compare with the perfumed femininity of her sister's quarters.

"Pan was my big sister," Jane pointed out, "so we loved and quarreled and fought and gossiped. She was the one who explained things to me when I had a crush on a young boy, this must have been in the fifth grade, and we were playing a game called 'Heads Up' where you throw the ball to someone. I complained to Pan that the boy kept trying to throw it to this one girl, and I heard him say, 'I'm trying to sex her up.'

"And I went home and asked my mother what it meant. She couldn't or wouldn't tell me. So I asked Pan and she told me the facts of life. She was the one I could watch when she was getting ready to go on dates. I would watch her in the bathroom when she put on her makeup

and she had big breasts. She was the flowering of woman-
hood and she was at the beginning of liking boys and
necking and I used to spy on her necking. It's nice to
have an older sister because you can sort of preview the
things to come."

If Frances would not discuss sex with her daughter,
there were many things she could do well. From her upstairs office she supervised the help that staffed her home.
She handled her investments, her husband's investments,
their real estate holdings, even the annual income tax
forms.

Frances kept office hours just as if she still worked in
Mr. Morgan's bank: seven-thirty in the morning until the
stock market closed in New York. She was the model of a
capable working woman who, along with a secretary, a
cook, two maids, a laundress, and a gardener operated
her home and her business properly and promptly.

"She tried hard to be everything," Peter said, "a
businesswoman, a wife, and a mother. In the afternoons
she'd often take us to the museums or to the beach."

Naturally Frances and Henry reciprocated the invitations they'd received by giving their own style of entertainment.

"Their parties were very un-Hollywood," Stewart reported.

"The Fondas gave informal barbecues for their close
friends. The host, generally, did the cooking himself, but
when there was a large group invited, Frances had the affair catered. The hot buffet dinner would be laid out on a
heavy wooden sideboard in the playhouse. Then the
guests would eat outside on rented tables lit by giant hur-
ricane lamps. Afterward they'd move about as they
pleased: swimming, dancing, playing games. No one
hovered over them suggesting group activity, although the
nights frequently wound up with about thirty people
gathered near the piano singing songs from the thirties
and early forties.

Dinah Shore's voice joined the others at one Fonda social gathering, and before she said thank you and good
night, Dinah invited Fonda to be a guest on her radio
program. Fonda accepted.

A motor car company sponsored the program, and the advertising agency representative asked the actor if he preferred a check for his appearance or a car.

"You have your choice of a small car, a medium-sized car, or a large one," the Madison Avenue man explained.

"Don't you people make tractors, too?" Fonda asked.

"Tractors? Tractors? I believe we do."

"I'll take one."

Up to now the Madison Avenue man thought he'd heard everything.

"Yup. That's it. That's what I want. I need it for my plowing."

A month later they delivered the prized vehicle complete with all attachments, plow, discs, rake, harrow. From then on, no matter how late he got to bed at night, he was up early in the morning, "and by eight A.M." as *House Beautiful* reported, "Hank's out in the field, plowing, planting, and looking after his fruit trees. He claims to raise the best apples in Los Angeles County—no small job—and his citrus grove keeps the family in oranges all year."

Most Americans had considered the wartime Victory Garden a temporary patriotic gesture and inconvenience. They were glad to return to their local fruit and vegetable markets. Not Fonda. His land and fields became a sanctuary for him. He liked the feel of the soil in his hands, the smell of the loam in his nostrils.

"June Walker recommended that I play The Farmer in 1934," Fonda says, "and by God, I never gave up the role."

Carefully, he followed the instructions laid down for compost in the *Organic Farmer*. Fonda was an environmentalist almost before anyone used the word.

"Let's be blunt and to the point," Fonda says. "Aged chicken droppings make things grow! It's pure gold. When I hear a guy say, 'That's a lot of chicken shit,' I want to ask 'Where? I'll use it on the lilac bushes.'"

A phone call from Pappy Ford put Henry Fonda back in the movie business. He stopped shaving, grew a handsome beard, turned over his land to the gardener, and started learning the lines for *My Darling Clementine*.

Clementine reunited Fonda and John Ford. It seemed fitting that Fonda's return to the screen should be in a western and that he should play the now-classic marshal of Tombstone, Arizona, Wyatt Earp. For the women in his family, Fonda's reappearance before the cameras caused little if any problems. Jane and Pan rode their horses on the bridle paths of the Brentwood hills. Frances worked upstairs with her secretary.

It was six-year-old Peter who felt rejected. Up early and home late, Fonda might just as well have returned to the Navy so far as his attention to his son was concerned.

Resentful, even angry that his father should leave after a few months, Peter and his best friend, Bill Hayward, son of Leland Hayward and Margaret Sullavan, made his own bid for attention.

"I'll tell you about that day with Peter and this buddy of his," Fonda says. "Peter'd never misbehaved any more than any other kid, so what happened was completely unexpected. Remember, I'd planted a lot of long leaf yellow pine trees even before we'd built the house. I'd taken care of them, given them the proper feed and they'd done well. They'd grown to fifteen or twenty feet, and were full and healthy. I'd planted clumps of pines and now they were groves."

When Fonda gets to this part of the story, he knits his brows and looks as though he'd like to bite a brass nail.

"Near the pines was a pasture," Fonda says, "and we'd irrigate it with huge sprinklers for a time, and then let the fields brown out. We'd cut the dry grass and rake it into haystacks. During this particular period the pasture was a tinderbox, and by God, if Peter and Billy didn't start fooling around with matches in the middle of it!"

The chief culprit's version varies slightly.

"My father had built these two miniature log houses on the land the family called the North Forty," Peter Fonda remembered vividly. "Adults could walk into them, but they were really for us. Bill Hayward and I were in the North Forty throwing rocks at each other. We had protective shields which were lids from garbage cans. Suddenly, we young gladiators came upon a book of matches. Rock warfare ceased and we started playing with these matches."

Hayward, co-conspirator in the great arson plot, confessed to a somewhat different tale.

"We got tired of throwing rocks at each other," William Hayward acknowledged decades later, "and we decided it was time to smoke cigarettes. Well—we not only lit up the cigarettes, we also lit up the bone-dry grass."

Both boys fought a gallant but losing battle in their attempt to extinguish or at least contain the fire. Seizing empty cans that formerly held three tennis balls apiece, the perpetrators rushed to the swimming pool, scooped up two cans of water apiece, and then ran back to the spreading fire. Total failure greeted their efforts. The expanding flames crackled and the conflagration soon burned out of control. The guilt the incendiarists felt was powerful but not so great that they were ready to disclose their culpability. Both boys agreed never to admit having any part of deliberately starting the fire. Bill, five years old at the time, a year younger than Peter, readily went along with the older boy's story.

"We were just playing up there," Peter Fonda tried to persuade his mother, "and someone left a book of matches. I stepped on it and there was a flash!" That was as strong an alibi as they could manage. Thirty-five years later, Peter realized his folly.

"No way, José," he said. "One of the firemen who answered the alarm got bitten by a rattlesnake and had to be taken away. My mother got so pissed at me. It became the most awful thing I ever did in my life: burning down the North Forty. I learned a lesson without having to pay a terrible price. Thank God my father's pine forest wasn't hurt or I'd have been in worse trouble."

As Fonda drove home from the studio toward Tigertail that evening, he breathed the pungent air and saw the haze of smoke that hung over his land.

"Everyone was in an uproar," Fonda says, "but no one more than Peter. It was a panicky experience for him. After I calmed down Frances and the girls and the help, I sent for my son. They couldn't find him for a while. He was petrified and I think he'd hidden in a closet.

"Anyway, when he finally came to me, I didn't spank him even though I was angry. I felt sorry for the little fellow. He stood there, trembling and crying. Like all children he'd been told not to play with matches. I intended to have a serious talk with him, but he looked so pathetic, I knew he'd had his punishment."

What concerned Fonda even more than the near disaster at the back of his house was the chilly, baffling atmosphere that had recently crept into his bedroom. Frances had moved her headquarters from her office to her bed. She offered no explanations.

"My God, I didn't like it, but I didn't beef about it," Fonda says. "Frances looked well. She could get up and go to a party, but otherwise—I really don't like to talk about it. There she was wearing beautiful dressing gowns, sitting propped up with lace pillows at her back. She carried on her business as usual. There were telephones on both sides of the bed, ledgers and date books piled high on the night tables. She could buy and sell, she could make deal after deal, she could talk to everyone except me. I thought to myself, 'Is this what marriage comes down to?' Many days I'd blame myself. Then I hinted maybe she ought to see a doctor or two. With Frances it didn't take much hinting."

This time, however, the Los Angeles diagnosticians found something more than hypochrondria. Unanimous medical opinion favored a hysterectomy. For reasons that remain her own Frances did not make this information available to her husband. During this period, she resolved not to complain. Instead she waited until Henry went on location to shoot a picture, and then, when a California physician recommended a surgeon at Johns Hopkins Hospital, she ordered the servants to pack for herself and her son.

"Maybe in Baltimore," she told her best friend, Eulalia Chapin, "they'll be able to discover why Peter is such a skinny little boy and what's wrong with his appetite."

"Never try to get me to Baltimore again," Peter Fonda pounded the table when he spoke years later. "I went

East with my mother thinking we were going on vacation. I thought the building we went into was a hotel. It turned out to be a hospital. The doctors there terrified me. During one examination they stuck a long metal object up my backside. It took three people to hold me down. It was so traumatic, it gave me a complex I have to this day. That's the one examination no doctor can do on me. If anyone tries I'll kill him!"

Of course there was nothing wrong with Peter except a neurotic mother. Frances returned home following her operation and was back in bed before Henry knew she had left.

Her resolution not to complain to her husband lasted as long as most resolutions.

To ease the image of Frances lingering on her pillows Henry instructed his agent, Lew Wasserman, to get him as many jobs as he could; pictures, radio, or a Broadway play. Fonda wanted his mind filled with the challenge of acting, not the anxieties he found centered in the shadows of that upstairs bedroom.

Between 1946 and 1948 Henry Fonda made seven films. *Clementine* turned out to be popular around the globe. When he visited Japan years later the Kabuki Players crowded about and had the interpreter compliment him on his brilliant acting as Wyatt Earp. "Ford did a fine job on that," Fonda says modestly.

On location, where Ford filmed *Clementine*, a new person had come into Henry's life. His name was Charles Bidwell. He'd been a United States Steel worker in Houston and he'd been fired in 1943. Bidwell decided to visit Hollywood for a couple of weeks and see the sights.

"I took a tour of the Fox Studios," Bidwell said, "and everyone kept telling me I looked like Henry Fonda. So when he got out of the service and was ready to shoot *Clementine*, Fox hired me as Fonda's stand-in. In those days, ten feet from the camera, you couldn't tell us apart.

"Ford's production manager took me over to him when we were on location and said, 'Mr. Fonda, this is your stand-in.' He stood up, shook hands with me, and said, 'Oh?' And that's the only time he said a word to me during the whole picture.

"Speaking of his silent moods, we finished early one day on another picture and the studio car drove us home. Naturally, they took him to his place first. I lived in Hollywood. When we got to Tigertail, Henry turned to me and said, 'Charlie, would you like to see the house? I'll take you home later.' I said, 'Sure.' We got out and went inside. We went from room to room and he didn't say a word. Finally, we wound up in the kitchen. He poured me a cup of coffee and sat there staring out of the window.

"I couldn't make any kind of conversation that he'd join in, so I finally said, 'Okay, I'm ready to go.' He drove me to the bus stop, dumped me, and said, 'See you tomorrow.'

"I've got to point out something," Bidwell added. "Don't think Mr. Fonda didn't like me. He kept me as his stand-in for thirty-five years. I watched all the kids grow up and I even get invited to all the family parties."

Another of the pictures Fonda made during this period was *Daisy Kenyon*.

"Love scenes are difficult for me," Fonda says, "not just because they're in front of a camera. I've never felt like a terrific lover on screen or in private. You know what it was to be out here in Hollywood? Christ! You'd go to dinner at Chasen's. There'd be Tyrone Power at one table with a knockout of a girl, and Bob Taylor at another table with Barbara Stanwyck. Those guys gave me a complex. They *looked* like lovers! Sure I had to kiss girls in pictures, Bette Davis, Barbara Stanwyck, Joan Crawford, Joan Bennett, but I wasn't any good at it."

"Maybe Henry lets on that he wasn't sexy," Dore Schary, playwright and onetime head of Metro Goldwyn Mayer, commented, "but I've heard stories that go just the other way. Hank will refuse to admit the truth. He's not a kiss-well-and-tell man. Joan Crawford used to laugh at an experience she had with her leading man in *Daisy Kenyon*. Obviously she found Fonda very attractive. When ordinary approaches failed to get a reaction from him, she asked the wardrobe department to make a jock strap of rhinestones, gold sequins, and red beads. Crawford gave the package to Henry on the set one morning, gift-wrapped.

"He opened it." Schary smiled when he thought about it. "Then Hank turned it over a couple of times. At last he figured it out. The next scene called for him to carry Crawford up the stairs, and she managed to whisper in his ear, 'How about modeling it for me later?' Hank stopped dead in his tracks. They had to shoot the scene over. 'He almost dropped me down those stairs,' Crawford told me."

"I don't handle a girl well physically on the screen," Fonda shrugs. "I don't kiss the way you should. I keep my mouth closed. People tell me, 'Shit, Fonda, you can't even kiss good.'" Then he hastens to explain, "Not a girl, mind you. No girl ever told me that. Maybe a director. You wanna know something? When I see two people on the screen kiss with their mouths open, I don't like to watch. It seems too personal for me.

"Well," Fonda says and slaps his thigh, "I succeeded in spite of the fact that I don't kiss good."

He didn't have to concern himself with kisses in his next film, *Fort Apache*. Shirley Temple was just growing into her first adult role and Fonda played her father, a stiff Army colonel. John Wayne was cast as one of Fonda's captains in the John Ford western.

The picture was shot on location in Monument Valley, and after they finished, Ford followed the custom of boarding his sailboat, the *Araner*, and headed for the warmer waters of Mexico. There, rumors persist, Fonda and John Wayne often took over the towns they visited.

"That's a crock!" Fonda says. "Twice, maybe three times after making a picture with Pappy Ford, I'd join him in Mexico. After *Fort Apache* we—that is, Ford, Duke, Ward Bond, and I—met in Mazatlán. Ford sailed with his wife, Mary; Wayne and I flew down and met them. I invited Frances. She showed no interest.

"The first four or five days Ford came to town with us. After that he was too drunk to leave his boat. We'd start at the Hotel Central, and then we'd pick up a three-piece mariachi band and go from bar to bar, saloon to saloon, whorehouse to whorehouse. You went to the whorehouses just to sit and drink and listen to the mariachis play. You didn't fuck. You didn't think you should. Those whores looked grungy.

"This one time there was just Duke Wayne and me and we were drinking only beer. We got drunk but not so drunk that we couldn't still walk. Wayne could outdrink any man. I couldn't keep up with him. The two of us were sitting at a table in the bar at the Hotel Central. A couple, who turned out to be newlyweds on their honeymoon, were sitting near us, and because they were Americans, we asked them to our table. Now Duke, who was a great talker and a great storyteller, was holding forth. He never talked politics. When we first made movies together, he couldn't even spell politics. Like Ford, it was impossible for him to say two sentences without using words that would put a dockworker to shame. He was telling a story to the young bride and her groom and suddenly out popped, '. . . and then, the cocksucker . . . oh, shit! I'm sorry.'

" 'Oh, shit! I'm sorry.' I fell apart laughing at that. I laughed so hard I practically passed out over two empty chairs.

"Now Duke squinted down at me lying there, and he'd heard that the pet of the Hotel Central was a boa constrictor about ten inches around and nine or ten feet long. It was a pet, loose like a cat.

" 'Would you,' he asked someone who worked there, 'get that snake I've heard about and lay it on my friend here?' I suppose the tip Duke gave him was big enough for the man to get the snake. Anyway, I'm waked up by someone stretching this ugly boa constrictor over me.

"Now I opened my eyes and saw this damn snake glaring at me, and for some reason, I'll never know why— probably I was anesthetized by the Mexican beer—I wasn't frightened. I just called out, 'Duke! Hey, Duke! Look!' Scared him to death. You know those long legs of his. Four steps and he was out of the hotel.

"Later that evening, after I'd gotten myself together, I wanted to sic that snake on someone else, and I found it in the kitchen. It was back of the stove where it liked to keep warm.

"Well, a curve of the snake was exposed and I tried

pulling the damn thing out, and again, still not sober, I didn't know any better. I was tugging away when someone came up, tapped me on the shoulder and said, 'Señor, do not do this. The snake, she do not like this. It make her mad.' I left. God knows, I never wanted to make a boa constrictor mad.

"That's as wild as it ever got for us in Mexico. Duke and the bridal couple and me and the boa constrictor. As for taking over a town? Jee-sus! I don't know how stories like that ever get started."

Upon his return from Mexico Fonda heard from his ever-constant enemy, Darryl F. Zanuck. The actor still owed the producer a picture. The relationship between the two men had begun with hostility and advanced to hatred. Zanuck had sent a script to Fonda's home. After reading it Fonda called Twentieth Century-Fox and asked to speak with the head man. Guarded by a platoon of secretaries, the studio head wouldn't let the actor see him for days. Finally, allowed into Zanuck's presence, Fonda charged in waving the script.

"This is the worst trash I've ever read!" Fonda said raising his voice for emphasis.

Zanuck ignored the outburst and tried talking to Fonda about another long-term contract. Fonda would hear none of it.

"In this business," Fonda pounded his finger onto the script, "the bottom line is the words, and if you don't get the words, I don't care what other talents you've got, you can't do much."

"Well, what kind of picture do you want to make?" Zanuck asked, his patience growing as thin as Fonda's.

"*Grapes of Wrath* was just fine."

"And?"

"*The Ox-Bow Incident*. That was a Darryl F. Zanuck production and a prestige film you didn't like but took bows for."

"*The Ox-Bow Incident?*" Zanuck asked as he thumbed through the pages of an account book he kept on his desk. "Come back here. Read this. See how well *The Ox-Bow Incident* did."

Fonda rounded the corner of the desk and looked

down at the figures. From the top of the page to bottom, every number was in red ink.

The actor stormed out of the producer's office not even glancing at the three doors he slammed as he left the building. He vaulted into his car, threw the gears into reverse, and backed out of the parking space allotted to him at the studio at a speed that removed at least a hundred miles of rubber from his tires. He ignored the guard at the gate and then he accelerated onto Motor Avenue, leaving, he fervently hoped, Twentieth Century-Fox and Darryl Francis Zanuck for the last time.

"I'm not difficult to anger," Fonda says in retrospect. "Principally, I get angry at incompetence. This isn't to say Darryl Zanuck did not know his job. His position at the studio was to make money, and if he had to do it by turning out eighth-rate films as well as fine ones, he did it. Zanuck was one of the top dogs of our business. What I am trying to say is that I had a bad relationship with him. I was unhappy with my contract. He didn't care. He wanted me to extend that contract, to make the kind of films he wanted to do and I didn't.

"I have no patience with people who drive me to anger. Very often I try to control myself. If it's something too close to me and involves me too much. I do blow up. A lot of people will tell you about me blowing up. Understandably, they don't like it, and probably they don't like me as a result.

"Can't help that. I don't forget quickly. I cling to my angers."

The late afternoon sun burned into his eyes. He took the first right-hand turn toward Tigertail.

"God!" he swore to himself, his rage at the system in Hollywood still growing. "I'm so tired of audiences made up of studio grips and gaffers. Isn't there any place left for a working actor?"

In a house in Connecticut his friend Josh Logan and a stranger Tom Heggen were pounding out the second act of an as yet untitled play.

CHAPTER
9

SCENERY for the *Mister Roberts* Company moved in large vans from the railway station in New Haven to the scene dock door of the Shubert Theater. During the journey through the streets of the small college town, a heavy snow began to fall. As the stagehands lifted the sets from the trucks into the backstage area, large flakes coated the canvas twofolds and threefolds.

Dismay struck Billy Hammerstein, stage managing his first major Broadway production. Snow settling upon his scenery could do untold damage. A stagehand gently pulled him aside and let him in on one of the many secrets of the legitimate theater.

"Kid," the carpenter advised, "don't let it bother you."

"Don't let it bother me?" a mix in Hammerstein's voice recalled fear, strain, and astonishment.

"Kid," the older man continued. "*Wet sets mean good luck.*"

Billy Hammerstein gaped at the stagehand. "Madness. Absolute madness!" he thought to himself. " '*Wet sets mean good luck.*' Complete garbage!"

After *Mister Roberts* opened William Hammerstein never again doubted the wisdom of that sound and very profound theatrical superstition.

The critics couldn't have written better reviews. The opening-night audience couldn't have been more enthusiastic. The only problem was that *Mister Roberts* ran forty-five minutes too long.

Seated in an old overstuffed purple armchair in his snug suite in New Haven's Taft Hotel, Henry Fonda observed with great satisfaction the stack of newspapers on the floor. All of them were open to the theatrical pages. All of them gave his performance and the play itself rave notices. To his right pyramids of unopened telegrams were piled high on the end table.

Fonda flicked his cigarette lighter, moved it to the tip of the Chesterfield between his lips, and took a long, satisfying drag.

This success had been his dream since the Community Playhouse in Omaha.

"Don't ever let anyone tell you it's a letdown once you reach a goal," Fonda says. "Remember the old song 'I'm Sitting on Top of the World?' That's it."

He had begun to memorize the role of Lt. (j.g.) Doug Roberts in the bedroom he shared with Frances on Tigertail Road in California. Autumn brought the Santa Ana winds. Generally, heat poured in from the upper and lower deserts. This year, however, cool onshore winds from the Pacific prevailed and the fireplaces had been lit in the Fonda home.

Pacing up and back on the hooked rugs, Henry, always a quick study, worked on the characterization of the young naval officer. During the war he had known hundreds of them. Frances cued him from her bed. As Fonda went through his lines he paused once in front of the bay window and glanced down.

The day before he and his wife had given away some of the litter that Peter's cat had kittened a few weeks earlier. The seven-year-old boy had been infuriated and now his father watched the result of that anger. Taking his Teddy bear and his little red wagon with him, Peter Fonda began the long and arduous task of running away from home.

Unaware that his father watched from an upstairs window, Peter went across the big field in front of the house, across Tigertail Road, and down to the neighbor's backyard. It had taken him at least three hours to cross

194

that big field, sneaking through the tall clover grass and mustard weed. Henry would stop repeating the lines of the script and frown as his son disappeared from view. He would pick up again when he saw the tops of the grass moving as the boy inched his way long.

Eventually, Peter arrived at his destination. Climbing underneath his wagon, he lay down and tried to sleep, but the neighbors came out.

"Would you like to come inside?" they asked the young nomad. "You'll feel a little warmer." By now darkness had fallen and Peter was glad to comply. Without his knowledge the neighbors telephoned the Fondas and Henry walked down and collected the boy, the bear, and the little red wagon.

After dinner the father mollified the son by giving him a large sheathed government-issue U.S. Navy knife.

Content that he had earned something for his trouble, Peter obediently trotted off to bed and Henry returned to the memorization of the dialogue of Lt. (j.g.) Doug Roberts.

Philadelphia was not quite the repetition of New Haven. Although the critics were appreciative and the audiences enjoyed the comedy, *Mister Roberts* was still fifteen minutes too long. And those fifteen minutes meant double time for the stagehands, and few if any plays can afford the luxury of running beyond eleven-thirty in the evening.

Even more vexing, Henry Fonda and the "flu" bug met in Philadelphia.

"They carted me right off to the hospital," Fonda says. "I ran a helluva fever and I felt simply awful. They kept me in bed for a week, but each evening around eight o'clock, they'd drive me to the stage door. I didn't miss a single performance, but after the curtain, back to sick bay I'd go."

Lying in his hospital bed in Philadelphia, Henry Fonda had ample time to remember his last night in California before he flew east to do *Roberts*.

"I hear you're going back to New York to do some

goddamn play," John Ford feigned scorn as he growled into the telephone.

"You hear right, Pappy," Fonda told him.

"Doing anything special tonight?" Ford asked.

"Not much."

"How about me and Duke and Ward and a few of the boys stopping by for a few games of pitch?"

"That'd be okay."

"Say about seven-thirty?"

"Seven-thirty's fine."

"Oh, Hank," Ford interjected, "there's this prick from the *Saturday Evening Post* who's following me around and wants to take a few pictures. All right with you?"

"Fine."

John Ford, John Wayne, Ward Bond, Frank McGrath, who'd been a stunt man on almost all of Ford's pictures, and a few other members of Ford's crew gathered at Tigertail after dinner.

"Oddly enough," Fonda says, "almost none of them had ever been to our home. Ford lived away down by the Hollywood Bowl, and Duke lived in the old part of Los Angeles past Highland. Maybe Ward Bond had dropped by once or twice during the day to swim because he lived not too far from us.

"Anyway I took the lazy Susan off the round table in the playhouse and covered it with a green felt cloth. And I made sure we had a big supply of silver dollars because that's what Ford liked to use to bet with in his pitch games. That's a form of high-low poker. Around seven-thirty, in they came.

"Pappy wore his brown sloppy felt hat and Duke wore a ten-gallon Stetson. Ward found one of Peter's toy Colts. It was plastic. Didn't even shoot caps, but for the benefit of the man from the *Saturday Evening Post* Ward laid it on the table beside him and we started playing cards."

After half an hour Ford addressed the photographer.

"All right, you. Split," Ford said.

Not at all insulted because he had been following Ford for days, the photographer left and the game continued. When the picture appeared in the *Saturday Evening Post*, Jane, during her rebellious years, would look at the pho-

196

tograph and label it "phony." But those years were yet to come. What occupied Fonda's thoughts most in Philadelphia was getting out of the hospital and making sure that not too many of his lines were cut so the curtain could come down before eleven-thirty.

Baltimore was more of the same—good reviews, good audiences, but a dire prediction.

All talent agents are endowed by their Creator with the right to sell the clients they represent. In addition, depending upon their station, they may add the right to tell their clients what to do, where to do it, and, if they are powerful enough, *how* to do it.

Lew Wasserman, executive officer of the good ship MCA, flew into Baltimore, caught one performance, and predicted the New York police would close *Mister Roberts* because of its filthy language. As agent for both Fonda and Logan, he had to be heard out.

"The line has to go," Wasserman pronounced with the authority of a sitting judge.

"What line?" Logan asked.

"You know," Wasserman warned sternly.

"What line, Lew?" Fonda pressed the agent.

"You know what line, Hank. The one after Pulver leaves."

"Jesus, that's my biggest laugh," Fonda protested.

"That's the biggest laugh in the whole show," Logan moaned.

"Boys," Wasserman pontificated, "*that line has to go!*"

Prior to Ensign Pulver's departure to manufacture a giant firecracker to shake up the Captain, he brags to Roberts that he intends to use fulminate of mercury for the charge.

Once Pulver exits, Roberts turns to Doc.

"That stuff's murder," Roberts says. "Do you suppose he'll use it?"

"Of course not," Doc answers. "Where would he get fulminate of mercury?"

"I dunno," Roberts muses. "He's pretty resourceful. Eighteen months at sea without liberty, where'd he get the clap?"

Wasserman, a good agent, dogged Leland Hayward until the producer convinced Logan, Heggen, and Fonda to make the cut.

To make further cuts, Emlyn Williams came down from New York and together with Logan trimmed *Roberts* to where the stagehands lived well but not extravagantly. The curtain came down before eleven-thirty.

The overwhelming success of *Mister Roberts* in New York changed the Fondas' way of living. Frances returned to California, but she flew into Manhattan for a weekend or two each month to be with her husband. Soon she and Henry decided their future lay in the East. The house and land on Tigertail Road would be put on the market for sale, and once the children finished school at the start of summer, the Fonda family would be reunited for a permanent stay on the East Coast.

Back in her element of a wheeling and dealing homemaker, Frances rented a house in Greenwich, Connecticut.

In June Frances, her children, and her two Japanese servants flew East.

For Jane, once she had resigned herself to the loss of her riding trails and her close friend Sue-Sally Jones, the flight to New York was exciting beyond belief. Their plane landed at La Guardia Airport at a late hour. Jane had never been permitted to stay up till that time. She reveled in the sight of the New York city streets, the lights, the people sauntering on the sidewalks enjoying themselves in the humid heat of the city.

Peter remained obdurate from the very start. He missed Tigertail immediately. The ride to Greenwich made him peevish and sullen.

Greenwich had been selected as a suitable living area because, "After nine and a half acres in Brentwood, I couldn't see my kids playing on the hard streets of New York," Fonda says.

"I HATE THE EAST," Peter Fonda wrote in large letters on every wall he could find in his new home. His friends were gone, his swimming hole, his log blockhouses on the North Forty, everything.

"When we left Tigertail," Peter continued, "it felt like we'd been booted out of Paradise. As for Greenwich, in those days I considered Greenwich the asshole of the world. I came home one afternoon and said to my father, 'What's a kike?'

"I thought he was going to take a swipe at me. Instead, he turned and bawled up the staircase. 'Frances! Where did this kid learn this kind of word? Frances come down here! You hear me?'

"Y'understand," Peter Fonda went on, "until Greenwich, I'd been just a country boy. I didn't know what the word meant. I'd never heard 'nigger' or 'wop' or 'mick' or 'polack.' All I knew was that my only friend at my new school, the only guy who would talk to me and didn't treat me totally different, had been called a 'kike' and I was too diplomatic or too timid to ask what it meant, so I went home and asked my Dad.

" 'Frances,' he was furious, 'where the hell did this boy learn such stuff!' I can hear him shouting to this day. I had no notion of what the fuss was about. But my father has a very clear idea of what it is to be a democrat. Small *d*, please. No party politics. But the concept of a democrat being a person who practices democracy as outlined by our constitution."

Peter found Greenwich inhospitable and difficult.

His sister, however, found certain conditions she liked. Until her family moved to Connecticut, Jane had been convinced that her mother had "an eagle eye, that she could see though walls and she would *know* if I was out of bed." Until they left Tigertail, Frances had insisted that her two younger children take naps for an hour every afternoon.

"She caught me out of bed enough times and spanked me for it," Jane Fonda swore. "It was a very rigid routine and it went on right through the sixth grade."

In Greenwich there were no more naps and no more governesses. It also had other compensations.

"As I remember," Jane said, "we moved into a big estate with a huge house that had an elevator in it and enormous grounds with lakes and swamps and apple orchards and a haunted house. Most of the time I explored.

I combed the hills and mountains and caves and paths and trails. What took my mind off California right away was this new kind of foliage. Trees and bushes and grass and these granite rocks that would occasionally poke up through the grass and these old stone fences and dog-wood—it was lush, lush, green.

"I liked the trees and the bushes and the stone walls and the bees and the wasps and all of that, and we lived within ten minutes of a stable. So it didn't take long for me to forget California."

During his investigations Peter discovered a room in the house to occupy his time and talent. Actually, it was more than a room. It was a huge walk-in safe, and Peter devoted the better part of the summer to working on the combination of the large round lock.

"Persevere ye." The Fonda motto finally paid off and Peter hit the numbers that opened the safe. Swinging the door just wide enough to slip inside, he fumbled for an electric light switch, found it, and flicked it on. Edmund Dantes, the Count of Monte Cristo, couldn't have been more excited. Three walls of the safe were lined from floor to ceiling with checks. Peter had never seen a check up close before. He simply knew they were pieces of paper that were as good as money. Immediately, he pictured himself wealthy beyond his wildest belief. His soaring imagination was quickly deflated when his father told him the checks were canceled and worthless. Suddenly, what was left of the summer had lost some of its fun.

Balancing the scales of Fonda's virtues were some of his lesser qualities, his temper, his aloofness, and the frequent and sometimes powerful silences he inflicted upon those near to him.

"I remember sitting in a box at the circus a few months after *Mister Roberts* opened," Radie Harris, the columnist, said. "Hank sat just to my right. With him were Jane and Peter, and not once during the entire performance did he say a word to either child. And either the children knew enough to say nothing, or they might have been too intimidated to speak.

"He didn't buy them hot dogs, cotton candy, or treat them to souvenirs. When the circus was over, they simply stood up and walked out. I felt sorry for all three of them."

Jane echoed the incident. She believed her father to be even worse than she was when it came to that anti-social, alienated, remote, puritanical coldness.

"I can remember long car rides where not a word would be spoken," Jane said. "I would be so nervous that my palms would be sweaty from riding in absolute silence with my own father."

Jane's emotions ran far deeper, but for an entirely new set of reasons.

"It was a rotten summer," Jane said. "To begin with, one day I was wrestling at the Greenwich stable with a boy named Jimmy. His father owned the place. I used to go there often. I did a lot of wrestling when I was ten or eleven. Well, Jimmy picked me up and threw me out the door and I landed on my arm.

"I went home. I bit my nails a lot in those days. It made my father very, very mad. He came into the room and I remember that my arm hurt so badly and I was afraid to tell him. It just hurt a lot and I had to sit on my hands because I was afraid he would see that I was still biting my nails.

"We sat down at the dinner table, and he asked me if I'd washed my hands. I said no. He got very angry and he took me into the little guest bathroom off the dining room. He grabbed my arm, turned the water on, and pulled my hands over the sink. I almost passed out. The pain was tremendous. The poor man had no idea what on earth was going on. They rushed me to the hospital. My arm was broken and they had to put it in a cast.

"As I said, it was a rotten summer. I broke my arm, I got blood poisoning, I had an ear infection from diving in the country club pool, and to top it all off, I realized my parents' marriage was falling apart. Oh, God, it was awful." With the instincts of an eleven-year-old Jane Fonda sensed that whatever they'd once had, the relationship between her parents was now almost finished.

Fonda drove to the theater in New York early each evening and returned each night. By August Frances became more and more withdrawn. Henry's silences which connoted anger were matched by Frances's ever-increasing sadness and lethargy.

"To be completely honest, as far as my mother was concerned, there was no closeness between us at all," Jane reflected. "I didn't like her near me. I didn't like her to touch me because I knew she really didn't love me." And then she added, "Maybe she wasn't capable of love.

"That summer of Forty-eight, I was sure my father didn't want to come back to Greenwich and be with us drags. You know, a wife who was getting sicker and sicker. She was going under. Even as a kid I could tell that."

Years later Jane Fonda met with Frances's psychiatrist to try to better understand her mother.

"My feelings have changed considerably," Miss Fonda confessed. "Now I realize she had tremendous potential. She was smart. She had a lot going for her, she was ambitious. But in those days her world had to do with being beautiful and being rich and being thin and being Henry Fonda's wife. She had nothing else, there was no other kind of structure to hold her in place. She had no creative and protective outlet beyond my father, and after the war, it wasn't there anymore. Her psychiatrist told me she became paranoid. She began to feel she was ugly. She became obsessed with the fact that she was poor and fat. She was neither. She was destroyed by bottled-up frustration. My father was her life—organizing the houses, having all the keys hanging in place, and the linens folded right. Yes, you can say I understand more, now."

As they had in California, Leland Hayward and Margaret Sullavan moved close to the Fondas in Greenwich. Brooke, Bridgit, and Bill were frequent guests at the Fonda home.

"We'd go over to the Fondas' for dinner," Brooke Hayward recollected. "We would eat quite early. The sun would still be out because Hank would be going in to do *Roberts* and he would sit at the head of the table, rather formal, unlike our household. Frances, however, would not appear. I never remember her coming to dinner at all. You could hear her typing.

"You'd hear the sound of the typewriter throughout the

meal. And at the very mention of her name the children would say, 'Well, you know Mother.' Meaning that she was in seclusion."

The master of the house was not indifferent to the conditions that existed beneath his roof.

"I can be a moody bastard," Fonda admits, "but at that point, what I probably had on my mind was a crumbling marriage. We didn't share anything anymore—not even a bed. I agonized over the idea of a second divorce. The first one with Sullavan had been rough enough for me. No, I decided, I'll live this way for the rest of my life."

Frances had begun the summer by having her hair lightened and changing its style, by browsing in antique shops along Madison Avenue and checking the galleries on Fifty-seventh Street for Early American art.

Frances had lunched with Eulalia Chapin at Pavillon, and then shopped for smart designer clothes. When she signed her name Mrs. Henry Fonda, she found salespersons clucking and fluttering about her. Frances seemed to relish the tide of attention that flowed her way, but by the time Jane entered Greenwich Academy, Pan went down to boarding school in the South, and Peter enrolled in the Brunswick School for Boys, Frances was sick enough to enter the Austen Riggs Foundation in Stockbridge, Massachusetts.

The children were at school, and as Fonda left the house for a Wednesday matinee, he shouted up, "Bye!"

"Wait," Frances called down. "I won't be home when you get back tonight, Hank."

Fonda stopped, and took a few steps back into the foyer of the house.

"Where are you going?" he asked. "A night on the town, a visit to your mother?"

He could hear Frances's blue satin mules click on the polished wooden floor as she advanced from her bedroom to the head of the stairs.

"No," she answered quietly, "I'm not going into New York, and I've asked Mother to come and stay in Greenwich for a bit while I'm away."

"Away?" Fonda asked. "Away where?"

"I'm afraid I've neglected to mention it to you, Hank. There's a popular sanitarium not too far from here. A lot of local people say it's wonderful."

Fonda walked a few steps up the stairs and turned his face up toward his wife.

"You're going to a hospital because some civilians recommend it?"

"Of course not," Frances shrugged. "I've consulted a doctor and he suggests I check in for a while, too."

Fonda could think of nothing to say. His mind raced back to the time in California when the hypochondriacal Frances had entered the Scripps Clinic. She had come out a much healthier woman. Perhaps this new place might be the answer to their marital problems.

His wife interrupted his thoughts.

"Don't fret, Hank. Stay in town more. That drive between here and New York must be a bore for you." Then, being the wife of an actor, she advised, "You'd better get going. You'll be late for the matinee."

Henry Fonda drove down the parkway toward New York.

Frances didn't return home for eight weeks.

During that time Sophie Seymour, Frances's mother, did indeed move into the Fonda home to look after her grandchildren, the management of household matters, and, of course, to oversee the comfort and care of her son-in-law.

"Sophie was a fine lady," Fonda says, "terribly bright, easy to be with. I was grateful she came."

Ticket buyers queued up in the lobby of the Alvin Theater in record numbers to buy seats for *Mister Roberts*. Even the preholiday slump so traditional to business on Broadway failed to affect the box office and mail-order sales.

Backstage, hilarity reigned. The all-male cast, with the exception of Jocelyn Brando and a newly appointed assistant stage manager, Ruth Mitchell, knew it was a long-running hit, and pranks and the ordinary theatrical humor were the order of the day.

"One time I went into New York with the Haywards. I was backstage climbing around on the main deck of the set, the one with the big hatch for the crew and the gun emplacements," Peter Fonda drew on his memory. "They were antiaircraft guns and I was in there when the damn turntable started to move. I knew I better duck because the next thing I saw were the spotlights pouring down and I knew that I was on stage. So I hunched down in the shadow of this gun emplacement, and then came the scene where everyone is called to General Quarters.

"Roberts is going to be chewed out by the Captain. There was no escape for me, and the klaxon in the sound system went, 'Ooh-ah-ooh-ah-ooh-ah!' and a boatswain on the PA called, 'Now hear this. Now hear this. General Quarters. Mister Roberts, report to the Captain.'

"Now with this, these big fuckers who man the guns came charging over the side, ready to go into action. I was scared to death those sailors were going to crush me as they jumped over. Downstage, to the audience, they were serious as hell, but upstage, seeing me scrunched down, they were laughing their heads off. I don't know how they worked it, but they swung out the guns without trampling me. Fortunately, they did not bust me to my father who would have found that to be very unprofessional and embarrassing. They kept their mouths shut. 'Loose lips did not sink that particular ship' that night. But I thought it was the end."

His father knew nothing of his son's first unscheduled stage appearance. In his dressing room backstage, in his car commuting to Greenwich each night: Henry Fonda was a very lonely man. There were autograph seekers outside the stage door after each performance, and letters of praise from friends and strangers alike. And every now and then when Jim Stewart and his new wife, Gloria, or Clark Gable or Pappy Ford stopped by to catch the show, Fonda would arrange with Bob Keith, who played the role of Doc, to reinsert the line about Pulver's resourcefulness that Lew Wasserman successfully managed to cut out of the show.

Other than that, his was a solitary life.

"Fonda was like a stoic," Davey Wayne said. "His performance never varied. If anything all our work kept improving week after week, and Hank set the example. But as far as he was personally concerned, at that time I always thought he was some poor son-of-a-bitch who had nothing in the world except those eight performances a week."

Frances returned from the sanitarium in Massachusetts good-humored and high-spirited. Henry felt he had reason to be optimistic about her health and their life together.

"His entire attitude changed when his wife came back," Wayne remembered. "He bought his son a set of electric trains for Christmas, but before they went under the tree in Greenwich, Hank set them up on the floor of his dressing room and ran them out into his sitting room.

"Between acts all of us'd crowd in there and play with the goddamn electric trains. I dunno if the kid got as much fun out of them as Hank and the rest of us, but until the night before Christmas, when he put 'em in the trunk of his car, Hank played Santa at the Alvin."

To amuse himself after Christmas Fonda collected a batch of the pastels that his children had discarded and took them into New York. During the long waits between the matinees and the evening performances, he drew. From the time he'd been a small boy Henry Fonda had been very good at sketching, He'd done the cartoons for the college paper at Minnesota. Now he turned to his true avocation: art.

A couple of days into the New Year Frances hesitantly informed her husband that she felt it best to reenter Riggs Sanitarium.

"The holidays take so much out of me," she told him. "I won't be gone long. I've already phoned Mother to come."

"We'd been widening the distance between us for months," Fonda says. "There was a helluva lot we couldn't say to each other. I could only wish her well."

After Frances left, Fonda bought a larger, more elaborate set of pastels and started to draw in earnest.

Although he applied himself to this new art form with all the energy and dedication he employs in everything he undertakes, there are those who claim Fonda was ready for anything—something more than painting. And along it came. Only it wasn't an anything. It was a something, something very special.

"One night backstage the phone rang," Billy Hammerstein recalled. "It was my sister, Susan. All giggly, she was very young—she must have been twenty."

"We're having a party," Susan told him. "Would you like to come after the show?"

This was a period when Billy Hammerstein had separated from his wife and he thought it might be fun to step out. There'll be a lot of young girls there. Much younger than himself, but, he thought, while it might be a bit silly, Susan *was* his sister and he liked her a lot.

"What the hell," Hammerstein said. "I'll come." That was the bait.

"Would you like to bring Mr. Fonda with you?" Susan asked. That was the trap.

"Jesus! Bring Mr. Fonda?" Billy replied. Well, he thought to himself, Hank is alone at this point in his life. Why not? "I don't know if he'll come, Susan, but what the hell, I'll ask him."

During the intermission, Billy Hammerstein knocked on Henry Fonda's dressing-room door.

"Come in."

Hammerstein opened the door and stuck in his head.

"My sister's having a little party at the house after the performance tonight."

The expression on Fonda's face was as usual completely noncommital.

"I'm going over. Do you want to come?"

"Fine. I'd love to."

"One day several weeks later," Hammerstein continued, "I'm riding down Seventh Avenue in a cab with Leland Hayward."

"What do you think of your sister and Hank?" the producer asked.

"What do you mean?" Hammerstein replied.

"What do you mean, 'What do you mean?' You don't know?"

"What don't I know?" Hammerstein demanded.

"Well, for Christ's sake," the producer answered, "they've been going together. Didn't you know that?"

"No," Hammerstein sighed. "Nobody tells me anything."

"What the hell is Billy Hammerstein talking about?" Fonda says. "I used to see Susan and Oscar Hammerstein's assistant, Shirley Clurman, backstage at the Alvin all the time. Susan was very, very pretty. Beautiful. Had that Alice in Wonderland quality. Long blonde hair that hung down her back. God! She was unbelievably attractive."

Susan Blanchard was the daughter of Dorothy Hammerstein by a previous marriage. As the young lady of the Oscar Hammerstein household, her position allowed her to ride the crest of New York's theatrical elite. Shirley Clurman described the couple.

"When Hank watched Susan, he glowed. She was an incredibly marvelous-looking girl, no make up, simple hairdo that was sometimes braided, frequently jeans and a T-shirt. She was the most honest and real human being I ever met. I can understand what drew Hank to her. Anyone could see. It was an extraordinary falling in love."

Susan found Henry Fonda "very guarded." Their courtship proved "very tentative." She was twenty-one. He was forty-four. The age difference wasn't the only problem. He was a very married man who took his obligations seriously. His middle-class, Midwestern background made no allowances for secondary romances. If he was stern with his children, he was sterner with himself.

And yet how could he resist anyone as lovely, as charming, as fun-loving, as confidence-building as Susan? The answer, in spite of his own wishes, his own inhibitions, was he couldn't. And he didn't.

"Henry is a controlled man," Susan observed in a frankly detached manner many years later. "He's an internal man, who's rather intolerant of imperfection. In himself, particularly, he strives for perfection. And my personality is such that I don't mind making a fool of myself."

Differences in temperament, differences in background,

differences in age were put aside. Neither could resist the attraction of the other.

At first only a few close friends knew they were seeing each other. And then, as these matters go, whether in New York or Chicago, in Manhattan or Milwaukee, the ripple effect began. It didn't take long to reach the Greenwich Academy where Jane was taunted for her father seeing a twenty-year-old "tomato."

At Jane's age it was difficult to formulate a defense against such gossip. Susan, only a handful of years older than Jane, found the going equally hard. Time and again she and Henry would break off their romance.

"I almost reverted to my teen-age personality," Fonda says. "Back to Omaha morality, back to the Boy Scouts. It wasn't an adult romance. My marriage and my guilt kept us at a most respectable distance."

When Frances came out of Riggs in the spring of 1949 she felt fine and showed much of her old verve and energy. She moved her family from the first house in Greenwich to a second sublet nearby. She called in architects to discuss blueprints for a new home. She announced the engagement of her daughter Pan. She planned the wedding, and in June Henry slipped out of the khakis of *Mister Roberts* into the formal attire of the father of the bride.

Frances approved of her son-in-law, even though Pan and her husband were only seventeen years old. The boy was heir to the Kreske Stores and came from a distinguished Main Line Philadelphia family. A disturbing prospect to Frances was the possibility of her becoming a grandmother.

Fonda faced a quandary of his own. By now he knew he was in love with "a remarkable girl," and not being a man who made plans to reserve dingy hotel rooms in out-of-the-way spots, he braced himself and entered Frances's bedroom one sunny afternoon in early autumn.

Frances's face was as composed as the neatly folded quilt that lay at the foot of her bed. She was calm, perhaps too calm.

"Hank was very sweet," she told Eulalia Chapin. "Hank was so dear. He came in and said he had something to talk to me about. I nodded and he put his arm around me."

"I'm going to tell you something, Frances," Fonda murmured to his wife, "and you're probably going to be shocked, but I want you to know that I'll always love you. There's a bond between us, and I'll always love you and our children."

Then he took a breath.

"Frances," he went on quietly, "I want a divorce. I've met someone."

Frances looked down at the birdbath in the backyard. It was empty.

"Well, all right, Hank." Then she buttoned her blue cashmere cardigan.

"Good luck, Hank," she whispered.

In retrospect, Fonda says, "I've got to tell you she was absolutely wonderful. I don't know whether she knew who it was, but it didn't seem to surprise her. She accepted it. She was sympathetic. She couldn't have been more understanding."

He hugged Frances for a moment and then left.

Henry Fonda closed the door to his wife's room. He stood there not knowing what he might hear: a gasp, a sob. He heard nothing.

"The knot that had been inside me for months began to unwind. The pressure I'd felt began to subside," Fonda says. "I had been honest with Frances, fair to my children, virtuous toward Susan, and, finally, honorable with myself."

A few days later he moved some of his clothes and personal effects into a one-bedroom apartment he had rented on the top floor front of a brownstone on East Sixty-seventh Street between Madison and Fifth avenues.

"After having spilled my guts to Frances I felt free now to know Susan more intimately. She was ready, too. Of course she still lived at home with her parents," Fonda says, "but my place was only four blocks away from the Hammerstein townhouse."

The morning after her husband asked for a divorce Frances made an unexpected appearance on the first floor.

"I had finished breakfast," Jane reflected. "I was on my way to school, and as I went out the door, Mum said, 'Come here.' And without even taking me into the living room and sitting me down, but just standing there in the entrance of the living room she said, 'If anybody mentions that your father and I are getting a divorce, tell them that you already know it.' Then she sent me to school."

That short speech must have been difficult beyond belief for Frances to get through. To speak to Peter about the previous afternoon's events evidently was impossible.

Peter knew nothing about the end of his parents' marriage until much later. Jane and Pan and Pan's husband, Bunny Abry, were getting into Bunny's Mercedes. Peter can still remember the rich smell of the upholstery leather, and the words that his two sisters were trying to aim over his head. Catching the single word "divorce," he surmised that it pertained to his parents. Peter's lower lip quivered as he got into the back seat.

"On Sundays," Fonda says, "I'd go up to be with the children. I'd take them hiking and fishing. Peter talked me—actually begged me—into buying him a twenty-two-caliber rifle. We compromised. I got the rifle and taught him to shoot, but when I wasn't there, the gun had to be placed in a locked closet and the key had to be kept by Grandma Seymour."

The fishing expeditions on Long Island Sound included Jane.

"Those fishing trips were awful," Jane recounted, "so awful because no one enjoyed them. Tension reigned on those little boats. Now while Dad was a good fisherman, I'm sure all he felt was guilt about being a visiting father, and Peter and I couldn't have cared less about fishing. We just wanted to be with him.

"Then there were those horrendous bloodworms we used to catch flounder. Peter did not like those bloodworms. And he did not like having to hook them. I didn't like it either, but I could do it. I always felt at that time I kind of had to protect Peter. He was three years younger and I felt that I had to butt in there. So it was like I was a daughter and a son."

Whether either of the two children or their father enjoyed themselves, they went out and participated. It was the price each had to pay for the failure of a marriage.

Frances had a price to pay, too.

"My mother was convinced the servants stood behind doors and spied on her," Jane grimaced. "This was what dinner was like. This was the worst one I can remember. We sat down, my grandmother, my mother, Peter, and me. We were all eating in silence, and I could see that she was crying. She was crying into her food, and I was so filled with tension and anxiety that I couldn't even ask her or my grandmother what was the matter. Everyone pretended that nothing was wrong. She sat there and cried into her dinner and no one said a word. That's an example. Polite suffering."

Eulalia Chapin frequently invited eligible men to her apartment in Manhattan. Frances always promised to come and meet them, but she never showed up.

The only man she did meet at Mrs. Chapin's was her lawyer. First off, Frances wanted her will to be changed. Executed October 18, 1949, it cut out Henry Fonda completely. The bulk of her estate was to go to her children.

The next logical step, the lawyer informed her, was to file for divorce. Frances hesitated, but allowed herself to become convinced it was the proper and necessary step to take. The stronger the demands sought by her lawyer upon her husband, the more agitated Frances became. She even accused Eulalia Chapin of siding with Fonda. While Mrs. Chapin protested she was completely neutral, the legal claims in the divorce action grew greater. Reservations were made for the plaintiff to leave for Las Vegas, Nevada, where she would establish residence.

At that point Frances Fonda suffered a complete nervous breakdown. Her mother took her back to the Austen Riggs Foundation, the sanitarium in Stockbridge, Massachusetts.

By the end of November 1949 Frances was virtually a permanent resident at Riggs. She visited with her family in Greenwich for short periods, always accompanied by a nurse, and then she would return to the place she now referred to as "home."

Eulalia Chapin noticed that Frances Fonda's eyes had lost their brightness. These days when Frances looked at people it was through dull brown buttons—unseeing, lifeless.

"So sad," Mrs. Chapin sighed. "She had been such a captivating personality, great poise, a brilliant woman. She was the gayest, most delightful human being in the world, but I was with Frances in a doctor's office during the Johns Hopkins period and I remember he cautioned her to try to keep on an even keel. When everything went well, she was high, so high. But if anything interrupted the smooth tenor of her life, she'd sink into an abyss of despondency. He told her to make an attempt not to be too easily affected by changing circumstances, but Frances couldn't control her reactions, her highs and lows."

In February a psychiatrist from Riggs made an appointment to meet with Henry in New York, Dr. Robert Knight used a New York Colleague's office on Park Avenue. They spoke for two hours; Henry asking questions, the doctor answering him. His prognosis for Frances was discouraging. At the end of the conversation, the psychiatrist pulled out a file and read it to Fonda.

"Emotional deterioration, extreme depression, suicidal threats," the doctor concluded.

Suicide? Her husband was shaken.

"I suggest, Mr. Fonda," Dr. Knight pressed on, "that your wife be transferred immediately to a hospital that offers increased security and more personal attention than we are able to provide."

The following week Frances Seymour Fonda was moved to the Craig Sanitarium, Beacon, New York.

In 1859 Joseph Howland, a Duchess County farmer, built a Victorian mansion far too elegant for the ninety-one acres that surrounded it. Complete with a pipe organ, rococo balconies and lattice work, Howland barely had time to move in when the Civil War broke out. A wealthy man and a strong supporter of the Union, he raised and commanded the 16th New York Infantry Regiment. He came out of the war a brigadier general, spent a few years playing his pipe organ, and died.

In 1915 Dr. Clarence Slocum, a pioneer in the field of American psychiatry, bought the Howland property and opened a clinic and sanitarium which he named Craig House after a highly respected open institution in Edinburgh, Scotland. By the time his son, Dr. Jonathan Slocum, took over following World War II, the hospital had over three hundred acres including a golf course, riding stables, and cottages and buildings small enough to house four to six patients apiece.

Craig House or Hospital was and is an execllent retreat for the upper classes to send the mentally ill members of their families. Loosely connected with the Austen Riggs Foundation, it sits above the east bank of the Hudson River. Behind it is the end of the Berkshire Chain. Across the narrowing Hudson, no longer the majestic river that flows past Manhattan, is the start of the Ramapo Mountains.

On February 3, 1950, as the sullen clouds met the snow-covered hills and the ice-choked river, Frances Fonda was checked into Craig. The building in which she stayed is a small hundred-year-old farmhouse whose buff bricks are painted white. Exclusivity went in hand with special care.

Referred by Dr. Knight to Dr. Slocum, Frances found herself with a friend. The Slocums, like the Seymours, were an old and distinguished New York family. In his youth as a Yalie Dr. Slocum had attended Frances's debut in Connecticut. The medical staff was happy to be of service to Mrs. Fonda, but her depression was so deep that at the time of her arrival at Craig she scarcely knew where she was.

Oscar Hammerstein II was the gentlest of gentlemen. If he raised his voice, no one in the theater will ever admit having heard it. If he had a temper tantrum so typical of Broadway, not a soul in show business will claim to have seen it. When he telephoned Henry Fonda one day and asked if he might meet with him, Fonda agreed at once, although he had no idea of what Hammerstein had in mind.

214

They met after a performance in Fonda's one-room apartment on Sixty-seventh Street.

"Hank?" the older man asked in the kindest of voices.

"Yes, Ockie?"

"I'd like to say this in the nicest way."

"Go ahead," Fonda bent forward to hear the other man's words.

"What do you think the future is for you and Susan?"

Fonda got to his feet slowly, almost as though his joints were thinking instead of his brain.

"Ockie," he said when he finally reached his full height, "I'm sure you're aware of the situation with my wife."

"I am," Hammerstein nodded.

"Then you also know I can't file for divorce from a woman who's as sick as she is."

Oscar Hammerstein II had many credits on Broadway. Hit after hit after hit. Many words have been employed to describe him. Understanding is not the least of them. He looked at Fonda and nodded his head in agreement.

"I can only tell you," Fonda concluded, "that I have nothing but honorable intentions toward Susan."

Hammerstein leaned his solid body back in his chair.

"Hank? Got anything to drink?"

"Yup."

"How about a ginger ale?"

"Fine. That's just about right for the occasion."

Locked in with the world locked out, Frances sat rocking, her head bowed, her hands folded in her lap. The nurse, tired of trying to make conversation, was turning the pages of a fashion magazine when Frances leaped up and dashed across the small carpeted room to a partly open window.

Before the nurse could prevent her, Frances tore off her wedding ring and threw it between the bars. The ring landed in a snow bank and disappeared.

For a second she wore a victorious expression, and then she seemed confused. She wanted her ring.

The staff had difficulty finding the small gold object. Frances was distraught until they returned it to her. She slipped the ring back onto her finger, sat down, folded her hands, and rocked and rocked.

On a Saturday in the first week in March Frances drove down to Greenwich with her companion. She knew that Henry would be in the city doing a matinee of *Roberts*. The children played jacks on the living room floor while the nurse and Sophie chatted. Suddenly, Frances arose and raced up the staircase. The nurse was puzzled. Frances had been home before and had behaved very well.

"Excuse me," she said to Sophie, "I think I'd better follow Mrs. Fonda."

Mrs. Chapin reported what happened next. "Her nurse saw Frances standing near her dressing table, and as she entered the bedroom, Frances was startled and dropped an object to the floor.

"I can't forget this ever, because what fell from her hand was a black-enameled box I'd once brought back from Europe as a gift for Frances," Mrs. Chapin said, stopping for a few seconds.

"The nurse grabbed the box, opened it, and looked inside. It was empty. I didn't learn about this until much later. You see, I could have told them. That's where Frances kept the tiny razor she used for underarm shaving, and that's the day she hid that razor on herself someplace. She obviously took it back into the sanitarium that night."

The personnel at Craig House didn't find it until it was too late.

Toward the end of March Mrs. Fonda's doctor reported her condition vastly improved. Her depression had lifted, she showed considerable interest in her surroundings. Frances played bridge and played it well. She gave the impression of a patient about to receive a one-way ticket home.

But on the morning of April 14, 1950, in a steady hand, Frances wrote six notes, one each to her three children, one to her mother, one to her nurse.

"Mrs. Gray," the message read, "do not enter the bathroom, but call Dr. Bennett."

The sixth and final note was addressed to her psychiatrist, Dr. Courtney Bennett.

"Dr. Bennett," Frances wrote, "you've done everything possible for me. I'm sorry, but this is the best way out."

Then she walked into her bathroom with the razor she had kept hidden for over a month. She had saved it for this moment.

Frances Seymour Fonda, on her forty-second birthday, cut her throat from ear to ear.

When the nurse arrived with Mrs. Fonda's orange juice, she found the written message on the floor. Dr. Courtney Bennett was summoned. Frances was still alive, but died a few minutes later. A tiny razor blade lay near her body.

Henry Fonda had an appointment for a publicity interview. He had already stepped into the elevator of his brownstone building and was about to push the button when he heard the phone ringing in his apartment. He considered not answering and then thought, "No, it may be important."

It was his mother-in-law's voice on the other end of the telephone.

"My God," Fonda gasped when he heard the tragic news. "I'm sorry. I'm so sorry. I'll pick you up right away."

At first he had trouble breathing. He thought he might faint. He couldn't. Sophie was waiting in Greenwich.

He went through every red light out of Manhattan and broke every speed limit on the parkway to Connecticut.

"I came home from school and put down my books," Jane remembered. "My grandmother stood at the top of the stairs. I really couldn't see her face.

" 'I don't want you to go out,' my grandmother said. 'Your mother is sick.'

"But then my mother was always sick. They were forever telling me that. I had a date with my girl friend, Diane, to go riding, so I left anyway."

217

When Fonda arrived, he helped Sophie gently into the car. Then he returned to the seat behind the wheel. As they made the dolorous journey to Beacon, they spoke in half sentences, softly, controlled.

"Our mother was gone most of the time," Peter Fonda said, his mind remaining vividly clear. "I'd started fantasizing that she would die, and Dad would marry my fourth-grade teacher, Miss Thompson. She was kind and nice, and I needed that.

"But then I came home from school that day, later than Jane. She'd gone down to the stables, which you could get to by foot, maybe a three-mile walk. I went into the kitchen and Katie, the maid, was polishing silver. She acted kind of odd. I asked her where everyone was.

" 'Well,' she said, 'they've gone to see about your mother at the hospital.'

" 'Is there something wrong?' " I asked.

" 'I don't know,' she said, but she said it in a strange way. It gave me a peculiar sensation in my stomach.

"I'd been so close to my mother in California. When I was afraid of the water, she'd stand in the pool and smile and encourage me, 'Jump into my arms, Peter.'

"I thought of that and I went into the living room. I think I could hear a clock ticking somewhere. That's all. I kneeled down at the end of the couch and I prayed to the Lord to take care of my mother so that she would come to no harm.

"Then I walked to my riding lesson. Jane and her friend were just leaving."

Perhaps it was April, but to Henry and Sophie the skies were leaden, the trees on the mountain overlooking the main building stood bare and forlorn.

A doctor sat behind his mahogany desk and explained that there was no way an incident like this could have been prevented.

"When a patient makes up his mind to take his own life," the doctor pronounced, "he finds a way to do it." Then he offered a few words of sympathy. Sophie and Henry got back into the car, and went to the village of

218

Beacon, to the McGlassen & Son Funeral Home. There they made plans for a brief service. Only the two of them attended. A hearse took Frances's body to Hartsdale, New York, to be cremated. The grieving pair drove back to Greenwich.

"In the car," Fonda says, "Sophie and I decided that the children were too young for the truth. Sophie suggested that since their mother had been away in a hospital for so long, we could just say she got sick and died there."

Following that discussion, they rode on in silence.

"When I came back, my grandmother was in a chair in the living room, and my father was on the couch," Jane Fonda said. "Clearly, something was wrong. I sat down next to Dad.

" 'Your mother has died of a heart attack, Jane,' Dad told me.

"I stood up. 'I want to go to my room,' I said.

"I sat on the edge of the bed and wondered why I couldn't cry. And I thought, 'How weird. I'm never going to see her again, and I can't cry.' I never cried. I went back downstairs."

"When I got back home," Peter said, "the entire family was there except for Mother. I had no idea what was going on. I crossed the room to them, and Dad said softly, 'Peter, Mummy is dead.' I turned away. The tears came down fast. I can still see myself crying."

At six-thirty in the evening, Henry Fonda put his arms around his two children. With his handkerchief he dabbed the tears from Peter's cheeks, patted Jane and her brother atop their heads, and started the drive into New York.

In the haunting shadows of the worklight on the stage of the Alvin Theater Billy Hammerstein had spent the better part of the afternoon rehearsing Fonda's understudy, Marshall Jamison. As a rule on Broadway understudies are underrehearsed. It is only when illness or some natural disaster strikes that they are quickly put through their assigned lines.

Marshall Jamison was as tall as Fonda but a good twenty pounds heavier. He had his own trousers, his own blouse, his own cap. What he needed was more work with his fellow actors. The few hours he spent on the stage each month, generally before a Wednesday matinee, wasn't really enough time to give anything resembling a polished performance. Hammerstein was still going over the scenes that involved Roberts when Fonda arrived at the theater.

He went directly to his dressing room. Leland Hayward, the play's producer, awaited him.

"Hank," Leland asked, "you're not going on tonight, are you?"

Even Josh Logan's sunlamps, used twice weekly by the actors, couldn't conceal the ashen color of Fonda's face.

The producer was sorry he'd even bothered to ask the question.

"There're a lot of reporters, Hank. They're waiting for a statement. Is this all right?"

He showed Fonda a single typewritten line.

"It's awfully hard to say how I feel," the quote read.

"Fine," Fonda nodded.

Hayward left and Fonda changed from his street clothes into costume. He glanced into the mirror. The mask wasn't there.

Leland Hayward returned to the dressing room followed by Joshua Logan and Billy Hammerstein. The halting, stumbling words of sympathy came out of the three men, and, finally, the twin questions came to the fore: Should a performance be given that night, and if so, should Fonda appear?

"Leland pointed out that maybe it wasn't the smartest thing to do," Billy Hammerstein remembered clearly, "at least, not from his point of view."

"Fonda just sat there, grim-faced, and without any doubt in his mind whether he should give a performance," Hammerstein added.

No matter how persuasively Leland Hayward spoke, in the end, the decision was Fonda's.

"I'm going on," the actor said firmly. "It's the only way I can get through the evening."

That decided it. The three men left Fonda's dressing room, Logan and Hayward went out front, Hammerstein continued on to dismiss Marshall Jamison.

Fonda looked into his mirror again. The mask was on.

"I was running the show that night," Ruth Mitchell, Billy Hammerstein's assistant, recollected, "and one of the things that sticks out in my mind is that no one knew what to say or do when he came into the theater that night. Hank looked terrible. He was upset beyond belief, but he tried not to show it.

"We always had a joke that we played as the turntable came around and he passed my desk. There was about a two-foot space where I could see him and I would always wave to him or blow him a kiss as he went past. That night, I thought, 'Oh, my God! What do I do? Do I do it tonight? Or does it seem like I'm making light of something that I know he's going through?'

"Well, Leland had said to us, 'Behave just as if nothing has happened. He's here and he wants to do his job and he wants to work.' So I did my little wave as Hank came by on the turntable. And just as he caught my eye, he saluted and went out of my sight."

"His performance that night, I swear to you," William Hammerstein stated, "was no different in spirit or essence or anything else than the performance he gave on opening night, except for a few little things he'd done over the years to improve it."

After the play Henry Fonda knew he could not spend the night in the tight little room atop the brownstone on East Sixty-seventh Street. Logan and Hayward took him to the Logan home in River House.

"Hank was silent and numbed," Nedda Logan recalled. "Josh was shocked and worried about the children, but Leland was very talkative and kept things up."

When Hayward left, quiet fell back into the Logan's sitting room. Without a word, Fonda went back into the bedroom he'd stayed in so many times during the run of the play. He took off his jacket and neatly placed it on a hanger in the closet. Then he walked into the bathroom and turned on both water taps over the sink. He didn't want the Logans to hear his sobs.

CHAPTER
10

FOR many people Easter is the time for resurrection, for hope and anticipation. Once again in 1950 New Yorkers clothed themselves in bright garments and brave spirits. Freshness lingered in the air.

Nature and people bestirred themselves.

Henry Fonda left the city and drove through the burgeoning countryside to be with his children in Connecticut. In contrast to the greening that surrounded the twin cement ribbons on which he drove, Henry Fonda was glum. He carried on the seat beside him two large Easter baskets that he had meticulously arranged for Jane and Peter, and a box of creamy chocolates for his mother-in-law. He also carried with him a load of guilt.

Since the death of his wife every mail that arrived at the theater contained unsigned, abusive crank letters. Tabloid columns attacked him with innuendoes on two fronts: his wife's despair and subsequent end, and his relationship with Susan. As the car rolled northward Fonda gave serious consideration to never seeing Susan again. They had broken off before, but the event that took place at Craig House could very well send their lives in opposite directions.

After two quiet days with Jane, Peter, and Sophie, Fonda returned to Manhattan for the Monday evening show. Even his relationship with his fellow actors had been strained. The *Roberts* cast controlled their loud laughter and bawdy speech when Fonda drew near. They lowered their voices and, sometimes, when he approached, they even stopped talking.

"Embarrassment, I guess," Fonda says. "They didn't know how to handle the situation."

That night in his mail cubicle below the company call board he found a long white envelope. It was postmarked Stockbridge, Massachusetts, and the chief of the Austen Riggs Foundation had dictated a letter to his secretary:

Dear Mr. Fonda:

I am writing to you both to express the sympathy of myself and my associates at the Riggs Foundation and to make some further comments which may help you in connection with your wife's tragic death.

Because of our having worked with Mrs. Fonda for several weeks we were in a position to know the extent and depth of her distress, and we were extremely sorry that we could not carry through with her treatment. Her death was a shock to all of us. We realize very well, however, the nature of the management and treatment problem which confronted the staff at Craig House. There is common agreement among experienced psychiatrists that if a patient is deeply determined not to live, all precautions can be circumvented by that patient; and, as I think I told you in our two-hour talk last February 2, Mrs. Fonda was so deeply disturbed and depressed that the protection of her against herself was going to be a very serious problem.

In my talk with you I was impressed strongly with your great good will and integrity with respect to her and the break-up of your marriage. Your good relationships with her mother and her lawyer were evidence of both good will and integrity. I wanted to tell you then—but I felt I shouldn't, and do feel I can tell you now, that Mrs. Fonda herself felt that your marriage had been on the rocks for a long time and was not on the rocks only because of your expressed wish to her to be divorced and to remarry. She was aware of many difficulties in herself that long antedated your asking for a divorce, and, as a matter of fact, it was because of the extent and intensity of her awareness of past personal difficulties that she was so desperately ill. Your asking her for a divorce was merely the immediate trigger for this distressing awareness, and not the cause. Apparently, she felt hopeless about coping with her personal conflicts and took her life in a mood of exacerbated hopelessness. This may even have come at a time when she appeared to be improving, as so many times happens. Her chances for reconstituting and readjusting herself were really not good, and she must have realized this.

Thus, while we wish to extend to you and to her mother and the children our sincere sympathy, we also wanted to assure you that you had done all you could, that you had been strong and tolerant through the troublous episode, and that you have no justification for self-reproach. May I also express the hope that you can now find the contentment and satisfaction that you had been seeking. Mrs. Fonda also said many times that you were a swell guy and that you deserved a happiness she knew she could not give you. So maybe she was also trying to help you when she arranged this solution for you both.

Sincerely yours,

Robert P. Knight, M.D.
Medical Director

The mist of gloom that had hung over him since Frances's death started to lift.

The next day he dialed Susan and read her the letter. They met for a late supper after the performance.

"Except for notes of sympathy," Fonda says, "almost all of my friends steered clear of me. Susan, on the other hand, offered consolation and tenderness. In Omaha we'd say, 'That's just what the doctor ordered.'"

In Greenwich, by the end of Easter vacation, Sophie Seymour and Henry Fonda determined the children should return to school, and it was in school that Jane learned the details of her mother's death, the hard way.

"I was with Jane when she found out her mother hadn't died of a heart attack," Brooke Hayward recaptured the scene. "Her reaction was amazing. She never said a word. Nothing. We were in art class at the Greenwich Academy and we were reading a movie magazine which we weren't supposed to do. There was an analysis of major movie stars, a synopsis of their lives. Each one had a little paragaph under his picture. And, of course, there was Henry Fonda. And it said his wife committed suicide. I read faster than Jane. I saw the piece, and I remembered flipping the page and she flipped it right back. I had to watch her read that. And then she turned the page over."

"Is it true?" Jane Fonda asked her friend.

"I couldn't answer," Brooke Hayward said.

Jane Fonda, some years later, spoke candidly of her immediate reaction to the magazine article.

"I was just stunned! It was dramatic. I mean it was a combination, and I'm being perfectly honest, it was a combination of horror and fascination. How much more interesting than a heart attack. When I got home I went to Mrs. Wallace. She was a nurse. My grandmother was sick and we had a nurse in the house for a while. I asked her to come up to my room. She was a formal lady and I asked her, and she told me yes, it was true.

"She also told me that my grandmother had received a letter from the doctors prior to the suicide. I remember the words she used, in fact. The doctors had said she's no longer behind the eight ball. They said she's coming out of it, she's okay, and they had taken some of the security away from her. The impression was that she was doing very well."

"Jane had given me no hint of being disturbed," Brooke Hayward said. "But that summer, we went to camp together in New Hampshire. Jane would wake up in the middle of the night screaming about her mother. I mean screaming so that the entire staff had to appear to calm her down."

Fonda never heard about Jane's nightmares. He didn't

even know she had learned the truth about her mother's death. Like many fathers he felt comfortable that he had properly protected his children from the anguish that facts would have brought them.

The only member of the immediate family Sophie Seymour told about Frances's death was Pan. And like her stepsister, Jane, Pan's sleep was filled with recurring visions of her mother lying on a chaise longue surrounded by blood.

By August natives of New York apologized to visitors by assuring them that the unbearable weather was a result not of the heat but of the humidity. People swarmed into that bit of land known as Central Park where they rowed boats on its lagoon, bought Italian ices, watched the seals in the zoo, and fed peanuts to the pigeons and squirrels. Others enjoyed a couple of hours of air conditioning and exceptional acting at the Alvin Theater.

Henry rented a larger apartment in Turtle Bay, did his eight performances, and sometimes spent his weekends in Greenwich. On one or two of the hottest Sundays of the summer, he took Susan and Peter to Jones Beach to stretch out on the sand or swim in the Atlantic surf.

Ten-year-old Peter eyed Susan with a bit of suspicion, but had to admit to himself that his father appeared in better humor when the pretty girl joined them.

Peter had a habit dating back to the days when his father was away in the Navy during the war. He would sneak into his father's closet, slip into Henry's shoes, and walk around in them. They were two or three inches too long, and Peter tripped over his feet, but it gave him a sense of being nearer to his dad.

He would get behind the wheel of the big black Buick that rested on blocks in the garage at Tigertail and pretend he was his father driving the car. Back in the bedroom he would open drawers in his father's bureau and smell the handkerchiefs and socks, anything to bring memories of his dad surging back into his senses.

Through the years Peter continued this secret but pleasurable pastime. In his father's apartment in New York he had fun examining his father's jewelry. All the cuff links were initialed. Peter pored over the Hs and the Fs.

"Then one day," Peter reminisced, "I opened up the cuff link box, and in it was a little heart on the end of a key chain, and inside the heart was an engraved heart with an arrow through it, and the engraving said, 'S' and 'H.' So I knew the 'S' had to be Susan and the 'H' was Henry, and I thought, 'Gee! He's getting married.' And I was very upset by it. Very upset.

"Well, I went right to my grandmother and told her about what I had found and what I was afraid of. And she said it was true. And I said, 'No! No!' I was mad."

"You need to have a mother," Peter's grandmother told him.

"But I didn't want one!" Peter recalled. "No way did I want one!"

Sophie never told Fonda of his son's objections, and Fonda continued to see Susan, appear in *Mister Roberts*, and, in the summer, play in the Broadway Show League, a series of softball games made up of teams of the various plays and musicals in New York.

"You'd think with all those brawny young sailors the *Roberts* team would win every game," Fonda says. "But no! We'd get whipped regularly by the chorus boys from *South Pacific* or *Gentlemen Prefer Blondes* or *Peter Pan*.

"In one game, though, when I was at bat, I punched a clean line drive smack into Walter Matthau's balls. He never to this day lets me forget that. He claims I was trying to put him out of commission, right there in front of everybody in Central Park."

Matthau's injury was temporary, but Fonda, during the course of one of the seven-inning games, slid into second base and twisted his knee. He continued in the role of Doug Roberts until the week after Thanksgiving. Then he checked into Doctors Hospital.

"Twenty years earlier I'd had an operation for the removal of cartilage in my knee," Fonda says, "and it was a bitch. They had me in a plaster cast for six weeks, and at the end of that time, I had to ride a stationary bicycle for months to get the leg back into shape.

"But now the operation had advanced to the point

227

where the day after surgery they had my leg dangling over the side of the bed and a sandbag hooked onto my toe."

"He wasn't very far out of the junk they'd given him in surgery," Peter Fonda smiled as he told the story. "The best way to talk to my father was when he was under the influence of some major drug, a serious downer so that he didn't have the chance to go after me the way he had ever since he'd come out of the Navy. 'Ah, Peter, did you hang the towels up straight? Peter, did you put the cap on the toothpaste?' I heard a lot of that in my life, and when Grandma took me to visit him in the hospital, he was a pussycat. He didn't ask me how my grades were, he didn't tell me not to make noise. I had a great time."

When Jane arrived two days later her father was in far better condition. This was when she first caught sight of Susan.

She had stopped by the hospital unexpectedly and there, beside her father's bed, sat a young woman. Henry introduced them and Jane knew that this lovely person must be the "tomato" her classmates had teased her about.

"She had blonde hair pulled back in a chignon," Jane remembered, "and she had light blue eyes. She was extremely beautiful. She had on a black skirt, a black velvet watchband, and an old-fashioned white blouse that had a high neck. I just couldn't believe it! She was warm and friendly and engaging. Susan was everything I wanted to be."

On December 28, 1950, Dr. Everett Clinchy, president of the National Conference of Christians and Jews, performed the ceremony that united Susan Blanchard and Henry Fonda. The place was the Hammerstein home on East Sixty-third Street.

For the Hammersteins, it was a busy day. Not only did they have a wedding and a wedding reception to give, but shortly after it was over, they had to slip away and attend the wedding of Elaine Scott and John Steinbeck.

The Fondas spent their wedding night at the Plaza Hotel.

The Steinbecks had rooms at the St. Regis Hotel.

"We behaved very silly," Mrs. Steinbeck recalled. "We

were in our suite drinking champagne, and they were in theirs, drinking champagne. And we called each other far into the night. We were like children, but we enjoyed ourselves immensely."

The next day the Fondas flew to honeymoon at Caneel Bay Plantation on St. Johns, Virgin Islands.

"It was a very attractive part of the world," Fonda says. "Ideal for a honeymoon, almost like a South Sea island. We'd planned to stay there for a week or two. But one night, well after dinner, just as we're getting ready for bed, someone came and knocked on the door of our cottage. There was a message for me at the office.

"I trotted down there and it turned out that one of the people who lived on the island permanently had a shortwave radio, and he'd heard a report from the Coast Guard that Henry Fonda who was known to be in this area was wanted. 'His son has been in a shooting accident!'

"My God! Susan and I packed immediately. The only way to get off the island was by skiff, and by the time we were ready to shove off, a pretty good surf was running. From Caneel Bay we took a launch to St. Thomas, and from there we took the feeder flight to hook up with Pan Am which took us to Bermuda. It wasn't the most direct way, but they assured us it was the fastest, and that's all that mattered.

"I worried myself sick. What kind of shooting accident? Could my boy be dead? What the hell happened?

"In Bermuda I finally got to a telephone and reached Grandma Seymour, and she told me Peter had shot himself accidentally and that he was in a hospital in Ossining alive and holding his own. By the time the Pan Am flight took off for La Guardia both Susan and I wondered how on earth a ten-year-old boy got a gun to shoot himself?

"I should have guessed. Ever since Peter was six he was a con artist. He could con almost anybody into almost anything. While Susan and I were away, he went to work on Grandma Seymour. He pleaded and he connived to get that twenty-two-caliber rifle out from under the lock in the closet. He told her he and two other boys were just going out and all he wanted to do was carry it. Look.

229

No bullets. No bullets, no shooting. He may have been skinny and little but he was smart as a bird dog during the hunting season. Before she knew it, Grandma Seymour took her key, unlocked the closet, and away scooted Peter with his rifle. What she didn't know was that the other two boys had pockets bulging with round after round of ammunition."

"Tony Abry, Pan's brother-in-law, and Reed Armstrong, her husband's nephew, had their grandfather's car and chauffeur," Peter disclosed, "and the chauffeur drove us over to the Abry estate near Katonah where there was a regular shooting range. One of the boys showed off an antique pistol that cocked when you broke it, just like a shotgun. The trigger laid up against the stem like a derringer. I put in the shell, and when I closed it, the whole fucking mechanism went around and discharged right into me.

"It went right into my belly, hit my rib cage, blew off a piece of my liver, tumbled through my stomach, just missed my abdominal aorta, slammed right through the center of my kidney, and made just a lump on the skin of my back right next to my spine.

"That chauffeur saved my life. I stumbled to the car, yelling that I'd been shot. And he didn't waste a word on me. He just shoveled me up and put me into the car, and drove like hell for the hospital in Ossining.

"Dr. Charles Clark Sweet, bless his name, was the prison physician at Sing Sing. He had puncture-wound and bullet-wound expertise, and he walked into the hospital from a hunting trip just as they brought me in. That's where the luck comes in. While they were prepping me, he scrubbed, and by the time he was ready, I was waiting on the table in the operating room, and he did some kind of job sewing and patching and stitching."

Despite the skill of the surgeon's knife, Death beckoned Peter Fonda. The surgeon emerged from the operating room to tell the waiting Sophie and Jane that the boy's heart had stopped beating. They'd managed to start it again, but he was dying, and unfortunately, there was not much else they could do for him.

"I remember when he was dying, I remember hearing

the doctor say, 'I don't know if he's going to pull through,' and I remember praying," Jane Fonda admitted. "That was the first time in my life I remember praying. 'Dear God,' I whispered, 'if you let him live, I'll never be mean to him again.' "

Henry Fonda arrived in his son's hospital room, well beyond midnight. All he saw was the narrow figure under the white sheet and the small, drained face with tubes coming out of his mouth and nostrils. There was nothing for the father to do but sit in a chair and watch his immobile child.

At three in the morning a compassionate nurse called him outside the boy's room and promised to telephone if any change occurred. It seemed better, she believed, for Fonda to have strength to face tomorrow and whatever it might bring.

Back in New York Henry Fonda caught a restless hour of sleep, and then made the return trip to Ossining. This routine continued for five days. On the sixth the doctors pronounced Peter had passed the crisis. Within a week he was considered in stable condition. Within another week he was out of danger and on the road back to chicanery.

"My sister," Peter recounted, "*was* a mean little girl. She was always so mean to me. Years later she told me, 'You know, when you were dying, I prayed to God that if He let you live, I would never be mean to you again. And you know? I was mean to you again right away.' "

"I couldn't help it," Jane explained. "He was a rotten kid in those days. He was back to being a brat before we knew he was well. I loved him anyhow."

Jane returned to the Greenwich Academy for her last semester. Peter spent a month in the hospital and a month recuperating at home.

"I went back to school after my birthday. In social studies the teacher brought in a cake. On it were the words, 'Happy Birthday to Lead Belly.' "

Around the beginning of February 1951 Henry and Susan Fonda flew to Pittsburgh where he took over the National Company of *Mister Roberts*.

Fonda is one of the few actors who enjoys trouping.

"*Roberts* was nine months on the road," he says, "and it was a wonderful tour for me. I enjoy touring for openers, and taking a good play with a good company out into the regional areas. In Boston or Philadelphia or Chicago they get first-class theater a lot. But to play Detroit, Pittsburgh, Kansas City, St. Louis, Portland and Seattle, when you took 'em something they loved, they wanted to hug you and say thank you. They didn't get it often enough. That's a great feeling and we were getting that wherever we went."

He opened in Pittsburgh, then played Cleveland, Columbus, Cincinnati, Madison, Des Moines, Minneapolis, Omaha.

"Let me tell you about playing my hometown," Fonda says, "not because it's my hometown, but because by the time we pulled out of Minneapolis and got as far as St. Paul, we were stopped cold by a small mountain of snow. The train couldn't move another foot. Abe Cohen, our company manager, got to a telephone and called Omaha. All the house manager had to say was that we were supposed to set up on Monday and open on Tuesday.

"Well, that was impossible. Our train was buried in a snowdrift that was higher than the smokestack of the engine, and by the time the snowplow came through, it was morning.

"We pulled into Omaha Tuesday afternoon. No scenery. No props. Just our uniforms. And a peek at the front pages of the local newspapers and we decided to give two performances. All they carried were *Mister Roberts* stories. That was the most important thing to hit that town in years and years.

"So we gave a six o'clock performance and a nine o'clock performance, and people are still talking, 'I saw *Mister Roberts* in Omaha, Nebraska, with no scenery.'

"Well, the play worked. I came out before we began and explained where the gun mounts were and where the hatch was, and the audience painted their own scenery. It was a wonderful experience."

After that the company moved on to Denver and Salt Lake City and from there to Seattle and then down the West Coast.

"Susan was marvelous," Fonda says. "If we stayed someplace that was longer than a week's stand, we'd take an apartment, and very often she'd cook my after-theater supper. The company doted on Susan. Everybody got along beautifully."

In San Francisco, the last stop before Los Angeles where the moviemakers were waiting, Joshua Logan arrived to spruce up the performances. It is almost axiomatic that on the road actors grow sloppy in their performances. They tend to throw away lines or, even worse, begin to add words of their own. Fonda didn't believe this happened with the *Roberts* cast.

"While I wasn't captain of the ship," he says, "I was head of the *Roberts* family. They'd come to me if they had any problems. I was proud that it worked out that way and that I'd earned their respect. We'd worked hard and well together to give audiences the best we had."

Logan saw the first performance in San Francisco and was appalled. Fonda, he recognized, remained perfect, but the other actors had fallen into the trap of playing Fonda.

"What I watched was a stage filled with Doug Robertses," Logan said angrily. "They had become so bland and so easy-going that, I thought, large portions of the ebullient comedy of the play had been lost."

Logan rehearsed the cast as much as he could, but time forbade a complete overhaul. They closed in San Francisco and Logan telephoned Fonda prior to the Los Angeles opening.

"I'm sorry," he told Fonda, "I couldn't stay any longer."

"Thank God for that," Fonda answered.

"You mean you didn't want me to bring it back to its original spirit?"

"No," replied Fonda, "I don't feel it's my play anymore."

"You bastard," Logan roared into the telephone. "It's *my* play."

For a moment there Josh Logan's name was added to Fonda's Darryl Francis Zanuck list.

"If you got too near to Hank during the next couple of days," a member of the cast reported, "you were in dan-

233

ger of getting frostbite. He was like dry ice. You could even see the steam."

Whosever play it was *Mister Roberts* opened in the "City of the Angels" where it met with the usual rave notices and the usual SRO sign on the box-office window. Sunlight and adulation thawed out Fonda.

Since school was over, Jane and Peter were shepherded onto an airplane and flown to the West Coast to be with their father and his new bride.

"I was very unsure when I married him," Susan commented recently regarding Fonda. "I was your typical Japanese wife. I wanted to do everything to please him."

If she had any concerns in terms of Peter and Jane, they were quickly dispelled. She and Henry met the children at the Los Angeles airport. Henry eagerly lifted his eleven-year-old son over the fence and scraped his knee. Susan's first job was to patch it up. Unlike Jane, Peter had originally opposed his father's marriage. Now, when the four of them moved into Ocean House, he reassessed his opinion.

"I adored her. She saved my act!" Peter emphasized. "She gave us so much of her valuable time and so much of herself. Dad was off doing his show, and Susan spent all of the matinee days and all of the evenings with us.

"The lipstick affair is a good example of Dad as opposed to Susan. I still liked to poke around in other people's bureau drawers. One day I came across a metallic tube. I didn't know what it was, but I opened it. It was a lipstick and Susan rarely wore lipstick. So I turned it till it came out and then I put a little of it on my fingertip to see what it looked like, how it smelled, how it tasted. Then, without rolling it down, I pushed back the top, squashing it. Susan never complained to me, never scolded me, but Dad got wind of it and he made me pay for that lipstick out of my twenty-five-cent weekly allowance. I tell you, it took a helluva long time for me to pay off, but my father taught me you don't go in there and squash anybody's lipstick. And I ain't ever gonna squash another lipstick tube in my life. But Susan was a very reasonable person, and my feelings toward her began to swing the other way that summer in California."

234

Jane proved even easier to win over. At thirteen Jane edged into adolescence and searched if not for a mother then at least someone after whom she might pattern herself. Her father's young wife quickly became her ideal.

"Susan was my role model," Jane Fonda admitted. "She was incredibly charming, funny, and outgoing. When I wanted to dress like her, she helped me dress like her. When I wanted to look like her, she helped me with that. She put in a lot of time with us, a lot of time. Thinking back, when I realize how young she was, I appreciate her even more."

As summer drew to an end, so did the final curtain of Henry Fonda's play. After the last performance Joshua Logan burst into the actor's dressing room, all thoughts of the San Francisco rehearsal differences forgotten. He seized Fonda's hand and pumped it enthusiastically.

"You son-of-a-bitch," he beamed, "you were better tonight than when you opened in New York!"

Next to "The part is yours," no sweeter words on earth exist for an actor.

CHAPTER
11

THERE was no doubt in Hollywood now, if there ever had been, Henry Fonda was the All-American hero. Screenwriters, in their cement bungalows on the studio lots, their brows furrowed, their fingers pecking away at their typewriters, turned out script after script for Henry Fonda. High studio chiefs, in their pickled-oak offices, sat behind their magnificent desks and fingered ivory letter openers as they spoke cajolingly to agents about scenarios for the man in the white hat on the white horse galloping forth for Metro-Goldwyn-Mayer or charging to the rescue of Twentieth Century-Fox. Harry Cohn had visions of Fonda riding the range and rounding up grosses for Columbia Pictures. Jack Warner was ready to offer him a sheriff's badge of twenty-four-carat gold. Henry Fonda graciously turned down their horses and heroines and signed for another play. It was the lead in Paul Osborn's adaptation of the John P. Marquand novel, *Point of No Return*.

Leland Hayward, who produced *Mister Roberts*, would serve the same function on *Point of No Return*. Hank Potter, whom Hank Fonda knew and respected in the University Players days, who had directed Hayward's first Broadway hit, *A Bell for Adano*, had been hired to repeat his work with the new play. Leora Dana, fresh from the New York smash *Happy Time*, had been engaged to play opposite Fonda.

Hayward spoke so glowingly of the play's future that

Fonda invested his own money, an absolutely unheard-of financial move for Henry Fonda.

Before they left for New York, Susan readied Jane and Peter for boarding schools in the East; Jane to Emma Willard, in Troy, New York, Peter to the Fay School in upper Massachusetts.

"Susan was my summer," Jane's voice filled with fond memory. "That was the summer that prepared me for going away to Emma Willard, and Susan bought me the clothes and went with me. And she was a mother to me. She must have been twenty-one. I couldn't have done that when I was twenty-one years old. Susan took responsibility really, really seriously, and I love her deeply for it."

Peter, packed off to the Fay School, forced to make up the sixth grade due to his shooting accident, was filled with resentment and resolved to return to his starring role as mischief maker when a sudden, unexpected emotion came over him.

"I needed to call somebody Mom, just like my grandmother had said," Peter remembered. "So I went to my math teacher at Fay and asked him the propriety of calling Susan 'Mom.' He told me I could if I wanted to and if she had no objection. So I wrote to her and she wrote back and said yes. I was happy as the devil must be when Sunday School lets out."

That was more than could be said for Peter's father. Somehow, during the trek back to New York, the script of *Point of No Return* seemed to have undergone a change.

"It read well in California," Fonda says, "but when we got on our feet in New York, I knew right off something was wrong with the play."

The large production had four heavy sets under construction from Jo Mielziner's designs, and while rehearsals went well, Fonda was unhappy.

Jane still laughs about a story Susan told her. "Your father is the kind of man who could stay in his art studio all day long, every day of the year. He never needed to see me. All he needed to know was that I was there.

"Once, when we were on the road with *Point of No Return* I thought I'd have some fun with Hank. I went

237

out and bought a garish red wig, and put it on. Your father came back to the hotel after the play, looked at me, and went right on talking without making a comment. Jane, that's a difficult man for a wife to understand."

Fonda was dissatisfied with the production in New Haven, he had insomnia in Boston, and shortly after the play opened in Philadelphia, he was so hoarse, Leland Hayward packed him off to a throat specialist.

"That doctor told me to open my mouth, looked down my pipes, and almost cracked," Fonda says. "He told me, 'You got, for Christ sake, volcano craters on your vocal cords. They're bleeding. Now you've got to go into a hospital, into a room where you're not allowed to open your mouth. If you have to communicate, you write notes!'

"So I went into the hospital. I always thought I'd blown my voice from yelling at Paul Osborn and Hank Potter. Potter left in Boston and 'Gadge' Kazan came in for a while, but like Potter, he had other commitments. What I'd been yelling for was an honest second act. What I got was a single bed in a hospital room and a notepad and pencil.

"The doctor told Leland that I had to miss the Friday and Saturday performances and the closing night in Philadelphia. At the time there was a big Army-Navy game in town and I'm sure most of the audiences thought, 'Well, that stinker must've gone to the game!'"

The production was trucked into New York. Preparations were made to receive it at the theater where *Mister Roberts* played to great notices, the Alvin.

Although Fonda remained on doctor-enforced silence, he and his producer kept up a bantering stream of communications, one verbal, the other written. Leland Hayward optimistically foretold a brilliant future for the play. Just as doggedly, Fonda dashed off notes of disaster.

"We're going to come into New York and be the biggest hit of the season," Hayward predicted. "The critics are going to throw roses at us."

"Leland," Fonda wrote furiously, "how can you say that? I can't believe you. You're the best producer in the theater. You're one of the brightest men I've ever met. Those critics are going to kill us!"

Hayward glanced at the actor's scribbles.

"Wrong!" he boomed. "They're going to be crazy about us."

Fonda started to write a fresh protest when the producer slapped his hand across the thinning scratch pad.

"Here's the deal, Fonda," Hayward offered. "If the majority of the notices are bad, I'll pay for the opening-night party. If they're good, you pay."

"Where's the party?" Fonda's pencil asked.

"The St. Regis Roof," came the answer.

Three nights later, with Fonda in full voice, *Point of No Return* opened to unanimously favorable reviews. At the end of the evening Hayward slipped a piece of paper into Fonda's hand. It was the bill for the party.

"It cost me five thousand dollars," Fonda winces. "Well, I didn't mind—much."

Point of No Return ran for 364 performances in New York.

"I was pleased that Dad was back in New York with a hit," Peter acknowledged, "but I had a terrible experience about this time at boarding school. I'd gone back to my room to pick up a book or something. Our mail was put on the bed by whatever boy had mail duty that day. There were three or four letters waiting for me, more than I generally received. I opened the top one and by God, I was floored. It said, 'Dear Peter,' and when I turned it over, it said, 'Love, Mom,' with a little face drawn like my mother used to draw on her notes. I couldn't move. I sat on the side of that bed and I thought, 'God, my mother's not dead! They were lying to me, and here I am calling this other woman Mom.'

"Guys came by and said, 'Come on. We have to go out.' And I told 'em to get the hell away from me.

"After clutching that letter for about an hour, I read it through. It didn't make much sense to me, and then I knew, it was for the boy in the next alcove, the next bed, Peter Teucher. I took it to him and mumbled, 'I'm sorry I opened your letter.' and I walked away. That experience practically blew my socks off. I wanted to talk to someone just to keep my sanity, but there was no one to talk to."

His father found few people to talk to during the run of

Point of No Return. Fonda's leading lady thought he might still have missed the riotous crew of *Mister Roberts*. More than that she learned something about the man himself.

"His acting was fantastic," Leora Dana noticed. "His precision was so perfect it made me want to be perfect. His relaxation was tremendous. I liked that. I admired that. I enjoyed playing opposite him. And then, one day, I touched him at a time when I wasn't supposed to be touching him. I just put my hand on his arm, and instead of that relaxed human being I felt steel. His arm was made up of bands of steel. His entire concentration was riveted onto the play."

During that run at the Alvin, two of New York's foremost musical comedy producers, Cy Feuer and Ernest Martin, approached Fonda. Feuer and Martin had presented *Where's Charley?* and *Guys and Dolls* among other commercial ventures. Ordinarily, this would have been enough to catch Fonda's attention. But Feuer and Martin came with an added attraction. They had acquired the rights to a John Steinbeck novel.

"There existed a kind of mystic bond between Steinbeck and Fonda," Robert Wallsten observed. The co-editor with Elaine Steinbeck of the author's letters went on. "A tremendous admiration and also a sense of destiny between the two men began with *The Grapes of Wrath* and continued till Steinbeck's death. John felt he and Fonda did good things together."

It was an unusual arrangement, tacit but strong. Fonda was Steinbeck's actor, Steinbeck was Fonda's author.

"John admired Hank more than anyone in the theater," Steinbeck's widow, Elaine, explained. " 'I keep your face and figure in my mind as I write,' Steinbeck typed in a letter to Fonda."

With their own credentials and Steinbeck's novel *Cannery Row*, Feuer and Martin met with Fonda. What they had in mind was a musical adaptation of the Steinbeck book.

"A musical?" Fonda's voice rose. "Boy's, I can't sing for shit!"

Feuer and Martin were prepared for that.

"*Knickerbocker Holiday*," Feuer pointed out. "Walter Huston couldn't sing a note and *September Song* is a standard still being done today, and that was over twenty years ago.

"Don't worry about your voice," Feuer pressed on. "We'll take care of that. What we're interested in is your acting. Steinbeck sees you in the part and he's going to write the book."

At the mention of Steinbeck, Fonda's interest perked up again. Still he had his doubts.

"Fellas," he began, "when I start to sing, people laugh. And it's the wrong kind of laugh."

"Will you let us decide?" Martin asked.

"Don't you think Ernie and I know our business?" Feuer echoed.

The next day Henry Fonda turned up on the empty stage of the Forty-sixth Street Theater.

"For the first time in years," he says, "I auditioned. It was funny. Those poor bastards, Feuer and Martin, sat in the dark theater in the front row. There was a piano player in the pit. I couldn't see him."

"What do you want to sing?" Feuer called up.

"Do you know any of the numbers from *Guys and Dolls*?" Martin asked.

"Sure," Fonda said.

"Well, sing 'If I were a Bell I'd Be Ringing.'"

Fonda sang. He rang no bells.

An embarrassed pause followed the last note. Then Cy Feuer ordered the piano player, "Try it in another key."

Fonda did the song again. Only the worklight pierced the gloom.

"Another key," Feuer called, but this time with less enthusiasm.

"He was just terrible," Feuer commented, "but he was absolutely perfect for the part. I could just picture him as Steinbeck's bearded hero."

Feuer and Martin retired to a side aisle for a hurried conference. When they returned, they both wore smiles on their faces.

"Call for help," Feuer instructed.

"God knows I need it," Fonda answered.

"No, no. Call to the top of the balcony for help."

Fonda projected the single word upward.

"Very good. Now sing it."

"Sing what?"

"Help. To the top of the balcony."

Fonda did as instructed.

"Great," lied Martin, "just great."

"Y'see, Hank, what's good in this business," Feuer explained "is loud." This was in the days before Broadway musicals utilized microphones for singers.

Then Feuer and Martin recommended that Fonda work with an experienced vocal coach named Herbie Green.

"He's great for loud," both men assured him.

Green's studio was a barren room fifteen by fifteen save for a piano and a bench. Three days a week, for as long as *Point of No Return* played in New York, Henry Fonda obediently went to Herbie Green and vocalized from falsetto to vibratto to basso. Then came the day when Feuer and Martin arrived with the composer, Frank Loesser. Three straight-back chairs had been added to the room's decor, and Feuer and Martin and Loesser sat down.

"I was as uptight as when I read in Dennis or Old Silver Beach," Fonda says.

The vocal coach struck a few chords and Fonda managed his way through the first chorus. He could see the expression of pain on the composer's face.

"Hank," Loesser's raw voice cut in, "we're not looking for a concert singer. Relax."

Then he pointed to a vase atop the piano. "Sing to that vase," the composer suggested. "That's the chick, that's the dame. Sing to her."

"I sang the second chorus," Fonda says and then I waved Herbie to stop. I looked straight at the three men. 'Fellas,' I told them. 'You've got to admit I'm bad.' I could see the composer was ready to agree with me, but Cy said, 'You're just what we're looking for. Keep working with Herbie."

"I told them I was taking *Point of No Return* on the road for a year. That didn't bother them. 'Just remember,'

Feuer said, clapping his hands together. 'When you get back, you'll have a show waiting for you!' "

"I went on tour," Fonda says, "with the fear of a musical hanging over me, but when I returned to New York, there was good news. John Steinbeck had decided not to write it, Feuer and Martin had sold the property to Rodgers and Hammerstein. The part of Doc, the marine biologist with the beard, that was supposed to have been mine, had been switched to a madame of a whorehouse. The madame was going to be played by Helen Traubel of the Metropolitan Opera Company. I tell you, that's the only time in my life I've been replaced by a soprano."

To celebrate this narrow escape, "from making an ass of myself to music," the Fondas went house hunting. They wandered through the streets of New York until they settled upon a house on East Seventy-fourth Street. Originally built in 1880, it had been remodeled several times and was then owned by the publisher of *The New Yorker*, Raoul Fleischmann. The Fondas bought the five-story townhouse in 1953. They planned to do the decorating together, but a new script came Henry's way and he left for California, and Susan had the job to herself.

Fonda's next project challenged his acting abilties and brought memories of the Navy rushing back into his mind. Paul Gregory, the producer, and Charles Laughton, the actor-director, had persuaded Herman Wouk, a Pulitzer Prize winner, to adapt a portion of his novel *The Caine Mutiny* into a play. Wouk, with a single purpose in mind, did the dramatization, most skillfully. Gregory and Laughton, having seen Fonda in *Mister Roberts* and *Point of No Return*, submitted the script to him and offered him three choices: he could play the role of Captain Queeg, the part of the defense attorney, Barney Greenwald, or, if he wished, he could direct the production.

"Jesus," Fonda says, "I hadn't directed a play since my little theater days. I decided on Greenwald because I thought I could do more with the character."

The producers filled the other leading roles quickly, Lloyd Nolan as Queeg, and John Hodiak as the defense counsel. Dick Powell was selected to direct the play.

"I had no reason at that time to pass judgment on Dick

Powell," Fonda says. "I didn't know him more than to say hello to, and whether or not he had any experience, I had no idea, and I figured Gregory and Laughton knew how to make that decision."

Rehearsals began in Los Angeles. It required a short time for the cast to learn that the director knew little if anything about staging a play. Hodiak, Nolan, and Fonda met during a lunch break and agreed the play was in trouble.

"I had no communication with Dick Powell," Fonda says. "We never exchanged a harsh word. I just believed I'd been doing plays long enough to know the company wasn't getting what it should be getting from a director."

Hodiak and Nolan were insistent, and Fonda agreed to see Laughton.

"I'm not sure if you and Paul Gregory are aware of what's happening," Fonda told Laughton, "but we're due to open in Santa Barbara pretty soon and we're in no condition to do that."

That afternoon Charles Laughton took over the direction and the actors buckled down to serious work. The playwright, Herman Wouk, recollected Fonda saying bitterly, "The trouble is that Queeg has a scene and Greenwald hasn't got a scene."

"But if Greenwald didn't have one," Herman Wouk said many years later, "Fonda surely gave him one. Fonda once said to me that there was no way to play the banquet monologue, technically; he had to get himself to believe it, and play it as though it were happening, which he could do only a few nights each week. On those nights he ended up in tears, and the effect was explosive. But from night to night no audience could have told the difference. It always seemed *brilliant*."

"I try desperately not to let the 'wheels' show," Fonda says with more intensity than usual. "Don't allow them to recognize that you're acting, conceal that acting until they totally accept you and forget they're watching a play. That's the essence for me.

"That last scene Wouk wrote was a demanding one. I could feel that audience when I had them. I was like a seaplane that takes off from the water: It's sluggish, but it

244

starts to taxi and then picks up speed, and then zoom! You get that great sensation of being airborne."

James Garner who played one of the "Silent Six," members of the court of Inquiry, had no lines at all in the play. "I learned about acting just sitting there night after night, watching Henry Fonda," Garner said. "That man's a total actor."

Testimonials after the fact were very gratifying, "but we opened in Santa Barbara," Fonda says, "and while the play was obviously a full and moving evening for the audience, we were all aware that Laughton had pulled that play together in ten days. And then he came to me and said, 'I've got to go. I have a series of solo engagements booked. I'm putting you in charge. Do anything you want to do. Don't cut the play, but tell the actors what you want out of them.'

"Well, hell!" Fonda says, "the bookings were all one-night stands. We'd drive the company from city to city by bus. I'd sit next to one fella and talk to him about the play as we rode along. We'd get up early, catch the bus, nap, hit the new town at four-thirty or five o'clock in the afternoon, eat, go to the theater, and do the performance. I hardly had time to write Susan and the children.

"We were getting ecstatic reviews from the critics, but always there'd be the same objection: the epilogue. It was anticlimactic, the drama critics all wrote. It was gratuitous. To sum it up, 'It ain't necessary.'

"Now Wouk had written the entire play just for that epilogue. I saved every review, and when Laughton and Wouk joined us in Boston, I went to Laughton's room in the hotel and laid it out before Laughton and Wouk, all the notices that told us how they didn't want the epilogue. It embarrassed them. I had the documentation. 'Well,' Laughton said, 'if we're going to have this epilogue, we better by God make the audience want to see it.' And Wouk and Laughton began adding a line here and a couple of lines there, and by the time we opened in New York, that audience went for the last scene the way a hungry man goes for groceries. They pulled it off, that author and that director. I have to give them all the credit in the world for that. I could just feel that audience in that last scene. I'd been waiting all season for it, and now I had 'em!"

Once in New York Henry had more than a hit on his hands. Fatherhood approached him for the third time, but not in the usual manner.

"Susan couldn't get pregnant," Fonda says, "and she and I both wanted a child very much. Nedda and Josh Logan helped us make arrangements for—" Fonda stops. "I don't like to say adoption, because the baby we got is *our* daughter, no one else's daughter.

"A doctor called on the phone one day and gave us the news, 'The baby has been born and is in a foster home in Connecticut. If you want we'll have the foster parents bring her to the adoption home. You can change your mind, if you like. You can say no.'

"It was a terribly emotional day. We hired a limousine and a driver to take us to the place. An attendant showed us to a small room and told us to wait. That wait seemed eternal.

"Suddenly, a door opened and a nurse came in carrying this eight-week-old baby in her arms. Well, shit! We fell in love with that child right then and I said, 'No way are we going to leave without her!'

"In the car we took turns holding the baby. When we arrived at our new house on East Seventy-fourth Street, we whisked her up to the nursery. We were completely prepared. Susan even had a nurse's name ready to call. Everything was set. We named the baby Amy, and let me tell you, I have to be reminded that she's an adopted child. She's our own.

"Something else wonderful about having Amy. I'd never had a chance to be a proper father to Jane and Peter when they were infants. I hadn't been allowed to touch them. But now, with Amy, I used to be the one who got up at five o'clock in the morning. I gave her the bottles and I burped her. I just had a ball!"

Fonda stayed with the New York production of *The Caine Mutiny Court-Martial* until his run-of-the-play contract expired on the last day of May 1954, when a film of great importance came along for him. Everyone wanted Fonda to stay in New York, but he couldn't see it.

"When I telephoned him to try to change his mind," Wouk said his memory was quite clear, "he put his refusal in a Fonda-like way. 'Herman, I don't want to be persuaded,' he said gently, and I gave up."

What got Fonda out of *The Caine Mutiny Court-Martial* was a telephone call from Leland Hayward in California.

"Are you sitting down?" the producer asked.

"No," Fonda told him.

"Well, you'd better sit down," Hayward advised. "You're going to be playing *Roberts* in the movie!"

Fonda couldn't believe it.

"You understand," he says, "I'd already resolved in my own mind that I was too old to play *Roberts*. I was almost fifty and Doug Roberts was supposed to be twenty-six, twenty-seven. I was reconciled to the producers talking about casting Bud Brando, Bill Holden, and a few others. But Leland told me over the phone that I was going to play the lead."

"You heard me, Hank," the producer informed him. "We hired Ford to direct and we said, 'Who do you want to play the lead, Pappy? Brando? Holden?'

" 'Bullshit!' Ford snapped. 'That's Fonda's part.' "

"Why not Josh for director?" Fonda asked Hayward.

"John Ford is money in the bank," Hayward warranted. "His name on this picture will bring 'em into the B.O. in droves."

"Well," Fonda says, "I knew Ford was a man's director, a location director, and that he was crazy about the Navy. Now, with him insisting that I play Roberts, I was ready!

"Starting in September, they were to shoot the picture off Midway Island in the Pacific. That gave me the summer off. I took Susan and the kids to Hawaii and we had one helluva summer."

"We had a lovely time," Susan reflected. "The children came with us, and we had a little rented cottage right on the water so that we could fall out of the house onto the beach. It was very pleasant and very easy."

As autumn approached Susan took the children and left for the mainland. Amy was turned over to her nurse while Susan prepared to deliver Jane and Peter to their respective boarding schools.

"I wanted to talk to their teachers," Susan coughed a nervous cough. "I was still terrified of teachers myself. I made a great effort to look at least forty years old, and I think I just about succeeded. I wore my hair pulled back in a tight bun, and I wore a black suit and a single strand of pearls. I was really scared to death, but I was devoted to Jane and Peter."

The Navy flew the *Roberts* company out to Midway where they were based on shore installations. Hayward, Ford, and their leading men were lodged in the Bachelor Officers Quarters. In addition to Fonda, James Cagney had been recruited as the petty but insidious captain, William Powell had been coaxed out of retirement to play Doc, and a new young man received the role of Ensign Pulver. His name was Jack Lemmon.

Ford had originally assigned a Broadway playwright, John Patrick, to do the screen version, but fell back on the efforts of Frank Nugent, a former film critic, for his working scenario. In one of the empty rooms of the BOQ, Ford had scripts passed among his actors and a reading took place on their first night on Midway.

"I didn't like it," Fonda says. "Josh and Tom Heggen had written an excellent play, and very subtly, the dialogue had been changed around. Not a helluva lot, but enough to lose the laughs and the nuances of frustration and pain.

"Midway is a marvelous place to shoot a movie about the Navy. The supply ship was swinging on the hook in the lagoon, the high Pacific sky is a sky you'd never get on a set on the back lot of Warner Brothers Studio in front of an old blue cyclorama. It seemed perfect.

"Anyway, a shore boat ferried us out to the ship and John Ford started setting up his cameras. I knew Bill Powell was nervous about his lines so I took him into a cabin off the main deck and we ran the lines we had in the opening scene. I'd say, 'Bill, how do you feel? Do you want to do it again?' And we'd do it over till Bill Powell felt he'd had enough.

"Now, when Ford was ready, the assistant director

called out and Powell and I took our places along the rail. Christ knows I was ready for Ford's way of shooting a picture. He was the original One-Take Kid. But just as Powell and I got about two minutes into our scene, a cloud drifted by and changed the light on our faces. We were in shadows. Powell hesitated. He'd been in films for years. He knew when a director should call, 'Cut!' so the crew could get set for a retake. But Ford didn't do that. He had the cameras continue to roll. Powell's timing was off from the very beginning, but that just made him even more unsure of himself. We plodded on. It couldn't have been worse. Now, I'd played this scene for three or four years, I knew how the timing should be, where there should be pauses, where there shouldn't be pauses. I don't want to dramatize it, but this scene just wasn't flowing. Everyone around us knew it. Everyone, that is, except Ford. That was the way he directed. And nobody dared to say a goddamn word or he'd be all over you in a second. He was the genius, he was the creator. And you just didn't argue with him. My heart ached for poor Bill Powell, but I said nothing.

"So—we moved on to the next scene, and the next one, and about three-thirty we began to lose our light, so we piled into the shore boats and packed it in for the day."

That night an uneasy quiet settled over the BOQ. All hands had chowed down and Fonda was sitting in his bedroom when Leland Hayward entered.

"Pappy wants to see you," Hayward announced.

Fonda stood up and walked with Hayward to Ford's quarters.

"There he was," Fonda says, "sprawled on a kind of chaise lounge holding a drink. I remember there were white rocking chairs, and there was a table next to him with a pitcher on it. Pappy, say what you will, was a sensitive man, and he couldn't help but realize that we were upset. Although I never said the first word, he couldn't have missed the fact. All he had to do was look at my face."

"I understand you're not happy with the work," Ford muttered.

"Pappy," Fonda answered immediately, "you know I

love you. We've worked on I don't know how many pictures, but you must understand that for Leland and me, who have been so close to this property for so many years, it has special meaning to us, it has a purity that we don't like to see lost. And I'm confessing that I'm not happy with that first scene with Powell.

"I must have said something else, something I don't recall, something that triggered his reaction."

Ford was not an old man. But because he'd been in love with the whiskey bottle for so long, he looked twenty years older than he actually was. He was also blind in one eye, five or six inches shorter than the leading man, and a good fifteen pounds lighter. Still, Ford flew off the wicker divan, crossed the room and swung at Fonda.

"I don't know what he hit me with," Fonda says. "It wasn't his fist. Maybe I ducked and he caught me with his arm, and it knocked me down. At least I staggered back and fell against the table and broke the water pitcher.

"Anyway, that was the end of the scene. I wasn't going to fight this man. He was older than me. I'm not a fighter either. I left and went back to my room. I couldn't have been more upset. I mean this is *Mister Roberts*, and we're just starting the movie. What's happening?

"Well, then, maybe fifteen minutes later, Pappy came to my door and stumbled into some sort of apology, and he began to blubber, and I said, 'For Christ sake, don't apologize! I can't stand it, Pappy. Just don't apologize to me. Not you!' And that was the end of that."

From then on, during all the filming on Midway, Ford turned to Fonda after each shot. It was embarrassing to the actor because the director had never before done that. It was always a glance, a suggestion of approval, a hint of "There. Does that satisfy you?"

"I don't know what was in his mind," Fonda says, "but I do know he was stricken by what he had done, by hitting me."

Fonda knew Ford's pattern. The director would stay away from anything alcoholic until he completed each picture. Then he would take off on his sailboat and drink himself into a stupor. On *Mister Roberts* the pattern was broken. Ford began to order the property men to have iced beer within reach. To Fonda's surprise he now drank openly. About two cases a day was his limit.

Leland Hayward was in no position to put a stop to Ford's drinking. The producer came down with a series of internal hemorrhages. He lost blood by the quart and had to be flown back to California.

Ford's constant companion, Ward Bond, tried to keep the cameras rolling when the director became too filled with beer. Bond would consult with Fonda, and between them, they managed to complete the work on Midway.

When the company returned to Honolulu, Ford went into the hospital to dry out, and the cast moved across the island to Kaneohe, where Fonda had studied during the war at the Navy's antisubmarine school.

Four weeks at Midway, four weeks at Kaneohe, and *Mister Roberts* returned to the Warner Brothers studios in California. A week later Ford was hospitalized and underwent major surgery for a kidney condition.

"It was one helluva spot for Leland and the rest of us to find ourselves in," Fonda says. "Most good directors would want anywhere from eight to ten weeks to study the script and look at the footage already done before they began shooting. As Josh has said, 'Taking over in the middle is like a cook taking over a soufflé. It's too delicate.'

"But we were lucky. Mervyn LeRoy has had more pictures play Radio City Music Hall than any other director living or dead."

Mervyn LeRoy had directed or produced *Little Caesar, Madame Curie, I Am a Fugitive from a Chain Gang, No Time for Sergeants,* and a score of other notable films.

"When do you want me?" Mervyn LeRoy asked Leland.

"Tomorrow?" the producer asked tentatively.

The next day LeRoy was on the set.

"Where do we start?" he inquired.

"Mervyn LeRoy didn't miss a beat," Fonda says. "What he did was try to shoot as much footage as he could from the original stage play. That made it just fine with me."

With great speed and skill, and with much effort,

LeRoy completed the film. His work was of such high quality that he received equal billing with John Ford as director.

At the party, following the last day of shooting, Mervyn LeRoy raised his glass and toasted Henry Fonda.

"He's a real pro," LeRoy beamed, "and when you have a real pro, how can you miss?"

The next day, after the toasts, after the empty bottles and glasses had been cleared away, after Mervyn LeRoy went on to another film, Jack L. Warner, in charge of production at Warner Brothers, ran a screening of a rough cut of *Mister Roberts*. What he missed in the John Ford version was the hilarity of the soap suds scene in which Ensign Pulver blows up the laundry. Also he missed the gratification in the scene where Pulver finally takes Roberts's place and tells off the Captain.

For this Joshua Logan received a call, and within a week, he reshot both scenes to Mr. Warner's satisfaction. For this, and the editing of other Ford scenes, Logan was given writer's credit with Frank Nugent.

"*Roberts* was my first experience with the biggies," Jack Lemmon reported with pride. "Hank turned all of us into a family and we stayed that way through the years. That rarely happens in movies. Ford tried to add a lot of crap for his own ego. Hank was rightfully upset about fooling around with the 'Bible.' None of it ended up in the film that was shown."

"Lemmon's talented as hell," Fonda says, "talented, sentimental, and funny.

"The movie went out, and it was a blockbuster. But I've said it before and I'll say it again, it was not the picture that Josh and Leland and I had dreamed it might be. You can't tell an audience who saw only the movie, 'You should've caught the play. You should've seen Bob Keith as Doc and Bill Harrigan as the Captain.' After a while, I stopped saying it and flew back to New York, where at the time I believed I belonged."

CHAPTER
12

TRAVEL agents, airlines, rent-a-car agencies, hotels, motels thrive on the lives of successful actors. Producers send for casts and ship them across continents and oceans without thought of the bookkeepers who try to keep the property reasonably within the budget.

Fonda spent the spring of fifty-five in his townhouse on Seventy-fourth Street with Susan and Amy and his painting. It was a halcyon period for the Fondas. Then he signed with N.B.C. to do a television program with Lauren Bacall and Humphrey Bogart.

"Back to Los Angeles I went for a week or two," Fonda says. "It was a Producer's Showcase of *The Petrified Forest*. The first night, the Bogarts gave a party and unfortunately I got more petrified than the forest. Frank Sinatra mixed up a drink he called a grasshopper. Well, shit! I'd never heard of it or tasted it. Where I come from grasshoppers are grasshoppers. I found the damn things delicious. I must have drunk more than I should because I remember very little about that night.

"Bogie and Frank carried me back to the Beverly Hills Hotel, undressed me, and put me to bed. I do recall thinking, 'I should be embarrassed, but I ain't. I'm too drunk.'

"As I crossed the lobby the next afternoon with a hangover that was a pip, a man I didn't recognize came up to me with another man.

" 'Mr. Fonda?' the first man asked.

" 'Yes?'

" 'I would like to introduce Mr. DeLaurentiis.'

"DeLaurentiis pumped my hand, and the other fella, the American, said, 'Mr. Fonda just finished the movie *Mister Roberts*,' and DeLaurentiis pumped my hand even harder. And I said, 'Good-bye,' and they said, '*Ciao.*' And I thought that was that.

"I wasn't in my room five minutes when the phone rang, and it was the fella from the lobby."

"I represent Dino DeLaurentiis," he told Fonda.

"Fine," Fonda answered laconically.

"Mr. DeLaurentiis is producing the movie *War and Peace*. His partner is Carlo Ponti."

"Fine."

"We wonder if we could send you a script?"

"Sure."

"Well," Fonda says, "in less than three minutes, a script arrived at my door about the size of a Manhattan telephone directory. Heaviest damn movie script I'd ever held, but I stretched out on a couch and started reading it.

"At first glance, it seemed like a perfectly good adaptation. I'd read the novel and I appreciated what work the writers had done. As I went through it, it gradually occurred to me that they wanted me to play the part of Pierre. I thought DeLaurentiis was out of his mind to want me, but I wasn't going to tell him that because it was one juicy part.

"Well, I called his room and I got the American and I asked if Mr. DeLaurentiis wanted me to play Pierre. And he said, 'Of course.'

"Who're the other actors?"

"Mr. DeLaurentiis has cast Audrey Hepburn and Mel Ferrer, and he is most anxious to sign you."

"Call my agents."

"It will be a pleasure," the man answered.

Upon his return to New York word awaited Fonda that a deal had been struck and the filming of *War and Peace* would commence next summer in Rome.

"I painted a lot and worked on the characterization of

254

Pierre," Fonda says, "and in a spare and foolish moment, agreed to introduce some celebrities on television. Those were the early days of live television for me and I was self-conscious. When that red light went on over one of the cameras I became stiff as the front of my dress shirt.

"The last person on my introduction list was Helen Hayes, and I slowly and somberly read the line right off the cue card, 'Ladies and gentlemen, the First Lady of the American Theater, Miss Helen Hayes.'

"When I got home that night, Susan just looked at me and shook her head.

" 'What's wrong?' I asked.

" 'Well, when you were introducing Helen Hayes you looked so sad I thought you were going to say, "Ladies and gentlemen, the First Lady of the American Theater, Miss Helen Hayes, just died." ' We both laughed, and the next day, I think, I called Miss Hayes and apologized for my funeral reading. She's a great actress. She said she forgave me and I believed her."

In June 1955 Henry and Susan attended Jane's graduation from the Emma Willard School.

"It was a lovely day," Fonda says, "and a proud one for Jane and all of us. But we weren't completely taken up with it because something had arisen a month earlier.

"The Omaha Community Playhouse had outgrown its theater and to raise money for a new one, they asked Dorothy McGuire and me to do *The Country Girl*, a play by Clifford Odets, about an alcoholic actor and his wife. Of course, Dorothy and I agreed. It seemed like a good vehicle for us.

"Now, shortly before Jane's graduation, my sister Harriet, who's been a supporter of the Playhouse since the time I first appeared there, called me in New York.

" 'Hank,' she told me, 'we're having a problem.'

" 'Oh?'

" 'We don't seem to be able to cast the ingenue for your play.'

" 'With all those pretty young girls in Omaha?'

" 'Why don't you bring out Jane?' "

"Have you lost your mind, Harriet?" Fonda's displeasure is rarely slow in coming. "I've got my own prob-

255

lems. This isn't an easy part, playing this drunk, and I have only three and a half weeks to rehearse, not as long as I usually like to get into the part. And worry about Jane? Forget it!"

"Please simmer down, Hank," his sister advised him. "I'll look after Jane. She can stay with us."

"Well, how do you know Jane wants to do this? She hasn't been on a stage in her life."

"Oh, I've already called her. She thinks it'll be fun."

That was the first time Jane Fonda gave any inclination toward an acting career. She had never discussed acting with her father, they had never talked show business. "Hank," Susan said, "could do anything he set his mind to, and Jane has that, too. He is extremely disciplined. I think if you asked Hank to build a bridge he would study the plans and build it, if necessary, with his own hands. And believe me, the bridge would hold. It might not be the most incredible bridge in the world, but it would hold. Now when I heard Jane was going to act I knew she could do it."

After graduation Susan returned to New York, and Henry and Jane flew to Omaha and began rehearsals.

"For someone who'd never appeared on a stage," Fonda says, "Jane did remarkably well. She surprised the hell out of me by bursting into tears on cue."

"It wasn't anything, really," Jane, now a seasoned movie actress, commented. "I had no technique or experience in those days, and in the third act, when I'm supposed to make my entrance crying, I asked one of the stagehands to whack me around, to slap me hard, and that plus the petrifying fear and trembling I had of acting on the same stage with my father turned the trick."

To Fonda, to Dorothy McGuire, to Jane, to the entire play, the critics gave enthusiastic notices. To the Omaha Community Playhouse enough money came in across the counter of the box office of the large downtown movie theater they had rented for *The Country Girl* to build a new home. Susan and Peter were on hand to attend the opening night, and after the sold-out performances, the entire Fonda family—Henry, Susan, Jane, Peter, and Amy—flew to Rome.

"Dino had arranged for us to stay in a villa off the Via Attica," Fonda says. "There was a fantastic swimming pool filled with naturally carbonated water. I remember the water had a sparkle to it, that is more than I can say about the summer. The place was in the country near Rome, about fifteen minutes from the studio.

"Dino, King Vidor, the director, and I didn't agree on the interpretation of my part. They wanted Pierre to be a romantic character. Tolstoy's Pierre wasn't romantic. He was a guy with two left feet, clumsy, a little too heavy, and not very good-looking. The wardrobe department wouldn't give me any padding, but I went out and bought my own pair of glasses. Whenever Dino saw me on the set, he'd have the interpreter tell me to take them off. It was a struggle the whole time.

"There we were in Rome," Susan said, "but just as in New York, we responded differently to life and to people. I was not very wise. Hank was obviously upset about the movie he was making, which made him upset about everything. There were no sharp arguments between us, but there was a great festering within me. I couldn't be myself. I wanted to discuss problems with him, and he'd turn a deaf ear. He had an ability to avoid confrontations with me.

"He did not like displays of temper in himself or others, but he would occasionally have them. Hank repressed, repressed, repressed, and when his anger broke out it was terrifying. Slowly it dawned on me that I had always been afraid of this man.

"After a few weeks of filming, about August 1955," Fonda says, "it was apparent that Susan had become disenchanted with our marriage. She wanted the kind of life a girl her age wants, and I couldn't manage the work and the social doings, too. We were invited out a lot, I couldn't go. We turned down most of the invitations, or sometimes Susan went alone. You could see the drift. We were drifting in opposite directions."

"She was unhappy, terribly unhappy," Henry Fonda's mother-in-law, Dorothy Hammerstein, believed. "She thought married people lived the way Oscar and I did.

257

She found out differently. When Susan left for Rome she had such plans and hopes, but her life was wretched."

Like Frances, Susan had to concede that her husband's true love was his work. It consumed him, and he became morose when the work wasn't going well. Fonda simply turned off on Susan. He didn't stop loving her, and she didn't stop loving him, but something stopped, like an old-fashioned gold timepiece that one forgets to wind.

"I had mistaken Hank's silent shyness when I met him," Susan admitted. "Perhaps I thought of him as an American Gothic. It was part of his attractiveness. Later, I understood it reflected a rigidity. His was a personality completely different from my own. There, in Italy, I felt I was being smothered. It took me back to an incident that happened on our honeymoon.

"We were at Caneel Bay. Hank owned a fancy watch that told the time and the moon and the date, and I took it off his wrist and left it up on a piece of driftwood, and then we went swimming. When we got back to the beach, the tide had come up and washed the watch away into the sea.

"I burst into tears. I wasn't prepared for my husband's reaction. He said, 'Stop crying. Your crying disgusts me.' Which, of course, made me cry more. I hid behind a boulder until I was cried out and then I joined him."

From the Caribbean to the Mediterranean, the Fondas' marriage hung together, but in Rome it reached an end.

One night Susan told Henry that she was going home to New York and not coming back. He was hurt and angry.

"I shouldn't have reacted so strongly," Fonda reflects, "but when she finally put it into words, it came as a shock to me."

"There was no big scene," Susan remembered. "I would have preferred to have it out, but Hank would have shuddered at the thought. He abhorred emotional expression. I liked to kick up my heels," she said. "It was as though Yente the Matchmaker from *Fiddler of the Roof* lived with Ibsen's uncompromising minister Brand."

The former Mrs. Fonda paused many years later, and then observed "I think there's a scream inside Hank that's

258

never been screamed, and there's a laugh that's never been laughed."

Fifteen-year-old Peter sat at the table eating hard rolls smeared with marmalade. He was alone in the enormous marble dining room.

"I usually had breakfast by myself," Peter noted. "Susan walked in and sat down across from me. She seemed very upset, but she came right out with it. 'Peter, I'm going to divorce your father.' I started to cry. No one should cry at breakfast. Then my dad walked in, walked through the room as though it was empty. He wore a look of betrayal. He went out to the pool. Susan got up and left the table. I couldn't stand the thought of our family breaking up again. I'm sure Dad felt the same way."

Peter went to Jane's bedroom. When she didn't answer his knock, he opened the door, and went to her bedside.

"I was distraught," Peter admitted. "I wanted us all to stay together, but then, after I shook her, Jane squinted at me, half asleep, and I blurted out the news. In a blasé voice she said, 'I've known that for a few days. They're too different, too incompatible.' "

"We had a heavy conversation," Jane reported. "Peter was awfully upset. He told me, 'We're so unlucky. First Mummy died, and now Susan is leaving us.' And I explained, 'Peter, you have to face certain realities. Dad is a wonderful man, but he's hard to live with. And Mummy didn't just die. She killed herself.' "

"Don't say that!" Peter shouted. "Don't say that. It's not true."

Peter was twenty years old before he actually accepted the facts of his mother's death. A sadistic patron of a bar near the summer-stock company in upper New York where he was working showed him a clipping. The yellowing newspaper article revealed that his mother had taken her own life.

"I ran out of that place, like a crazy man," Peter said, full of anguish. "Jane had told me the truth back in Italy and I hadn't believed her."

After a month at the villa Susan and the children returned to New York.

"I'd go home after a difficult day," Fonda says, "and

now I was alone. There were servants Dino had hired, too many for me, a maid, a cook, and a man who drove me to the studio. The chauffeur couldn't speak a word of English, and every time I tried speaking Italian, instead of a lilt, it came out flat Midwestern.

"*War and Peace* took longer to shoot than any picture I'd ever done.

"I'd call up Susan regularly and beg her, really beg her to reconsider the divorce. Each time she told me the same thing. She wouldn't be coming back, our marriage was no good, and there was no future for us together. I'd hang up from every conversation more and more heartsick. I was ashamed as hell that a guy with a solid background like mine kept screwing up his personal life.

"Well, I finally learned to say about six expressions in Italian: 'Please pick me up in the morning at seven-thirty,' 'I'll need you at the studio at eight o'clock tonight,' things like that. Just enough to get up and back. Tony Quinn once told me that if you really want to learn a foreign tongue, shack up with a girl who doesn't speak anything but the local language, and by God, you'll learn it.

"Shacking up with another girl didn't even enter my mind. That August and September were the pits. The weekends were the worst. Then one afternoon an agent who ran the MCA office in Paris invited me to a party. I didn't want to go, but Audrey Hepburn had been invited, too. What the hell, I thought, it might be better than being alone, studying my lines, and writing letters, and calling New York.

The sister of the hostess, a twenty-four-year-old daughter of a Venetian nobleman, gazed across the room at Fonda. She was engaged to be married to the heir of an Italian dukedom, but her fiancé happened to be in Milan.

"Henry Fonda stood against a wall and said nothing," the Italian woman asserted. "I thought he was divine immediately. Absolutely divine. He didn't say anything to me at all. I tried everything possible. All my charms. I didn't do anything obvious, you know, because I was engaged.

"The next Sunday that nice Jean Stein who wanted to rent my flat in the Via Monte Brianzo called and asked if she might stop by with a friend. He had nothing to do, and his wife and children were in New York. His name was Henry Fonda.

"Henry Fonda . . . the divine one. . . . 'Bring him. Yes. Bring him.' And my mind began to go click . . . click . . . click . . . click."

CHAPTER
13

for instance. After leaving her native Venice, she trav-

PARIS was the social and cultural center for Americans living or traveling in Europe after World War I. Following World War II, Rome took that place. Either the French had grown disenchanted with having their Gallic coals pulled out of the Teutonic fire twice in half a century or the fresh faces in Rome provided more competition than the Parisiennes had anticipated. In Paris the Ugly American was viewed with undisguised distaste. In Rome he was greeted with open arms.

Sophia Loren, Gina Lollobrigida, Anna Magnani, Vittorio De Sica, Marcello Mastroianni, Roberto Rossellini, Fellini, Antonioni, DeLaurentiis, Ponti, names that meant nothing until the end of the war became an Italian industry during the years of peace that followed. The glory that Il Duce had promised the Romans arrived on the casters of a thirty-five-millimeter motion picture camera.

To the Venetian Baron Raimondo Franchetti, six-foot-six and known throughout Italy as a great explorer, movies meant nothing. His four children were named Nanook, after the Eskimo; Simba, after the lion; Lorian, after the swamp in Africa where the animals go to die; and Afdera, after a volcano in Ethiopia.

Afdera Franchetti's eyes seemed to hold secrets that went back to Eve and the apple. An effervescent, sensuous-looking girl, she was as volatile and mysterious as an active volcano. More than that she had blonde hair and a tongue that could hail a taxi or converse with a general in six languages. After leaving her native Venice, she traveled about with one or two Italian theatrical groups, and then settled in Rome where she quickly became popular with that particular group known as the International Set, later labeled the Jet Set.

With his wife and children gone, Fonda had only *War and Peace* to occupy his time. When he wasn't busy filming, he liked to wander through the back alleys of Rome. In a shop owned by a Signor Bubbuino he found three small paintings of nuns by an artist named Canavari. The first nun played tennis, the second nun sold watermelons, the third nun engaged herself in a similarly unreligious occupation. Fonda admired the three paintings and promised to return. When he did, he found the third painting had been sold. He promptly purchased the remaining two.

When Jean Stein, the writer, took him to see the flat she had rented, Fonda saw the painting of the third nun hanging on the wall. It had been bought by Afdera Franchetti. A similarity in artistic taste was the first thing they shared.

That second time the actor met the future duchess he recognized her vivacity and gaiety, and for a man as dissatisfied with his work and his personal life, he needed cheering up. As it turned out he had come to the right person. At the start their relationship was purely platonic. If he wanted a companion to wander through the art galleries, Afdera made herself available. Later if he needed a companion for a dinner, he escorted her.

"Week in and week out I had nothing to do," Fonda says, "so I'd call her or she'd call me and we'd go out. Nothing more."

"Go out!" Afdera exclaimed. "Never! I would hardly call it that. We were always hidden away. Dear God, he was married and I was engaged. Can you imagine what the paparazzi would have done if they'd caught me with Fonda? We'd have a bite or two in an out-of-the-way place and he would take me to my door and that was it. I was one of the first girls in Rome to have my own bachelor apartment. I had to be careful."

"She lived in a very old part of the city, ancient, I suppose, you could call it," Fonda says. "She had two or three of the top floors."

Jean Stein vanden Heuvel described the apartment more colorfully. "It looked out on the Tiber, and across the river was the Castel Sant' Angelo. It was straight out of *Tosca*. Her terrace was in the shape of a boat."

And there the willowy Afdera, when she wasn't renting it out, held court. Johnny Agnelli, owner of the Fiat Motor Works, Bolivian tin magnates, Milanese politicians, French statesmen, Florentine artists were only a cluster of those who glittered in the tiara of La Franchetti.

Ultimately, Fonda and Afdera gave up their rendezvous for the better-known restaurants in Rome. Afdera took him to the Italian theater which, while he didn't understand the dialogue, impressed him with its fluid acting style. Slowly, what began as a casual friendship, slipped into something more.

In New York Susan took steps to secure a divorce, and while her lawyer and Fonda's people quibbled about settlements, in Rome, his friendship with Afdera ripened.

"Rebound, it's called," Fonda says. "I was old enough and I should have been smart enough to stay away from Afdera, but she was a totally unpredictable and glamorous woman."

By the time *War and Peace* finished filming, Afdera suggested they visit Venice. He agreed, and they took the train "to a stop just this side of Venice where her family's palazzo stood. It wasn't a palace," Fonda says, "but it was a big villa with long, winding driveways, not well kept up, but there it was. Centuries old, probably. Anyway, Afdera brought me into a library that was stacked with books, and she went up to visit her mother."

It was fortunate for Fonda that Afdera's brother, Nanook, was away on a hunting trip with Ernest Hemingway. The brother favored his sister's marriage to the duke's son. The mother, the dowager baroness, in seclusion since her husband's death, surprised the entire household. She had heard of Henry Fonda and wished to meet him. To the amazement of the staff the baroness left her quarters and came downstairs for the first time in twenty years.

"We sat and talked for fifteen minutes or so," Fonda says, "and then Afdera and I left for Venice. It was her city, and even though winter had come, she showed me everything that could be seen—the opera, the theaters, the wonderful restaurants. It was very different for me, this Omaha boy, seeing Venice."

Different, too, became the relationship between Afdera Franchetti and Henry Fonda. Back in Rome he told her he planned on returning to America. She had never been there. He invited her to join him for Christmas. This posed a problem for Afdera, but she solved it easily. She convinced her fiancé she wanted a few days of freedom before she married him. He agreed she could go to New York.

Fonda boarded the plane in Rome before anyone else. Italian authorities were always partial to the wishes of American actors. When the other passengers walked onto the plane, Afdera took the seat beside Fonda.

In New York he stayed in his house on Seventy-fourth Street. She stayed in a hotel. International tongues wag almost with the speed of light, and when word got back to Rome that la Signorina Franchetti was seeing Henry Fonda, the duke's family insisted the engagement be broken. It was a matter of honor.

"I returned my little pearls and my little gifts to my fiancé," Afdera spoke frankly, "and he's a very happy man now. We are still good friends, and his wife, who never wanted to meet me, likes me very much today."

What caused this social upheaval, her trip to New York, was of short duration. Christmas 1955 came and within a few days Afdera went back to Rome. Letters between Henry and Afdera were exchanged almost daily and transatlantic telephone calls almost as frequently.

During a break in the filming in Manhattan of *The Wrong Man*, an Alfred Hitchcock picture, the long-distance conversations did what absence is supposed to do.

"Where are you, Hanky?" Afdera asked during one telephone call. In those days she always called him Hanky.

"New York," he answered.

"Why don't we compromise?"

"On what?"

"I will meet you halfway. I will fly to London if you will fly from New York."

"Fine."

This was more than a compromise for Afdera. She loved trains and detested planes. She was one of those "white-knuckle fliers" who needed a drink or two before she could get herself onto an airplane. But to see Fonda again she managed quite easily.

A long weekend in London and Fonda returned to America to start the only picture he ever produced in the nearly one hundred films he has made since *The Farmer Takes a Wife*.

12 Angry Men had been a television program written by Reginald Rose. Fonda saw it in a Hollywood projection room, and when United Artists urged him to make the TV show into a movie, he went them one step better and agreed to produce it.

In an art form called theater, in an industry named movies, in a world which for a lengthy time thrived on fads and style, Fonda always looked for substance. He found it in *The Grapes of Wrath, The Ox-Bow Incident, Mister Roberts, The Caine Mutiny Court-Martial*. Now he believed he could reach it again with *12 Angry Men*.

Returning to New York, he contacted the author and learned that Reginald Rose had cut twenty minutes from his original teleplay. No need existed to pad the screenplay. Next, Fonda engaged a young director, Sidney Lumet, and together they interviewed actors. In addition to Fonda the remaining eleven included Lee J. Cobb, Ed Begley, E. G. Marshall, Jack Warden, Martin Balsam, Jack Klugman, and Robert Webber.

The entire action of the film took place in a jury room. Fonda, accustomed to theater work, had the cast rehearse just as it would for a Broadway play. During the two weeks the actors worked on their parts, Lumet, eager to make good on his first film, and his Academy Award-winning cameraman Boris Kaufman moved constantly through the room setting up shots.

"Fonda came into the project a little uptight," Lumet said. "He had to deal with problems he didn't want to deal with. I knew rehearsals were going very well, but two or three days before shooting, I could feel his tension building. One afternoon we stood at the elevator. He turned to me abruptly and with marked irritation said he was dissatisfied with everything. My heart leaped. The star, the producer was unhappy.

"We walked into the studio. Only worklights were on. Hank went pale. The exterior was a shot of the other buildings outside the courthouse in Foley Square. Now, we could have had a huge photo blowup made, but this was a low-budget picture, so we opted for a compromise, a painted backdrop from a photograph. It didn't look great hanging there. You could see all the paint marks."

"Christ!" Fonda exploded before the director. "When I worked with Hitchcock the backings were so real you'd walk into them because you thought they were three dimensional."

"My heart sank," Lumet continued. "I've been told it'll work, Hank."

"You've been told. I tell you it looks terrible! Christ, I don't want to be a fucking producer."

After Fonda left the cameraman assured Lumet that with the proper lighting the drop would look genuine.

"We started shooting the following morning in Manhattan," Lumet said. "The first shot was a very complicated one, over the blades of the fan from a crane. The lighting turned out to be a phenomenal problem. We waited from eight-thirty to four in the afternoon. Hank doesn't sweat, but that was about as close as he's ever come.

"We went to the rushes the next noon, and he said, 'Sidney, what am I going to do? I can't stand seeing myself on the screen. I never go to rushes, and sometimes I wait two years to see a finished film I've made. Sometimes I never see them.'

"Hank steeled himself, walked into the projection room and sat down behind me. He watched for a while, and then he put his hand on the back of my neck and squeezed so hard I thought my eyes would pop out. He leaned forward and said quietly, 'Sidney, it's magnificent.' Then he dashed out and never came to the rushes again.

"What is so fascinating to me about Fonda as a talent

is I don't think if you took a stick and beat him he could do anything false, he's incapable. As a performer, as a man, he's pure. He's like a barometer of truth on the set. Fonda has the inner resource to make the lines deeply true. Great actor. I don't use that term often."

"I hired Sidney," Fonda says, "because he had the reputation of being wonderful with actors. We got a bonus that nobody counted on. He also had incredible organization and awareness of the problem of shooting and not wasting time."

It required seventeen days to get the action of *12 Angry Men* onto the celluloid. The film Fonda produced came in at a ridiculously low three hundred and forty thousand dollars, a thousand dollars under budget.

"Rose, Lumet, and I realized we had something special when we saw the first rough cut," Fonda says. "We dreamed of putting it into a small East Side movie house, the kind that held a few hundred people at the most, and we hoped that word of mouth would spread just as it had built with Paddy Chayefsky's *Marty*.

"Well, that never happened. I got a phone call from the head of United Artists, Arthur Krim. 'What're you doing? We want you. Get down here just as fast as you can.'

"When I got down to Krim's office," Fonda continues, "there sat Bob Benjamin and the other heads of the Loew's Circuit. They'd seen our picture and they'd flipped out. They wanted it for Easter Week for all of their flagship theaters across the country. I told 'em I'd like to think on it a while."

"Are you out of your ever-loving mind?" Krim thundered. "All you'll have to do is sit back and hire people to take the wheelbarrows of money to the bank."

As United Artists had put up the financing for the film, Fonda felt he had no alternative.

"The Capitol Theater was Loew's flagship in New York," Fonda says. "It's been gone for some time now, but in case anyone's forgotten, it had over forty-six hundred seats. The opening day *12 Angry Men* barely filled the first four or five rows. They pulled it after a week."

Henry Fonda decided never to produce a picture again. He thought the failure would be a reflection on him at the box office. There was no second release for his film. No third release either. Could it be that he, too, might suffer irreparable harm?

And then *12 Angry Men* was shown at the Berlin Film Festival. It won first prize. It won prizes in Japan, Australia, Italy, Scandinavia. Krim and Benjamin had been wrong. Fonda, Rose, Lumet, the movie critics, and the public had been right. Fonda breathed with relief and did something highly unusual for him.

"I had the summer free," he says, "and I wanted to be with the kids and go where it would be good for them, and where they'd have fun. I brought 'em together and said, 'You pick the spot. Pick anyplace you want.' Jane and Peter had a conference and then came back and told me. Hyannisport on Cape Cod.

"Peter knew a couple boys from his boarding school who would be there, and Jane found out that some Ivy Leaguers would be hanging around the Cape. She also had a crush on a Yalie who had been hired as stage manager for the Dennis Playhouse, next door to Hyannisport. The boy's nickname was 'Goey,' but you probably know him as James Franciscus.

"Anyway, I flew up to the Cape, looked at some houses, and rented one. We had Amy with us, too. Susan always let me have Amy in July and August. Well, I was without a mother for this gang, so my darling sister Harriet came on from Omaha to live in the house with us for the summer."

Within a week Jane came to her father.

"Dad, I think I'd like to join the apprentice group at Dennis," she informed him.

"Now, I didn't think this meant any theatrical ambition on her part," Fonda says. "Just an urge to be with a certain group for a couple of weeks. Jane had never shown real interest in show business. On the other hand, Peter, when he was only thirteen, wrote a play, designed the sets, directed, and acted four parts. He named it *Stalag 17½*. It was a satire about prep school life."

Peter shrugged when he spoke of his youthful efforts.

"Christ! I only did it to get out of being in the damn chorus of *The Pirates of Penzance*. They always had me playing a girl."

Jane received a bit part in a Restoration comedy and invited her father, her aunt, and her brother to it. She played the role of a maid, and had no dialogue, but the moment she made her first entrance, her father noticed the reaction of the audience.

"Nobody knew who she was or that she was related to me," Fonda says, "but you could hear the audience react. Something physical happened to the people in that theater. They sat up, they sucked in their breath, they straightened up in their seats. She had presence. You either have it or you don't have it, and Jane had it. I knew it that afternoon.

"One day I got a phone call from the house manager in Dennis. 'As long as you're in the neighborhood, why don't you come over and do a show with us?' I said, 'Are you kidding? I'm on vacation. I'm down here with my kids to relax.' Well, they wouldn't let up. They insisted *The Male Animal* would be a perfect vehicle for me, and they added, 'Jane can play the ingenue.'

"I took them up on it, Jane and I played together again, and this time, she really knocked me over. None of the amateur self-consciousness. She was absolutely delightful, charming, and natural. I watched her from the wings and I thought, 'If that girl ever wants to do this professionally, she'll make out all right.' I didn't even hint it to her."

Jane knew she impressed her father, though. One night she spoke her exit line, walked off stage, and he stood frozen staring after her in admiration.

"The last time I went up in my lines was at the University Players, twenty-five years before, when Margaret Sullavan came on in a seaweed brassiere," Fonda says.

Toward the end of August Afdera cabled that she would be arriving on Cape Cod to spend a few days.

"I thought she'd be out of place on Cape Cod," Fonda says, "but I should have known better. She was at home every place in the world. To Afdera Hyannisport was just another Lido."

They sat on the beach, made sand castles and big plans. Perhaps Henry had too much of the sun or perhaps Afdera was really a golden girl with a siren's touch, but before the baron's daughter returned to Rome, she and Henry walked out on the Hyannisport pier at sunset and decided they would marry as soon as his divorce was final.

John Houseman, a close friend of Fonda's, stated with great insight, "He's a very uxorious man. I think he's probably gotten laid a few times, and after he goes to bed with a girl, he usually marries her. He needs to be married, and he very much *wants* to be married. He feels obligated to women he's taken to bed."

"Obligated," Fonda nods. "Houseman's right. If I made penetration, a proposal was the next step."

Afdera returned to Rome, and within a few days the summer ended. Henry went to Hollywood to make *The Tin Star*, Jane to Vassar, and Peter to the Wesminster boarding school.

"It started innocently enough," Peter said, making a fist as he spoke. "There'd been a radio announcement that my dad was engaged to be married. I took the usual kidding from a couple of friends, and that's all. Then the fellows told me that one of the masters wanted to see me in his rooms. 'You're always late for chapel,' he taunted. 'You have no religion! You live in a community of one hundred thirty-six people and you don't live up to their standards.'

"There were a few more insults exchanged," Peter continued, "and by God, all of a sudden, he shouted at me, 'You're no good, like your father. Anyone who's been married as many times as he has and is getting married again is a son-of-a-bitch!'

"I nailed him smack on the side of his head," Peter added. "I wanted to make hamburger out of his face. I threw every bit of my one hundred two pounds straight to my left hand. He was out like a light. Boom! Wham! On the floor!

"The whole corridor could hear what was happening. The master of my section, Jake Nolte, ran in, grabbed me

271

around the body and stopped me from hitting him again. Actually, he stopped me from killing him.

"The school didn't kick me out, but they made me feel that I might not be a permanent resident. When Dad heard about it, he wrote an indignant letter to the head of the school, and as there'd been other complaints about this one teacher, they eventually dismissed him. Dad offered to let me change schools, but I told him to forget it. I'd try to stick it out."

Conditions were even worse in Rome. Five days before Afdera packed to go to New York for her wedding, her brother Nanook burst into her apartment.

"You really going to marry an actor?" he demanded.

"Yes," Afdera told him.

"A man who has been married three times before this?"

"Yes."

"A man who is not even a Catholic?"

"I am."

"And you are not going to marry the man I selected for you?"

Afdera shook her head.

To emphasize his displeasure Nanook beat her soundly.

"I didn't have to put ice on my face for too long," Afdera said, "but I was beaten up."

A badly bruised bride-to-be arrived in New York accompanied by her lady's maid, a four-foot-ten-inch Italian girl named Fidalma and her husband, Giuseppe. Giuseppe had been a grocer in Rome and Fidalma had ordered provisions as often as twice a day so Giuseppe could deliver them. When Afdera invited Fidalma to accompany her to New York, the maid agreed on condition that she marry the grocer and that the two of them serve as a couple.

"They were the only dowry I brought Fonda," Afdera said ruefully.

The wedding was held on March 10, 1957, in the library of the Seventy-fourth Street townhouse. Peter and Jane were among the limited guest list. Peter, in fact, served as his father's best man. He sulked during the proceedings.

A New York Supreme Court justice performed the ceremony and the newlyweds flew to a drafty chalet in Canada for a thirty-six-hour wedding night. As a honeymoon it was about as successful as *Spendthrift*, which Fonda made for Paramount in 1936 and doesn't seem to remember. The bride hated the airplane flight, she still suffered the effects of Nanook's fury, and Fonda had a heavy cold with chills and fever.

"Both of us couldn't wait until it was over," Afdera told her friends. "The only good thing to come out of it was that he promised me we would have a second honeymoon."

When her wedding photographs arrived, Afdera noticed that her eyes were swollen from crying. Her brother's anger had done its work. With a cuticle scissor she carefully cut out her eyes from every available picture.

Back in New York Fonda went to work on the motion picture *Stage Struck*, a remake of Zöe Akins's play and film *Morning Glory*. Sidney Lumet, now a favorite of Fonda's, directed the script written by Ruth and Augustus Goetz, a husband-and-wife team of highly successful playwrights. Starring with Fonda was the girl who had created a sensation on Broadway in the title role of *The Diary of Anne Frank*, Susan Strasberg.

"I had seen him play *Mister Roberts*," Miss Strasberg commented, "and I revered him as an actor. Both Sidney Lumet and I were rather hyper in those days and Hank kept everyone under control. He was very kind to me although everyone on the set thought he was removed, aloof, and remote. What he really was was terribly professional.

"I was a little self-conscious playing love scenes with him. Listen, if you had to stand on an apple box wearing four-inch heels in order to kiss Henry Fonda, you wouldn't remember it. You're just happy you didn't fall off the box."

During the shooting of *Stage Struck* Fonda was offered a new play. It was written by a man who never had a production on Broadway, produced by a man whose only experience had been in television, and directed by a man who until then had never directed a Broadway play.

273

"I was really impressed with the talent those men had," Fonda says, "and I thought the play was marvelous. But it was only a two-character play and I felt the part of the man was not fully developed."

"I've got a girl who'll be absolutely wonderful," the producer, Fred Coe, told Fonda. "Let me bring her over and have the two of you read together."

"Jesus, don't do that," Fonda balked. "If she doesn't get the part, she'll think it's because I didn't like her."

"Please, let me bring her to your house," Coe persisted. "The author, Bill Gibson, will come, too. You and the girl will read an act."

Over Fonda's protests, Coe, Gibson, and a young girl who had never set foot on a legitimate stage arrived at Seventy-fourth Street. Her name was Anne Bancroft.

"After the first act," Fonda says, "I didn't want to stop. She was just great. When we finished reading the play, Bill Gibson said it was the most wonderful experience of his life. I thought the woman's part was very impressive, but I was more convinced than ever that the man's role had problems. Gibson and Coe understood. And I told them I could make no decision until the rewrite was done. I was going to Europe when I was through with the movie I was making, and if they wanted, I told them where I'd be and they could send the new material to me."

When *Stage Struck* ended shooting in New York, Fonda made good on his promise of a second honeymoon. He and Afdera flew to Venice. Elsa Maxwell, the society party giver, was holding a masked ball, and Henry, to the dismay of his wife, spent three entire days and nights in their hotel making masks for them to wear.

"I was so furious," Afdera said. "I wanted to show off my American husband, and there he sat, twisting wires and gluing feathers. It was humiliating!"

"It was one of my better efforts," Fonda says. "When I finished, she looked like a fawn."

"Sometimes," Peter Fonda said, clasping his hands behind his head, "I'm on the edge so much, I think I own it.

"After Dad and Afdera left for Europe I sort of wigged out at school. They wouldn't let me stay alone in New York on my own, I had to go someplace, so my Aunt

Harriet told me I could come to Omaha. Poor Harriet. She was very Republican and I was a radical-off-the-wall freak. I'll never be able to repay her for everything she did for me, and all the bad things I did for her.

"I actually fled to Omaha, not only to be with my relatives, but I'd befriended a fellow at my boarding school, Westminister. He came from Omaha, too. His name was Eugene Francis McDonald III. Everyone called him Stormy. He was crazy but terrific. The local paper ran a piece on him that said he was worth $21,189,000. Rich guy, poor guy. Father dead, mother in Chicago always trying to break his dad's will."

One of Harriet's first moves was to arrange for Peter to have an appointment with a psychologist. The doctor gave him a series of tests. After a few visits he announced the results to Peter and his family: Peter's IQ was well over one hundred sixty, in the genius class; only a small percentage of Americans are in the group.

"Dad was flabbergasted when he heard," Peter reported. "And when the University of Omaha wrote me that they intended to put me directly into my sophomore year in the fall, my father was fractured. I hadn't finished high school."

It was difficult for Fonda to brag about his son as he spoke no Italian, the season had scarcely begun, and few Americans were in Northern Italy.

From Venice the Fondas went to the South of France. There an estate agent secured a three-month rental on a house overlooking the Mediterranean, near Villefranche, and Henry and Afdera moved in for the summer.

"It was a large white stucco villa, lots of rooms, guest houses, swimming pool," Fonda says. "It stood on a cliff maybe a hundred feet over the water. Below was a little beach that could be reached by a steep set of stairs going down."

If Afdera thought she would be alone with her husband she was mistaken. Peter and one of Peter's companions were invited, and Jane and eventually "Goey" and Amy and her nurse and Fidalma and Giuseppe. All of them arrived in record time and took up residence.

If Henry thought he would spend the summer in the

bosom of his family he, too, was mistaken. Afdera immediately began a series of luncheons and cocktail parties and dinners and late-evening suppers that left Fonda wishing for the comparative quiet of a Hollywood sound stage or a Broadway rehearsal hall.

"Twenty guests for lunch was nothing," Fonda says, "and there'd be more for dinner and on into the night. I got the full treatment from the Jet Set, and by God, I wasn't knocked for a loop. Not by a hell of a shot!"

The most fun Henry Fonda had that summer was on the Fourth of July.

"The French celebrate Bastille Day on July fourteenth," Fonda says. "That meant I could get all the fireworks I wanted.

"Anchored in the harbor was an American cruiser, and as the light faded, I thought I'd give the Navy as well as my own family a touch of Independence Day the way it's celebrated back home. I'd bought two or three hundred dollars worth of skyrockets, Roman candles, pinwheels, and I said to myself, 'By God, those boys on that cruiser are going to know there's an American here!'

"Well, I sent up the first rocket, and wham! One came up off the cruiser. I sent up another one. They sent up one. It was like Indian messages going back and forth.

"Of course, I'd forgotten about the United States Navy. They must have had a hundred thousand dollars worth of fireworks aboard, and long after my last rocket went off, they were still firing 'em in our direction. It was a great night!"

While Fonda was celebrating the Fourth, three men—Bill Gibson, Fred Coe, and Arthur Penn, the director—worked on the rewrite of *Two for the Seesaw*. At that point they had no road bookings, no theater in New York, and most importantly, no financing for the play. Gibson kept writing and rewriting, urged on by the producer and the director. It became increasingly clear that if the play was to hit the boards Fonda's presence in the cast was essential.

In Villefranche Fonda led a life not to his liking.

"Afdera's friends were as far from me as I could possibly get," Fonda says. "I didn't fit in with them. If there

276

was a big ball given by a grandee in Madrid Afdera would be one of the first four hundred invited. I'd have to tag along. If there was a fete in Paris given by some guy whose name I don't even want to remember Afdera would insist on going and drag me along. I always felt that they were just putting up with me. Afdera was their friend and I was almost like a consort. I had nothing in common with any of them, and I was always uncomfortable. It was the craziest, most insane marriage anybody ever got into."

"He really was a husband," Afdera admitted. "I was not a wife."

"It was sort of fun for a while to have this frothy, fascinating, slanty-eyed Italian 'contessa' for a stepmother," Jane reflected. "She opened up a whole new world: Italian aristocracy, Capri. Later on I hated the fakiness, and those people who pull the money strings. They were dull!"

"I didn't appreciate Afdera at all," Peter spoke openly. "At a difficult time in my life, when I could have used my father's friendship, when I needed contact with him I felt she effectively alienated us."

"I was good to Jane. I should have been nicer to Peter. He needed love, but I wasn't a maternal woman," Afdera conceded. "Amy was adorable, sweet, tiny. I wasn't maternal to her either."

Not all was bleak that summer. The family got to meet Jean Cocteau, the filmmaker, and watch Picasso paint and order his people about his studio.

"Garbo came to lunch and visited with us many times. She was one of the few bright lights of that summer," Fonda says. "Here was someone I could relate to. She'd come with the nutritionist, Dr. Gaylord Hauser. Sometimes she'd bring Johnny Agnelli. She was a sweet woman, darling. She wasn't difficult to talk to. She was very friendly, very open, very relaxed.

"I remember she used to ask if she could go swimming and I'd say, 'Sure.' And she would go inside and change either into a bathing suit or sometimes nothing at all and come across the lawn in a robe and go down the steep steps and dip in the blue waters."

Even a talking Garbo couldn't make matters easier for

Fonda. The social life of the Riviera proved too much. A story in the Paris *Herald* advised him of the annual running of the bulls at Pamplona, Spain. He rented a Fiat Familiare, the Italian version of an American station wagon, packed his family into it, and started for Spain.

"We got as far as Marseilles," Fonda says, "and the Fiat gave out. I rented an old Nash and we got to Pamplona. We couldn't get rooms together because Pamplona, when they run the bulls, is like a town during the World Series. Our rooms were spread out all over: Peter in one place, Jane in another, Amy, Afdera, and me in a third. But we would meet for meals and watch them run the bulls through the streets. Except one morning we couldn't find Peter. Well, we ate and then we watched the bulls and the young men who dashed out in front of them, daring the bulls to catch them on their horns. And that morning who do we see running in front of the bulls? Peter! That's how wild he was.

"Anyway, it was an unforgettable three or four days, and then we drove back to Villefranche."

Awaiting Fonda were the revised first two acts of *Two for the Seesaw*. Always an early riser, he read the new version on the temporarily deserted terrace. He still didn't feel the play was right for him, but perhaps he felt uncomfortable on the Riviera, or perhaps he longed to be at work again. In either case, he cabled Fred Coe:

START IT ROLLING. I AM YOURS.
FONDA

CHAPTER 14

IF a witch doctor had cast the bones for the new project they would have come up trouble. But the theater employs no witch doctors, and the production went forward.

Solely on the strength of Fonda's cablegram, Fred Coe contracted for the best house in New York to stage an intimate play, the 783-seat Edwin Booth Theater. With that same cablegram in hand he raised the backing of the play and set the out-of-town bookings.

By September 1957 Fonda and his family left the Riviera with a variety of emotions: Henry was bored with life in the sun and the rounds of parties after dark, Afdera was sorry to leave her friends and their social activities. Peter sided with his father, Amy was a small child who enjoyed the attention paid to her, and Jane was ready for fresh fields.

Her two years at Vassar had not been ideal. Stories of her mischievous behavior in college, riding motorcycles through the halls of the dormitories, when run to ground proved largely apocryphal.

"I felt I wasted my two years at Vassar," Jane admitted. "I didn't try, I didn't succeed. There are nights now when I dream I'm back there. You must understand I'm the kind of person who likes to finish what I start."

Instead of returning to college, Jane asked her father if she might study at the Sorbonne.

"I would have liked to have studied art in Paris in my

junior year," Fonda says. "I agreed. Then we found out that you just don't walk into the Sorbonne. What we decided was that Jane should rent a room and live with a very respectable family in Paris, learning the language and studying at the Beaux Arts."

When they left Villefranche the Fondas went to Paris to make certain Jane was in good hands. Then they flew to America.

"Typical," Peter Fonda said with a hint of resignation in his voice. "Jane got to live in Paris and I went back to Omaha."

Life was not as grim as the seventeen-year-old Peter made it appear. His father understood that it was necessary, if not necessary certainly desirable, for a college man to own an auto.

"I had hoped that my father would fork over his Thunderbird," Peter said. "He hardly ever drove the sucker. I had souped the engine up. I did everything to that car and he never knew what was in it. If he didn't give it to me, I'd hoped he'd lend it to me. Not a chance!"

"I don't want you driving that kind of car when you're going to college," Fonda told his son. "I want you to be like everybody else. And everybody else doesn't have his own Thunderbird."

"Well," Peter mused, "I thought maybe he'd get me an old used car. I didn't care, as long as it moved and it had a heater that worked because it was cold back in that neck of the woods.

"One day my father called my room and said, 'Let's go shopping.' Well, Henry hates to shop. He'll go buy one tie, one shirt, one sport coat, one pair of trousers, one pair of socks, and one pair of shoes. And that's it. He doesn't realize he might need another pair of socks. So I wasn't sure what he meant by shopping and he didn't elaborate.

"When I got down to the lobby and met him I said, 'Where are we going?'

"To look at cars."

"Jesus!" I thought. "A foreign car! A sports car? A Ferrari was not part of the deal, but I knew there was a chance. We were in Paris. Well, we jumped into a taxi and he handed the driver a piece of paper with the address he wanted to go to. And this fella drove us down Car Road, which is beyond the Arc de Triomphe. We stopped at this German car place and went in. Of course in the front of the showroom were Mercedes. I didn't even slow down to admire them. Then there were the Porsches. Fabulous Porsches. They're real good cars. Jeez! I'd get a Porsche. Dad walked by the Porsches, and the next cars in line were Karmann Ghias which I'd never heard of before. What the hell! They're not bad looking. There was a convertible in one place and a coupe in the other. Not bad. I started to check them out when Dad dragged me away.

"Then came these very strange-looking cars that I'd never seen before. They were nicely done. They had some chrome on them, not too much, but we went by them, too.

"We reached the back of the shop. There stood some funny-looking cars with nothing on them at all. No chrome on those suckers. They had nothing. No radio, no gas gauge. It was your basic 1957 Volkswagen. The Bug. The Bug with the small window in the back.

"Needless to say," Peter continued, "my spirits dropped a bit, but not too far, because, in fact, Dad was giving me a car and it did have four wheels and it was brand new."

"Peter," Fonda advised his son, "I want you to have a car that won't stick out like a sore thumb at a Midwestern college."

"They shipped it to Omaha in a crate," Peter said. "I was proud of that car because it was my car, but I was embarrassed because it looked funny, so weird. But at least I had transportation. I found out pretty fast that I would have been better off if I arrived in a Thunderbird or a Ferrari. They didn't expect Henry Fonda's son in the Bug. They would have preferred me driving a Rolls-Royce.

"But no. Those Cornhuskers thought that car was the silliest thing they'd ever seen. They made a wreck out of me because of it. I'd go into a movie house and come out and find the goddamn thing had been put on the sidewalk.

I mean sixteen jocks would come along, pick up the car and turn it around so that it was parked in the other direction, and I'd get a ticket for parking illegally. One time they picked it up and carried it into the lobby of the Dundee Theater. I couldn't believe it.

"It was a masterpiece of engineering but it didn't have a gas gauge, and I'd run out of gas when I was out with my dates. I'd like to apologize right now to all those girls I used to date. Believe me, most of the time I didn't run out of gas deliberately."

In New York Fonda began work on the new play. *Two for the Seesaw* is about a Nebraska lawyer, Jerry Ryan, adrift in New York, and his affair with a girl from the Bronx, Gittel Mosca.

"From the very beginning," Fonda says, "I felt the man's role was weak and underdeveloped, but I thought any son-of-a-bitch who can write a part as good as Gittel can do better by Jerry Ryan. Both Fred Coe and Arthur Penn agreed with me. What's more important the playwright, Bill Gibson, felt the same way."

The problem, seen through Gibson's eyes in his chronology of the play, *The Seesaw Log*, was that throughout rehearsals, the try-out on the road, right up to the opening night, Gibson, Coe, Penn, and Bancroft balanced themselves on one side of *The Seesaw* and left Fonda perched precariously on the other.

Professional as he is, Fonda favored the traditional "freezing" of the play three or four performances prior to the New York opening. The process of "freezing" the production is to make no further changes. The dialogue and the movement on stage remain the same so the actors can feel sure of what they say and do by the time the play is finally seen by the critics. But Gibson continued to write new material, and Penn continued to insert new scenes right up to the day *Two for the Seesaw* gave its first performance for the New York critics on January 16, 1958.

"Bill Gibson has always been a nice, polite, dear man," Fonda says, "but when he stuck his head inside my dressing room door on opening night, I lost my temper like I never had before in the theater. 'You get your ass out of here,' I told Gibson. 'I don't ever want to see you again. Don't come into my dressing room to wish me good luck. You've been of no help to me!' "

Despite his anger, Fonda recovered and the play went very well. His wife and a few friends repaired to Sardi's second floor to await the critics' notices while Gibson, Coe, Penn, and Bancroft went off to a party of their own. Afdera felt the tension at the table. When Vincent Sardi passed around the morning papers that contained the reviews, Fonda's wife attempted to break what seemed to her an intolerable strain.

"I thought I would take his mind away from the show," Afdera said.

Her husband's attention was riveted to the theatrical page.

"Hank?" she asked.

His answer was inaudible as he switched from the *Times* to the *Tribune*.

"Hank, I would like a fur coat."

No reply.

"Will you buy me a fur coat? Please?"

Fonda continued to read.

"I have something in mind, Hank."

Without answering he reached for the *News* and the *Mirror*.

"What I'd like is a new color of mink," she plunged ahead. "Light gold mink."

"Jesus!" Fonda rose from his chair, "I never expected reviews like this!"

Suddenly, everyone at the table was talking, shaking hands, congratulating Fonda. Four hits in a row. Incredible!

As for the blonde mink coat, Afdera never got it.

"Thank God," she said fervently years later. "Instead he bought me a painting, and eventually I sold it and lived on it for quite a while."

Despite the critics' plaudits, those pundits on Broadway knew once Fonda's run-of-the-play contract expired he would clear out of the Booth like a fall leaf in a high wind. And he did. *Seesaw* ran on but without Fonda. It made a star out of Anne Bancroft, but without Fonda it folded in England, France, Italy.

William Gibson's next play also starred Anne Bancroft. Playing opposite her in place of Fonda was a little girl called Patty Duke. The play was called *The Miracle Worker*. And somewhere that play is still running.

"I had a contract with Twentieth Century-Fox to make two movies in 1958," Fonda says. "So I took my whole gang out to Malibu Beach for the summer. Afdera was very social, as usual, rarely home. The kids spent most of their days on the beach or driving around. The Lee Strasbergs lived about six houses away from us. They had their two kids, Susan, about Jane's age, and Johnny, about Peter's age. It made it pleasant for the young people. I was working, but on weekends we generally got together for a barbecue on the beach. I guess I should mention Marilyn Monroe was there. The Strasbergs were getting her ready for *Some Like It Hot*. That girl wouldn't move an inch without asking them. Monroe was a fragile little thing in person. We all saw each other, we weren't close, but we saw each other. Susan kept suggesting to Jane that she consider acting as a career. Nedda Logan had mentioned the same thing. It must have sunk in because at the end of the summer she came to me and said, 'Dad, I think I'd like to study with Lee Strasberg.' I said, 'Okay,' and when we went back to New York, she started taking private lessons. Within a short time, she was accepted by the Actors' Studio.

"I had visited the Studio once. Dorothy McGuire told me it was not only interesting but instructive. Well, there we were in a large room with bleachers, six, seven, eight tiers. Lee Strasberg sat in the first row. The rest of the room was empty except for a table and a few chairs. Well, some guy talked for a while, then he got off his stool and carried it to the side. He put a record on the record player. It was swing, and we sat. Now, there were five fellows and five girls lounging against a wall. After the music started we waited. Nothing happened for a long time. The idea is, don't do anything until you feel like it. I gather this is one of their laws.

"Anyway, finally one of the girls wandered slowly onto

the acting area, sort of walked around. You've never seen anybody as aimless in your life. At last she stopped and started to pantomime. I didn't know whether she was washing dishes or peeling potatoes, but every now and then, she would look up and say, 'Hello, four o'clock, hello four o'clock.' She said it about twenty times. I don't know how I kept from falling off the bench. They call it The Method, and many fine actors swear by it. Jane does.

"I watched Jane out of the corner of my eye, one afternoon. I was at home reading a script, and every now and then, I'd take a quick look at Jane. She had a glass of orange juice in front of her, and each time she took a sip, she'd wear a different expression. Later I found out it was an exercise for class. Some days she'd come home and seem really disheartened, like she didn't know what it all meant. I could see a question mark in the space over her head, like you see in a balloon in the comics, but by God, one day it took, and there was no question mark above her head. There was a thousand-watt bulb, and it all made sense to Jane. The next year she would do two plays and a movie. She was off and acting."

Somewhat reluctantly, wooed only by the promise of cash on the barrelhead plus residuals in the future, Fonda returned to Hollywood to make the first of his two television series, *The Deputy*.

"I think my wife's got her eye on an emerald she wants very badly," Fonda told an interviewer. Afdera, by then, had become newsworthy in her own right. Instead of being referred to as Mrs. Henry Fonda, the tabloids joyfully called her the "Contessa Afdera Franchetti."

"She wasn't any more a contessa," Fonda says, "than my flannel shirt."

"I inherited no title," Afdera confirmed. "My sister had one. She married a count."

For a pair of commoners, however, the Fondas did quite well in the social whirl. The previous summer, thanks to the good offices of Douglas Fairbanks, Jr., they were invited to a garden party given by Her Majesty Elizabeth II at Buckingham Palace. In August 1959 Fonda dropped his gun belt and set aside *The Deputy*'s star and flew to Rome. There he and Afdera met the brilliant

British author, actor, and director Peter Ustinov. Together with Ustinov's then wife, they embarked on their host's fifty-eight-foot ketch for a cruise of the Greek islands.

"Peter's boat had a crew of three," Fonda says, "and what he didn't know and what I didn't know and what the captain didn't bother to tell us when we set sail was the mistral was blowing. That's a wind that blows from the north and makes the waters rougher than the bark on a Norway pine. If you're going to do the Greek islands, sail before the end of June or after the end of August."

"Fonda was absolutely marvelous when we encountered high seas," Ustinov said. "The girls went below and huddled in the cabin, frightened and quivering. Afdera bobbed up for a second to ask if we were in danger. I pretended we were giving consideration to abandoning ship. She made the mistake of speaking Italian to a Spanish crew member with the result that he merely said, 'Si.'

"Terrified, the two girls clung to their bunks below while Fonda bravely stood on deck and sang 'Nearer My God to Thee.'

"We weathered the storm all right and the women joined us. Afdera proved to be a most interesting person. She had kind of a surprised look. A little bit like a Botticelli, but more surprised at being a Botticelli than not. She bought a carpet in Delphi and had it transported by two boys to where we'd put into port. It's a long walk. I should judge eight miles through quite a steep grade through the olive groves. When they spread it out on the quay before her, she said she didn't like it and to take it back. Her position, I dare say, was that the Romans had conquered the Greeks several centuries earlier and she felt she still had a certain authority over them.

"I saw a flash of exasperation on Hank's face, but no more. I think the expression on my face was disbelief."

"When we were in Greece, Peter'd talk Greek. When we were in Turkey, he'd amaze me by speaking Turkish," Fonda says. "Now when we tied up in various ports, there were always parties, and Peter was the perfect host. He outdid Afdera in German, French, Spanish, the Balkan languages, and he guided us on tours of ruins and

286

monasteries. And with all that to do, he was also writing a play, writing a novel, writing twelve pieces for the *Atlantic Monthly*. And he did them. The play was eventually produced, the novel was published, and all twelve pieces came out in the magazine on schedule!"

In return for Ustinov's hospitality, Fonda, who snapped photographs throughout the cruise, had them developed, mounted, and bound in an album that he named *The Cruise of the Metchevo*, after Ustinov's sailboat.

"It was lovely, very lovely," Ustinov remarked, "except for the fact that Mrs. Fonda had taken a pen knife and cut out all of the faces of herself that didn't please her. Curious. No?"

Curious or not, Afdera grew more independent and provided better copy for the society columns of New York, London, Paris, Rome, and, of course, Hollywood.

"I took New York by storm that season," Afdera said. "New York was so social. We were this couple, so popular, so in demand. I think Hank's friends considered I was at least interesting."

"Afdera was very chic, very affected. She looked like an exotic bird you see in a natural history magazine," noted costume designer Lucinda Ballard Dietz.

Kent Smith: "A likable nut."

Mel Ferrer: "Afdera was a flamboyant social climber and an *arriviste*."

Edith Atwater: "She was a bit flakey."

Peter Ustinov: "She could be most engaging, but she'd probably admit herself that she was rather spoiled."

Nedda Logan: "Afdera was an extrovert. Very extravagant, practically threw money out of the window. So attractive she could have been a fashion model."

Most of those who met her acknowledged that Afdera was fun loving and good-hearted.

"She was the biggest party giver ever," Fonda says. "Our house in New York was the scene of one enormous gathering after another."

"In the years we were married," Afdera shrugged, "I never went into the kitchen. I didn't have to. Hank babied me. I didn't even know how to write a check. I didn't have a checkbook."

Fonda took care of most matters, but he certainly did not need to send out invitations.

"Oh, the dinners I gave started out cozy," Afdera said. "Then they snowballed and many people came because Italians are like that."

The house had been redecorated to match the feminine occupant. It resembled a Venetian palace—heavy Italian antiques, an antique mantle, even hand-painted frescoes on the walls from floor to ceiling.

"Fonda fitted into those affairs like a grandfather clock in a Louis Quinze salon," Lucinda Ballard pointed out. "He was a tall Early American type, surrounded by these small, chattering satin-covered, overexcitable Mediterraneans." To better describe the group Ballard quoted an acquaintance who said, "The closest these people got to speaking English was French."

Fonda spoke as much French as he did Italian, and he watched in dazed disbelief as the elite of the Jet Set threw ice cream and chocolate syrup against the walls.

"I think it happened only twice or three times," Afdera said, "but Hank sometimes would come home tired from the theater and it was too much for him. He was a good host, though. He didn't complain; he never became rude."

Perhaps not, but he spent as few hours on Seventy-fourth Street as he could. He hurried to rehearsals of his new play *Silent Night, Lonely Night*. He'd get there early and stay late, trying to avoid Afdera's perpetual open house.

Weeks before, the distinguished author Robert Anderson had submitted his new drama to Henry Fonda. He heard nothing from the actor until both men moved to California.

"Early one morning," Anderson said, "I was awakened by a terrible pounding on the door of the little house I'd rented. I got up and looked. There stood Fonda, banging away with my script in his free hand. 'This is the play I was born to play,' Anderson remembered Fonda telling him. 'How the hell do you know my life that well?' "

The playwright later learned that Fonda referred to the institutionalizing of his wife, Frances. When autumn arrived in New York, so did Fonda, Anderson, and rehearsals of the play. It was during those rehearsals that Henry skipped a few hours to see his son's latest appearance on the stage.

"I took a day off to fly to Omaha," Fonda says. "Peter was appearing in his college's production of *Harvey*. He didn't expect me. I just settled into a seat in the back row and watched. It was the damnedest series of performances by a group of actors I'd seen in years. Here were these college kids, eighteen to twenty-two, playing people in their fifties. They were playing the parts as though they were ninety-nine. Elwood P. Dowd's sister wouldn't turn her head when another actor spoke to her. She'd pause and then slowly turned her entire body. The lawyer, supposedly in his late forties, came creeping in on a cane.

"My boy Peter was smart. He played it straight and landed every single laugh. By God, his name isn't Fonda for nothing!"

After his father's compliments, Peter made up his mind he wouldn't spend another year in school. It would be the actor's life for him. He confided this only to his close friend, Stormy.

Back in New York Henry continued rehearsals of his own play. The cast also included Barbara Bel Geddes and Lois Nettleton. The director was Peter Glenville, a very tasteful man who lost interest in the play, according to Fonda, within two weeks.

"Bob Anderson, who is still a very good friend," Fonda says, "had written a play about two extremely lonely people on Christmas Eve. In spite of Glenville's apparent indifference, we opened in December and ran." The applause came regularly at the Morosco each night. So did his problems with Afdera.

"If she wasn't entertaining at the house," Fonda says, "I'd meet her after the performance at a chi-chi restaurant. She'd be having a dinner date with some Englishman or Italian. And I'd sit there like an intruder while they sipped their wine. I didn't belong there at all. It made me miserable."

"I was a widow every night from seven to eleven," Afdera said, "so I needed to go out all the time. He objected that the phone was ringing a lot. I had lots of men friends, but they were not lovers."

Neighbors reported that when Fonda left the house, his wife lowered the window shade and visitors appeared, only to leave before her husband returned.

"Nasty gossip," Afdera said, looking hurt. "They were not lovers, I tell you. I could feel, all of a sudden, Hank didn't want to remember our good times. He wanted to put me in a drawer and close it."

New Year's Day 1960 arrived and like most Americans Henry Fonda wished this year would be a better one than the previous. Afdera still slept. She'd been to a round of parties and hadn't gotten in until six A.M.

Henry put down his morning newspaper and turned on the radio. The weather . . . the sports . . . and then a bulletin, "Margaret Sullavan, star of stage and screen . . . dead. Suicide suspected."

"I switched off the radio," Fonda says, "I couldn't listen anymore. That lovely woman, gone. The room wasn't as bright as before."

A mutual friend had once referred to Sullavan as an innocent savage. He would miss the innocence and the savagery. He'd never hear that throaty laugh again, see that devilish wink. The phone rang with more information. It had happened in New Haven, on the road with a show. The play wasn't up to expectations, neither was Sullavan. Apparently, she had been unable to sleep for nights. Fonda knew that feeling. It had happened to him during *Point of No Return*. Rest, she needed rest. She got it . . . from a doctor's syringe and too many sleeping pills. No one ever learned if it was deliberate or accidental. This New Year's Day it didn't make much difference to Henry Fonda. That vivid light was gone, along with a part of his youth.

That next June and July Mr. and Mrs. Henry Fonda lived two entirely separate summers, both of them in Los Angeles. "In a sensational house, Ty Power and Linda Christian had built it," Fonda says. Henry continued with his television series and Afdera with her social engagements. There were far more social engagements than episodes of *The Deputy*. Sooner than Afdera wanted, she and her husband returned to New York. This time Henry had a pair of projects to juggle. John F. Kennedy had been nominated for the Presidency and Ira Levin had written a play Fonda wanted to do.

In previous elections Fonda had teamed with John Steinbeck to support Adlai Stevenson. Steinbeck wrote the speeches and Fonda traveled throughout the East to deliver them. Bitter was the taste of defeat. In 1960 Fonda thought he'd picked a winner and supported him strongly. He had fought Senator Joseph McCarthy's red-baiting activities in the fifties. Although his passport had been revoked for a time, his friend and fellow actor Eli Wallach considered Fonda to be "in the very center politically." Ten years later, he gave as much of his time as he could to Kennedy.

Right before the election, Bridget Hayward died.

"I was sick," Fonda says.

"I don't know how deeply Peter felt about Bridget, but he was damned fond of her. He had been for years. She was the prize of the Hayward children, and that's something, because they are all great. Bridget was unique in every way.

"She almost looked bloodless, white skin, straw-colored hair, and she had a striking personality. Bridget took her life, ten months after Peggy. Leland discovered her body. It was a tragedy for her family, and for Peter, too."

"In the south of France," Peter said, "when the all-night parties kept me awake, I'd reach for a pen and paper and write my most intimate thoughts to Bridget. I told her how when Afdera wanted to get rid of me in the evenings, she'd make Dad give me money to go out, but instead I'd pocket the money, and sneak into the kitchen where Fidalma and Giuseppe would feed me. I learned to speak Italian that way. I'll tell you how close I felt to Bridget, Brooke, and Bill. As far as I was concerned, they were my sisters and brother.

"Bridget was like a piece of Meissen china, even more than that, porcelain, the finest porcelain that would crack if you breathed too hard on it. The color of her eyes was a mysterious blue, shivering blue, silver blue. I loved her.

"I remember right after Bill Hayward's wedding in Topeka, Kansas. Brooke and Bridget and I spent hours in a motel room just talking. I fantasied that Brooke would go to sleep, and I'd run away with Bridget and we'd make love all night.

"I ended up with one of her gloves and I kept it for years. Bridget was quite a girl. She pulled her ticket early. Life breathed too hard on her, I guess."

Following the blow of Bridget's death came the close but heady victory of John F. Kennedy at the polls. Fonda was in his final week of rehearsing *Critic's Choice*, when a handwritten letter arrived from the future First Lady:

Dear Hank,

I could never express to you my appreciation for your being on our Calling For Kennedy program—I know that this last week in rehearsal for you is exactly like the last week of the campaign for Jack—There simply isn't one minute to be spared for extracurricular activities—and yet you spared two whole, frustrating mornings—with endless patience and good nature.

I feel so strongly that your participation gave it the distinction it so badly needed—it could have been a corny amateurish home-movie sort of thing where we would have looked like fools, and given people something like Checkers to laugh about—

But you saved us from that—and our gratitude is boundless—I saw it this afternoon with 200 ladies who were wildly enthusiastic—and I felt so proud you had been on it with Jack—You both bring the same quality to your different fields—

A million thanks again—
Jackie

"I wanted to help Kennedy," Fonda says, "I liked him a lot. I felt awful the two times Stevenson didn't make it. I will always regret that this country didn't get a chance to benefit from that man. But I admired Jack Kennedy, too. He and Jacqueline used to come to our house on

Seventy-fourth Street for dinner or late suppers when they were in New York. They stayed at the Carlyle. Close by. I did everything I could to help Jack. In one of my pieces of advice, I warned him to go easy on his voice. I wasn't about to forget that Willkie lost his election because he strained his voice. The last month of the campaign he croaked. And I said to Jack and to Bobby, who was his campaign manager, 'Be sure your P.A. system works. Don't tax your vocal cords, don't scream your speech or you'll do a Willkie.'

"I knew Jack better than Jacqueline. She wasn't that easy to know. She was not cold, but she didn't let herself be too open with people she wasn't close to. How do you like that? It sounds as though I'm describing myself. Well, anyway, I think a lot of Jacqueline. She's an exceptional woman, and it always gave me a kick to be with Jack Kennedy and hear him talk." Fonda sighed, "I expected great things from him."

"Christmas, 1960." Peter smoothed his moustache with pleasure. "I'll always remember that Christmas dinner at our home in New York. Afdera piped up, 'You know, Hank, we've been married three years now, almost four.'

"Dad put down his fork, looked at her, and said, 'Seems more like seventeen years to me.' I pretended not to hear, but inside I thought, 'Petey Boy, you're on the verge of getting one of your wishes.' "

On the night of January 20, 1961, while Fonda played at the Ethel Barrymore Theater in New York, Afdera danced in Washington with the new President of the United States.

Upon her return to New York, Hank and his wife discussed a divorce.

"Things had gotten pretty fiery," Fonda says, "And the fights between us became more and more frequent. I wasn't the husband for her. And she must have been aware that I wasn't the kind of guy who could lead her kind of life forever. I didn't want that marriage to fall apart. I didn't want to fail again. I thought if there's any way to compromise, I'll compromise. I was ashamed to go through another divorce. But there was no way to avoid the break."

"Fonda is what he is," Afdera said. "He's a strange man in the sense that he has this block and you can't reach him anymore. He has his whole private world. He could have been a monk. If I had married him ten years later, I would have been a good wife to him, and understood him and never let him go. He could have been a friend, he could have been a father. Certainly he was a lover. Everything. I didn't give him a chance."

Although it was his house, Fonda moved out and took rooms at the Croyden Hotel on Madison Avenue and Eighty-sixth Street. Afdera allowed him to take a few of his favorite paintings to make his sitting room more homey.

Through the efforts of a pair of attorneys, Fonda bought Afdera a cooperative apartment on Park Avenue. She carted out the paintings he'd given her, and Jane's four-poster bed. This required ripping away two windows and lowering the bed to the street and then re-cementing the windows. Upon his return to the house on Seventy-fourth Street, Fonda asked Afdera to send back Jane's bed. Again the windows had to be removed, the four-poster hoisted to the third floor, and the windows resealed.

In Juárez, Mexico, where Afdera went for her divorce, the court inquired as to the grounds for the dissolution of the marriage.

"There are none," Afdera Fonda murmured.

"There must be," the court instructed her.

"Nothing. He did nothing wrong. It was me. I was too young. I was too headstrong. I was immature."

Mrs. Fonda's lawyer approached the bench. A few soft words and the decree was granted.

"Incompatibility," ruled the court.

On East Seventy-fourth Street Fonda took the news calmly. He not only had his house again, he also had Afdera's dowery. Fidalma and Giuseppe had decided to remain with him.

On the morning the divorce papers arrived, Fidalma, as

was her custom, entered the dining room and asked, "*Signor, posso offrirle la prima colazione?*"

"Fidalma," Fonda said with a grin. "From now on we speak only English in this house."

La dolce vita was over.

CHAPTER
15

ONE thing Henry Fonda knew for certain: He would never marry again. In light of his past record he convinced himself he simply was not a man to wear a wedding band.

Of more concern was his career. At fifty-six years of age many of his contemporary leading man were finished in films. Most of the leading ladies who had played opposite him had either retired or become character women.

Fonda and James Stewart stepped out of a movie house one evening in the early sixties. They had seen a showing of Stewart's latest film.

"Know something, Hank?" Stewart asked in his Indiana, Pennsylvania, twang. "I'm depressed. I don't know if I'll ever get another picture again."

"You, too?" Fonda muttered. "That's the way I feel."

Neither man need have worried.

For the record, between 1961 and 1971 Henry Fonda made twenty-one pictures and appeared in five plays. Chroniclers of Hollywood films list Fonda in the roles of President of the United States, candidate for the Presidency, Secretary of State-Designate, an Admiral, a General, a Lieutenant Colonel, a spy, a widower, a sex symbol, a police officer, a prosecuting attorney, and eight variations of a westerner.

The first westerner he played in 1961 was in *How the West Was Won*. It was one of those Cinerama extravaganzas that utilized two directors, John Ford and Henry Hathaway, and a cast that boasted not only Fonda, but Spencer Tracy, James Stewart, John Wayne, Richard Widmark, Gregory Peck, George Peppard, Robert Preston, Karl Malden, Eli Wallach, Raymond Massey, Lee J. Cobb, Andy Devine, and Henry Morgan as just *some* of the men. Among the women were Carroll Baker, Carolyn Jones, Debbie Reynolds, Agnes Moorehead, and Thelma Ritter.

Fonda saw little of the impressive cast thanks in large part to his new friend George Peppard.

"They'd chartered a plane for us to fly up to Rapid City, South Dakota," Peppard said. "I went to the airline lounge and there was this very attractive blonde lady. Now, at that particular time I seized upon any opportunity that might be available. I told her I was an actor about to make a picture and she asked who was in it. Well, I rattled off as many names as I could, Tracy, Stewart, Wayne, Peck, Widmark, but when I got to Henry Fonda, I knew I'd made a mistake. She lit up like the torch on the Statue of Liberty at night. I couldn't make any time with this girl at all.

"Now Hank wasn't married then, so I said, 'Well, the thing to do is come up and visit us.' And she said, 'Really?' And I said, 'Certainly. Hank would be delighted to meet you.' And she laughed and said, 'Do you really think so?' And I said, 'Trust me, or I don't know my man.'

"When Hank got to the lounge, I said, 'Guess who wants to come up and visit you, Henry? And he said, 'Who?' And I said, 'That gorgeous creature over there.' And he said, 'Really.' Fonda's always underplaying everything, you know."

"In Rapid City, South Dakota," Fonda says, "we settled in and started shooting. And within a few days, damned if that girl didn't show up. She took a room in the old wooden motel the company was staying in. We all had drinks that night and then dinner. And when dinner was over, she came up behind my chair and whispered, 'Come to my room.'

"This motel had several wings, and between her room

and my room were seven porches and seven railings. Well, I didn't want to go out in the public hall so that meant I had to climb over all those railings. But she made it worthwhile.

"Next night after dinner was a carbon copy. 'Come to my room.' I climbed over those same seven railings again."

"After a few days," Peppard reported, "the phone rang. It was Fonda."

"What did you do to me?" Fonda asked. "I've got a problem with this girl."

Fortunately for MGM, the studio producing the picture, the young woman had only a week's vacation. Fonda had enough strength left for the remaining scenes and then went to Washington where he played the Secretary-of-State-designate in Otto Preminger's *Advise and Consent*.

"I don't know how that girl got word of where I was staying," Fonda says, "or what my telephone number was, but she checked into the same hotel and we began all over again. 'Come to my room.' And I did. Every night. I don't know how I resolved it, but after the picture was over I never saw or heard from her again."

At the film's conclusion Fonda returned to New York for his son's debut as an actor on Broadway. *Blood, Sweat, and Stanley Poole* opened on October 5, 1961. Young Fonda's reviews were excellent.

"Now I can stand on my own two feet," Peter declared, "and dispense with anybody who comes up to me and says, 'You are here because of who you are and not because of your talent.'"

Three days later Peter and Susan Brewer, stepdaughter of Howard Hughes's good right arm, Noah Dietrich, were married at St. Bartholomew's Church. Eugene Francis "Stormy" McDonald III served as Peter's best man. A reception was held at the Hotel Pierre, familiar nuptial territory to Fonda.

A month later at seven-fifteen on the morning of November 5, 1961, the Bel Air fire broke out. Fanned by the high Santa Ana winds that swept in from the deserts to the east, the fire roared without restraint all that day and throughout the night. Overhead the sky glowed orange and pink and the dense smoke drifted over everything.

The flames jumped across hastily bulldozed firebreaks, defying the combined efforts of all neighboring fire departments. Equipment from pumpers to specially equipped airplanes that unloaded countless gallons of chemicals on the fire failed. It raged mindlessly, fiercely through the dry grass and scrub in the canyons, lit on the roofs of houses, and reduced them to charred rubble within minutes.

By the next afternoon aid from nearby Army and Marine bases helped bring it under control. Although there were no deaths, hundreds of the most expensive dwellings in Bel Air and nearby Brentwood burned to the ground. Three thousand people were left homeless.

The house on Tigertail Road that Pan, Jane, and Peter once thought of as home had nothing standing except the stone chimneys. The trees that Henry had planted and nurtured so carefully were gone.

Not only did the former Fonda residence burn, but Grandma Seymour's place went, too, and with it went the letters that Frances Fonda had written to each of her three children during the last hours of her life.

After *Blood, Sweat, and Stanley Poole* closed Peter and Susan flew to Los Angeles. He asked a friend to drive him up to Tigertail. Nothing remained except ashes. Peter kicked them helplessly, and just as helplessly tried to buy the land from the woman to whom his father had sold it in 1948. He offered all of his inheritance from his mother, but even that wasn't enough.

"I was willing to live there in a tent," Peter said, "but she wanted a million dollars for the burned-over land."

"That woman held out," Henry says, "and eventually sold the property to a real estate developer. Where Tigertail had been, eighteen houses now stand."

Henry Fonda, in France for a cameo role in *The Longest Day*, learned of the Bel Air fire from a fellow actor who had saved his home by spraying it with a hose filled with water from his swimming pool. Edmund O'Brien brought the news to Fonda, and although Tigertail hadn't been his for over a dozen years, a sadness came over

299

Fonda. So much planning, so much love had been poured into that house, and now nothing remained.

Back in New York Fonda went directly into rehearsal of *A Gift of Time*, the play written and directed by Garson Kanin from the book by Lael Wertenbaker.

"The first actor I sent it to was Henry Fonda," Kanin said. "I thought then and I think now that there is no better American actor."

"Gar can write like an angel," Fonda says. "The script was beautiful."

The sensitive and talented Olivia de Havilland was his leading lady, but that was not enough. The play was the true story of a man who faced death from cancer and whose wife helped him kill himself. While the notices were filled with praise, ticket buyers stayed away.

"It's the only show I've ever been in," Fonda says, "where they didn't applaud at the final curtain. People found the play too painful to accept. Instead they waited outside the stage door to tell me how grateful they were in hushed voices."

Fonda retreated to his life as a recluse, drawing with his pastels by day, or taking long walks down Madison Avenue to look in at the art galleries. To keep him company during the evenings Sydney Chaplin, the actor, and Orson Bean, the comedian, started taking Fonda to singles bars.

"They thought those places were great. I didn't like them, but I met this girl there," Fonda says. "She was a fashion coordinator for a photographer. I began to see a lot of her. I lived on Seventy-fourth Street. She lived on Seventy-fifth. It was convenient. She was very attractive and I liked her, but I was far from being in love with her.

"I took her to the premier of *The Longest Day*. It was a black-tie affair, and the studio provided me with a chauffeur and a limousine. What was memorable about that night was a tall girl who looked at me as I got out of the car. She saw me and did a double take. She didn't have a clue who I was."

"I'll never forget that night," the tall girl who stared at Fonda said years later. "I wore a long black jersey evening dress because a young actor friend had invited me to

300

a formal opening of a movie in New York. As we reached the entrance to the theater I saw this gorgeous man helping a woman out of a limousine. I didn't recognize him.

"When we got inside it turned out he sat across the aisle from us and back about four rows. I must admit I spent most of the evening glancing over my shoulder. My date began to notice it."

"What's wrong?" he whispered.

"Who's that?"

The young actor turned.

"You don't know who that is?" he asked.

She shook her head.

"Shirlee, that's Henry Fonda."

She hadn't seen many movies. The name didn't mean much to her. Shirlee Mae Adams was a full-time airline stewardess in her mid-twenties. When she wasn't flying, she modeled in Dallas, Los Angeles, and New York.

"By the wildest coincidence," Shirlee recollected, "a few days later, I was in a furrier's waiting for some alterations. I told the furrier I had to have the jacket now because I was flying back to Los Angeles the next day."

" 'Los Angeles,' " a woman who'd just come in said. " 'I wish I were going. My boyfriend's out there.' "

" 'Who's your boyfriend?' "

" 'Henry Fonda.' "

"I looked over at her. It was the woman he'd taken to the opening."

A week later a member of a Beverly Hills public relations firm called Fonda and asked him to dinner at La Scala to discuss an upcoming minor award.

"I wasn't too eager to go," Fonda says, "but I'd been eating alone so often. It's difficult for anyone the public knows to have dinner by himself in a restaurant. One day I was sitting at a counter taking a big bite out of a sandwich and a woman came up to me and said, 'Oh, dear. Mr. Fonda.' I asked her what was wrong and she said, 'You look so unhappy, poor man.' Well, my God! You can't eat and smile at the same time. You'd look like an idiot.

"Anyway, before he picked me up, this press agent

called an airline stewardess and told her that Fonda was a quiet man and he needed some help with him."

"Knowing that I was a talker who could keep the conversation going," Shirlee said, "he asked me if I would come along, and I said, 'Would I?! Absolutely.' "

"So," Fonda says, "he brought Shirlee Adams. It took me half the meal before I figured out she wasn't engaged to him or even his date. All I knew was that she was tall, slim, looking just a couple of years older than Jane, and had a face with great bone structure. She also had eyes I felt I could drown in, and she was as refreshing as spring water.

"At the end of dinner we said good-bye to the press agent and went for a nightcap at someplace on the Strip near to where she lived. I don't know how long we talked, but by the end of the evening, I knew I was smitten."

Like Fonda, Shirlee Adams came from the Midwest, Aurora, Illinois, an hour's drive from Chicago. She'd been a religious girl, a faithful churchgoer. She didn't believe in smoking, liquor, coffee, tea, dancing, movies. She was allowed to swim in the summer, skate in the winter, and bowl in between. Everything else, they taught her, was a sin. She went from the Presbyterian Church to the Baptist Church to the Lutheran Church to the Church of God. The reason for these denominational changes was that at the age of four, Shirlee Adams was placed in the Mary A. Goddard Juvenile Home. "An orphanage is not the easiest place to spend a childhood," she said, but it was there that Shirlee became a "belonger." She filled the sugar bowls on the tables in the dining room, she went to Sunday School, attended the Young People's Meetings, and sang in the choir.

"We had to clean our plates or we couldn't get up from the table," Shirlee said. "I'd sit there so long I'd fall asleep. When I'd wake up, I'd have to eat what was left, even if it was ice cold. I was this skinny little thing, and I was almost forced to eat. I mean I wasn't being spoon-fed, but I had to clean my plate before I could leave the dining table."

By the time she was eleven years old, the major portion of Shirlee Adams's character had been formed. By the time she completed high school, the need to belong was a set part of her personality. As soon as she could she entered American Airlines Stewardess School. Flying was an adventure, a great escape from the sugar bowls and the ice-cold vegetables she hadn't wanted to eat at the orphanage.

"I loved flying," Shirlee said. "I'd recommend it to every young girl. It was particularly good for me because I was very insecure. Out of the orphanage I felt unwanted and unloved. And I *had* to be loved, wanted, accepted. That was *my* plane in the sky. The captain had the cockpit and I had the cabin. I had my passengers and I took care of them like they were the only ones on the plane. I learned their names, I wanted to know everything about them.

"A trip across the country, before I flew jets, took nine hours. So I had time to get to know everybody. It got to the point where I couldn't stand at the front door deplaning passengers because I would cry. I liked them so much, I'd have to go hide in the coach section."

She still doesn't smoke, but that is because she doesn't like the smell of tobacco. She doesn't drink because she is allergic to alcohol, and it's no contest between a cocktail and a migraine headache.

Henry Fonda claims to be an agnostic. Not an atheist but a doubter. He smoked, he drank, he danced, but there was a quality in Shirlee Adams's background that was similar to his. They shared the same elements of honesty, the same sense of values. Mutual attraction and respect began their relationship.

"I know a lot of attractive men," Shirlee said, "but I think Fonda is the most attractive man in the world. I love to look at him. I love to look at his face, not only because he's handsome, but because he had wonderful expressions. He's a study. His whole being is a study. I love to watch what he does with his hands when he's acting, painting, whatever. His hands are always in motion. Henry's always in motion. I love to watch him walk, sit, read. I even like to watch him sleep. He's so special." Shirlee paused and gazed off into the distance.

"It took him a while to find me, and it took me a while

to find him, but when we did find each other, that was it. We never wanted to be apart. Now, I really belonged to somebody."

Henry Fonda shakes his head, almost in disbelief at his good fortune. "I never saw the girl from the singles bar again. Shirlee is a fantastic woman. She's almost my opposite, in the sense that she is outgoing, charmingly so," Fonda says. "She makes friends so easily. People fall in love with her right on sight. She has a marvelous quality which I don't have. It's difficult for me to meet new people. I'm not easy to talk to. I don't have ready conversation. Shirlee does. I still marvel at how easily she can talk to a stranger, animatedly. Well, I feel we complement each other beautifully. I guess that's the way love is supposed to be. After I met Shirlee I felt like a kid again. I wanted to send her valentines every day of the year.

"Of course, I made it clear at the very beginning," Fonda adds, "that there'd be no more marriages for me."

"I never really thought about getting married," Shirlee said. "When I was a young girl I imagined myself wearing a white gown and having bridesmaids, but as I got older and started to date, I didn't stop to figure, 'Is he a potential husband?' And I suppose now, the reason I never thought that way was because none of them were really potential husbands for me."

In 1962 Henry Fonda switched agents, going from the initialed giant MCA to the new and more youthful CMA.

"Same letters," Fonda says, "a little scrambled. Anyway, Edward Albee wrote a play and wanted me for the leading male role. He sent it to my new agents. John Foreman read the script and sent a memo to his colleagues. 'This no-balls character is not for my Henry.' They turned it down without even telling me.

"Foreman isn't my agent anymore. He's my friend and a fine producer, but he doesn't like to be reminded that he turned down *Who's Afraid of Virginia Woolf?*

"When I saw the play in New York I flipped. I went home and wrote one of the few fan letters I'd ever written to Arthur Hill, the lucky actor who got the part. In Hollywood Bette Davis and I were considered for the film, but when Richard Burton and Elizabeth Taylor said they wanted it, they got it.

"To make up for this CMA, in the persons of David Begelman and Freddie Fields, got me a picture called *Spencer's Mountain*. As far as I was concerned, it set the movie business back twenty years, but it was a financial success and everyone was satisfied with it.

"The only two pleasures connected with that picture," Fonda says, "were the location, Jackson Hole, Wyoming—I swore I'd go back there one day to do some fishing—and the telephone calls I made to Shirlee Adams. Just hearing her voice picked me up.

"After *Spencer's Mountain*, I did go back to Jackson Hole. I was fishing on the Snake River, casting for trout, when I, the experienced angler, did the same damn thing Jim Stewart had done twenty, thirty years before in Indiana, Pennsylvania. I whipped the fly rod back, and by God, the hook caught me in the right eyelid.

"Well, my boatman blanched. He had to cut the line. The hook was hanging from my eyelid, but I felt no pain. We went downriver till we found a ranch where we could go ashore and get some woman with a station wagon and two kids to drive me to the hospital. I sat in the rear seat, and those two kids—a boy about five, and a girl about seven—knelt in front goggling at me. They kept looking at my closed eye with the hook in the lid probably wondering what kind of new jewelry I was wearing."

Shirlee continued to fly, Fonda continued to make films, *Fail Safe,* directed by Sidney Lumet, and *Sex and the Single Girl*, the adaptation of Helen Gurley Brown's book.

"Our first big date," Fonda says, "was the opening of *It's a Mad Mad Mad Mad World*."

"I had a special dress made for that evening," Shirlee said. "It was a full-length light blue satin. The front was covered with hand-sewn bugle beads. Probably cost me more than a month's salary. It was one of the loveliest gowns I've ever seen. I still have it."

"Photographers were all over the place," Fonda says, "and I was proud as hell of Shirlee."

Henry Fonda made it a policy when flying from coast

to coast to fly on Shirlee Adams's flights. If she worked in coach, he rode in coach. If her post was in first class, he made sure to get a seat up front.

In 1963 Peter's wife, Susan, presented him with a daughter. The child was named for Peter's earlier love, Bridget.

In that same year Henry rented a house on the very top of Summit Drive overlooking Beverly Hills. When she wasn't flying, Shirlee spent a goodly amount of time there. She and Henry could look down on the lights of the movie colony and beyond. On misty nights only the street lamps of the major thoroughfares could be seen. When the night sky was clear, lights flickered down the hills and into the valley beneath them.

"I came home from the dentist on the morning of November twenty-second and found Shirlee riveted to the television set. John Kennedy had been assassinated," Fonda says. "For three days neither of us left the TV set, watching that terrible story unfold."

After the days of national mourning, life reverted to regular schedules for most Americans. Henry Fonda, who had known and liked the late President so well, felt unable to return to everyday pursuits. Instead he bought a set of oil paints, closeted himself, and went to work in a new medium. Just as his pastels had been detailed realism, his works in oils were equally realistic.

"I can't paint what I don't see," Fonda says. Two tomatoes on a weatherworn windowsill, a lantern hanging on the side of a barn; when Fonda painted, it seemed as though he saw his objects through a magnifying glass. Nothing was eliminated. If he saw it, his brush copied it. The Dutch blood in Henry, consciously or unconsciously, had him copying the style of the old masters.

In 1964 Fonda made another western, *The Rounders*, and another Navy picture, *In Harm's Way*.

"One of the houses I sublet and lived in with Shirlee for a couple of months was on Benedict Canyon in Bel Air," Fonda says. "Does that street name ring a bell? Remember the place where Sharon Tate and her friends were massacred? Remember the guest house? That's where we stayed during the summer of sixty-four. It was a pleasant place. I did a lot of painting there. I had to drive in and park in the area where those violent people parked that night. I'd walk down the same path below the main house to the guest house. That's where the young guy was murdered when he made an exit at the wrong time.

"My God, timing is *everything*, even *outside* the theater."

A more personal tragedy took place on a raw February night in 1965 in Tucson, Arizona.

"I was sitting in a little disco in Beverly Hills," Peter Fonda recalled. "With me were my wife, Susan, and Mia Farrow. I knew Stormy was in trouble because he had called me every night for the last five nights. He was very agitated and upset. I listened to Mia and Susan talk, and at eleven-fifteen at night, twelve-fifteen his time, my eyes filled with tears. I couldn't figure it out. It shocked me. I thought maybe I was having a reaction to something I'd eaten or drunk. As soon as I got home, I called Stormy. There was no answer.

"I was getting ready to go the next evening and I asked Susan to try one more time to reach Stormy. I heard her dial. Then I heard her say, 'Stormy?' Then she handed me the phone.

"'Hello,' I said into the phone. 'Who is this?' And a voice on the other end said, 'Who is this?' I said, 'This is Peter Fonda,' and the voice said, 'This is the sheriff.' There was a pause, and I said, 'He killed himself, didn't he?' And the sheriff said, 'How did you know?' And I said, 'Well, I was his best friend. I think I know a little about the fellow.' There was another pause, and the sheriff said, 'Can you identify him?' And I said, 'Yes,' And I flew down there. They met me and drove me out to Stormy's.

"Boy, he sure wanted to die because he cut his wrists. He sat in the tub, and when that wasn't happening quickly enough, he got out of the tub, and you could see the blood that trailed behind him. He went to his closet, took out a pistol, shot himself with one bullet. He put it right in his head."

This awful news greeted Henry Fonda upon his return to California. The death of the McDonald boy, his son's dearest friend, moved him deeply. For the first time since Peter had been a small boy, Henry put his arms about his son.

"It really twisted Dad around," Peter said. "He had one helluva reaction."

His father says, "There's been so damn much tragedy floating around me since I've been an adult. I didn't want my son to have that, too."

Work has always occupied a major portion of Fonda's life, and with the solace offered by Shirlee, Henry was able to help himself and his son through the days following the suicide of Eugene Francis McDonald III.

In March 1965 Fonda took Shirlee to Spain. In Segovia he made *The Battle of the Bulge*, a film dealing with the last great German offensive in World War II.

"We were together in Spain for maybe ten weeks," Fonda says. "We had a wonderful time doing all the tourist things between working days. The film was shot in the snow up in the mountains, and when I was off, we'd rent a car and drive down to Toledo or down the Costa Dorado, the Costa Brava, or the Costa Del Sol. We did everything you're supposed to do when you're in Spain. It wasn't the first time for me, but it was for Shirlee. Anyway, they were wonderful days and we were together. And that's what made it wonderful, being with Shirlee."

The summer of 1965 turned out to be a summer of surprises for Fonda. Susan, as usual, allowed him to have their daughter for July and August. This year Fonda rented a house at Malibu, a house with only two bedrooms, and Shirlee moved in with Amy. In Rome, Pan married an Italian diplomat.

A third surprise came when his oldest child moved into a house a mile up the beach. With her was her "live-in companion," the French film director Roger Vadim.

Jane had made much progress since her first movie, *Tall Story*, and her first play, *There Was a Little Girl*. Both were in 1960 and both were masterminded by her father's old friend Joshua Logan.

"I remember Jane's opening night on Broadway," Fonda says. "I was appearing with Barbara Bel Geddes in *Silent Night, Lonely Night*. I went to my theater, put on my makeup, and then put on a coat and walked over to her theater and stood in the back of the house. In those days the curtains for openings were at eight o'clock and the curtains for the other Broadway plays that were running were at eight-forty. That meant I got to see Jane's first act.

"Afterward, I joined her at some party the producers were giving over on the East Side near River House. But Jane, who had heard about going to Sardi's after opening nights, said, 'I'm going to Sardi's.'

"I said, 'Jane, are you sure?' because she had no way of knowing what could happen. And she nodded yes, so I went with her. We split from the producers around midnight and when we reached the restaurant the crowd was beginning to thin out. There was the usual applause actors receive who've just opened in a play, and then we sat down at a table up in front. In a very short time, you know what happens in Sardi's, the headwaiters came in with stacks of *The New York Times* and passed them around. They came to our table and Jane took one and I took one, and Jane was across the table from me, and I'll never forget the review because it was devastating, and that's what I wanted to save her from.

"Anyway, she read the notice and she looked up at me, because now everybody in the place was reading it and pretending she wasn't there. It was an experience Jane didn't need. God! It's an experience *no one* needs." Jane went on to do Authur Laurents's play *Invitation to a March* and picture after picture that made her more and more successful.

"Jane is scaringly bright," Fonda says, "but she had a—well, I wouldn't call it an affair, it was an involvement with a man for a couple of years that almost made me accuse her of being stupid. I felt that he was a user and a parasite, a would-be director, and somehow, he deluded Jane into believing she needed him; I also felt that he had no talent, but he played Svengali to her Trilby. He came to her movie sets and tried to tell her what to do. The directors would steam and kick him the hell out, but he'd go straight to Jane's dressing room and wait for her there. They'd discuss the scenes in between takes.

"He even lived with her in her New York apartment for a while, and one day I heard she was very sick and couldn't eat anything. I phoned her, he wouldn't let me talk to her. Shit, I wanted to help get her well, and a friend had given me a recipe for sort of a tonic. I went to a butcher on Third Avenue and bought a thick sirloin steak.

"In my kitchen on Seventy-fourth Street I took a big hunk of the meat, put it in a mason jar, sealed it, and then placed the jar in boiling water on the stove. After cooking like that, the meat was swimming in its own juice. Then I removed the stewed meat, covered the jar, and grabbed a cab to Jane's apartment.

"That son-of-a-bitch answered my knock, snatched the package out of my hands, and said, 'Oh . . . thank you very much,' and closed the door in my face. He wouldn't even let me see my daughter. Thank God, Jane eventually outgrew him. It was a black period for me."

To Fonda's relief Jane met Roger Vadim, and by mid-August, 1965, without telling her father, Jane and Vadim got into her car and drove to Las Vegas where they were married.

"I was glad when I heard about it," Fonda says. "Vadim is a very civilized man." Following his daughter's marriage, Fonda left for New York to start rehearsals for a new play, *Generation*. Amy returned to her mother. Shirlee closed up the house. "And now," Shirlee asked herself, "what's going to happen to this wonderful relationship?"

Fonda was quick to tell her. He wanted her to join him in New York.

"I'll get you an apartment," he promised.

"That's like being a kept woman," Shirlee replied, "and I've never been kept."

"Look," Fonda said, "I've got this five-story townhouse. It has seven bedrooms. Take your pick, take a floor, take two floors. I'll move up to the top of the house and you can have the rest of it."

Shirlee Adams thought it over. She was through flying as a stewardess. If she did go to New York, she'd start looking for work as a model. She'd go back to the Ford agency or try Wilhelmina. One way or another, she'd get a job and a place of her own. But when she arrived in New York Fonda insisted she go on the road with him for the pre-Broadway tryout tour. New Haven, Boston. Old stuff for Fonda. Very new for Shirlee.

Generation opened at the Morosco Theater early in October, 1965.

"I played a confused father," Fonda says. "I was a living authority on the subject."

He was also an authority on marriage, but after making it clear to Shirlee early in their relationship that he never intended to enter into that state again, he let the matter rest. Then came the afternoon Shirlee Mae Adams hadn't expected.

"I'd been out walking," Shirlee said. "I came in around four-thirty. That's when Fonda generally takes his afternoon nap before he goes to the theater. But he wasn't asleep yet. He was in his office with sort of a funny look on his face. He asked me how I'd spent my day, we were talking, and in the middle of the conversation, he suddenly stopped."

"Do you want to get married?" Fonda asked quietly.

"Do *I* want to get married?"

Shirlee experienced a sensation of lightheadedness.

"Well, do you want to marry me?" his voice grew even softer.

"Yes. Of course I do. When?"

"Any Friday," Fonda said. "You pick it."

"You mean any Friday?"

"Yup," Fonda said. "Would you like to get married next Friday?"

"No," the new bride-to-be answered, getting more control of herself and the situation. "I want to do it like a real wedding. I want somebody to stand up with us."

"Who do you have in mind?"

Shirlee thought for a moment.

"Let's ask Elizabeth Ashley and George Peppard."

Peppard was on location filming in Ireland, and the wedding had to be delayed once or twice to accommodate his shooting schedule.

"I wasn't too shook up when I heard," Peppard confessed. "He'd met this sexy stewardess, Shirlee. I liked her. I've always liked Shirlee. I was dating Ashley when Hank started going around with Shirlee. Most people think of Hank, because of his looks and his integrity, most people think he's dominated by his intellect. The fact of the matter is that Hank is dominated by his passions.

"Well, Hank called me and told me he was going to get married, and would I be his best man. I said sure."

"We wanted to soft-pedal it as much as possible," Fonda says. "So my lawyer picked a judge outside of Manhattan."

Mineola, Long Island, is a couple of towns south of Oyster Bay and north of Rockville Center. Through it each day pass thousands of commuters to and from what they call the "City." Its permanent population is smaller than the number of transients, but it was large enough to boast a justice of the New York Supreme Court named Edwin B. Lynde. Judge Lynde was selected because prior to his being elevated to the bench, he had engaged in amateur theatricals and had continued a deep interest in the legitimate theater.

"I rented a limo," Peppard said, "got a bottle of Dom Perignon, put it in an ice bucket, bought a jar of beluga caviar, picked up some flowers, and stopped by for Ashley. She played the best lady."

"Elizabeth was wonderful," Shirlee said. " She had something old for me, a blue garter, something new, and something borrowed. I wore a white brocade dress designed by Galanos and off-white ballet-type slippers that had my name inside. George and Elizabeth gave me a nosegay before we went into the judge's chambers."

Justice Lynde had waived the customary three-day waiting period and concluded the simple double-ring ceremony by pronouncing, "I've been marrying couples for ten years, and I've never had one break apart. I don't expect you to either."

"It was a pleasant ceremony," the best man said, "but considering the length of his earlier marriages, I didn't figure it would last sixteen years. But if it made Henry that happy, it was okay with me."

In addition to Miss Ashley and Mr. Peppard the only other guests at the wedding were Fonda's close friends, John and June Springer. Springer, Fonda's personal press representative for years, had tried to cooperate with Henry's wish to "soft-pedal" the event, but there was no holding back the reporters and photographers. A battalion of them awaited the couple as they returned to Seventy-fourth Street.

Fonda gritted his teeth. He intended to crash through the assembled press and reach the safety of his front door.

Springer flinched. He knew his client only too well. When he first went to work for him after the war, about all Fonda would say to reporters was, "Yes," "No," and "Shit!" Springer had brought him a long way from that, but the crowd of reporters asking questions and the popping of the photographers' flashbulbs seemed too much. It was then that the new Mrs. Fonda turned on enough warmth to melt her husband's frosty facade.

"Let's invite them all in, Henry," she jollied him.

He eyed his bride and thought, "Why not? I want everyone to know about Shirlee. Come on, boys." And he led the press into his home. Reporters told one another they'd never seen Henry Fonda so outgoing.

He made the announcement himself, introduced his wife, looked at his watch, and said, "Fellas, you can stay as long as you want. I have a curtain to make."

After the theater Ashley and Peppard took the bridal couple to Orsini's for a late supper. Fonda sat back and sipped his drink. He couldn't have been happier.

"After stepping up to bat five times," he said, "I finally hit a home run."

CHAPTER
16

"AND we lived happily ever after . . ." Henry Fonda says contentedly. "Every day I wake up and take a look at Shirlee and think, 'This is it. She was worth the wait. I really feel she's the only wife I ever had.'"

The Mary A. Goddard Juvenile Home in Aurora, Illinois, is gone. Not a sign of it exists. But if any of the former administrators of that orphanage have moved on to other guardian institutions, they might take pleasure in hearing what a distinguished former resident, Shirlee Fonda, thinks of the sanctuary of her youth.

"It was a wonderful, wonderful large brick home," Shirlee said, "and it gave me a sense of being loved, being secure, being taken care of. Belonging. Try not to regard me as silly, but I'll always live in either a stone or brick house. They are safe havens for me. It sounds strange, I know, but after Fonda and I moved into his townhouse on Seventy-fourth Street, it was as though there were three of us, my husband, our house, and me. All necessary to each other."

After *Generation* ended its run, Fonda received a telephone call from an executive of the USO. The war in Vietnam had heated up and American servicemen in the Southeast Asia Theater of Operations needed the sort of help that performers could provide.

"They were sponsoring what they called 'Handshake Tours' in Vietnam," Fonda says. "They told me Charlton

Heston, Bob Mitchum, Jim Stewart, and other actors had already been there.

"'Well,' I said, 'you've got the wrong guy, I don't approve of that action.' The fella who called said, 'That has nothing to do with it, Mr. Fonda. Our boys are there and they need their morale picked up. It helps when they see a recognizable face from home. Just go and talk to them. Sit with them while they eat in their mess halls, and listen to them talk in their barracks.'

"Well, they persuaded me. We fixed a date for April. I was to be in Vietnam for about twenty-three days. In the weeks before I left, I kept thinking, 'What the hell am I going to do? I'm not an entertainer. I'm no Bob Hope. I'm not even good at mixing with people I don't know.'

"Suddenly, a gimmick occurred to me. I'd buy a Polaroid camera, have somebody take pictures of me with the soldiers, give them the autographed prints, and they could keep them or send them home. Well, that's what I did. I bought a bagful of film, a camera, and off I went to Saigon. Damn long trip. It's the other side of nowhere.

"A Major met me. He'd been assigned as my guide and to accompany me on the whole tour. I had quite an itinerary. A different place every day. Sometimes two, sometimes three, sometimes more. We flew by helicopter from one spot to another. I told my Major about the Polaroid and he thought it was a marvelous idea.

"We'd arrive at a base and get taken from one location to another—recreation halls, the mess, officers' club, enlisted men's club, hospitals. I had a terrible time controlling my emotions when I looked at those hundreds of casualties. And I did have to control myself. You wouldn't want the boys to see you upset. That was the roughest part of the trip.

"Whenever I had the chance, I'd stand with a soldier or a Marine, and my buddy, the Major, would take our picture. Then I'd sign it. The fellas got a boot out of those snapshots. I ran out of film in two days, but luckily, it was available in the PXs. I must have bought hundreds of dollars worth during those three weeks.

"The Navy flew me to the aircraft carriers the *Ticonderoga*, the *Kitty Hawk*, and the *Bennington*. You can't

315

imagine what it is to land on an aircraft carrier. It's like landing on a domino. It gets larger as you get closer, and then wham!, you're brought to a stop by a cable. That was exciting. I'd give in-house interviews over the ship's closed-circuit television system. Would you believe they were showing Jane's *Cat Ballou* when I visited the *Ticonderoga*?

"I sacked out at ten o'clock in the evening. That's twenty-two hundred hours Navy time. At oh-six hundred, right after they fed me breakfast, I was catapult-launched off. Never eat before that happens!

"They took me to every fucking ugly town you've read about and forgotten. Dozens and dozens of towns, each more lice ridden, more burned out, worse smelling than the other.

"Hugh O'Brian's brother met me in one of those forsaken places. Jack Kelly, the actor who worked with Jim Garner in *Maverick*, had breakfast with me one morning. Finally, the Major and I left in a jeep for Bien Hua. At the airport I watched tired but eager troops boarding TWA planes for the States. Fresh, frightened-looking troops landed to take their places.

"My flight going south was delayed by bad weather and motor trouble. A doctor took me over to a Vietnamese hospital. They had three or four people in each bed. One section was filled with children. A lot of them had been mutilated by booby traps. Jesus! I didn't know whether they'd been hit by *our* booby traps or North Vietnamese booby traps. I was afraid to ask.

"Well, the monsoon blew in and teemed rain every morning. It cleared some during the days, but stayed hot and muggy. I couldn't sleep well at night. Too hot, too many mosquitoes. I couldn't stop scratching.

"The helicopters we rode in generally flew at treetop level and we got shot at quite a few times. Scary.

"We went back to Saigon and ran into Mike Douglas and three CBS men. I was really dragging. A General debriefed me, I did an Armed Forces Radio interview, and left from the Saigon airport at ten-forty-five A.M. I carried dozens of enlisted men's telephone numbers. When I got back, I made damn sure to call every one of their families.

"It was a trip this sixty-two-year-old man didn't want to take, but I felt I had to, not for any of the political or military ramifications, but for the guys sweating it out and dying in the rice paddies and jungles. It was a different kind of war that I had fought—different and dirtier, and as usual, I was damn glad to be home."

Back in California Henry went directly into a film with Lucille Ball, while Shirlee went out to find another "safe haven."

The picture with Lucille Ball was called *Yours, Mine and Ours*. It was a comedy dealing with a widower and his children, a widow and her children, and the children resulting from their union.

"Henry's terrific to work with," Lucille Ball said. "Once he settles on 'Yes, I will do it,' 'Yes, the director is fine,' he does his job, but he tries not to become involved with the production. He says, 'Just pay me and let me get the hell out.'

"Well, I owned a piece of this picture, there were some problems, and I needed Henry's advice. So I went to his dressing trailer. It's really a sitting room and a bathroom and a makeup room. 'Knock, knock, knock,' I said. 'Henry, may I talk to you?' "

" 'Yeah.' "

"I went in and there he sat doing his crewel work. That's a kind of embroidery with heavy yarn. He does unbelievable crewel work, maybe better than women do. Makes huge canvases and pillows and rugs. He likes to do this on the set. You can pick it up and put it down. He couldn't drag his paintings back and forth. There he was doing his crewel.

"Well, Henry, this is happening and this is happening and they've cut out this and they've cut that and some of it are your scenes."

Henry didn't raise his eyes.

"It'll all work out. Believe me."

And he returned to his hobby.

"Two days later," Miss Ball said, "I was sitting over there, and I heard a man's voice. 'What!' And everybody on the set got very quiet."

"What do you mean?" Henry Fonda said to the direc-

317

tor. "How can you do that if you don't do that? Well, that's not the way I understood it!"

"And," Miss Ball added, "he walked.

"I whipped back to his trailer, and I said, 'Knock, knock, knock.' I was afraid he was ready to junk the whole picture. Instead he taught me a lesson I've used many times since. He said, 'Lucy, let's cool off. Relax. Easy does it. I'll go and talk to that director. I'll get him to make the changes. It'll be better on the next take.'

"I felt like I'd won a great victory," Miss Ball said. "Not only was I right, but Henry Fonda had become involved at last."

As Fonda shot his movie Shirlee searched for a permanent living place in California. After miles of driving through the twisted roads of Brentwood and the neatly lawned streets of Beverly Hills with real estate agents, she found a house on a hilltop on Chalon Drive in Bel Air, a Spanish hacienda made of stones and bricks.

They told her another family was ready to buy it that evening. When Henry returned from the day's filming, Shirlee drove him up to see it. The sprawling, airy old house appealed to him. So did the two and a half acres surrounding it. Henry considered the possibilities; he could have a "North 40" and a "South 40" again. Without even examining the guest house and the chauffeur's quarters, he uttered three words, "Let's take it."

At United Artists a few days later Lucille Ball asked, "Did you buy that place?"

"The money's in escrow."

"Well, be sure to have the plumbing checked," she warned.

"What?"

"The plumbing. Be sure and have the plumbing checked. I know that house. It was built over fifty years ago. Always check the plumbing."

"Come on, Lucy. We let other people handle that sort of thing."

"Well," Lucille Ball said, wearing a self-satisfied expression, "two days after they moved in, a weak place which they'd been assured was copper tubing gave out, and the entire driveway just rose and separated. It cost him about forty-eight, fifty-eight, sixty-eight thousand dollars."

"That's why *I* do crewel work," Fonda says, "and Lucy owns the studio.

"Shirlee hired one of the finest decorators in the country, Peter Short, and we furnished the place from scratch. All we had in a twenty-room house was Shirlee's king-size bed, a beaten-up refrigerator, a few odd chairs, and a table."

"It was a real hodgepodge," Fonda's wife said. "When we bought it, everything was painted shiny white and shiny black. The floors were covered with gold carpeting. Well, we had that pulled up and then we sandblasted the beamed ceilings and stripped all the doors."

As the house underwent a transformation, so did Henry Fonda.

"Shirlee turned me around," Fonda says. "I'm easier with her than I've ever been with anyone before. Maybe I'm mellowing with age. Maybe with Shirlee I'm more willing to compromise."

"His whole life," Nedda Logan observed, "opened like a rose coming out from a tiny, tight bud. Shirlee gave him confidence, and now he's even loquacious. He has a whole new personality, and I feel like saying, 'Where were you all those years?'"

"Shirlee is quite a remarkable woman," Jane Fonda said. "My father likes to play the hermit act, but Shirlee doesn't allow him to get away with it. He is the center of her life. She's exactly what he needed and she won't let him. I mean, she's on to him all the time, all the time, all the time!

"My father needed to be plugged in. By himself he could just go floating away. I understand him so well, because I'm so much like him. I can see him sort of drifting farther and farther and farther into some hermitic kind of situation. His wives have had several things in common. They've all been blondish, extremely outgoing, very social, very effervescent, very energetic, and then he could tune out safely. Shirlee is the one woman who won't let him tune out. And she puts up with a lot of abuse, and she puts up with it because she knows underneath it all he

319

loves her, he really loves her, he adores her, he worships her, he needs her, he relies on her. And he has an incredible way of striking out cruelly at the people he loves. She has put up with it and I really respect her for it."

"Jane hit it on the nose," Fonda says. "I don't really like myself. Never have. People mix me up with the characters I play. I'm not a great guy like Doug Roberts. I'd like to be but I'm not.

"I'm petty about certain things. I can't stand to see anything wasted. When Sinatra or Streisand invite us to their openings in Las Vegas, we go, but I will not gamble at the tables. You see, *I hate to lose.*

"Those early days in New York when I had to struggle left their mark on me. When you've been poor, you can't stand waste. I bug Shirlee sometimes. We go shopping together at the market and Shirlee buys too many fresh vegetables at one time. And four days later there's some broccoli that's four days old, and I make a fucking big deal about that. My point is don't buy fresh vegetables if you're not going to use them. I shouldn't carry on, but I still have that thing. Don't waste."

"A lot of women in this part of Los Angeles were jealous of Shirlee in the beginning," her friend Muriel Slatkin said. "I think she was aware of it, but eventually, she won them over the way she does everybody."

"She won me over," Peter Fonda said. "My first judgment on Shirlee was totally wrong. I try to stay clear of value judgments on people, but from time to time, dealing with your family, you can't help it. One day I was using the telephone in Shirlee's bedroom. Well, you know my weakness. I'm nosy. Her closet door was open so I looked in. There must have been four hundred pair of shoes. Most of them unworn.

"I thought, 'This is ridiculous. This woman is a banana!'

"Well, I told a couple of people about it, and the comment got back to Shirlee. The next time I went by the house, she called me aside."

"I heard what you said about my shoes," Shirlee told him. "I want to explain it to you, Peter, because I was hurt when word got back to me. And then I asked myself, 'Why *do* I have all these shoes?' I couldn't figure it out.

"And then I came across this photograph of myself at the orphanage. Take a look at it, Peter."

"She handed me a shapshot," Peter said. "She was a little girl, and she had on a pair of shoes and the soles were flapping, like an old pair of clown's shoes."

"When I saw that picture," Shirlee told him, "I said to myself, 'That's never going to happen to me again.' And I remembered that the shoes in that picture weren't really mine. They were just put on my feet for the photograph."

"I was very touched that she included me in her life by telling me that story," Peter said. "I empathized with Shirlee because of the traumas I'd suffered as a child. My mother's death left me disturbed, so disturbed that shortly after I was married, I took my wife, Susan, and drove clear to Beacon, New York, walked through the sanitarium where mother'd spent her last days, and asked questions of the psychiatrists. It didn't help much. I wrote a poem about the way I felt in 1966.

Here comes the past,
Passing by my eyes,
Passing by my ear,
Passing through my heart.
Oh, the pain will never end
Until my past is past.

"My dad wanted me to be perfect. I'm afraid I wasn't. There had been an article from a paper in my baby book that I wanted to show Shirlee, but it was torn out. My baby book is filled with holes, just like my life."

"Peter had a bungalow in the San Fernando Valley," Fonda says. "It was really more of an office for him, but he let two of his buddies live there, and without Peter's knowing about it, they grew some marijuana in the backyard. The neighbors reported it and the police arrested the two boys, and since the house was in Peter's name, they busted him, too.

"I was in Arizona making *Welcome to Hard Times* when I heard that my son was to go on trial in Municipal Court in downtown Los Angeles for drug possession. Well, I flew into town, put on my most conservative suit, and drove to the courtroom. Grandma Seymour, Eulalia Chapin, who'd come out from New York to help Peter, the three of us sat quietly among the spectators.

"When Peter was called to the stand, he couldn't have been a worse defendant. Every time the prosecutor asked him a question, Peter gave him a wisecrack and then turned to the judge or the jury to see if he'd landed a laugh. He didn't look at me because I would have given him the signal to stop it and play it straight.

"But he went on like that for the better part of the morning, trying for laughs instead of trying for an acquittal. When the court adjourned for an hour, Grandma Seymour, Eulalia Chapin, Peter, and I started out for lunch.

" 'Listen,' I told him, 'you're handling this in the wrong way. You're dressed crazy enough to make them believe you *are* on drugs. If you think you're going to win over those twelve good men and women in the jury box, you're out of your head. You've got to persuade that judge and jury that you're honest, sober, that you're an upright citizen, not some kind of comic. If you want them to be on your side, don't be a smart ass!'

"Peter got the message. He listened to me and said, 'You're right, Dad.' After lunch he played the scene just as I told him—straight.

"Then it was my turn. I'd never been in a courtroom before. Well, maybe in a movie or two. But this was the genuine article. I was sworn in and sat down in the witness box and answered their questions, not like a movie actor, but like an ordinary taxpayer, same as they were. I mean I was back in the Navy. 'Yes, sir. No, sir. I've never had any trouble with the boy, sir. Never.' They understood that kind of talk, and pretty soon they 'sirred' me right back. By the end of the day Peter was found not guilty, and I think the other two boys may have drawn a year's probation. And that's the last time Peter caused me any trouble.

"Jane was a relatively slow starter when it came to trouble," Fonda says. "She seemed to be happily married, she had a career that few young people in Hollywood or anywhere else could match. She'd done so many really successful films, I can't remember them all. *Cat Ballou, Any Wednesday, Barefoot in the Park, Barbarella.*"

Barbarella was a shocker—to Fonda—and to almost everyone else who saw it.

After her mother's death, Jane had become a compulsive eater. She'd rush home from school and go through mounds of toast and jam, candy, and cake.

"I'd sit in front of the television set and watch 'Howdy Doody,'" Jane said, "and I'd gorge myself with all the sweets I could lay my hands on."

The result was predictable. Jane Fonda became chubby Jane Fonda. When she spent the summer with Henry and Afdera in Villefranche, she appeared in a bikini one day. Her father, noticing the skimpy bathing suit and his daughter's generous figure, casually advised the teen-aged girl not to wear anything so tight. That was enough for Jane. That and peer pressure did the trick. From then on Jane went on a series of sensible diets. To this day she eats sparingly and works out regularly and strenuously.

Barbarella was the movie where Jane Fonda discarded her concerns about her body. Not only did she have a beautiful face, but a figure to match, and she was ready to act in a film that displayed both.

Perhaps it displayed too much. Women's groups around the country protested Miss Fonda's exploitation as a sex symbol by male chauvinists.

That didn't last too long because by then Jane had pitched into political activism. Living in Paris, she was exposed to France's opposition to America's involvement in Vietnam. The French, after two hundred years of colonialism in Southeast Asia, went down to inglorious defeat at Dien Bien Phu. Rather than venting their anger upon the Vietnamese, they turned on the Americans for picking up where they left off.

"Peter and Jane," Fonda says, "were successful very young. Their rebellion against me as a parent didn't last too long. They willingly admitted, 'I'm sorry, Dad, for the hurtful things that were said.' Jane said plenty of hurtful things to the press. She told one reporter she grew up in a completely phony atmosphere.

"Well, I don't have to tell anyone about Jane Fonda.

She's been front-page material for years. Her name is more recognized than mine ever was. Lots of times I had to turn pages pretty fast. I wasn't Harry Truman. I couldn't write letters to the editors. I just bit my lip and lived through it all. They called her 'Hanoi Jane,' a traitor, they wrote unsigned letters urging me to send her back to Moscow. I stewed a lot about her. I was afraid she might be in danger from some maniac.

"Y'know, when she was married to Vadim, she got into this whole business and some of his friends sold her on the idea that America's position in the Vietnam war was wrong. To tell you the truth, in many areas, she's been vindicated. That war was obscene.

"They labeled her a Communist. She did have a couple of friends who believed in that system. I know because she lived with Shirlee and me during most of this. When Jane had Angela Davis over to the house, I began to wonder about her. I was not happy. But Jane was that kind of girl, the poor American Indians, the poor Indian Indians, the poor Black Panthers, the poor people in the ghettos. I've always been for the underdog, but I personally believe that communism is full of lies. I am definitely anti-Communist.

"Jane today will be the first to admit that she made many mistakes, things she said and things she did. She changed into a militant almost overnight. It was too fast for anyone to handle."

"My rebellion against my father really ended when I went to Europe," Jane said. "It was then that I became my own person. Maybe that's even why I went. Maybe going had to do with trying not to be Henry Fonda's daughter anymore. Go to another culture. Prove myself on my own. It was so far removed from his background and his upbringing and his world views, the world I entered into there. And I got over him as a problem-figure in my life. Now, later, when Vadim and I split up, I came back and lived with my father and Shirlee. There were difficulties because I was becoming a political activist. I was way over my head, you know, plunging in as I have a wont to do. And at the very time when the Plumbers were being sent out by Nixon to deal with people like me. Well, the impact of that fell squarely on my father. After all, I was living in his house, and that's where the FBI came and questioned me. So that created tremendous tensions between us.

"Dad and I would argue about what I was doing. Dad would say, 'You're dead wrong,' and I'd say, 'No, I'm not.' And he'd say, 'If you can prove to me that what you're saying is true . . .' And then I would bring home soldiers from coffeehouses and who'd been in Vietnam, and have him listen to them. And Dad and I would fight. And he was worried. Obviously, he thought, 'What foreign agent is manipulating my daughter?' Until slowly he realized what a lot of parents did, we weren't crazy."

"I can remember," Fonda says, "one emotional scene Jane and I had on the terrace outside the den. We were talking. It was around sunset. I looked at my beautiful, darling daughter, and I thought, 'Am I being duped? Has she really been seduced by that bunch?' And right then and there I decided to level with her.

"I said, 'Jane, if I ever discover for a fact that you're a Communist or a true Communist sympathizer, I, your father, will be the first to turn you in. I fought for this country, and I love it.' And tears trickled down her cheeks. She shook her head, 'No.'

" 'Jane, there are less human rights in Russia than in America. Maybe we do have some inequities, but it's worse over there.'

"She nodded in agreement, but her tears wouldn't stop."

"I've blacked out on that night," Jane admitted. "I can't even recall it, but my father was a worried, concerned parent. We don't fight the way we used to anymore. Dad's loosened up, he's more at peace with himself, more affectionate. He wouldn't have had the power over me if he had been ice cold. You see, the thing about my dad is, if you like someone, and I like him, and he doesn't give a whole lot, when he does give, however oblique it may be, oh, I mean, it's like the sun. You can go for months on it!"

"Let me kill a rumor," Fonda says. "I've never stopped talking to my kids. I've got exceptional children. I'm very lucky. There are many friends of mine who've had nothing but pain from their kids. Jane and Peter have given me pain, sure, but mostly they've given me pleasure.

"Peter has suffered a great deal from being Henry Fonda's son, but Peter tells me that if he had to choose a father, he'd still want me.

"There are a lot of liberal activist women in America, but if Jane hadn't been my daughter, she probably would have been in for less hounding from the media, the public, and the authorities. My kids are smart, talented, and successful, and they take time out for me always.

"Of course, Amy is the white sheep of the family. I don't see her as much as I'd like. She attends school in San Francisco where she's studying to be a doctor of clinical psychology."

"I didn't want to be an actor," Amy Fonda said, "not because I felt I couldn't act, but because I felt there were too many actors in the family already, and if I started it, I'd have to be better than any of them."

"Even Pan keeps in touch with us," Fonda says. "She's a delightful woman. I never think of her as a stepdaughter, and Peter calls her his sister."

"It's a good thing to be surrounded by young people," Fonda says, "because inevitably, as you grow older, you lose friends."

On December 20, 1968, John Steinbeck died in his home in New York. His grieving widow, Elaine, sat with Nathaniel Benchley, the author, and drew up a list of pallbearers for her husband's funeral.

"I called St. James Church," Elaine Steinbeck said, "and asked them if the strict Episcopal service might permit three short poems to be read by Henry Fonda. They told me it could. We lived on Seventy-second Street and I thought Hank was in his townhouse on Seventy-fourth. Nat got him on the phone and asked him if he'd do it. Of course he said yes. What I didn't know was that he was in California making a movie."

"God! I was distressed by the news," Fonda says. "John was a man of gigantic talent and a fine person. I said to the director and the producer of whatever movie I was making, 'Boys, count me out for a day or two, shoot

326

around me, do whatever you have to because I'm going to New York.'

"At the church I did my bit, three short poems by Synge, Tennyson, and Robert Louis Stevenson. After the service, I went home with Elaine. She took me into John's room."

"He wanted you to have this," she said as she held out a silver box.

"Actually," Fonda says, "it was an old tobacco can that John, who was almost as gifted with his hands as his fingers were on the typewriter, had converted into a jewel case. The interior of the box was lined with felt."

"John wanted you to have these, too," she said, lifting the lid. Inside were the pearl studs Steinbeck had worn in his dress shirt when he accepted the Nobel Prize for Literature.

"I've never worn them," Fonda says, "but I treasure the studs for what they represent, and the jewel box because John Steinbeck made it. I still have both."

In the late sixties he signed for a trio of westerns. Westerns mean horses, and all of his life Fonda has had a feud with horses. Going back as far as the big one that tossed him across the hood of an oncoming car in Mt. Kisco, New York, right through every cowboy picture he ever made, Henry Fonda had problems with the ponies.

"I was afraid one would bite me or stick his foot in a gopher hole and break his neck or mine," Fonda says. "They couldn't get me on one of those animals today, not with a derrick. Y'see, I never really learned to ride. As a kid growing up I might have gone out in the fields and gotten on bareback and been bucked off, but I didn't really ride until I came here to do movies.

"They'd send me over to the stables in the Valley. Wranglers handled the horses, and I was supposed to ride one and get used to him and he was supposed to get used to me. That's a crock! I never felt secure. I may have looked okay, but I wasn't any good.

"The hardest part was mounting. The director would tell me, 'Don't worry. He'll stand still.' The hell he will. Those beasts rarely cooperated. I was swinging up on a horse in one of my movies, he moved, and I landed on my ass on the ground. Rattled all the teeth in my head.

"Once, making *Jesse James*, I played a real tough guy. They had a group of us who had just escaped from jail. We'd mount the horses that were waiting for us on the dirt street. The director wanted us to have our guns in our hand, shoot in the air, rear the horses, and start off. He made us do it over and over. My arm got tired from putting the gun back in the holster, then raising it and shooting it in the air. This one time, I lowered my hand without uncocking the gun, the horse wiggled his rear end, and my gun went off. I'd shot myself! No bullet, but a full charge. I sure as hell had powder burns. They tore my trousers and burned by leg so badly I had to be taken to the emergency room of a hospital in Kansas City for a tetanus injection and dressing.

"Jim Stewart and I played together in a thing called *Firecreek*. You know, someone had the bright idea of making me the villain. I played a bad guy who tried to kill Jim Stewart. Now, any man who tries to kill Jim Stewart *has* to be marked as a man who's plain rotten. You can't get much worse than that.

"I did though. I was the meanest man you ever saw in a spaghetti western called *Once Upon a Time in the West*. A spaghetti western is an American cowboy picture shot in Italy or Spain. The script wasn't much as far as I could tell. It was written in Italian and then someone made a literal English translation. It was awkward. I didn't dig it, and I turned it down. I told the fellas I was lunching with that some Italian producer was flying in to try to talk me into doing it. 'Who?' they asked.

"Sergio somebody."

"Sergio Leone?"

"I said yes, and they all fell down. Seems Sergio Leone had made the three biggest box-office pictures to come out of Italy. Next to Clint Eastwood's father, he personally had done more for Clint Eastwood than anyone else.

"Well, I went home and called an old, valued friend, Eli Wallach. He'd been in *Mister Roberts* with me and he'd done one or two of those spaghetti westerns. I told him I wasn't wild about the script."

" 'Pay no attention to the script,' Eli told me enthusiastically. 'Just go. You'll fall in love with Sergio. You'll have a marvelous time. Believe me!' "

On the strength of Wallach's recommendation, Fonda and Shirlee went to Italy where he learned that Claudia Cardinale and Charles Bronson were to appear in the film with him. To portray a truly villainous type, Fonda grew a mustache and a beard and had brown contact lenses made for his eyes.

"When I walked onto the set," Fonda says, "Sergio, who spoke no English, took one look at me and let loose a volley of rapid-fire Italian, gesturing wildly with his hands and arms as he spoke. An interpreter stood beside him, and the first word in English I heard was 'Shave!' And the next thing was, 'Throw away the brown eyes. Where are the big blues? That's what I bought.'

"I did what he asked, and in the first scene in the picture, not the first scene we shot but the first scene the audience sees, there's this happy rancher and his family. They're getting ready to eat outside their cabin, smiling, laughing. A shot rings out and the eighteen-year-old daughter of the family falls dead with a bullet through her eye. Her father looks up and a bullet gets him right in the forehead. The mother screams and she's blown away. A sixteen-year-old youth comes out of the barn and *bam!* He's dead. That leaves a nine-year-old boy standing in the middle of the worst massacre you can imagine.

"The camera cuts to a long shot and from behind the sagebrush on the desert come five ominous figures, all wearing gray dusters, black, wide-brimmed hats, and they're carrying rifles and side arms. Slowly, they converge on this little boy. Cut to him. Cut to the advancing men. Cut to the terror in the kid's eyes. Cut to the back of the central figure of the five desperados. Very slowly the camera comes around and that's what Sergio was going for all the time. The main heavy, Jesus Christ, it's Henry Fonda!

"We finally stop in front of this frightened little boy.

" 'What'll we do with this one, Frank?' Jack Elam, one of my henchmen, asks.

" 'Well,' I say as I spit in the dirt, 'now that you called me by my name . . .'

"A bell chimes once in the distance," Fonda says. "I draw my pistol slowly from my holster, the innocent nine-year-old looks up at me pleadingly, and I shoot him dead.

"That picture ran four years at the same theater in Paris. The identical thing happened in Berlin. It was one of the all-time grossing pictures in Europe, South America, and Japan. But it didn't pull a dime in America."

Audiences at home simply would not accept Henry Fonda shooting a helpless child in cold blood. The film may be seen on late-night television in the United States, but just as Fonda draws his gun, stations all over the country cut to commercials. Shooting Stewart, not fatally, but shooting Stewart, was bad enough, but Fonda killing a child is totally unacceptable to American audiences.

What did receive high recognition by Americans with cheers and incredibly long lines at the nation's box offices was a Fonda film made not by Henry Fonda, but by his twenty-eight-year-old son. With *Easy Rider* Peter Fonda fixed the seal of approval on a whole way of life.

"The plot," Henry says, "that's hard to describe. Two guys make a big push. They sell a lot of 'coke,' split with the money, and they're going to Florida on their motorcycles. When they get there, they plan to have an easy ride for the rest of their lives. They never reach their goal. Reviewers compared Peter to James Dean and Clint Eastwood."

"We started rolling at twelve o'clock on a Friday—Good Friday," Peter said, "and I wasn't aware until after the day's 'shoot' that it was my birthday, and *Easy Rider* was quite a birthday present.

"The first week we went to New Orleans during the Mardi Gras. We shot in sixteen millimeter, and Dennis Hopper, who directed the picture, had me out in this fuckin' graveyard, and everything is buried above ground because you dig a foot and you have water. There's this big Italian statue. A seated woman with a shield and a spear, and I'm to sit in her lap. I didn't want to climb up there, but Dennis grabbed me by the shoulders.

330

"'You've got to do it,' he yelled. 'I'm the director. You've got to do it for me. I want you to pretend that she's your mother. Now this is supposed to be an acid trip we're on and you can stretch a lot when you're dealing with acid.'

"I said, 'Dennis, you can't ask me to do that just because you happen to have inside information about my own background. That's called dirty pool.'

"'Just do it!'

"So I climbed up and asked this cold statue questions I have never asked in my life. 'Mother, why did you leave me?' 'Mother, I hate you.' 'Mother, I love you!' I really got into it. I was shouting. It came flooding out of me.

"Afterward, I thought, 'God, when my sister and my father see this they're going to come unglued.'

"I went to Bert Schneider, the guy who gave me the money to make the movie, and I said, 'Bert, we've got to take that scene out.' And he asked, 'Why?' And I said, 'That's too fuckin' close.' And he said, 'So what? It's great. It's heavy stuff.'

"Well, I affected a great deal of public opinion in my own little way. That movie was not about the war, just about attitudes. . . . I look at it as my *Grapes of Wrath*. I don't say my acting was anywhere near where my dad's acting was; it was a different style, a different stanza, a different piece of music, but it was still music. It affected an entire culture and it continues to. I have accomplished in my sweet, short life what most people connected with films dream about doing."

The first thing *Easy Rider* did was win the Cannes Film Festival Award. After that full-page ads in the newspapers trumpeted it, as one critic raved, "the little movie that killed the big picture."

According to latest estimates, *Easy Rider* grossed sixty million dollars. As the producer, the leading man, and one of the three co-authors, Peter Fonda walked away with twenty-two percent of the picture.

"I am in awe of this boy," Fonda told Leonard Probst, the drama critic. "He is more knowledgeable in a technical area of his business than I will ever be. He is a hyphenate, actor-director-producer.

"Can you imagine Peter and Jack Nicholson and Hopper smoking joints and saying, 'Man! Man!' and capturing not only the mint but the reviews, too? *Easy Rider* cost pennies, made a fortune, and Peter didn't even have to get on a horse."

Henry did. His next picture was a western with his friend Jim Stewart. *The Cheyenne Social Club* dealt with a pair of down-in-the-pocket cowpokes, one of whom inherits a house of ill repute.

Cheyenne wasn't filmed in Wyoming. It was made on location in Santa Fe, New Mexico. Unlike Fonda, Stewart had no dislike for horses. Quite the contrary.

"I had a horse I'd been riding in the movies for twenty years," Jim Stewart said. "His name was Pie and the girl who owned him only let *me* ride him. Now, I'd been advised not to take him to Santa Fe because of the seven-thousand-foot altitude, but I felt so close to Pie, I didn't want to make a western without him."

"Well," Fonda says, "they took Ole Pie in a horse trailer and they brought a double along. Old Pie damn near died. They had to stop along the way at a vet's. They saved him and finally trucked him to our location.

"The picture was rolling along just fine," Fonda says, "when Jim and his wife, Gloria, suffered the worst kind of loss. Their older son, Ronald, was killed in action with the Marines in Vietnam. Here we were, making this comedy, when the Defense Department notified them. Jim tried hard not to spread his grief through the company. He and I avoided discussing the war before the tragedy. Now, I did everything I could to take his mind off it.

"We chawed about old times at the Madison Square Hotel in New York, and our early bachelor days living together in Brentwood.

"After lunch each day I noticed that Stewart would slip away with an apple or a piece of watermelon or a carrot in his hand. And I learned that he'd walk two or three blocks to the corral where the horses were kept and he'd give a 'goodie' to Pie.

"That's when I began to realize what Pie meant to him. His boy was gone, and I couldn't do anything about that, but now seeing the expression on Jim's face when he reached for something to take to his horse—I had an idea.

"On Sundays, when we weren't working, I'd trek over and have the wrangler bring Pie out and stand him in front of the barn. And then I made sketches of the horse, the barn, a carriage, and the gate. I planned it to be a surprise for Jim. I finished the watercolor after I got home. I had it framed and gave it to Jim. He was surprised all right. He just dissolved when he saw the painting. He's got a light over it now, like it's a shrine. Ole Pie died about ten days later."

During the campaign to publicize *The Cheyenne Social Club*, Fonda ran into heavy flak regarding his daughter Jane's activities.

"We were in Salt Lake City," Jim Stewart said, "to do a television promotion to plug the picture. The man who was going to interview us said, 'Is there anything you'd rather not talk about?' And Hank said, 'Well, I'd just as soon not get into a discussion about Jane and her politics. I'd just as soon stick to what we're here for, the picture.'

" 'Well,' the man said, 'I see. All right.' And so we went on the air, and the first question the man asked was, 'Mr. Fonda, I understand that your daughter Jane sort of looks upon herself as an American Joan of Arc. Is that true?'

"And Hank, never changing his voice or expression, said, 'Yes. It's true. And I don't think she'll be satisfied until they burn her at the stake!' Well, the guy hemmed and hawed and then went on to *The Cheyenne Social Club* for the rest of the program. Hank handled it well."

John Swope's wife, Dorothy McGuire, referred Fonda to a nutritionist in the Valley. The good doctor recommended vitamins, niacin, lecithin, yeast, and other assorted natural products. Henry believed they added to his already considerable energy and passed the word on to his daughter. After attending a rally in Canada, she reentered the United States at the customs office in Cleveland.

"Because she was Jane Fonda," Henry says, "the finger was on her."

A customs official opened her bag and found capsules labeled, "B," "L," and "D."

"That's breakfast, lunch, and dinner," Jane pointed out quickly. But the official pondered the possibility that the "B" might be an "S" and that spelled "LSD," and that meant trouble in the city beside Lake Erie. The young woman was hauled out of line and placed in custody. She kicked a policeman in the shins, found herself in handcuffs, and the entire incident was pumped up out of proportion.

Several similar happenings occurred before she was allowed to return to the relatively normal life of a movie actress. Other events made it possible, too. The end of the war in Vietnam, Watergate. Jane didn't turn around as much as America did.

By 1971 Jane Fonda won an Oscar for her performance as the prostitute in *Klute*. The Motion Picture Academy, in making the award over national television, ran the risk of airing the same kind of inflammatory statements made by previous recipients. Oscar nominees had failed to appear or had harangued audiences about their favorite causes. If ever a nominee had causes by the dozen, it was Jane Fonda.

When the presenter tore open the envelope and made the familiar announcement, ". . . And the winner is . . ." Henry Fonda's daughter, elegantly coiffed and gowned, stood, walked to the stage, took her Oscar in one hand, and to the delight of all, made a short, gracious, and polite speech, and exited with her chin slightly tilted upward.

Henry Fonda had not voted for his daughter. Henry Fonda does not believe in Oscars.

"I've been at too many private parties on Oscar night," he says. "When the winner is announced, three quarters of the people in the room slap their foreheads and moan, '*Oh, no!*'

"Well, I wouldn't want that to happen to me. I wouldn't want to walk up there thinking people all over Hollywood are saying, 'Henry Fonda? *Oh, no!*'

"Besides, I don't believe in that kind of artistic competition. Take the best performances of Laurence Olivier, Richard Burton, Jack Lemmon, Dustin Hoffman, and

Woody Allen, and you tell me how anyone can possibly pick the best one. It's an absolute impossibility."

"You know what vacation is to me?" Fonda asks. "A vacation is when you can go somewhere with some nice people and act in a good play. Well, Martha Scott got in touch with me. She told me she was organizing the Plumstead Players and the Plumstead Playhouse on Long Island. She wanted me to be on the board and act in their shows whenever I had a little free time. I took her up on it.

"That gave me a chance to act in *Our Town, The Front Page,* and *The Time of Your Life.* Alfred de Liagre and Ed Sherin directed. Robert Ryan and I got to be pals. Eventually, Plumstead was able to acquire its own playhouse in Connecticut. I had fun and I had vacations."

In 1973 both Jane and Peter asked for and received divorces. Within a month, Jane married the writer and political theoretician Tom Hayden. Peter waited three years and then married Portia Rebecca Crockett, the great-great-great-great-granddaughter of the man in the coonskin cap who killed a bear in Kentucky, went to the House of Representatives, and met his end with Jim Bowie at the Alamo.

Fonda, meanwhile, went on to do a TV series which he disliked, a western in Spain about which he felt indifferent, and signed a seven-year contract to do the GAF commercials.

"It was like hitting three bars on a slot machine," he says. "Money just kept pouring out."

All during this time Edward Albee blew hot and cold on a play for Fonda. He started it, hit a block, stopped, returned to the typewriter, paused, began work anew. Having missed out on *Virginia Woolf* by a chance negative nod from an agent, when Albee's producers, Dick Barr and Chuck Woodward approached John Springer, Springer called Fonda who instructed him not to let the Albee play go to someone else.

On his way back from Spain Fonda asked if the Albee play was ready. His schedule for the forthcoming year had been cleared and he was itching to return to the theater. Yes, the Albee play was ready at last, but it was being mimeographed. Assured he would have it within three days, Fonda and Shirlee continued on to California.

"Three days later," Fonda says, "I went out to my mailbox and there was a large envelope with a script in it from Barr and Woodward. There was a lot of other mail and I took it all in my den, flopped down on the couch and read the Albee play. It was great. I didn't understand certain sections of it, but it was well written and I knew Albee could explain any questions I had. I called Springer to tell him I'd do the play, but Springer wasn't in.

"I glanced at the other mail. There were a few bills, and then I came across a large brown envelope from Mike Merrick and Don Gregory. A script was inside. It read, 'Darrow, by David Rintels, from the book Clarence Darrow for the Defense by Irving Stone.'

"I picked it up and leafed through it. I was into it for pages before I realized it was a one-man show. Well, the more I read, the more I fell in love with the character of Clarence Darrow and the idea of doing the play. It was a beautiful conception.

"When I finished, I called New York and told Springer to get in touch with Merrick and Gregory and book me into Rintels's play for the next year.

"Then I stood up and thought, 'What the hell am I going to say to Edward Albee?' "

It took Fonda a week to compose a letter to Barr and Woodward, hoping they would pass its contents along to Albee. Fonda's choice was inevitable. He identified completely with the character of Darrow. Both the lawyer and the actor came from Midwestern backgrounds. Fonda's father had taken him to see a black man lynched in Omaha; Darrow's father had smuggled slaves to the North via the Underground Railroad. Fonda spent two years at college, Darrow one. The two men held similar ideals regarding the poor, the disenfranchised, the underprivileged.

Once he made the decision, Fonda met with the author of Darrow, the producers, the director, and started to work. The original script was three and a half hours long.

"My dad wouldn't have any problems learning the lines," Peter said. "That son-of-a-gun could memorize a phone book, both ways."

Memorization didn't bother Fonda, but after a couple of weeks with the director, Henry grew uneasy. He doubted he'd made the proper choice.

"I wasn't comfortable," Fonda says.

"And he's always right," the author maintained. "If a line doesn't sound honest coming out of Fonda's mouth, it means the line isn't true. He had an unerring sense of what is right."

Even Shirlee came to a rehearsal and confessed to certain reservations about the show. A decision was reached; they would get a new director, and see if it made a difference.

The producers sent for John Houseman, another hyphenated man, director-producer-actor-author, and a person who knows how to handle a fellow actor.

"When Mr. Houseman and Mr. Fonda got together for the first time," Rintels said, "they were like two lions. It was clear that there was a lot of size in that room. Houseman let Fonda boil over, he agreed with him every now and then, sometimes he said, 'No, no. That will play all right. It's just a little awkward, you'll see.' Houseman was completely on top of it."

"He made it work for me," Fonda says. "Absolutely."

"I simply gave him confidence to go on," Houseman contended. "Apparently, Hank always reaches a point in a production when he becomes insecure and loses faith in the project. All you have to do is to get him over that hump. Then he picks up and by opening night he's perfect."

On the road tour Rintels cut and changed, Houseman advised and admonished.

When Henry Fonda opened in New York in March 1974 the audience forgot there was a lone actor on the stage talking to props and furniture. He looked like Darrow. He spoke like Darrow. He was Darrow. He was also the prosecuting attorney, the judge, the jury, and the accused.

William Wyler, the distinguished film director, went

backstage and embraced Fonda. "You were *all* wonderful," Wyler said.

The next morning's *New York Times* urged ". . . everyone, man, woman, and child interested in justice and America, to see this play." *The Times* ended its review with ". . . if Clarence Darrow was not like this, he should have been."

Fonda was back on Broadway, with another hit.

His friend Peter Ustinov commented, "He's got that quality of a great wine that suddenly begins to do unbelievable things as it gets older. What interests me is that he has a sense of life being a marathon and of keeping something in reserve for the final stretches."

CHAPTER
17

In 1960 Archer Winsten, the critic, wrote, "His face has weathered a little, rather than aged. His eyes are young and clear. He changes less with the years, or more slowly, than most people." At fifty-five Fonda looked forty.

"And even more important," Fonda says, "I felt great. Someone, maybe Johnny Swope, had convinced me that all men at about fifty should have annual physicals, not just in an office, but a real examination in a hospital, and that's what I did. Dr. Rex Kennamer or his assistant, Dr. Gary Sugerman, took care of me in California. I never had any complaints. I'd pass the tests and get a Grade A diploma each time. Disgustingly healthy, that's what I was.

"Whenever I got to Manhattan, I'd walk from Fifty-seventh Street to Eighty-ninth Street, up one side of Madison Avenue and down the other, doing museums and galleries. That's a long haul. Well, Alex Cohen chose me as a co-host for the Tony Award Show in 1974. It was a Sunday, my day off from *Darrow*.

"Everyone was rehearsing on the Shubert Theater stage, and in between numbers they'd tell me, 'Go upstairs to the chorus dressing room, we'll send coffee and sandwiches. You can relax.'

"I started up those stairs and felt like I was climbing a mountain. When I reached the dressing room I was out of breath. That surprised me, an active person doesn't generally have that trouble. I didn't think too much about it, though. I sat down and recovered right away. I had to make the same trip three, four, five times during the day, and each time I'd remark to myself, 'Goddamn, what's the matter?'

"Anyway, we did the Tony show. It went fine. The next day I had to tape a radio spot for the Red Cross. It was at a studio not too far from our hotel, and I started walking. I got to the corner and I had to stop and rest. I walked another block and found myself leaning on a lamppost. Crazy. I couldn't understand.

"Well, I finally managed to do the radio spot, and then I remembered that I had an appointment with a doctor the Kennedy family had recommended. I'd asked them to give me a name, because I thought I had an allergy. My nose kept dripping during my performances. I could get away with it in *Darrow*. I'd keep a handkerchief in my hand, but it was a real nuisance. I checked the doctor's address in the phone book. East Seventy-seventh Street. Wilbur Gould.

"Now, while I was in with Dr. Gould, I told him about my nose, and I also mentioned being out of breath.

"He left the room, came back, handed me a prescription and said, 'Have this filled later to use as a nasal spray, but I've just made an appointment for you, Mr. Fonda. I want you to go straight to another physician. I've called him. He's expecting you.'

"I went down in the elevator, hailed a taxi, and found myself in this other doctor's office before I had time to be concerned.

"The new man, Dr. Elliott Howard, a cardiologist, had me sit on the examining table with my jacket and shirt off, and he used a stethoscope on my chest. He asked me a few questions. I answered, and Dr. Howard said, 'You're fibrillating.' I didn't know what the hell that meant. Well, he explained it. My heart was way out of rhythm, very irregular. Long pauses, and then a lot of fast beats. In other words it wasn't pumping the way a heart should. I told him I had a performance that night, and he said, 'I'll give you some capsules to take.'

"I got to the theater, I fixed my hair to look like Darrow's, my dresser helped me into the padding, and a sensation hit me like a right hook to the stomach. Nausea. I vomited until I thought my insides were coming up. I couldn't stop. The stage manager called, 'Fifteen minutes, please.' I knew there were about twelve hundred people out there and I didn't want them to be sent away. I was so weak I could barely get around the wings to make my entrance. But I did it. The curtain went up and I walked on."

Henry Fonda gave an extraordinary performance. The author went backstage afterward to tell the actor that he had surpassed himself that night.

"He had given the role an extra dimension," David Rintels said, "but I worried about him. Fonda's face was the color of putty. He didn't even have the strength to change out of costume into his street clothes. He was coughing and choking. A car and driver took him home."

Fonda and Shirlee waited for the morning light, and then he telephoned Dr. Howard.

"Get right to Lenox Hill Hospital," the medical man told Henry, "and don't waste any time. I'll meet you there."

Lenox Hill Hospital is a collection of conflicting architectural styles occupying the land between Seventy-sixth and Seventy-seventh Street between Lexington and Park avenues. The admission desk faces Seventy-seventh Street, and it was there that the Fondas waited until the arrival of Dr. Howard. The good doctor whisked them through admissions up to the fifth floor where a series of tests were run on Fonda while Shirlee sat in the mini-sized waiting room staring at the impersonal color of the hospital walls.

"That was the first time," Shirlee said, "that I'd ever seen the man sick, and it was my first experience in a hospital, too. I was more frightened than anything else. I didn't think I could ever be that frightened. And I had to act brave and strong, as though I wasn't scared at all.

"I kept thinking, 'This isn't really happening. It's going to be all right tomorrow when I wake up.' But it wasn't."

It seemed like endless hours before Fonda returned in a

wheelchair pushed by an orderly and was assisted into bed. His wife joined him and their talk revolved about the theater and the problems of refunding ticket money to audiences rather than zeroing in on the real problem confronting them. At last Dr. Howard appeared and announced he had called in a heart surgeon for a consultation.

Shirlee immediately sent for Peter and Jane in Paris. While she telephoned, Fonda listened to the heavy breathing of the patient on the other side of a white cotton curtain that divided the small room.

"I don't think I could have made it without Shirlee," he says.

Upon examining the patient, the surgeon, Dr. Simon Stertzer, gave his opinion that a temporary pacemaker might give Henry needed relief from the symptoms he was experiencing.

"Mr. Fonda was taken to the cardiac catheterization laboratory," Dr. Stertzer explained. "He was equipped with a temporary pacemaker which goes in from the outside of the body and is attached to a generator that hangs from an IV pole standing beside the patient's bed."

"It was strange," Fonda says. "They could turn it on or off and monitor me."

By the time Peter and Jane arrived, one of his doctors told the children that their father's condition was such that an operation seemed unlikely. Peter returned to France where he was making a picture, Jane continued on to California to be with her family.

"That night Fonda's heart fibrillated again," Shirlee said, her voice wavering. "The doctor advised, 'For precautionary reasons, we'd better put in a permanent pacemaker tomorrow.' Now, here I was alone. Most of my friends were out of town, Jane and Peter had left, and I was anxious and so was Henry.

"Early in the morning, I met with Dr. Stertzer, the key man for this kind of surgery, and I met with Dr. De Pasquale, the head of the heart department at the hospital. And they showed me exactly what they were going to do. I had confidence in both surgeons and in Dr. Howard, too.

"Henry signed the consent form and they wheeled him out of the room. I paced the halls. My head throbbed."

"The procedure is relatively simple," Dr. Stertzer said. "The electrode going into the patient's heart is a little bit thicker than the lead of a pencil. The generator attached to the wires that go within it is about the size of a cigarette case."

Two days later Fonda, discharged from Lenox Hill Hospital, returned with Shirlee to the Wyndham Hotel. Their townhouse had been leased out and they made their temporary home at the small hotel on West Fifty-eighth Street.

"That day he came back," Shirlee said, "I thought, 'This man isn't well.' He had moments when he got very pale and short of breath again. We went out for dinner that night. We walked because Trader Vic's was almost right across the street. He could barely drag himself to the restaurant. We had to stop and start. It took forever to get there, and I said, 'Fonda, there's something wrong. This isn't normal. I know you've been in a hospital and I know you're weak, but there's something terribly wrong.'

"The next day he called Dr. Howard and went to his office. Sure enough, Fonda's pulse wasn't doing what it should have been doing. They put him right back in the hospital. One of the electrodes of the pacemaker wasn't reaching into the lining of his heart. I don't know technically what they had to do, but they corrected it within two days and we flew to California.

"That was my first introduction into Fonda not being the healthy, energetic, hard-to-keep-up-with guy that I'd known. He took all this sort of the way you'd expect him to take it. In the beginning he didn't want to accept the reality of it. It was as though he was saying to his own body, 'Hey, this can't happen to me. I'm not going to let my heart attack me.'

"When he finally came to grips with it, he said, 'Okay. What am I going to do about it? I'm going to get well.' That's always been Henry's attitude. If he's told to blow up a balloon ten times a day, he's going to blow up a balloon ten times a day. He's not going to let a day go by without blowing up that balloon. That's just how he is. Very disciplined."

"The pacemaker they put in me was the newest one at the time," Fonda says. "I could recharge the battery every week with an apparatus about the size of a typewriter. It had a pad made of a kind of material that I stuck around my chest, and I'd sit there, plug it in, and start the timer. Then I'd read or fall asleep or anything for an hour, and the battery recharged. At the end of the time, the bell rang, and I was all set for another week."

Alternating rest and tending his fruit trees or his hive of bees, Fonda recuperated within a month or two. He reopened *Darrow* in Los Angeles and played to capacity.

At the invitation of the American Bar Association, he and Shirlee flew to Honolulu where he performed before packed houses filled with lawyers and their wives. The size of the auditorium, twenty-seven hundred seats, did not seem to be ideal for an intimate one-man show, but for a week Fonda made Clarence Darrow come alive before large audiences each night.

This led to his return to New York where he opened *Darrow* at one of the new and larger musical houses, the Minskoff, and "turned 'em away."

London beckoned and the Fondas crossed the Atlantic. No actor is ever weary of applause, but the two most important events in Britain were his reunion with Jim Stewart, who was there playing *Harvey*, and the malfunction of the recharging apparatus for his pacemaker. Fortunately, he obtained similar gear in London, and despite a virus attack, he finished a successful run.

Back in Bel Air, at the urging of Shirlee, he paid a visit to his internist. The physician, after a thorough examination, recommended that he report to Cedars-Sinai Hospital. Fonda went home, found the house empty, packed a bag, called for a taxi to take him to the hospital, and wrote a note to Shirlee. It read:

Darling—
  I'm in the hospital—I'm taking a cab because there's nobody home—I'm at Cedars-Sinai where Dr. Fields is going to replace my pacemaker—Mine

isn't working—He's doing it tonight and I may be home tomorrow.

> Love,
> Your husband

When the taxi failed to appear, Fonda added a postscript to the note to his wife.

> P.S. The cab company can't make it for half an hour so I'll drive myself. You can come to bring back my car.

Dr. Joshua Fields, his surgeon in California, inserted a lithium-operated pacemaker. Because it was a new device, no time period could be estimated for the life of the battery.

To monitor it he returned to his physicians every three or four months. They employed X rays, stethoscopes, and a variety of instruments to check on the size of his heart and to determine whether excess body fluids had collected.

During one of these visits the physicians decided that an excess of fluids had apparently built up in one of his chest cavities. Once again, he entered the hospital where his surgeon, after administering a local anesthetic, injected a long needle into the area where the X ray had shown a shadow. It was the surgeon's intention to draw off the fluid.

"Mr. Fonda, it's not fluid in there," the surgeon told his patient. "It's a tumor."

"I took a deep breath," Fonda says, "And waited for the rest. It wasn't long in coming."

"I've got a piece of it," the surgeon said. "I'll do a biopsy and let you know."

"God Almighty!" Fonda says. "I thought I'd had enough of hospitals and doctors and operating rooms and nurses, but no! I had to wait for the result of a biopsy on a tumor somewhere inside of me.

"Forty-eight hours later he called. It was benign. Good. I can unwind."

"No," the surgeon said, "it's got to come out."

"More X rays followed," Fonda says. "There was quite a large tumor growing out of my diaphragm.

"They cut through my ribs and went way down, and when they got it out, it was the size of a grapefruit and weighed a pound and a half. It took a long while for me to recover. I was in intensive care longer than anybody should be. And they put these tubes down my throat. Well, it was a bad, bad time for me. Not the worst as it turned out, but bad enough."

"It was tough for both of us," Shirlee said. "It was a rough operation further complicated by his having a pacemaker. Fonda was in the intensive care unit of the cardiac area for about ten days. He had to be monitored all the time. I got to see him five minutes out of every hour, and I was quietly going crazy. Being there in the hospital as often as I was, week after week after week, I spoke softly, I walked about softly. I got to know everyone's symptoms and conditions. I didn't want anyone to think my husband was really that sick. I put on this big act, like everything was fine. I brought cheese and fruit for the other patients, and candy for the nurses, and we'd sit around and we'd talk, and I'd hand out magazines. I got to know everyone's case, and I really made light of Henry's illness because that's what I have a tendency to do when I get scared. I don't let people know I'm nervous or worried, particularly Fonda. I always make him think, 'Oh, it's nothing. It's a piece of cake.' Listen, you don't fly on airplanes for as long as I did with birds flocking into the engines or propellers going wild and let the passengers onto what's happening. You just play it cool.

"He was there for a long time, and eventually, to our relief, they discharged him."

"I don't know whether it was the tubes they kept down my throat while I was in intensive care," Fonda says, "but now my voice wasn't what it should have been. It sounded strangled and sometimes it would be embarrassing to have people listen to me. It drove Shirlee mad.

"I'd go to throat specialists and they'd tell me nothing was wrong with my vocal cords, but when I'd ask why I sounded like I did, I'd get a pat on the shoulder and a lot of explanations I didn't or couldn't understand."

346

"Now around that time Peter made a movie called *The Trip*," Fonda says, "about a kid on LSD. Peter took LSD himself. More than once, under controlled conditions, to see what it was like.

"Later he was a devotee of pot, which to me had been reefers fifty years before. Peter assured me marijuana wasn't dangerous or habit-forming, and every now and then, he'd suggest that I try it. Never!

"Well, we were at dinner and I complained that I couldn't sleep for more than two or three hours. I'd wake up in the middle of the night and not be able to get back to sleep. And Peter said, 'Dad, I'll lay it on you.' God, you need an interpreter for some of his dialogue. He went out to his car and came back with a test tube containing what he called 'Good Shit.' He doled some out and put it in those make-it-yourself cigarette papers. Now I'd given up smoking when I met Shirlee, but I thought, *this* is medicinal.

"Well, let me tell you. It didn't work. I was awake all night looking at sort of a kaleidoscope of flashing colors. I was relaxed all right, but I couldn't sleep and the side effect it had on me was that I was thirsty, and I couldn't see to get up and get water. I never tried it again. The only pot I like has flowers blooming in it. Another funny thing, Peter developed an allegy to the stuff and doesn't use it any more."

Shirlee became aware of a new problem. At first she thought it was connected to his vocal cords. Then she suspected something else was wrong with her husband. She'd speak to him in a normal voice.

"What did you say?" Fonda began to ask. "I can't hear you, darling."

"Fonda," Shirlee raised her voice, "will you please go to a hearing man?"

"Why, for Chrissake?"

"You're getting deaf."

"I am not getting deaf!" Fonda protested. "You don't speak up, that's all."

The difference of opinion continued until Shirlee won out. Fonda went to an otolaryngology specialist who examined him carefully.

"You've lost forty percent of your hearing in both ears," the doctor told him.

"No point in arguing anymore," Fonda says. "I asked him what could be done and he sent me to a hearing-aid man. I've got several kinds. Mostly, the average person doesn't know I'm wearing hearing aids. They're in my eyeglasses, and when I don't wear those, I've got tiny little buttons that fit inside my ears, and unless you know what they are, you can't see 'em."

"Once that got settled," Shirlee said, "Fonda signed to do a film and we went on location in northern California."

"We were shooting a picture called *Last of the Cowboys*," Fonda says. "Thank God there were no horses. I played a truck driver. It was a six-week location, and after a while I began to notice the incision where they took out the tumor. It turned a little red at first, and then the redness increased, and then it became really inflamed."

"The area where they operated was very angry looking," Shirlee said, "and the incision had become quite swollen. I made Fonda go to a doctor in Oroville, and the doctor said he felt it was a suture that hadn't dissolved and was trying to push its way out. He gave Fonda a medicated salve to put on it. Well, nothing cleared it up. It stayed there. He got through the film. He wasn't tired. As a matter of fact he felt okay, but when we got back to Los Angeles, he went right to the doctor who'd operated, and it wasn't a suture at all."

At Cedars-Sinai, a newly constructed gigantic mass of glass and masonry spread over a matter of blocks, they put Fonda under a fluoroscope to look for the suture. After probing about in various areas, the elusive thread could not be located. The surgeon did catch hold of something and tugged, and the pain almost lifted Fonda off the table, but the answer was still to be found. Fonda went home despondent. Shirlee was in despair.

George Peppard, who was making "a bomb at Fox," telephoned one afternoon. He thought Fonda's voice sounded dry and croaky.

"Hank," Peppard asked. "What the hell's the matter with you?"

"Oh, I feel terrible."

"Jesus, you really sound bad."

"I am."

"Well, I ought to cheer you up."

"Try."

"Okay, I will."

Peppard visited him every day for two weeks.

"He wasn't doing any of the things he normally does," Peppard said. "He wasn't listening to Shirlee, he wasn't painting, he wasn't doing his garden. Normally, he is articulate and specific and when riled meaner than hell. When he gets mad, he looks like a cartoon of somebody with steam coming out of the end of his shirt, out of his collar, and out of his ears. There's even a slap sound to his voice.

"But I couldn't even get him angry. He just dug in, and his stubborness stopped everyone from doing anything for him. Ordinarily, he's not encased in a little glass capsule as many film actors are.

"I cussed him out pretty good, and I think I may have gotten through to him a bit. He was cranky as hell with everybody else. Well, I decided it was his circulation so I got him a masseur, and every day he'd have his massage."

Peppard helped his spirits, but not the condition that was draining Fonda's strength. His weight dropped from one hundred seventy pounds to one hundred thirty-two. His body was bent and he shuffled as he walked. Finally, medical science triumphed when his physicians and surgeons decided Fonda's ailment was caused by an infection.

Back into the hospital he went.

"When they'd taken out the tumor," Fonda says, "they had to place a piece of surgical gauze over the hole they'd cut in my diaphram. A staphylococcus infection developed in that netting and for months it incubated and grew inside me until it burst out. They had to open me up again and go way back in there to get that piece of netting. That surgery was harder to recover from than the regular operation. And Shirlee will tell about those nightmares because she was the one most concerned. I didn't care whether I died or not."

"They told us he was going to be there for three weeks," Shirlee said, "that it was going to be a simple op-

349

eration. Almost a patch-up job. It wasn't. It was a complicated, involved, long-healing operation. They kept him in intensive care for about twelve days. He had to stay in Cedars for seven weeks. Generally, I'm an optimistic person, but then I was terribly, terribly down.

"I'll never forget because I spent the holidays there with Henry. When I'd arrive at the hospital every morning, I'm sure my smile looked as artificial as the Christmas decorations. The silver-covered cardboard Happy New Year signs made me want to run, to scream. Instead I'd pull myself together, go to his room, talk light chitchat for a while, and give his private nurse time off to get coffee or a snack for herself.

"When she'd leave, because I didn't want Henry to feel humiliated, I'd take care of him. If he'd messed the bed or if he'd had an accident, I'd get it all cleaned up because I didn't want the nurse to know that anything had happened. That's unfair of me, but that's the way I am. I would have almost apologized for my husband being sick. That's wrong, but I couldn't help it. I wanted everybody always to think Henry was perfect.

"Then, I'd make sure he ate. I'd force him to eat. I was really a monster. I would say, 'I'm not leaving, I'm not going. You have to eat that lunch. I don't care whether you're hungry or not. You have to have it.' And he was wonderful. He'd try. Some days he'd manage to get down the food. Some days he couldn't. But slowly, painfully for him, I know, I got him well.

"After he was discharged from the hospital, it took three or four months before he felt like himself."

And then came the medicine most helpful to Henry Fonda. It arrived in a ten by thirteen manila envelope. Jerome Lawrence and Robert E. Lee had written a play called *First Monday in October*.

The plot concerned itself with a glimpse of the inner workings of the Supreme Court of the United States. Crusty Mr. Justice Snow, patterned loosely after William O. Douglas, is appalled when the President appoints a woman to sit on the Court. The conflict arises not because she is a woman but because she is a conservative from Orange County, California. Fonda, of course, played

Snow. Opposite him was the daughter of his childhood friend from Omaha, Bart Quigley. Quigley had gone to Central High School with Fonda, met up with him at the University Players where he painted scenery and acted a bit before returning to Harvard and medical school. His daughter, Jane Alexander, whom Fonda calls, "my other Jane," played the Justice from Orange County. More than that, her husband, Edwin Sherin, who had supervised two previous Fonda productions, directed *First Monday*.

Fonda rehearsed with his usual eagerness, but not with quite as much energy. He had been advised by his doctors not to work too strenuously.

"I was in a panic," Fonda says, "that my voice would tighten up again. Shirlee was the only one I told."

"Shirlee hovered about," Ed Sherin said, "and was, as usual, completely supportive of Hank. When she watched him now, she sometimes wore a slight expression of concern."

Slowly, as Fonda's health and strength returned, Shirlee sighed a few sighs of relief, made luncheon dates, and felt that life was almost back to normal. Fonda's children "touched base" while the company was in Washington.

"Peter is my best friend," Shirlee emphasized. "I love Peter. If anybody said anything against me, Peter would get them. Jane cares about me a lot, and it's mutual. We're really girl friends. I like Amy, too. I'm really fortunate to have stepchildren like them. In fact the whole Fonda family is special. I always say, 'I'm going to prove I'm a Fonda and have the Fondas accept me and be glad that I'm part of their family.'"

"She doesn't have to worry about that," her husband says. "My relatives would rather spend time with Shirlee than with me."

"The *First Monday* company was a compatible one," Ed Sherin recalled. "And why not? We don't breed actors like Henry Fonda in this country anymore. We breed them to be the best television actors in the world. Henry likes the stimulation of that live audience, that edge of excitement. It's like a blood transfusion to him. He brings those people into his world and makes them believe intrinsically in what he's doing. It's an incredible experience

351

to direct him. In the beginning of the show I don't tell him too much. He has such good impulses. In the initial stages the less the better. Later I'm very precise with him, very specific. I give a load of notes and he absorbs every one and he never fails to do exactly what you tell him, no matter how subtle the suggestions are."

The authors, Jerome Lawrence and Robert E. Lee, added their voices to Sherin's enthusiasm.

"That man doesn't change a writer's comma. Not a comma, ever," Lawrence said.

They opened at the Eisenhower Theater in Washington, D.C., just after Christmas 1977.

During the course of the engagement, eight of the nine Justices came to see the play. Everyone wondered if Mr. Justice Douglas had taken offense because Fonda's character had been based on him. On the contrary. One evening word seeped backstage that Justice Douglas was in a box in the theater. Whether he would remain for the entire evening was debatable due to the poor state of his health. At intermission, information arrived to the effect that Mr. Justice Douglas would be pleased to meet the cast after the performance.

Following the final curtain call, the company assembled in the Green Room.

"I was at the door," Fonda says, "and I was the first to greet him. He came in a wheelchair pushed by a young man. We shook hands and he said some nice things to me, and then he introduced the young man.

"This is my son, Bill," Justice Douglas said. "He's an actor."

"I said 'Hi' and Bill explained that he'd studied mime in Paris. He was a pantomimist, but as far as his father was concerned, he was an actor.

"The entire company lined up and Justice Douglas greeted each one. Then he said, 'Would you and Mrs. Fonda have tea with me in my chambers one day?'

"Of course," Fonda told him.

"Less than a week passed and my phone rang and a woman said, 'This is Justice Douglas's secretary, Miss Judge.' Sounded like the name of a Sinclair Lewis character, but I bought it. She asked if Shirlee and I would come to tea and if any of our friends would like to come along?

"I asked 'How much room do you have?' I pictured his chambers as being the average size room. 'We're moving it into the conference room,' Miss Judge said. 'We can take about two hundred.'

"Well, I told the whole company we were going to tea at the Supreme Court. We showed up and there he was in his wheelchair with his wife, Kathy, beside him. And all the other justices and their wives, and senators like Ted Kennedy, Speaker of the House 'Tip' O'Neill, and other VIPs, filled the room."

After a goodly amount of socializing Justice Douglas went off for his afternoon nap. It was then that Chief Justice Warren E. Burger approached Fonda.

"Would you like to see *our* backstage?" the Chief Justice asked.

Of course he would. Henry, Shirlee, and Jane Alexander followed the Chief Justice behind the bench of the United States Supreme Court. The courtroom was empty but the big black leather high-back chairs were there. Fonda gestured toward the middle one, Mr. Burger gave his approval, and Henry Fonda seated himself in the Chief Justice's chair.

"May I steal a paper clip?" Fonda asked.

"Of course."

"May I take a rubber band?" Shirlee asked.

Again the Chief Justice concurred.

"I still have the paper clip and the rubber band," Shirlee said. "A month later Henry received a personally inscribed photograph of Mr. Burger. It hangs in his office at home in California."

"*First Monday* ran six weeks, and then, because Henry was told to go easy," Robert E. Lee said, "we closed down, and sent Henry and Shirlee back to California."

"When I was thirty-seven years old, an important event happened in my life," Peter Fonda said. "I'd phone Dad from Montana a couple times a week. One night we were talking, and I had an urge to make the connection. I thought, he's my father, he's been sick, and it's about time we're able to be with each other and hug one another and look down the barrel and say, 'I love you.' I knew if I tried the direct approach in person it would floor him, and he wouldn't know how to deal with it. He has to be led to water even if he's thirsty.

"Well, there I was, on the phone having this nothing conversation, and I blurted out, 'Listen, Dad, I just want you to hear something before we say good-bye.' He asked, 'What's that?'

" 'I love you,' the words came tumbling out of me. He practically choked. I'd attacked his defenses. He murmured a sentence or two and hung up.

"I sat there for a long period. I could picture him going through the same thing on the other end. I was sorry if I'd made him uncomfortable, but you have to start someplace. The egg has to be laid, and get sat upon, and then hatched. If it's fertile, it will bear fruit.

"The following phone call I didn't preamble it at all, I just said, 'I love you, Dad.' A pause, and then I heard, 'You too, son,' and he crashed the phone. Not out of anger, out of sheer terror. Because of that tender phrase, 'I love you, Dad.'

"Now, he tells it to me and Jane and, I think, Amy, in an easy, pleased manner. He's delighted that he can speak the words that were stuck inside him, unverbalized all those years. I'll tell you one thing, I know my father loves me, and it's a great feeling."

"I sure do," Henry says, "and Peter's right. I was very tentative about telling him at first. I thank Peter for making it all possible."

"What Peter did was good," Jane said, "because you can't change *yourself*. Saints and prophets, maybe, but average people, and Dad's average, just as I am, you can't do it by yourself."

While Fonda rested up for his next stint in *First Monday*, his son signed to direct and star in a movie with Brooke Shields. It was called *Wanda Nevada*, and Peter had an idea.

"He invited me," Fonda says, "to play a bit part, just for fun. He asked me to go on location in Colorado Canyon, and I had to get up there and work about two or three hours, one scene. Well, I'm as impressed with Peter as I am with Jane. As a director he was in command completely, not with a big stick, but in a relaxed way. He knew what he wanted, he knew how to get it, and everyone on that location respected him."

"It was tremendous working with Dad," Peter said. "I played opposite him in the scene. He was this beaten-up, old character. They put so much makeup on Henry you couldn't recognize him. Well, the cameras rolled. Dad came on, gave me a side glance, and said, 'I reckon one of us got up a little late this morning, and it weren't me.' And then he spit tobacco.

"That line was terrific, because it reminded me of when I was six years old, and I'd come running downstairs, and he'd say, 'Reckon you forgot to put the top back on the toothpaste. It's all dried up.' What a kick to be able to direct him."

Henry Fonda expressed his own feelings about that experience in a letter to Peter.

15 July 1978

Dear Son:

I started thinking about this letter flying home a week ago, but the crowded days have passed so quickly, I never seemed to get to it. I got up at six o'clock this morning before another dynamo day goes by. I felt so badly about the phony makeup. I wanted you to know that I fully understood if you found that you couldn't use the scene. It meant a lot to me that you asked me to participate, and I so wanted it to be meaningful to the picture. . . . It would have been such a gas if it had worked. . . . Anyway, I want you to know how proud I am of you. Your whole company so obviously worships you, and it's a beautiful thing to see. And I haven't seen it so often in 43 years that it doesn't impress me. And you're a very good director. . . . You are a thoughtful man, and I love you.

Your Dad

First Monday in October had played Los Angeles, took a break, and then opened in October 1978 in New York. Robert E. Lee said, "*First Monday* and Fonda broke all records for a straight play at the Majestic Theater. One week the gross was over $168,948. That record still stands."

"The audiences stampeded to see Fonda, Lawrence said. "They ate him like ice cream."

"I remember Hank at a ladies luncheon," Jane Alexander reminisced, "when someone asked him why he preferred the theater to the movies he didn't even stop to think. 'If the hackles rise once on the back of my neck when I'm making a film,' he told her, 'I consider myself fortunate, but it happens every night to me on the stage.'

"Did you ever see Henry exhibit that elfin quality of his?" Miss Alexander asked. "Right before curtain time," when we were in our places, he'd get a mischievous glint in his eye and start to tell a story to the actors on stage. He would time these tales so that just about the punch line the curtain would rise. He'd never tell us the end of the story," his "Other Jane" said. "The trick worked every night. He had us relaxed."

After three completely sold-out months in New York, *First Monday* moved on to Chicago where another three-month stand was anticipated. Miss Alexander had a contract to do a movie. Her replacement was Eva Marie Saint, the girl who had been let go as the nurse in *Mister Roberts* because she had been too attractive. As a glimmering Hollywood luminary, she opened opposite Fonda at the Blackstone Theater in Chicago.

Henry and Shirlee settled into a duplex apartment at the Tremont Hotel on the Near Northside. Two bedrooms and a bath upstairs and a sitting room and kitchen downstairs.

"Now," Fonda says, "I'd been feeling like a million. I'd been having a ball doing old Justice Snow. We'd played there for a couple of weeks, and I woke up early one Sunday morning. We were due for brunch at Margie Korshak's. I looked over at the clock and knew I had time to luxuriate and stretch. It's fun to do. You see dogs and cats stretching like that. I stretched and *Whop*! Something snapped in my left hip. It made a strange noise. It didn't hurt as I lay there, but when I tried to get up, my left leg collapsed. It simply would not hold my weight. Well, somehow, using a chair, I propelled myself through the bathroom and called to Shirlee."

"I'd been expecting trouble," Shirlee said. "In California Fonda had developed a painful on- and off-again limp. A doctor examined him and thought it might be arthritis or tendonitis. His sister Harriet recommended a chiropractor for an adjustment. But then the California doctor decided it was definitely tendonitis. He gave Henry some pills and sent him off to Chicago.

"While the show was previewing, a friend and I met at a restaurant near the Loop, and Henry walked in at lunchtime to join us. As he edged his was to our table, his leg gave out. He was on the verge of tumbling backward, the people near him gasped. A nearby journalist sitting in the corner saw Henry stagger, and the next day printed, 'Henry Fonda must have had a few too many drinks. When he came to meet his wife, he almost fell on the floor.'

"Well, when he woke me that Sunday morning, I wanted to send for a doctor, but Fonda wouldn't hear of it. Then I asked him if we should cancel our brunch date. 'Absolutely not,' he said. 'Whatever it is will pass.' Well, we dressed, I don't know how."

"I even managed to get down the stairs," Fonda says, "by going down one step at a time on my butt. Then Shirlee phoned Margie. She's a lovely woman who handled all the press for *First Monday* in Chicago."

"I told Shirlee not to worry," Margie Korshak Ruwitch reported. "My father and brother are both bigger than Hank, and they were already on their way to pick up Eva Marie and the Fondas.

The Ruwitch home is in suburban Glencoe. After an uncomfortable forty-five-minute drive, Marshall and Sydney Korshak helped Fonda out of the car and into the house.

"Great food," Fonda remembers. "Lox and bagels and creamed cheese. I wasn't feeling pain, at first, just sort of a weakness. Of course I still couldn't stand up on my own. After lunch the pain hit me."

"Let's call Dr. Newman," the hostess suggested. "He's a good friend and the best doctor in Chicago."

"But this is Sunday."

"I know, but let's give him a call." Margie Korshak Ruwitch reached Dr. Edward Newman, and he promised to see Fonda back at the hotel.

"What's the story?" Dr. Newman asked after meeting his new patient.

"I told him everything," Fonda says.

The doctor listened to him, then shook his head.

"We're in trouble."

"What kind of trouble?" Shirlee's voice was apprehensive.

"I've got to get your husband to the hospital."

"The hospital!" Fonda howled. "You mean, I've gotta go to another goddam hospital?"

The doctor nodded.

"You know, don't you, that I have to give a performance tomorrow evening?"

The doctor nodded.

"Well, you've got the rest of this afternoon and all of tomorrow, but by Monday night I damn well better be on the Blackstone stage."

The doctor nodded a third time and dialed the phone for an ambulance.

"Two attendants came and put me in sort of a chair," Fonda explains. "Y'see the elevator was too narrow for a stretcher and they couldn't get me down otherwise."

"It was a pair of unusual experiences," Shirlee said. "Number one, I've never seen my husband being taken away in an ambulance. Number two, I've never ridden in a car with a doctor chasing an ambulance. We went through every red light. I was more wretched than Fonda."

"My husband rode inside with Henry Fonda," Margie Korshak said. "It was an occasion he's never forgotten. Ted is a very conservative, buttoned-down business executive. Listening to Fonda made him wonder what on earth he was doing there."

358

"I was stretched out," Fonda says, "and I looked at those two guys in the white suits and I said, 'Hey, fellas, this is the first time for me. I want the full treatment. I want mouth-to-mouth resuscitation. I want the siren, everything.' They eyeballed me like I was out of my mind. They didn't know I was making a small joke instead of whistling like a kid does in the dark. Anyway, they humored me and turned on the siren, and they went through all the lights. If I propped myself up on an elbow, I could see Shirlee and Dr. Newman in the car behind us weaving from side to side. For Shirlee, it was torture. She hates to ride in automobiles as a passenger. And Dr. Newman was tearing around corners, and dodging oncoming traffic like a stunt man in the movies."

"When a police car joined us," Shirlee said, "we went even faster. I thought I would end up in the bed next to Fonda."

The small but speedy caravan arrived at Michael Reese Hospital, a large array of buildings constructed over many years along Lake Michigan on Chicago's South Side. The emergency staff rushed Fonda up to a private room, and just as quickly into X ray.

"They took pictures of me from here to here," Fonda says, indicating an area from his waist to his knees. "When they finished, the X rays were sent to be developed. Then I was wheeled out on a bed on casters. They pushed me down the hall to another place. Shirlee was there with Dr. Newman, and a few other medical men. It didn't take long before the radiologist delivered the wet X rays. They slapped them on to a glass backed by fluorescent lighting. Dr. Newman, pencil in hand, pointed out various aspects of the picture to the other doctors.

"I remember those X rays. They were huge and, of course, I didn't have any idea how to read them, and neither did Shirlee. Eventually, Newman turned to us and said, 'You see this area? That's white. Now, you see this other area? That's chalk white. There's a difference.' Now, I didn't know what the hell he was talking about, but I had a feeling it was bad."

"Dr. Newman told Fonda he didn't think they'd be able to send him home just yet," Shirlee said. "It was five in the afternoon, and they couldn't contact all the consulting specialists because it was Sunday. They really needed him for more tests early in the morning."

"Fine," Fonda said.

"You may be able to play the show on Monday night," Dr. Newman told him cautiously. "Have you ever been on crutches?"

"Only in films," Fonda answered confidently. "I'll be able to handle them."

"Oh, no," the doctor said. "There's an art to using crutches. You have to know what you're doing or you can hurt yourself. After your tests tomorrow, we'll send in a therapist, and she'll teach you the fundamentals."

"Please get me some crutches tonight, doctor," Fonda asked. "I haven't anything else to do." The staff at Michael Reese rustled up a pair of crutches and a therapist almost immediately.

"Mr. Fonda," the woman in the starched white uniform said, holding the crutches away from him, "it will be days before you'll be able to move around on these."

"Give 'em to me," Fonda said, and in three or four minutes, he was up and using them as though he'd been doing it for months. With Shirlee's encouragement Fonda became more proficient in their use, but the better he became, the more he realized he'd be unable to appear.

"*First Monday* had moving platforms," Henry says. "I'd have to race from my chambers clear around backstage to Eva Marie's chambers in less than a minute, and in no way was I going to be able to do it on crutches. So I asked Shirlee to call the company manager and cancel the performance. She did just that."

Early in the morning, orderlies wheeled him back into X ray. By now there were five or six specialists waiting to read the pictures.

"What I liked about Michael Reese Hospital," Shirlee said, "was they didn't just take one doctor's opinion. They had five doctors' opinions. They brought in a heart specialist, an orthopedic specialist. I felt we were on a really good team."

Fonda was rolled back to his room while the team consulted. Shirlee walked beside his bed. Once inside, the attendants disappeared and Fonda and Shirlee waited. It didn't take long. It just seemed long. A knock at the door and Dr. Newman entered.

"You saw that chalk white area on the X ray," he said soberly. The Fondas waited again.

"And then he came straight out with it," Shirlee said.

"There's a malignant growth, a nodule," Dr. Newman continued. "It's not very big."

For a few moments only the sounds of the corridor were heard in Fonda's hospital room. Dr. Newman's voice cut through the void.

"It's a small nodule on the prostate gland," he said. "A few splinters have gone into the hip bone. But if we can stop it, you're going to be in good shape."

Fonda mumbled something about having to cancel the entire engagement. The doctor agreed. Shirlee opted for having the surgery done at Michael Reese. The doctor disagreed.

"I think you should go home and consult your doctors there. I'll call them and write a full report. You'll recuperate better at home, Mr. Fonda."

"When he left the room," Shirlee said, "I sat down on Fonda's bed."

"Honey . . . I've got cancer . . . and I'm scared."

"We put our arms around each other," Shirlee said. " 'Everything's going to be okay. Everything's going to be okay,' I told him. Then we held each other tighter and began to cry. It was the first time I'd seen Henry break down and cry like that. I've seen him cry, but to really show fright and fear and to be really unsure, Henry's never been unsure. He's always been on top of situations. At least he makes you think he is.

"But now, when there was no doubt about what he had, when he said the word 'cancer,' the two of us were the most terrified couple in the world. That single word devastated us. And then the nurse walked in. Two masks came down over our faces. I guess I learned that trick from Henry. In an instant we were all lovey and wonderful and talking like we hadn't even had this conversation seconds before."

Fonda spent an anxious night at Michael Reese. The hospital switchboard had been alerted not to allow incoming calls to go through to his room. At one o'clock in the morning, Chicago time, a long-distance call came from Jane Fonda in California. Better than half the patients and personnel in the hospital had watched the Academy Awards on television. Jane was telephoning to tell her father that she had won her second Oscar for Best Actress in *Coming Home*. The switchboard operator was so excited she rang Henry's room.

Fonda had seen the awards. He congratulated her and told her how happy he was for her. He did not tell her that he and Shirlee were flying back to Los Angeles the next day. Nor did he tell her why. He hung up the telephone and allowed the medication he had been given to resume its effect.

Dr. Edward Newman wrote:

> Mr. Fonda was seen with acute left hip pain on April 8, 1979, and was hospitalized at Michael Reese Hospital, 29th Street and Ellis Avenue, Chicago, Illinois, on the same date for evaluation, diagnosis and treatment.

> Mr. Fonda's discharge diagnosis was carcinoma of the prostate with metastasis to the left hip—confirmed by biopsy, X ray, and nuclear studies.

With this information and his own medical evaluations Dr. Joseph Kaplan performed the operation at Cedars-Sinai. It was a success. Within a short time, Fonda moved about on crutches. Then a cane. Finally, he walked again with what critic Jack Kroll called, "the long stride, with the heel landing decisively before the toe in that deliberate yet syncopated Fonda rhythm."

"I didn't feel as though my feet were even touching the ground," Fonda says.

At the end of April he went back to his hilltop home in Bel Air. The sky seemed bluer, the air fresher, the fruit trees gave off a sweeter odor than he remembered. Best of all Shirlee's smile was sunny again.

"That told me what I needed to know," Fonda beamed. "I was well."

CHAPTER
18

THE bees, the chickens, the compost heap had all been looked after by Fonda's yardman, but no yardman, however conscientious, can care for the "North 40" and the "South 40" with the devotion the organic farmer can give to his spread. Gradually, Fonda recuperated from his operation and began to work the land again. Each day he grew stronger until the day he put down the hoe and picked up the telephone.

His friend of fifty years, Johnny Swope, was dead. Swope had been with him at the University Players, Swope had lived with Fonda, Jim Stewart, and Josh Logan in their early days in Hollywood. Swope had married Dorothy McGuire, the girl Fonda had chosen from a crowd of youngsters auditioning in Omaha. Swope's path had crossed Fonda's when both men served in the Navy. The Swopes and the Fondas saw each other at least once a week whenever the two couples were in California.

"The Swopes were two of our dearest friends," Fonda says. "John died in June, 1979. He shouldn't have died. He wasn't old enough to die. But then, I don't think I'm old enough to die, either.

"John had left instructions to be cremated, and since he was such a lover of the sea, Dorothy arranged for a launch, a small launch, one that could only take about eight people. There were Dorothy, their children, Topo and Mark, and John's sister. Shirlee, Jim Stewart, and I were the only ones outside of the family invited to the services.

"I don't like funerals," Fonda says, "and it's in my will that there won't be one, not even a memorial.

"But that day on the launch was terribly moving. We went pretty far out to sea, maybe ten, fifteen minutes, and then Dorothy told them to make a big, wide circle, about two hundred feet. She signaled Mark, John's son, that it was time. He'd been holding on tight to the box with his father's ashes since we left the house. Dorothy said, 'Now,' and Mark and Dorothy opened the box over the end of the boat."

Fonda leaned back in his chair, and tried to compose himself.

"Oh, my God," he says, "the ashes came out in their hands, and the breeze carried the ashes down into the water. The boat was going very slowly, and Dorothy had brought a long wicker tray of flowers from their home, bougainvillea fresh from the vines, gardenias, other colorful flowers. Dorothy gave all of us some to toss into the ocean. I knew it was tough for the family, so afterward I went under a little protective area, away from the others, to pull myself together.

"It's been difficult for Dorothy. She's had days when she couldn't see anyone, or days when she wouldn't answer the phone. I felt helpless, so a while ago I wrote her a letter."

Dearest Dorothy,
Although we talk to you almost every day and see you frequently and think of you constantly, I never feel that I have really expressed my great feeling about John. But then, that's the story of my life. For reasons that are too deeply buried for me to understand I have never been able to articulate my emotions. Only recently, Peter has been ending his phone calls by saying, 'I love you, Dad.' And of course, it has forced me to say, 'And I love you, son.'

He knew I did. But he was making me say it. And now, it's coming easier. I loved John. I truly did. I was just 23 when we first became friends and I don't think I originally appreciated how much his outgoing, giving, resounding personality affected me in a positive way.

But it wasn't too long before I recognized that he was truly unique. And what an experience. What a pleasure it was for me to be in his company. I have never known a man to so thoroughly enjoy life as John did and to live it as fully. His enthusiasms were contagious. You always felt better for having been with John.

Today, it is hard for me to accept the fact that he isn't available any more. There isn't a day that I don't think to myself . . . I have to talk to John about this and ask his advice about something.

Just last night, he was with me in the most realistic dream, surrealistic, really. A rowboat, a beautiful rocky coastline, a majestic, pounding surf. We were both young and strong and unafraid. I think it will always be like that. I'll miss the hell out of him. But I'll always see him in dreams and my wonderful memories.

I don't know how well I've said it but I wanted to say it to you because you completed John's life. And it was beautiful and inspirational to watch. I count one of the blessings of my life that it so often touched yours.

> All my warmest and dearest love,
> Henry

"People who read that letter can learn about Fonda and friendship and idealism," Dorothy McGuire Swope said. "Henry has been a guiding star in my life. He's given me perimeters and guidelines and structure. He's a good man, a caring man.

"I once heard a woman make a comment about an actor in his forties. With disdain she told me, 'He always plays so young.' And I explained to her an actor doesn't have a time barrier. He doesn't have to rock in a chair and pull a shawl over his shoulders. He goes with his energy. And thank heavens, that's what Hank does. After he mended, he started working again, and he's never been better."

Fonda's agent, his business manager, his press representative constantly received plays, film scenarios, television scripts, and a host of requests from people for the actor's participation. Most of these were sent on to Fonda and he thumbed through them searching for his next project.

One script that caught his eye was *Gideon's Trumpet*, written by the author of *Clarence Darrow*, David Rintels.

Clarence Earl Gideon, a Florida drifter, had found himself in jail six times in his life. A loser, if ever one existed, Gideon read the law books in the libraries of his various prisons and eventually petitioned the Supreme Court of the United States to overthrow his conviction of burglary because he had not been able to afford counsel. The court ruled in Gideon's favor, Martin Agronsky did it as a documentary in 1964, Anthony Lewis turned it into a book, and Rintels wrote it as a play for television.

Fonda was ready to act again. He changed his tortoise-shell glasses for Clarence Gideon's steel-rimmed spectacles, trimmed his hair, and donned the prison shirt and jeans.

The locales of the film shifted from California's Chino Prison to the old courthouse in Santa Ana. There are no class distinctions with Fonda. When the cast and crew broke for lunch, they'd run down the steps to the catering tent. Fonda loped down the same steps and got into line.

"Come on, Mr. Fonda," the crew called to him. "You go to the head of the line."

"I'll wait my turn same as everybody else," Fonda replied.

Fonda made an arrangement with his elderly chauffeur, Ben Jones. One day, Ben would get the coffee, the next day Fonda would go for it.

"People kidded Hank about it," David Rintels said, "but Hank would answer them out of the side of his mouth in a W. C. Fields voice:

"I wait on the son-of-a-bitch hand and foot."

On the last day of filming in the Santa Ana courthouse, the camera focused on the jurors. They were supposed to listen to Fonda's summation and react. What they actually heard was the sound track of Fonda's voice. It was late in the day, and most actors would have gone home. But the leading man stood up, took off his Henry Fonda glasses, and put on his Clarence Earl Gideon glasses. The script girl was surprised.

"Mr. Fonda," Mae Brown said, "you don't have to do that. You're going to be *behind* the camera."

"The jurors can see me," Fonda said. "I want them listening to Clarence Earl Gideon, and looking at Clarence Earl Gideon. There isn't one of them that has a line in the show. They're day extras, but by God, they're actors and I'm going to give them the same courtesy they gave me."

"All actors can't sit on a patio beside their swimming pools," Fonda says. "I've spent a lifetime on stages and in sound studios with people who rode busses and subways instead of driving to work in foreign automobiles. The smell of honeysuckle may be up here. Down there it's pollution. But we all belong to the same unions, Equity and the Screen Actors Guild.

"I went back East through Grand Central Station years ago. They were holding an automobile show, and there, sitting in the cars, were some of the same fellas I'd pounded the pavements with back in the early thirties. I'd made it and they hadn't. Living models, that's what they were. And seeing them broke my heart."

Critics, producers, directors, to say nothing of his peers, substitute the word talent for luck. They translate good fortune into taste and integrity. Fonda sticks with luck.

"Without it," he says, "I might have been sitting in one of those cars. And I haven't forgotten yet how hungry I was when I went to that art exhibit in Grand Central. I can still smell the food, I can taste it, but somehow, no matter how badly I wanted it, I couldn't get myself to take it. Maybe if things had gone differently, maybe today I would have snitched a sandwich or two. I dunno. I hope I'll never know."

Another member of the Fonda family who believes in luck is Shirlee. One wedding ring isn't enough for her. She acknowledges that every year she is married to Fonda is special. The result is that every year she adds a thin gold band. Presently, her eight fingers carry fifteen little talismen of their marriage.

"And it's a miracle," Fonda says, "because I'm a goddamn hard man to live with!"

Although she is wildly in love with Fonda, Shirlee admits their life together isn't always a mixture of orange blossoms, glittering Hollywood openings, and sophisticated New York dinners.

"Crabby," is how Shirlee describes Fonda when he shows his dark side. Peter will second that motion readily, and Jane and Amy will agree.

"Of course, Henry was happy to come through those six operations," Shirlee said, "but he hates the food he has to eat to stay well—food that contains the very minimum amount of salt. I am very firm in following doctors' orders, and Fonda kicks, swears, and complains."

"One day, if I get mad," he says, "I'll throw away all my medicines and OD on Chinese and Japanese food!"

Fonda's pet peeves have never lessened over the years. Although Peter has long since learned to put the cap on the toothpaste and straighten the towels in the bathroom, he is quick to claim, "Dad has absolutely no patience with me when I'm late. He chews me out like I'm an eleven-year-old, not a man of forty-one."

"As a grandfather," Jane reflected, "let's put it this way. There is something awesome about him that make his grandchildren fascinated and they like to be around him, but they don't know him very well. He doesn't bounce them on his knee. I don't think Dad knows what a grandfather is supposed to do. But they all love him very much anyhow, my two and Peter's two."

In rehearsal for a play recently, a prominent actor who was in the cast with Fonda made his entrance one beat too early.

"Goddamnit!" Fonda exploded and turned upstage. "Don't you ever do that again. That's a laugh line I have there, and I want that laugh to peak. *Then* you can come on." It might be unnecessary to add the actor never made that mistake again.

Before *Gideon's Trumpet* was aired, Fonda went to

Dallas to the campus of Southern Methodist University, where he participated in the first "live" television drama N.B.C. had done in eighteen years.

In the title role of *The Oldest Living Graduate*, Fonda played the cussing, cantankerous Colonel J. C. Kinkaid, the oldest living graduate of the Mirabeau B. Lamar Military Academy. Aided by Cloris Leachman and George Grizzard, the television play received critical cheers.

"One performance for such a fine production?" the cast asked one another. Together they answered, "Nonsense." They signed with the producer, David Rintels, to play a converted movie palace in Los Angeles, the Wilshire. The Colonel took the town.

They might still be there if Ernest Thompson hadn't written a play called *On Golden Pond*. The first time Fonda heard those three words was in Washington at the Kennedy Center's Eisenhower Theater. He and Shirlee had gone to a screening of a few episodes of *Roots*. The center held a cocktail reception in the lobby, and Fonda spotted the head usher. He knew her well since he had acted in the theater many times. He waved and then pushed through the crowd to say hello to her.

"Mr. Fonda," the head usher said, "we have a play running here that you must see. It's as though it was written for you, and Katharine Hepburn has been here three times to see it."

The Fondas didn't stay there long enough to attend a performance, but Arthur Cantor, the producer of *On Golden Pond*, called Henry to tell him the script was on its way to Fonda's New York residence.

"I read it and got fired up," Fonda says. "The leads were an elderly husband and wife. It takes place at their country home in New England. They think it might be their last summer there."

Jane heard of her father's enthusiasm and asked to read the script.

"It's wonderful," Jane told her father. "I want to play the daughter."

"I can't understand why," Fonda said. "It's a small part."

"I don't care how small it is," Jane answered. "You

play the father, I'll play the daughter, and because of their relationship, it'll work."

Jane had enough faith in the property to raise the money and co-produce it.

"Then came the movie adaptation," Fonda says. "The best I've ever read. Finally, it was set. Jane met with Hepburn. She was scared of Katharine. Can you imagine Jane being frightened of anyone?"

Eventually, lawyers drew contracts, parties of the first part and parties of the second part signed them, and production got under way. Miss Hepburn flew out to California to meet with Henry; Jane's co-producer, Bruce Gilbert; and Mark Rydell, the director. The meeting was held in a conference room at Twentieth Century-Fox.

"Katharine came in, held out her hand, and said, 'Well, it's about time,'" Fonda says. "We'd never met in all those years."

"I've never met *many* people," Katharine Hepburn conceded, "but I'm sure I must have said, 'How do you do?' to Henry Fonda at one time or another. I felt as though I knew him."

"We had a stimulating session," Fonda says. "We talked about the script for about two hours. Katharine had a lot of ideas and suggestions. They were all good."

The only hitch came when a month or so later Miss Hepburn entered a New York hospital for surgery on her shoulder.

"Well," Miss Hepburn reported, "my doctors told me, 'You cannot do the picture.' And I knew the film was dependent on the Fonda part being lazy, and not working, and not wanting to do a lot of physical things, and also not able to do a lot of physical things. The wife, my part, had to carry the wood, carry the canoe, carry all the luggage, do everything, and here I am with an arm that's really bad. Well, I tried to get out of the picture, but Fonda said, 'No, you'll be fine. You'll do it. We won't get anyone else.' He stuck to his guns, and in July, 1980, we found ourselves on location in New Hampshire."

Few towns are more representative of New England than Laconia, New Hampshire. Slightly over 700 feet above sea level, slightly under 12,000 in population, surrounded by four lakes, Laconia is a place that swells in the summer with vacationers and tourists. Its spring-fed lakes are bordered by cottages and lodges, and these, in turn, are separated by firs of many species as well as by birch, poplar, elm, maple, and oak.

It is a place of beauty, and the *On Golden Pond* company shot all of its footage in and around Squam Lake.

"The first day," Fonda says, "I was sitting in one of those high director's chairs with some of the company. We were between the cottage that was supposed to be our summer house and the lake. Shirlee was there, the makeup people, the crew, a few members of the cast. And around the corner came Katharine Hepburn. Now, Hepburn is a presence wherever she is. In a room, she is the only one in it. In a big area, she doesn't do anything to dominate, she just does and is. But as people saw her, she was gesturing for them to move away, and they sort of just melted in front of her, just disappeared. By the time she got to me, I was alone. I was aware this was happening, but I wasn't quite sure why or how it happened. She came up to me holding her outstretched, cupped hands in front of her. Something crumpled was inside those hands but I didn't know what it was. She came right up to me and stood there."

"I want you to have this," Katharine Hepburn said to Fonda. "This was Spencer's favorite hat."

"My God! What a gracious thing to do," Fonda says.

"It was the exact hat that John Ford wore while he directed pictures. And I knew Ford and Spencer Tracy had been close friends, hard-drinking Irishmen. It was Ford's good-luck hat. He had several of them, and I suppose Spencer had several of them, too, because eventually they'd get lost. But they don't ever get dirty or too old. That's the kind of hat it is. I was thrilled with it. I put it on, Katharine approved, and I wore it in the first scene we shot that day.

"While we were making the picture, Katharine asked me to do a painting for her, sort of a memento of our working together."

Fonda was no longer a weekend dauber. His friendship with the famed American artist James Wyeth furthered

372

his use of oils and led him into the dry-brush technique. In 1973, Shirlee had been on the board of directors of the Neighbors of Watts, a charitable organization formed to give aid to the black community in Los Angeles. Annually, a large auction is held at the local Sotheby Parke Bernet.

"It's half social, half serious," Fonda says, "in the sense that they do auction off really fine items. Everybody donates. That year, Frank Sinatra gave an engraved solid gold cigarette case. An antique dealer came through with a Louis Quinze settee. A travel agent contributed a trip to Acapulco. One of the great ranches in northern California gave the colt of a thoroughbred."

Shirlee walked into their Bel Air billiard room, which Henry uses as his studio, and announced, "Fonda, I promised the girls on the Watts board that you'd do a painting for them."

"Okay," I said. "But somehow I never came round to doing it."

"Fonda, I'm not going to be able to face my friends if I don't have a picture," Shirlee told him.

"I went out and picked two tomatoes from my garden," Fonda says. "It was a little early and they weren't quite ripe yet. They were red but there was still a touch of green in them. I placed them on the windowsill. The outside of the house was black, the way it had been when we bought it. The black was peeling, and you could see the peeled paint, and the white underneath, and the putty around the glass falling off. Beyond that was the stone wall. It's got a character to it. So all of this was white stone, stucco, and shadows and textures and two not-quite-ripe tomatoes. The only other color was a pale blue, the sky reflected in the window glass.

"Well, I finished the painting, got it framed, and over to Parke Bernet just in time. I called it 'Ripening.' The night of the auction, Shirlee and I went with the Yul Brynners and two or three other couples. Everyone we knew was there. We sat in the third row, the place filled up, and the auction began. They'd handed us programs and I noticed that my painting was number forty-eight of the fifty-three items.

"The first things put up went for almost nothing. It was like stealing. I mean, the race horse that was worth thousands went for a few hundred. The Louis Quinze settee went for a tenth of what it should have brought. Outright robbery. I got madder and madder and I thought, 'Fuck! I'm not going to let them steal my painting. I'll buy it back. I'll buy it and give the money to the Neighbors of Watts!' Well, it went on and on and things brought less and less. Finally, they put up my painting. I squirmed.

"The auctioneer started. I got ready to hold up a finger when some son-of-a-bitch beat me to it. The first bid was seven thousand dollars, and it put me into shock!

"Then it jumped to eleven thousand dollars before I could make sure it was my painting on the easel. Shirlee fidgeted with excitement. I sank down in my seat just like I had in Omaha during my first movie where I played a bare-assed Indian kid. Both Yul Brynner and Irwin Allen dropped out at twelve thousand dollars. After thirteen thousand dollars it narrowed down to two bidders. Both of 'em were in back of me. I had no idea who they were and I didn't want to turn around. They continued to bid against each other until it was knocked down for twenty-three thousand dollars. Whew!

"On the way out, someone whispered to me that Jennifer Jones and Norton Simon had bought it. The next day, I wasn't home when Norton called and talked to Shirlee."

"Just want to say how happy Jennifer and I are to have it," Norton Simon, one of the great private collectors of art, told her. "But also give Hank a tip. You don't ripen tomatoes in the sun. You ripen them on the vine."

"And this is a guy who knows," Fonda says. "He made his first bucks in Hunt's Tomatoes. His collection contains works by the finest artists who've ever used a brush, and by God, in the middle of them all, is a Henry Fonda.

"Hepburn hadn't heard the story, but I was very flattered that she wanted a painting of mine. I promised to do one for her because I consider her someone very rare. You don't come across a person of her caliber often."

"Henry Fonda's not one to make new friends, and neither am I," Katharine Hepburn said, "but we got along okay. He has his own world. He likes to sit and fish, I like to walk through the woods alone. We are quite similar. He doesn't waste time. No small talk. And I hate to have idiotic conversations. We found we could act together just like *that!*" Katharine Hepburn snapped her fingers several times rapidly. "And we really did it.

"Jane was a good daughter for me and for him. I was a good intermediary between them. Therefore, the story comes out powerful. Hank was just deliciously cast. He did something that no one else could do better, and he was so funny and so moving that all the men up there were really mad about him. He behaved so well. He had to do very, very, very uncomfortable things on cold evenings, in the wind, and sitting out in an open boat. He had to sit out in the bright sun, and he has skin like mine, can't take the sun at all. He never uttered a complaint. You know, I would have shot someone.

"The men in that company were nice but tough, and they had real regard for Henry. He has the capacity to inspire that in a bunch of men. He got on fine with Jane, too, but a bit awkwardly, I would say. And Shirlee," Miss Hepburn observed, "she didn't mind if he came back after twelve hours away and picked up his fishing rod and went down to the dock and sat there holding the goddamn thing when he knew there were practically no fish. It's a wonderful marriage. She knows enough to let him alone, let him sing his own song the way he wants to sing it.

"I think Hank has gotten to be a better actor, richer, more direct, more vulnerable. The whole cast is perfect."

"Six actors," Fonda says. "Six actors, every grip, camera operator and assistants, focus man, costume, wardrobe, makeup, they were all wrapped up in the picture. Every scene was better and more fun than the one we did the day before.

"You want to hear about Katharine Hepburn? She swam every morning and after work. She'd have her dinner, and go to sleep at eight o'clock, get up at three or four and study her lines.

"The last five weeks, Shirlee and I lighted fires in our bungalow fireplace. We wore winter long-johns, and used electric blankets at night.

375

"At the end of September, when it was bitter cold, they catapulted the fourteen-year-old boy and me into the water. The company was more nervous than I. They thought, 'This old son-of-a-bitch is going to have a heart attack,' but I fooled 'em. I had a wet suit on under my wardrobe. Katharine had to dive into the water, too, but she didn't even wear a wet suit. Eventually, Jane and I did the father-daughter scene in which she indicates it's time we become friends."

"I knew what that woman in the movie was feeling," Jane said. "My father could still evoke the same emotion in me as he evoked when I was young. Here was this forty-three-year-old woman whose dad determined her life. We were supposed to look at each other at one point with a tremendous amount of intensity and hostility."

"I hung around," Miss Hepburn confessed, "to peek at their scene where they have a big reconciliation. It's really shattering, and done with a great depth of meaning behind it. Of course, these days, Jane and Henry mean a great deal to each other. They're both reaching for something they think they've missed. We all reach for something we think we've missed, don't we?"

"We got through that scene," Fonda says, "and there wasn't a soul on that set not crying. There were at least thirty people on that dock, and they couldn't control themselves. As for me, I've said it before. A Fonda can cry at a good steak.

"Later, there was another scene where the boy said good-bye and taught me, just like Peter had taught me, to really let go. He grabbed me and hugged me. And it touched me. Then he left me alone with my daughter, and she said, 'Good-bye, Dad,' and I hugged her because the kid had shown me how. Wow! There wasn't a dry eye.

"I'm not a religious man, but I thank God every morning that I lived long enough to play that role. *On Golden Pond*, how can I describe the experience? Magic, I think. Magic!"

Another pleasant week awaited Fonda on Cape Cod. He made a fast television movie. This time the delightful Myrna Loy played his wife.

"There I was," Fonda says, "back on Cape Cod where

I'd started. Life is strange. It's like a big circle. After the film, Shirlee and I headed back to Bel Air.

"Now, I didn't have the faintest notion of what the subject should be for Katharine Hepburn's painting, but after we returned home to California the wardrobe department sent my costumes back to me. I opened the overstuffed cardboard box and three objects tumbled out. Right then and there, I knew exactly what to paint for Katharine."

Three of Fonda's hats, neatly arranged, are done in dry brush. On the left, is Spencer Tracy's favorite, a battered, brown, crushable felt. In the middle, is Fonda's rain hat, a little deeper in color than tapioca pudding. Finally, on the right, is his tan fishing hat, complete with fisherman's flies in the band over the brim.

Like *On Golden Pond*, it was as good as anything Henry Fonda had ever done.

"When I was five, my mother woke me up and took me to the window on the landing. She showed me Halley's Comet streaking across the sky. She told me to remember it always, because, my mother said, it comes around only once every seventy-six years. And seventy-six years is a long time.

"Well, that's almost how old I am now—seventy-six. The years seem to have gone by as fast as Halley's Comet. But I don't think of myself as old."

He grinned that Fonda grin.

"I still think of myself as the boy on the landing looking out of the window."

CHAPTER
19

"IF you survive," Fonda says, "you can collect enough awards on paper to cover the wall in a fair-sized room, and more than enough metal to build a stove. I've been fortunate to gather up my share."

Few actors have received the plaudits bestowed upon Fonda by his admirers, his peers, and his country. Still, Henry, as usual was a slow starter, picking up velocity and esteem as the years sped on.

His initial opportunity to receive an Oscar came from his memorable performance in *The Grapes of Wrath*. The ceremonies held on February 21, 1941, made for an unusual evening. Franklin Delano Roosevelt became the first President of the United States to address the Academy of Motion Pictures via closed-circuit radio. The luminous Lunts, Lynn Fontanne and her husband, Alfred, handed out the Oscars for the Best Leading Lady and the Best Leading Man. The people seated in the Biltmore were dressed in the last finery many of them would wear until the end of World War II. They waited in suspense for the words, "The envelope, please . . . And the winner is . . ."

Jane Darwell won her Oscar for Best Supporting Actress in *The Grapes of Wrath*. John Ford was named as the Best Director for his production of Steinbeck's novel. A trend appeared to be shaping up. Tension built as the final selection approached.

For the Best Actor, the nominees were Charles Chaplin

for *The Great Dictator*, Raymond Massey for *Abe Lincoln in Illinois*, Laurence Olivier for *Rebecca*, James Stewart for *The Philadelphia Story*, and Henry Fonda for *The Grapes of Wrath*.

People in the ballroom leaned forward, millions listening to their radios at home held their breath. The nominees tried to betray no emotion. Henry Fonda didn't give it too much thought. He was aboard John Ford's boat, the *Araner*, fishing for marlin in the warm waters off Mexico, watching the burnished brass sunset sink into the Gulf of California.

"I was too embarrassed to go," Fonda says. "I was much too embarrassed. If I'd won, I'd have been speechless. If I'd lost . . ." and the words trail off. His friend Jim Stewart's name was in the envelope and Fonda was pleased. Aboard the *Araner*, the fishing was good, the weather was perfect, and the Mexican beer was its own reward.

After the war, he was deluged by honors: the Straw Hat Award for outstanding contribution to summer stock, Broadway's coveted Antoinette Perry Award. In 1979, Alexander H. Cohen, who produces the Tony Awards, knowing of Fonda's innate reticence, lured him to the Shubert Theater on the pretense that Henry and Jane were to be co-presenters of an award to Joshua Logan. While Fonda stood in the wings, his daughter walked out onto the stage before the television cameras. Jane announced the Tony was for her dad and his outstanding contribution to the American theater.

"Dumbfounded! That's how I felt," Fonda says. "I knew Jane was a fine performer, but I didn't know she could carry off a stunt like that.

"I've always opposed competitions where one actor's performance is pitted against another's," Fonda said later. "When it comes to a body of work, that's different."

In keeping with that, Fonda accepted honorary doctorates from three universities and laurels from the American National Theater and Academy West; his favorite of all theaters, the Omaha Community Playhouse, paid tribute to him more than once.

When the American Film Institute saluted him in 1978,

James Stewart confessed to Fonda he admired his performance as Tom Joad in *The Grapes of Wrath* so much that he'd voted for him in 1941.

"Of course," Stewart added wryly, "I also voted for Alfred Landon, Wendell Willkie, and Thomas E. Dewey."

When Lloyd Nolan spoke to the AFI, he said, "When Charles Laughton told me who was going to play Barney Greenwald in *The Caine Mutiny Court Martial*, I told him, 'You've got to be kidding. Henry Fonda is about as Jewish as Cardinal Spellman.' As an actor, I should have known better."

March 30, 1981, the Los Angeles Drama Critics Circle honored Henry Fonda with a lifetime achievement award. That broke tradition: no other actor had ever received the Critics award and the Oscar in the same year. Two nights later, after a pre-recorded message from President Ronald Reagan, Johnny Carson stepped to the rostrum and the 53rd Academy Awards presenation began. Before the close of the ceremonies, Robert Redford introduced Fonda and on behalf of the Board of Governors of the Academy presented him with an honorary Oscar that read, "Henry Fonda, the consummate actor, in recognition of his brilliant accomplishments and enduring contribution to the art of motion pictures."

Gratefully, Fonda thanked the Academy, took his Oscar, and with Robert Redford, exited stage right out of the glare of the lights. He could not fail to remember a gala weekend a pair of years earlier. That time, the setting was not Los Angeles, but Washington, D.C.

The Potomac flowed silently in the darkness. On its southern bank stood the Lee Mansion, high on the hill overlooking Washington. On its northern bank, the Kennedy Center blazed with light on a crisp winter evening.

Saturday, December 1, 1979. A grand occasion. The huge crystal chandeliers sparkled eighty feet above the red plush carpet. Upstairs, five hundred persons dined in a room atop the building. They were there to honor five Americans: Aaron Copeland, Ella Fitzgerald, Henry Fonda, Martha Graham, and Tennessee Williams.

Roger Stevens, chairman of the Kennedy Center, spoke briefly after dinner. While Shirlee's former bridesmaid,

Elizabeth Ashley, read a paragraph about the cultural contributions of each of the five, Stevens went from recipient to recipient and placed a medal that hung from a multicolored ribbon around their necks.

"I was busting with pride," Fonda says.

The next night marked a sharp contrast to the simplicity of the first evening.

The cream-colored card bore the Seal of the President of the United States. Beneath the golden crest was an engraved invitation for Mr. and Mrs. Henry Fonda to attend a reception at the White House at 7:00 P.M. on the night of Sunday, December 1, 1979. In a lower corner were the words, "Black Tie."

A limousine picked up the Fondas at their hotel and sped them to 1600 Pennsylvania Avenue. The Marine Band, "The President's Own," played, and leathernecks in dress blues motioned with their white-gloved hands to point the guests to the staircase. In a corridor between two of the large public rooms, the first lady, the Vice-President, and Mrs. Mondale greeted those who had been invited.

The five honorees were then escorted into the East Room where they stood on a small platform. The President welcomed each one and congratulated them upon their awards. Because Americans were being held hostage in Iran, he excused himself and left the remainder of the evening to Mrs. Carter and Vice-President and Mrs. Mondale. Long tables ladened with hors d'oeuvres and punch were in another room. The band struck up again, but before long, White House ushers led the guests to the door.

A procession of limousines took them from the Executive Mansion to the Opera House in the Kennedy Center. Every seat in the huge auditorium was filled. Aaron Copeland and Ella Fitzgerald received their accolades.

Then Alan Alda strode to the microphone.

"I join you tonight in honoring a genuine original," Mr. Alda said, "an actor who has been as thoroughly true to the characters he's played and at the same time, so thoroughly true to himself, that we've almost come to take for granted that shining excellence, that richness of humanity that has been his gift to us.

"He has a standard in his own profession that we admire and reach toward, but that precious few will ever match. All of us remain in your debt, Mr. Fonda, for your dignity, your honesty, and your strength."

A scene from *My Darling Clementine* flashed upon the screen, followed by a scene from *The Grapes of Wrath*.

"He has played cowboys, playboys, and most everything in between," Alda continued, "starring in nearly ninety pictures. . . . The stage is still his first love. When the right part comes up, he always comes back. He has become an American symbol of the unbiased, uncorrupted man."

A scene from *The Ox-Bow Incident* followed, and Joshua Logan advanced to the podium.

"Fonda has always had such a burning," Mr. Logan said, "a true burning light inside of him which is the thing he prays to in the theater . . . In this night of superlatives, I would like to make one statement. I've been through a lot of ups and downs in the theater, and I've seen a lot of actors come and go. And I've known them in England and all over the world. And tonight, as far as I'm concerned, Henry Fonda is the greatest actor in the world."

With that, the entire audience rose to its feet and applauded.

Jane Alexander spoke in conclusion.

"Among many things I've learned from him," Miss Alexander said, "I learned from him how to listen. I learned that professionalism means being sensitive to the needs of others in this most collaborative of all arts. And I learned how to grow through his generosity. None of this was ever told to me by Hank. He doesn't talk much. He just does. And he doesn't act much. He just is."

Another round of applause from the audience, and the curtains parted revealing ninety Midshipmen of the Naval Academy Glee Club. The traditional Navy song, "Anchors Aweigh," came from their lips.

"That darling man, George Stevens, Jr., who produced the show with Nick Vanoff, warned me there would be a surprise that would knock me over," Fonda says. "This was it. A serenade by the Navy. Wow!"

Fonda, seated in a box with Shirlee, William S. Paley, Chairman of the Board of the Columbia Broadcasting System, and Mrs. David Bruce, widow of the American Ambassador to the Court of St. James, clapped his hands enthusiastically as the young men started to harmonize.

Midway through the refrain, Fonda's eyes misted over. He remembered his years as a Lieutenant in the Navy. When the Glee Club segued into a familiar ballad, he leaned back to Shirlee, and in a choked voice whispered, "My God, they're singing 'Red River Valley'!"

At that moment, millions of people watching television saw Henry Fonda's mask slip off. He wasn't Tom Joad or Barney Greenwald or Clarence Darrow or Wyatt Earp. He was Henry Fonda, and he couldn't stop the flow of tears.

After the theme from *The Grapes of Wrath*, he listened as the Midshipmen sang "America the Beautiful."

   . . . God shed His grace on thee . . .

When the vocalizing was over, cheers thundered through the Opera House and the band started to play a spirited orchestration of "Anchors Aweigh." A Midshipman walked to the microphone, looked up at Fonda, saluted smartly, and spoke clearly.

       "Thank you, Mister Roberts."

And then, each member of the Glee Club, as he left the stage saluted and repeated,

       "Thank you, Mr. Roberts."

"It absolutely broke me up," Fonda says. "It wiped me out, but Shirlee's kiss made me raise my head. I couldn't believe what I saw."

The entire audience was on its feet. They turned toward Henry Fonda's box and gave him an ovation. "I didn't really deserve all that," Fonda says. "God! How many guys get the chance to work at what they want for fifty years?

"If those people in the orchestra and in the balcony had quieted down, and if I'd been bolder and more in control of my emotions, I might have told them, 'To the audience in this theater, and to audiences all over, I'm in your debt. It's my turn to applaud . . . and my turn to say:

" 'Thank you.' "

The last time I saw Henry Fonda he sat stiff-backed in an armchair in his Bel Air home. His face had the leathery quality that made him typical of the American characters he'd portrayed. He wore jeans and a denim shirt and bedroom slippers. Down the hall his cowboy boots stood empty in his studio alongside a crumpled shirt and a worn jacket. They were the subjects of an unfinished still-life he had started painting many months earlier.

On the day before his seventy-sixth birthday, May 15, 1981, he had undergone an exploratory heart operation. He spent his birthday in the cardiac intensive care unit at Cedars-Sinai Hospital in Los Angeles. His physician, Dr. Rexford Kennamer, considered his condition grave. Yet when Jane came in briefly to see her father, he lifted his head and said, "I thought, at least, you'd bring me a root beer float to celebrate."

Six days later he underwent his eighth operation in seven years. The surgeon, Dr. Jack Matloff, inserted a new type lithium pacemaker into his damaged heart. To the surprise of his doctors, to the delight of his wife, Shirlee, his strength slowly returned and within three weeks he was back home.

When I got up to leave after a half hour's visit with Henry, his handshake was firm and strong, and his eyes, "the big blues," were as clear as they had ever been. His voice, however, was soft and thin, not the deep commanding sound I had grown to expect.

Shirlee walked me to the door. She spoke eagerly of their plans for the future. I remembered she'd once described how she handled fear. She "played it cool, made light of it."

I crossed the cobblestone courtyard and thought of Fonda's letter to Dorothy Swope after his best friend's death.

"Just last night, he was with me in the most realistic dream, surrealistic, really," Henry wrote. "A rowboat, a rocky coastline, and a majestic pounding surf. We were both young and strong and unafraid. I think it will always be like that."

I got into the car, and drove the narrow, winding road from Fonda's hilltop house. As I braked for the sharp curves, I thought of his words—young and strong and unafraid. They cheered me. I found myself humming "Red River Valley." And suddenly, there was the street sign. It read *Sunset Boulevard*. Sunset.

H.T.

ACKNOWLEDGMENTS

The vast amount of time Henry Fonda spent talking with me into a tape recorder provides most of the basis for this book. Weekly conversations we had over the telephone were, with his permission, taped. They added further information and helped me check and recheck facts Fonda had supplied earlier.

Henry also made it possible for me to interview many members of his family, friends, and fellow workers. The list of people I want to thank for their cooperation and kindness is a lengthy one. It includes:

Susan Ades
Jane Alexander
Robert Anderson
Edith Atwater
Erik Barnouw
Lucille Ball
Lucinda Ballard
Denny Beach
Joan Bennett
Charles Bidwell
Jocelyn Brando
Anthony Burton
Kathleen Cavanaugh
Eulalia Chapin
Sybilla Clark
Shirley Clurman
Imogene Coca

Alexander H. Cohen
Marc Connelly
Leora Dana
Betty Davis
Fred de Cordova
Frances Corrias
John Dinkelspiel
Shirley Eder
Mel Ferrer
Cy Feuer
Posey Feuer
Afdera Fonda
Amy Fonda
Douw Fonda
Henry Fonda
Jane Fonda
Peter Fonda

Shirlee Fonda
Arlene Francis
James Garner
Janet Gaynor
Frank Gilroy
Ruth Goetz
George Grizzard
Margaret Hamilton
Dorothy Hammerstein
James Hammerstein
William Hammerstein
Joseph Harris
Radie Harris
Helen Hayes
Brooke Hayward
William Hayward
Katharine Hepburn
Norris Houghton
John Houseman
Garson Kanin
Dorothy Keith
Marjorie Korshak
Jerome Lawrence
Cloris Leachman
Robert E. Lee
Harvey Lembeck
Jack Lemmon
Mervyn LeRoy
Ira Levin
Joshua Logan
Nedda Logan
Myrna Loy
Sidney Lumet
James MacArthur
Fred McMurray
Ruth Mitchell
Mildred Natwick
Patricia Neale
Millicent Osborn
Paul Osborn
Elizabeth Paige

William S. Paley
George Peppard
Lucilla Potter
Otto Preminger
Harold Prince
Dr. Bart Quigley
Muriel Resnick
David Rintels
Nancy Sackson
Dore Schary
Patricia Scoll
Ted Sherdeman
Edwin Sherin
Sylvia Sidney
Leonard Sillman
Muriel Slatkin
Dr. Jonathan Slocum
Betty Smith
Kent Smith
John Springer
Barbara Stanwyck
Elaine Steinbeck
James Stewart
Dr. Simon Stertzer
Roger Stevens
Dorothy Stickney
Susan Strasberg
Dorothy McGuire Swope
Day Tuttle
Peter Ustinov
Jean vanden Heuvel
Eli Wallach
Robert Wallsten
Harriet Warren
David Wayne
Jane Wayne
Watson Webb
Irene Windust
Herman Wouk
Max Youngstein

Gratitude must go to Walter Kerr of *The New York Times* and Dan Sullivan of the *Los Angeles Times* for permission to quote from their writings. Also, Henry's good friend for many years, John Springer, must be singled out and thanked for his complete cooperation and generosity.

I am obliged to Maureen Bronson of the Academy of Motion Picture Arts and Sciences, Deborah Davidson Boutchad of the American Film Institute, Leo Sullivan of the Kennedy Center of Performing Arts, Tony Magner of the Antoinette Perry Awards, Carol Fox of the Bettmann Archives, and Susan Feleppa of the American Broadcasting Corporation.

Greater thanks must go to Joan Sanger, Editor-in-Chief of NAL Books, for her editing of this book and for providing her constant encouragement and support during its writing. Also, my appreciation to Mrs. Sanger's assistant, Alison Husting, for her patience and aid. Also, my appreciation to Irene Yuss, Vice President and Director of Production, and Julian Hamer, Chief Designer, for their creative contributions toward the design of the book. It goes without saying how much we are indebted to Herbert Schnall, chairman of the board, and Robert Diforio, president of the New American Library.

I owe a very deep bow to Morton Janklow for his acumen and ability in making all arrangements between Henry Fonda, our publisher, and me. Further thanks go to Arthur Klebanoff and Anne Sibbald of Mr. Janklow's office for their most useful contributions. My gratitude also goes to Candida Donadio for representing me with concern and consideration.

Betty Davis, of the Omaha Community Playhouse, contributed hours of work. She never said "no" to my many requests for information and photographic material. My thanks go to her.

Henry's sister, Harriet Warren, was particularly beneficent and courteous and deserves an extra amount of recognition.

Eileen Kelly, my secretary, deserves her own share of gratitude. Also, Constance Ernst Bessie, David Tebet, Anthony Burton, Paul Bonner, Janet Jacobs, Anne and

Irving Schneider, Irene Selznick, and Roz Starr must be thanked for their efforts toward the completion of this work.

I should like to acknowledge the dedicated work and ever present support of Judith Steckler. Not only did she do the research, she also typed and retyped the hundreds of pages of manuscript that comprise this volume. I am in her debt forever.

Finally, I thank most profoundly my devoted wife, Evelyn, without whose ability and actual collaboration this book could not have been written.

H.T.

INDEX

Abe Lincoln in Illinois, 379
Abry, Charles (Bunny), 211
Abry, Tony, 230
Academy of Motion Picture Arts & Sciences, 334, 378, 380
Actors Equity, 52, 94
Actors' Studio, 284
Adams, Shirlee Mae. *See* Fonda, Mrs. Henry
Adamson, Harold, 54
Advise and Consent, 298
Agnelli, John, 264, 277
Agronsky, Martin, 367
Akins, Zoë, 273
Albee, Edward, 304, 335–36
Alda, Alan, 382
Alexander, Jane, 351, 353, 356, 382
Alexander, Ross, 61, 88, 102, 104, 109
Alexander, Mrs. Ross (Aleta), 61, 88, 102, 109
Algonquin Hotel, 19, 84
All Good Americans, 82
Allen, Gracie, 107
Allen, Irwin, 374
Allen, Woody, 335
Alvin Theater, 2, 5, 7, 13–18, 21, 204, 208, 219, 226, 238, 240
Ameche, Don, 142
American Film Institute, 379–80
American National Theater & Academy West, 379
Anders, Glenn, 84
Anderson, Maxwell, 122
Anderson, Robert, 288–89
Anderson, Sarah, 16
Androcles and the Lion, 45
Annabella, 114–18
Antoinette Perry Award, 339–40, 379
Antonioni, Michelangelo, 262
Any Wednesday, 323
Appointment in Samarra, 4
Araner, 133, 189, 379
Arden, Eve, 83

Armstrong, Louis, 123
Armstrong, Reed, 230
Arnold, Edward, 142
Ashley, Elizabeth, 311–13, **381**
Astaire, Adele, 85
Astaire, Fred, 8, 85, 90, 177
Astaire, Mrs. Fred (Phyllis), **177**
Atkinson, Brooks, 19, 122
Atlantic Monthly, The, 287
Atwater, Edith, 287
Austin Riggs Foundation, 203, 206, 209, 212–14, 223

Bacall, Lauren, 253
Baker, Carroll, 297
Ball, Lucille, 108, 317–18
Ballard, Lucinda, 287–88
Balsam, Martin, 266
Bancroft, Anne, 274, 282–84
Bankhead, Tallulah, 76–77, **86**
Barbarella, 323
Barefoot in the Park, 323
Barker, The, 46
Barnow, Erik, 63
Barr, Richard, 335–36
Barretts of Wimpole Street, The, 63
Barrie, Sir James M., 60, 61, 93
Barry, Philip, 31, 122
Barrymore, Ethel, 37
Battle of the Bulge, The, 308
Bean, Orson, 300
Beckhard, Arthur, 75–76
Begelman, David, 305
Begley, Ed, 266
Bel Geddes, Barbara, 289, 308
Bell for Adano, A, 8, 236
Benchley, Nathaniel, 326
Benchley, Robert, 86
Benjamin, Robert, 268
Bennett, Dr. Courtney, 217
Bennett, Joan, 188
Benny, Jack, 107
Benny, Mrs. Jack (Mary Livingston), 107
Berlin, Irving, 125

Beverly Hills Hotel, The, 91, 125, 253
Beverly Wilshire Hotel, The, 92
Beyond the Horizon, 43
Bickford, Charles, 103
Bidwell, Charles, 187–88
Billings, George, 39–41
Blood, Sweat and Stanley Poole, 298–99
Blore, Eric, 108–09
Blow Ye Winds, 129
Bogart, Humphrey, 76, 110, 253
Bond, Ward, 189, 196, 251
Booth, Clare. See Luce, Mrs. Henry
Booth Theater, 65–66, 279, 283
Boy Scouts of American The, 30, 209
Boyer, Ben, 94–95
Boyer, Charles, 114, 119
Brando, Dorothy, 31
Brando, Jocelyn, 7, 204
Brando, Marlon, 7, 31, 247
Brent, Romney, 45–47, 51
Brentwood Town & Country Day School, The, 155, 162, 165, 172
Brokaw, Ann, 126
Brokaw, Frances de Villers (Pan), 117, 123–24, 126, 130, 140, 143, 146, 151, 155, 163, 166, 174, 181, 184, 186, 198–99, 203, 209, 211, 299, 308, 326
Brokaw, Frances Seymour. See Fonda, Frances
Brokaw, George Tuttle, 116–17, 126
Bromfield, Louis, 86
Bronson, Charles, 329
Brother Rat, 124
Brown, Helen Gurley, 305
Brown, John Mason, 122
Brown, Mae, 368
Bruce, Mrs. David, 383
Bruce, Nigel, 142
Brunswick School for Boys, 203
Brynner, Yul, 373–74
Brynner, Mrs. Yul (Jacqueline), 373
Burger, Warren E., 353
Burns, George, 107
Burns, Millicent, 41–42
Burns, Brinker & Company, 41
Burton, Richard, 305. 334
Byington, Spring, 108

Cagney, James, xii, 248
Caine Mutiny, The, 150, 243–44
Caine Mutiny Court Martial, The, 247, 266, 380
Campbell, Alan, 18
Candida, 45
Caneel Bay Plantation, 229, 258
Cannery Row, 240
Cantor, Arthur, 370
Cape Playhouse (Dennis), 43, 45, 47, 49
Cardinale, Claudia, 329
Carmichael, Hoagie, 178
Carrie Nation, 75
Carrillo, Leo, 142
Carson, Johnny, 380
Carter, Jimmy, 381
Carter, Mrs. Jimmy, 381
Cat Ballou, 316, 323
Cedars-Sinai Hospital, 344, 348 50, 362, 384
Chad Hanna, 166
Chapin, Eulalia, 101–02, 116, 187, 203, 209, 212–13, 216, 322
Chaplin, Charles, 378
Chaplin, Sydney, 300
Chapman, John, 19
Charles Darrow for the Defense, 336
Chasen's Restaurant, 188
Chayefsky, Paddy, 268
Cheyenne Social Club, The, 332–33
Christian, Linda, 290
Clarence Darrow, 336–41, 344, 367
Claudia, 7
Clinchy, Dr. Everett, 228
Close Up, 54
Clurman, Shirley, 208
Cobb, Lee J., 266, 297
Coca, Imogene, 85–86
Cocteau, Jean, 277
Coe, Fred, 273–74, 276, 278–79, 282–83
Cohen, Abe, 232
Cohen, Alexander H., 339, 379
Cohn, Harry, 236
Cole, Nat King, 178
Columbia Broadcasting System, 75, 236
Columbia Pictures, 142
Coming Home, 362
Connelly, Marc, 92–95, 99
Constant Wife, The, 37
Cooper, Gary, 3, 95, 100

Copeland, Aaron, 380–81
Coquette, 37, 89
Cornell, Katharine, 63
Cotten, Joseph, 73
Country Girl, The, 255–56
Coward, Noel, 17–18, 63
Craig Sanitarium, 214, 222–23
Crawford, Joan, 136, 142, 188–89
Creative Management Associates, 304–05
Crews, Laura Hope, 45, 57
Critic's Choice, 292
Crouse, Russell, 8, 9, 10, 17, 122
Crouse, Mrs. Russell (Anna), 17
Curtis, U.S.S., 158–62, 168–69, 175

Daisy Kenyon, 188
Daddy Longlegs, 100
Dale, Esther, 75
Dana, Leora, 236, 240
Darwell, Jane, 137–38, 378
Davies, Marion, 176–77
Davis, Angela, 324
Davis, Bette, xii, 37–38, 129–30, 188, 304
Davis, Bobbi, 37–38
Davis, Mrs. Harlow, 37–38
Dean, James, 330
de Havilland, Olivia, 300
De Laurentiis, Dino, 254, 257, 260
De Liagre, Alred, Jr., 335
De Mille, Cecil B., 64
Denham Studios, 114, 116
De Pasquale, Dr. Nicholas, 342
Deputy, The, 285, 290–91
del Rio, Dolores, 107
De Sica, Vittorio, 262
Devil's Disciple, The, 45
Devine, Andy, 108
Dewey, Thomas E., 380
Diary of Anne Frank, The, 273
Dietrich, Marlene, 17
Dietrich, Noah, 298
Dinkelspiel, John, 159, 169
Doctors Hospital, 130, 227
Doty, Glen, 30
Douglas, Mike, 316
Douglas, William O., 352
Douglas, Mrs. William O. (Kathy), 353
Douglas, William O., Jr., 352
Drums Along the Mohawk, 166
Duke, Patty, 284

Easthampton Playhouse, 71
Eastwood, Clint, 328–30
Easy Rider, 330–32
Eddy, Mary Baker, 22
Edmond, Walter D., 94
Eisenhower Theater, 352, 370
Elam, Jack, 329
Elitch's Gardens, 49
Elizabeth, Queen of Great Britain, 285
Elser, Frank P., 94
Emma Willard School, 237, 255
Enola Gay, The, 170
Enright, Sara, 73
Essex, U.S.S., 157

Fail Safe, 305
Fairbanks, Douglas, Jr., 285
Farmer Takes A Wife, The, 94, 98, 100–01, 103, 108, 183, 266
Farrow, Mia, 307
Fay School, 237
Faye, Alice, 142
Fellini, Federico, 262
Ferrer, José, 98
Ferrer, Mel, 254, 287
Feuer, Cy, 240–42
Fiddler on the Roof, 258
Fields, Dorothy, 125
Fields, Freddie, 305
Fields, Dr. Joshua, 345, 348
Fields, W. C., 367
Finian's Rainbow, 10–11
Firecreek, 328
First Monday in October, 350–53, 356–57, 360–61
Fitzgerald, Ella, 123, 380–81
Fitzgerald, F. Scott, 37
Fleischmann, Raoul, 243
Fleming, Victor, 103–04
Foley, Gregory, 31, 39
Fonda, Afdera Franchetti, 260, 263–65, 270–81, 283, 285–91, 293–95, 323
Fonda, Amy (daughter), 246–47, 253, 256, 269, 275, 278–80, 308, 311, 326, 351, 354, 369
Fonda, Bridget (granddaughter), 306
Fonda, Douw (cousin), 23
Fonda, Frances Seymour, 3, 14, 19–20, 101, 116–28, 130–33, 139–46, 151, 154–55, 162–67, 172, 177–82, 186, 189, 194, 198–99, 202–04, 206–07, 209–19, 222–26, 258, 259, 321

Fonda, Harriet (sister), 22–25, 28, 34–35, 42, 94–97, 125, 146, 155, 167–88, 256, 269, 274–75, 357

Fonda, Mrs. Henry (Shirlee), xiv, 132, 300–08, 311–14, 317–24, 329, 336–37, 341–51, 352–53, 356–63, 369, 370, 372–76, 380–85

Fonda, Jane Seymour (daughter), 3, 130, 139–41, 143–44, 146, 151, 154–55, 163–67, 172–74, 179–81, 184, 185, 196–204, 209–11, 216–19, 222, 225–26, 228–29, 230–31, 234–38, 246–48, 255–56, 259, 269–70, 278–80, 284–85, 294, 299, 308–10, 316, 319–20, 322–26, 331, 333–35, 342, 351, 354–55, 362, 369–71, 375–76, 379

Fonda, Jayne (sister), 22–25, 34, 94, 125, 146, 167

Fonda, Peter Henry (son), 3, 140, 143–44, 146, 151, 155, 162, 166, 172–74, 177–82, 184–87, 194–95, 198–200, 203–05, 211–12, 216, 218–19, 222, 226–32, 234, 236–39, 246–48, 256, 259, 269–75, 277–79, 284, 289, 291–93, 298–99, 306–08, 321–23, 326, 330–32, 335–36, 342, 347, 351, 353–55, 365, 368–69, 376

Fonda, Portia Rebecca Crockett (daughter-in-law), 335

Fonda, Susan Blanchard, 207–10, 215, 222, 224–29, 231–37, 243, 246, 247–48, 253, 255–60, 269, 308

Fonda, Susan Brewer, 298–99, 306–07, 321

Fonda, Ten Eyck (grandfather), 21–22

Fonda, William Brace (father), 21, 23–28, 33–34, 42, 59, 94, 97, 336

Fonda, Mrs. William Brace (Herberta, mother), 23–27, 31, 34, 36, 42, 59, 94

Fontanne, Lynn, 63, 122, 378

Foran, Dick, 110

Ford, John, 132–38, 159, 183, 188–90, 196, 205, 247–52, 297, 372, 378–79

Ford, Mrs. John (Mary), 189

Ford, Patrick, 132

Foreman, John, 304

Forsaking All Others, 76

Fort Apache, 189

Forty-sixth Street Theater, 96, 97, 241

Fox Studios. See Twentieth Century-Fox

Foy, Eddie, Jr., 142

Franchetti, Afdera. See Fonda, Afdera

Franchetti, Lorian, 262

Franchetti, Nanook, 262, 264, 272–73

Franchetti, Baron Raimondo, 262

Franchetti, Simba, 262

Francis, Arlene, 76

Franciscus, James, 269, 275

Freel, Aleta. See Alexander, Mrs. Ross

Frohman, Daniel, 47, 51

Front Page, The, 37, 333

Gable, Clark, 3, 102, 144, 205

Game of Life and Death, The, 58

Garbo, Greta, 8, 67, 106, 110, 277–78

Garland, Judy, 8, 94, 107

Garner, James, 245, 316

Gaynor, Janet, 100, 103

Generation, 310 11, 314

Gentlemen Prefer Blondes, 221

Ghost Train, The, 67

Gibson, William, 273–74, 276, 282–84

Gideon, Clarence Earl, 367–68

Gideon's Trumpet, 367, 369–70

Gift of Time, A, 300

Gilbert, Bruce, 371

Gill, Susan, 61

Glenville, Peter, 289

Goetz, Augustus, 273

Goetz, Mrs. Augustus (Ruth), 273

Gone With the Wind, 103

Goodbye Again, 75

Goodman, Benny, 79

Gordon, Max, 92–95, 101

Gould, Dr. Wilbur, 340

Graham, Martha, 380

Grapes of Wrath, The, xv, 135–39, 142, 191, 240, 266, 331, 378–79, 382

Great Dictator, The, 379

Green, Herbert, 242

Greenwich Academy, 203, 209, 225, 231

393

Gregory, Don, 336
Gregory, Paul, 243–44
Grizzard, George, 370
Guys and Dolls, 240–41

Haight, George, 49
Hamilton, Margaret, 94, 95–96, 108
Hamilton, Nancy, 85
Hammerstein, Oscar, II, 17, 208, 210, 214–15, 228, 243, 257
Hammerstein, Mrs. Oscar, II, (Dorothy), 17, 208, 210, 228, 257
Hammerstein, William, 5, 9, 15–17, 19, 193, 207–08, 219–21
Hammett, Dashiell, 8
Hanighen, Bernard, 48–49, 54, 55
Hanmer, Gahan, 7
Happy Time, 236
Harrigan, William, 252
Harris, Jed, 68–69
Harris, Radie, 200
Harrison, Rex, 241
Hart, Moss, 122
Hart, William, 96
Harvey, 289, 349
Hathaway, Henry, 297
Hauser, Dr. Gaylord, 277
Hayden, Tom, 335
Hayden, Mrs. Tom. See Fonda, Jane
Hayes, Helen, 37, 255
Hayward, Bridget, 202, 284–85
Hayward, Brooke, 112, 139–40, 202, 225, 291–92
Hayward, Leland, 6–7, 9, 15–18, 57, 89–91, 93–95, 101, 124, 126–27, 135, 139, 166, 184, 198, 202, 205, 207, 220–21, 236, 238–39, 247–48, 250–52, 291
Hayward, William, 184, 202, 205, 291
He Who Gets Slapped, 45
Hearst, William Randolph, 177
Heggen, Thomas O., 4–6, 9, 11, 18–19, 192, 248
Hellman, Lillian, 8
Hemingway, Ernest, 8, 264
Hepburn, Audrey, 254, 260
Hepburn, Katharine, 86, 370–77
Hersey, John, 8
Heston, Charlton, 314–15
Hill, Arthur, 304
Hitchcock, Alfred, 265, 267

Hodiak, John, 244
Hoffman, Dustin, 334
Holden, William, 247
Holman, Libby, 86
Hoover, Herbert, 59, 74
Hoover, John H., 156, 159–60, 169–70
Hope, Bob, 166–67, 315
Hopper, Dennis, 330–32
Hotel Pierre, 125, 298
Houghton, Norris, 51
House Beautiful, 183
Houseman, John, 271, 337
How the West Was Won, 296–97
Howard, Dr. Elliott, 340–43
Howard, Leslie, 62
Howard, Sidney, 122
Howdy Doody Show, The, 323
Howland, Joseph, 213–14
Hudson, Rochelle, 108
Hughes, Howard, 298
Hunter, Glenn, 37
Huston, Walter, 241

I Am a Fugitive from a Chain Gang, 251
I Dream Too Much, 108
I Loved You Wednesday, 76
Ile de France, 114, 119
Immortal Sergeant, The, 146
In Harm's Way, 306
Invitation to a March, 309
Is Zat So?, 51
It's a Mad, Mad, Mad, Mad World, 305
Ivanov-Rinov, Goury, 62, 64

Jamison, Marshall, 219–20
Jesse, James, 142, 328
Jest, The, 50
Jezebel, 130
Johns Hopkins Hospital, 186, 213
Johnson, Nunnally, 135, 137
Jones, Ben, 367
Jones, Carolyn, 297
Jones, Jennifer. *See* Simon, Mrs. Norton
Jones, Sue-Sally, 198
Journey's End, 81

Kanin, Garson, 300
Kaplan, Dr. Joseph, 362
Kaufman, Boris, 266–67
Kaufman, George S., xiii, 92, 100, 122
Kazan, Elia, 238

Keating, Fred, 76
Keith, Fay Devereaux, 117
Keith, Robert, 16, 205, 252
Kelly, George, 48
Kelly, Jack, 316
Kennamer, Dr. Rexford, 339, 384
Kennedy Center, 370, 380–81
Kennedy, Edward, 353
Kennedy, John F., 291–93, 306
Kennedy, Robert, 292–93
Kern, Jerome, 125
Kerr, Geoffrey, 92
Kerr, Walter, xi, xiv
Keyser, Irving, 8
Kiss for Cinderella, A, 60, 61
Klugman, Jack, 266
Klute, 234
Knickerbocker Holiday, 241
Knight, Dr. Robert P., 213–14, 224
Korshak, Marshall, 357–58
Korshak, Sidney, 357
Krim, Arthur, 268
Kroll, Jack, 362

Lady Eve, The, 132, 143
Landon, Alfred, 380
Lane, J. Russell (Rusty), 16, 18
La Scala Restaurant, 301
Last of the Cowboys, 348
Laughton, Charles, 243–45, 379–80
Laurents, Arthur, 309
Lawlor, Marvin, 86
Lawrence, Gertrude, 63
Lawrence, Jerome, 350–52, 356
Leachman, Cloris, 370
Leatherbee, Charles, 50, 54, 58, 60, 62, 65, 71
Lee, Robert E., 352–53, 356
Lembeck, Harvey, 8–10, 16, 18–19
Lembeck, Mrs. Harvey (Caroline), 10, 16
Lemmon, Jack, 248, 252, 334
Lenox Hill Hospital, 341
Leone, Sergio, 328–29
LeRoy, Mervyn, 351–52
LeRoy Institute, 140
Levin, Ira, 291
Lewis, Anthony, 367
Life, 175
Lillian Russell, 142
Lillie, Beatrice, 96
Lindsay, Howard, 8, 9, 17, 122
Lindsay, Mrs. Howard (Dorothy

Stickney), 17
Little Caesar, 251
Little Shows, The, 89
Lloyd, Harold, 107
Loesser, Frank, 242
Logan, Joshua, 4–6, 9, 11–13, 14–15, 17–19, 48–49, 52, 56, 61–62, 65, 68, 72–76, 79, 80, 104, 110, 124, 192, 198, 220–21, 233, 235, 246, 248, 251–52, 308, 364, 379, 382
Logan, Mrs. Joshua (Nedda), 4, 12, 18–19, 60, 221, 246, 284, 287, 319
Lollobrigida, Gina, 262
Lombard, Carole, 102
Lombardy Hotel, 1, 4–5, 19
Long Valley, The, 135
Longest Day, The, 299–300
Loren, Sophia, 262
Los Angeles Drama Critics Circle, 380
Los Angeles Times, xiv, 154
Low and Behold, 83
Loy, Myrna, 102, 376
Luce, Mrs. Henry (Clare Booth), 116, 126
Lumet, Sidney, 266–68, 273, 305
Lunt, Alfred, 63, 122, 378
Lynde, Edwin B., 312
Lyons, Leonard, 87

MacDonald, Jeanette, 110
Mad Miss Manton, The, 132
Madame Curie, 251
Madison Square Hotel, 83, 97–98, 106, 123, 152, 332
Magnani, Anna, 262
Malden, Karl, 297
Male Animal, The, 143, 270
Man Who Came to Dinner, The, 79
Marquand, John P., 236
Marshall, Alan, 110
Marshall, E. G., 265
Martin, Ernest, 240–42
Martin, Freddie, 108
Marty, 268
Mary A. Goddard Juvenile Home, 302, 314
Masaryk, Madame Jan, 50
Marx Brothers, 176
Massey, Raymond, 297, 378
Mastroianni, Marcello, 262
Mata Hari, 67
Matloff, Dr. Jack, 384

Matthau, Walter, 227
Maverick, 316
Maxwell, Elsa, 274
Maytime, 45
MCA. *See* Music Corporation of
    America
McCarthy, Joseph, 291
McCormick, Myron, xiv, 60,
    67–68, 74–76, 104
McCrea, Joel, 100
McDonald, Eugene Francis, III
    (Stormy), 275, 289, 298,
    307–08
McGowan, Kenneth, 133
McGrath, Frank, 196
McGuire, Dorothy. *See* Swope,
    Mrs. John
McMurray, Fred, 177
McMurray, Mrs. Fred (Lillian),
    177
Mercer, Johnny, 178
Merchant of Venice, The, 45
Merrick, Michael, 336–37
Merton of the Movies, 33, 37,
    100
Metro Goldwyn Mayer, 85, 105,
    136, 142, 148, 188, 236, 298
Michael Reese Hospital, 359–62
Mielziner, Jo, 18, 237
Miller, Marilyn, 85
Mills, Ogden, 80
Miracle Worker, The, 284
Mister Roberts, 2, 4–6, 8–9,
    10–19, 193–94, 195–96, 197–98,
    200, 202, 204, 209, 216,
    220–22, 227, 231–34, 236,
    238–40, 243, 247–54, 266, 273,
    328, 356
Mitchell, Margaret, 62
Mitchell, Ruth, 204, 220
Mitchum, Robert, 315
Modern Virgin, A, 65
Mondale, Walter, 381
Mondale, Mrs. Walter (Joan),
    381
Monroe, Marilyn, 284
Montgomery, Robert, 144
Moon's Our Home, The, 111
Moore, Helen, 29
Moorehead, Agnes, 297
Morgan, Henry, 129, 297
Morning Glory, 273
Morris, John, 79
Moss, T. R., 14
Mr. Pim Passes By, 45
Music Corporation of America

(MCA), 8, 197, 260, 304
My Darling Clementine, 183, 187,
    382
My Fair Lady, 241

Nathan, George Jean, 122
National Broadcasting Company,
    75, 79, 253, 370
National Cathedral School, 53
National Junior Theater, 53, 58
Natwick, Mildred, 53, 60, 88
Naughty Marietta, 45
Neighbors of Watts, 373–74
Nettleton, Lois, 289
New Faces of 1934, 85, 90
New York *Daily News*, 19, 283
New York *Herald Tribune*, 283
New York *Mirror*, 283
New York *Sun*, 99
New York Times, The, xii, 19, 92,
    109, 135, 283, 309, 338
New Yorker, The, 243
Newman, Alfred, 137
Newman, Dr. Edward, 358–62
Nicholson, Jack, 332
Nimitz, Chester William, 156–57,
    160
Nixon, Richard M., 324
No Time for Sergeants, 251
Nolan, Lloyd, 243, 380
Nolte, Jake, 271–72
Northwestern Bell Telephone
    Company, 29
Nugent, Frank, 248, 252

O'Brien, Edmund, 299
Odets, Clifford, 255
O'Hara, John, 4, 12
Oldest Living Graduate, The, 370
Olivier, Laurence (Lord Olivier),
    334, 379
Omaha Community Playhouse,
    21, 31–33, 40, 43, 58–59, 194,
    255–56, 379
Omaha *World Herald*, 40
On Golden Pond, 370–72, 375–77
Onassis, Jacqueline Kennedy,
    292–93
Once Upon a Time in the West,
    328
O'Neill, Eugene, 43, 62, 84, 122
Organic Gardening & Farming,
    144, 183
Orsini's Restaurant, 313
Osborn, Paul, 236, 238
Our Town, 335

Ox-Bow Incident, The, 143, 145, 191, 266, 382

Paramount Pictures, 143
Paris Herald, 278
Parker, Dorothy, 18–19
Patrick, John, 248
Peck, Gregory, 297
Penn, Arthur, 276, 283
Peppard, George, 297–98, 311–13, 348–49
Perkins, Osgood, 109
Peter Pan, 227
Petrified Forest, The, 111, 253
Philadelphia Story, The, 379
Picasso, Pablo, 277
Pickford, Mary, 87
Pidgeon, Walter, 177
Pidgeon, Mrs. Walter (Ruth), 177
Plaza Hotel, 228
Plumstead Players, 335
Point of No Return, 236–37, 239, 242–43, 290
Pons, Lily, 108
Ponti, Carlo, 254, 262
Porter, Cole, 96, 125
Potter, Henry C., 49, 71, 236, 238
Powell, Dick, 243–44
Powell, William, 107, 248–49
Power, Tyrone, 3, 83–84, 116, 144, 166, 188, 290
Preminger, Otto, 298
Preston, Robert, 297
Private Lives, 63
Probst, Leonard, 331
Provincetown Playhouse, 42

Quigley, Dr. Bart, 351
Quinn, Anthony, 260

Radio Keith Orpheum (RKO), 132, 143, 144
Raffles, 45
Rain Before Seven, 4
Rains, Claude, 58
Ready Money, 45
Reagan, Ronald, 380
Rebecca, 379
"Red River Valley, The," 137, 383, 385
Redford, Robert, 380
Retail Credit Company, 33, 36, 59
Reunion in Vienna, 63
Reynolds, Debbie, 297

Ridley, Arnold, 67
Rintels, David, 336–37, 341, 367, 370
Rio Rita, 37
Ritter, Thelma, 297
Riviera Riding Club, 181
Road to Rome, The, 90
Rodgers, Richard, 17, 243
Rodgers, Mrs. Richard (Dorothy), 17
Rogers, Ginger, 108
Rogers, Henry, 116
Rome Haul, 94
Roosevelt, Franklin Delano, 77, 378
Roots, 370
Rose, Reginald, 266–68
Ross, Shirley, 105
Rossellini, Robert, 262
Rounders, The, 306
Ruwitch, Ted, 358
Ruwitch, Mrs. Ted (Margie Korshak), 356–58
Ryan, Robert, 335
Rydell, Mark, 371

Saint, Eva Marie, 6, 356–57
St. Regis Hotel, 228, 239
Sardi, Vincent, 283
Sardi's Restaurant, 11, 73, 309
Satterlee, U.S.S., 150–52, 171
Saturday Evening Post, 196
Schary, Dore, 188–89
Schneider, Burt, 331
Schoentgen, John, 167
Schoentgen, Mrs. John. See Fonda, Jayne
Schuster, Harold, 114, 117
Scott, Elaine. See Steinbeck, Mrs. John
Scott, Hunter, Jr., 35–36, 130
Scott, Mrs. Hunter, Sr., 35–36
Scott, Martha, 335
Scripps Clinic, 142, 204
Seesaw Log, The, 282
Selznick, David O., 101
Seventh Heaven, 100
Sex and the Single Girl, 305
Seymour, Eugene Ford, 123
Seymour, Mrs. Eugene Ford (Sophie), 117, 123, 179, 204, 211, 216–18, 222–30, 299, 322
Seymour, Ford de Villers, 124
Seymour, H. Roger, 124
Seymour, Marjory Capell, 124
Shearer, Norma, 107

Shelton, James, 89
Sherdeman, Ted, 72
Sherin, Edwin, 335, 351–52
Sherwood, Robert E., 111, **122**
Shore, Dinah, 182
Short, Peter, 319
Shubert, Lee, 65, 84, **86**
Shields, Brooke, 354
Silent Night, Lonely Night, **288,** 308
Sillman, Leonard, 83–86, 89
Silver Cord, The, 45
Simon, Norton, 374
Simon, Mrs. Norton (Jennifer Jones), 374
Sinatra, Frank, 253, 320, **373**
Skelton, Red, 107
Skinner, Otis, 37
Skinner, Richard, **79**
Slatkin, Muriel, 320
Slocum, Dr. Clarence, 214
Slocum, Dr. Jonathan, 214
Smith, Kent, 52–54, 66, 68, **287**
Sockman, Rev. Ralph, 124
Some Like It Hot, 284
Sotheby Parke Bernet, 373–74
South Pacific, 74, 277
Southern Methodist University, 370
Spellman, Francis Cardinal, 380
Spencer's Mountain, 305
Spendthrift, 273
Springer, John, 313, 335–36
Springer, Mrs. John (June), **313**
Stackpole, Peter, 175
Stage Door Canteen, **144**
Stage Struck, 273–74
Stagecoach, 132
Stanislavsky, Konstantin, **62**
Stanwyck, Barbara, 132, 188
State of the Union, 8, 9
Stein, Jean. *See* vanden Heuvel, Jean Stein
Stein, Dr. Jules, 8
Steinbeck, John, xiv, 135–37, 228, 240–43, 291, 326–27, 378–79
Steinbeck, Mrs. John (Elaine), 228, 240, 326–27
Stertzer, Dr. Simon, 342
Stevens, George, Jr., 382
Stevens, Roger, 380
Stevenson, Adlai, 291–92
Stewart, James, xiv, 3, 12, **73,** 74–76, 81–83, 97–98, 104–14, 144, 148, 175–78, 182, 205, 296–97, 314, 328, 330, 332–33,
344, 364, **379**
Stewart, Mrs. James (Gloria), 205, 332
Stewart, Ronald, 332
Stone, Irving, 336
Strange Interlude, 58, **84**
Strasberg, John, 284
Strasberg, Lee, 284
Strasberg, Susan, 273, 284
Straw Hat Award, The, **379**
Streisand, Barbra, 320
Strictly Dishonorable, 65
Sugerman, Dr. Gary, 339
Sullavan, Margaret, 6–7, 54–58, 61–62, 65–71, 76, 78, 81, 87–89, 97, 105, 111–13, 126, 139–40, 184, 202, 270, 290–91
Sullivan, Dan, xiv
Summerville, Slim, 108
Sunny Side Up, 100
Sweet, Dr. Charles Clark, 230
Swan, The, 92
Swope, John, xiv, 17, 67, 106, **110,** 112, 166, 176–77, 333, 339, 364–66, 385
Swope, Mrs. John (Dorothy McGuire), 6, 17, 60, 166, **177,** 255–56, 284, 333, 364–66, 385
Swope, Mark, 364–65
Swope, Topo, 364–65

Tall Story, 308
Tate, Sharon, 307
Taylor, Elizabeth, 305
Taylor, Robert, 144, 188
Temple, Shirley, 189
Teucher, Peter, 239
That Certain Woman, 129
Theater Guild, The, 58
There Was A Little Girl, 308
Thompson, Ernest, 370
Tiffany's, 117
Time of Your Life, The, 335
Tin Star, The, 271
Toland, Gregg, 137
Tommy, 37
Torchbearers, The, 48
Tracy, Spencer, 297, 372, 377
Trail of the Lonesome Pine, 111
Traubel, Helen, 243
Trip, The, 347
Trotti, Lamar, 133
Truex, Ernest, 142
Truman, Harry S, 172, 324
Tuttle, Day, 79–81, 88–89, 92, **129**

398

12 Angry Men, 266–69
Twentieth Century-Fox, 13, 101, 103, 106, 108, 136, 143, 187, 192, 236, 371
21 Club, 176
Two for the Seesaw, 276, 278, 282–83

Under Cover, 45
United Artists, 268, 318
United Service Organization (USO), 314
U.S. Naval Academy Glee Club, 382–83
Unity Settlement House, 29
University Players, 12, 49–50, 55, 58, 60–67, 71–72, 75, 79, 236, 270, 364
Universal Studios, 132
University of Minnesota, 29–30, 38, 54–55, 206
Ustinov, Peter, 286–87, 338

Vadim, Roger, 308, 310, 324
Vallee, Rudy, 96
vanden Heuvel, Jean Stein, 260, 273
Vanderbilt, Mrs. Cornelius, 79
Vanoff, Nick, 382
Variety, 46
Vaughan Brothers, 26–28
Victoria, H.M.S., 152
Vidor, King, 257
Vinegar Tree, The, 90
Virginian, The, 129
Vogue, 124

Walker, Danton, 87
Walker, June, 92, 95, 100, 183
Wallach, Eli, 291, 297, 329
Wallsten, Robert, 240
Walters, Charles, 85–86
Wanda Nevada, 354
Wanger, Walter, 91, 101, 110–11
War and Peace, 254–55, 260, 263–64
Warden, Jack, 266
Warner Brothers, 75, 102, 109, 143, 248, 252–52
Warner, Jack L., 91, 236, 252
Warren, Mrs. M. J. *See* Fonda, Harriet
Wasserman, Lew, 13, 187, 197–98, 205

Watson, Minor, 45–46
Way Down East, 108
Wayne, David, 5, 10–13, 19, 205
Wayne, Mrs. David (Jane), 10, 11, 13, 19
Wayne, John, 3, 132–34, 189–91, 196, 297
Wayne, Melinda, 10, 11
Wayne, Susan, 10, 11
Weaver, John, 47
Webb, Clifton, 85
Webber, Robert, 266
Weber and Fields, 142
Welcome to Hard Times, 321
Wertenbaker, Lael, 300
Westchester Playhouse, 79, 87–90, 92, 129
Where's Charlie?, 240
Who's Afraid of Virginia Woolf?, 304, 355
Why Men Leave Home, 45
Widmark, Richard, 297
William, Warren, 142
Williams, Emlyn, 198
Williams, Tennessee, 380
Willkie, Wendell, 293, 380
Wiman, Dwight Deere, 89–90
Winchell, Walter, 87
Windust, Bretaigne, 48–50, 55, 58, 62, 65–66, 71, 84
Wings of the Morning, 114, 118
Winsten, Archer, 339
Wister, Owen, 129
Wizard of Oz, The 58 94
Wood, Peggy, 45–46
Wooden Kimono, The, 61
Woodward, Charles, 335–36
Woollcott, Alexander, 86
Woolley, Monty, 79
Wouk, Herman, 150, 243–47
Wrong Man, The, 265
Wyeth, James, 372–73
Wyler, William, 105, 112, 337–38

You and I, 31
Young, Gig, 144
Young Mr. Lincoln, 133
Yours, Mine and Ours, 317

Zanuck, Darryl Francis, 136, 142–43, 146, 191–92, 233
Ziegfeld, Florenz, 37